Reading Instruction for Today

Reading Instruction for Today

Jana M. Mason
University of Illinois, Urbana-Champaign

Kathryn H. Au
Kamehameha Schools, Honolulu, Hawaii

Scott, Foresman and Company
Glenview, Illinois
London, England

Acknowledgments

Excerpt from "Reading the World and Reading the Word" from a *Language Arts* interview with Paulo Freire, Vol. 62, #1, January 1985, pp. 18–19. Reprinted with permission of the National Council of Teachers of English.

From *Independent Application of SEARCH in Reading and Language Arts* by Roselmina Indrisano, Number 12 of the *Ginn Occasional Papers*. © Copyright 1983 by Ginn and Company. Used with permission.

From "Think Aloud: Modelling the Cognitive Processes of Reading Comprehension" by Beth Davey, October 1983 in the *Journal of Reading*. Reprinted with permission of Beth Davey and the International Reading Association.

Dixie Lee Spiegel, *Reading for Pleasure: Guidelines*, p. 39 and p. 54.

Acknowledgments continue on page 452

Library of Congress Cataloging-in-Publication Data

Mason, Jana.
Reading instruction for today.

Bibliography.
Includes index.
1. Reading (Elementary)   2. Children—Books and reading.   I. Au, Kathryn Hu-Pei.   II. Title.
LB1573.M376   1986   372.4'1   85-27752
ISBN 0-673-18010-7

4 5 6 7 - RRC - 91 90 89 88 87

PREFACE

The research of the past decade has greatly increased our understanding of effective reading instruction and of how children learn to read. Much of this research has centered on the critical area of reading comprehension—understanding the meaning of what is read—which, after all, is the whole point of reading. While those of us in reading education have long recognized the importance of comprehension, we previously did not understand the process of comprehension or how to teach it. Now, research has made that knowledge available. Thus, while *Reading Instruction for Today* was written to meet the practical needs of prospective teachers, the material presented is based upon current research theories and findings, including much valuable information about reading comprehension. It includes topics now recognized to be important but generally not covered, or only touched upon superficially, in other textbooks. Among those topics are early literacy, writing, vocabulary, reading in the content areas, and teaching students with special needs.

The book is intended as the main text for a semester-long course on elementary school reading instruction. It is typically used with courses for second or third year undergraduates, or occasionally for returning master's level students, and assumes that prospective teachers have had no other reading instruction courses.

Because of the rich research base, there is more for prospective teachers to know about reading than about any other part of the elementary school curriculum. Reading and reading instruction are also complex topics. For these reasons, we have made every effort to organize and present the material clearly. Each chapter is introduced with a quotation from another author, highlighting an important concept in the chapter. Each chapter is then structured around four or more key concepts, which are summaries of the main ideas covered. The key concepts will aid prospective teachers in learning and retaining the information presented. Under each key concept we begin with an overview of issues and relevant research. We then provide the prospective teacher with instructional guidelines and activities consistent with current knowledge of the area. New terms are defined when they first appear in the text.

Another of our concerns has been to provide prospective teachers with complete information on how instructional activities should be carried out. To meet this need we have provided detailed descriptions (often in a step-by-step form) of techniques for all aspects of teaching. These aspects include preparing, planning, and organizing lessons; sequencing skills, topics, and materials; asking questions; and evaluating students' progress.

Each chapter in *Reading Instruction for Today* gives comprehensive treatment to a particular topic and may be read independently of the other chapters. There are, however, blocks of chapters that cover closely related topics.

Chapter 1 stands alone. It is an introduction to the reading process and to children's learning to read and is best used as the introduction to the book. Chapter 2 covers the teaching of reading in kindergarten or to very beginning readers. Chapter 3 provides an extensive treatment of the teaching of word identification skills, including phonics. Vocabulary, a topic closely related to word identification, is the subject of Chapter 4. Because it includes a discussion of teaching students to learn word meanings, Chapter 4 provides a natural bridge to the next chapters, which are on comprehension.

Chapter 5 introduces the comprehension process, picking up themes introduced in Chapter 1, and outlines principles in the effective teaching of comprehension. Chapter 6 focuses on methods for helping students to comprehend stories and appreciate literature. In a parallel manner Chapter 7 focuses on the comprehension of expository text and on study skills. Chapter 8 is devoted entirely to the topic of how teachers can strengthen students' reading ability through writing activities.

Chapter 9 covers the teaching of reading to students with special needs and serves as a bridge to the next block of chapters. Chapter 10 presents explanations of testing and assessment, while Chapter 11 provides an overview of reading methods and materials. Chapter 12 describes ways to organize and manage the classroom for effective reading instruction. Finally, Chapter 13 discusses reading in the school, home, and community, pointing to the importance of looking at reading beyond the walls of the classroom.

Other features of this textbook the reader should find valuable include lists of further readings, visual aids, and a complete index. An Instructor's Resource Book and test bank is also available.

For their valuable comments, we wish to thank colleagues who took the time to review various chapters of this book: Victoria Chou-Hare, University of Illinois at Chicago; William Kirtland, Boise State University; Jane Hansen, University of New Hampshire; Eunice Askov, Pennsylvania State University; Elizabeth Sulzby, Northwestern University; Sam Sebesta, University of Washington; Judith Meagher, University of Connecticut; Jerome Harste, Indiana University; Donna Ogle, National College of Education; Karen Wixson, University of Michigan; Yetta Goodman, University of Arizona; Taffy E. Raphael, Michigan State University; Cathy Roller, University of Iowa; and Susan M. Kershman.

We are especially indebted to Richard C. Anderson, University of Illinois; Rosalinda B. Barrera, New Mexico State University; Janet R. Kendall, Simon Fraser University; William Nagy, Center for the Study of Reading; and Janice Stewart, Rutgers University. Our thinking has been greatly influenced by the work of colleagues at the Center for the Study of Reading at the University of Illinois. At the Kamehameha Schools, Alice J. Kawakami, Jo Ann Wong-Kam, and Kori Kanaiaupuni gave us many good ideas and much needed assistance. We are grateful to Marjorie Y. Lipson for her fine work on the Instructor's Resource Book. Finally, we have appreciated the encouragement and wise counsel of Christopher Jennison, and the good sense and organizational ability of Anita Portugal, our editors at Scott, Foresman and Company.

To teach reading effectively is one of the greatest challenges facing today's elementary school teachers. We hope the material in *Reading Instruction for Today* will be a resource teachers will recall and act upon when seeking to meet this challenge.

Jana M. Mason
Kathryn H. Au

CONTENTS

Reading and Learning to Read

If we think of education as an act of knowing, then reading has to do with knowing. The act of reading cannot be explained as merely reading words since every act of reading words implies a previous reading of the world and a subsequent rereading of the world. There is a permanent movement back and forth between "reading" reality and reading words—the spoken word too is our reading of the world. We can go further, however, and say that reading the word is not only preceded by reading the world, but also by a certain form of writing it or rewriting it. In other words, of transforming it by means of conscious practical action. For me, this dynamic movement is central to literacy.

Thus, we see how reading is a matter of studying reality that is alive, reality that we are living inside of, reality as history being made and also making us. We can also see how it is impossible to read texts without reading the context of the text, without establishing the relationships between the discourse and the reality which shapes the discourse. This empha-sizes, I believe, the responsibility which reading a text implies. We must try to read the context of a text and also relate it to the context in which we are reading the text. And so reading is not so simple. Reading mediates knowing and is also knowing, because language is knowledge and not just mediation of knowledge.

Perhaps I can illustrate by referring to the title of a book written by my daughter, Madalena. She teaches young children in Brazil and helps them learn to read and write, but above all she helps them know the world. Her book describes her work with the children and the nature of their learning. It is entitled *The Passion to Know the World*, not *How to Teach Kids to Read and Write*. No matter the level or the age of the students we teach, from preschool to graduate school, reading critically is absolutely important and fundamental. Reading always involves critical perception, interpretation, and "rewriting" what is read. Its task is to unveil what is hidden in the text. I always say to the students with whom I work, "Reading is not walking on the words; it's grasping the soul of them."
(Freire, 1985, pp. 18–19)

OVERVIEW

We begin this chapter by giving you an understanding of the reading process as it is seen in mature, competent readers. We show why reading is defined as the process of constructing meaning from text and discuss why reading is defined as reading as a psychological process. Next, we look at reading as a social process, highlighting its importance in our daily lives. We discuss the purposes people have for reading, and the importance of considering not just the text, but the social context surrounding the reading event. We then describe how children develop as readers during the elementary school years. Three phases of reading development are outlined. Finally, we lay out broad goals for the elementary school reading program.

Chapter 1 is organized around the following key concepts:

Key Concept #1: Reading may be defined as the process of constructing meaning from text.

Key Concept #2: Reading is a social process, one of the means people rely upon to communicate with one another and to make sense of their world.

Key Concept #3: Children can be seen to go through three broad phases in developing as readers.

Key Concept #4: The overall goal of the elementary school reading program is to give students a foundation for lifelong literacy.

PERSPECTIVE

KNOWLEDGE OF THE WORLD

The background knowledge readers bring to the act of reading is what allows them to "grasp the soul" of the words, or arrive at meaning. This is why Freire emphasizes that every act of reading words is, in a sense, preceded and followed by a reading of the world. Only by applying their knowledge of the world can readers make sense of text.

In contrast to this view, reading was once thought simply to be a matter of identifying words. We now know that reading requires much more than that. Reading is a highly complex mental activity. This complexity is highlighted by Anderson, Hiebert, Scott, and Wilkinson (1985):

FIGURE 1.1 **Aspects of the Reading Process**

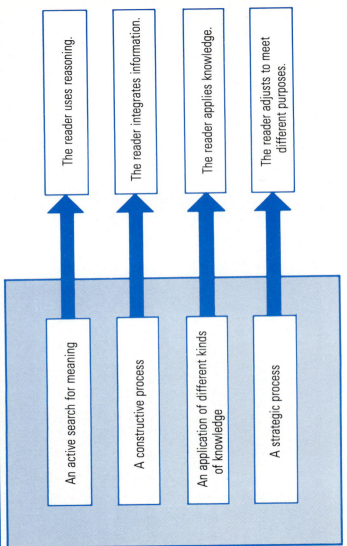

Reading can be compared to the performance of a symphony orchestra. This analogy illustrates three points. First, like the performance of a symphony, reading is a holistic act. In other words, while reading can be analyzed into subskills such as discriminating letters and identifying words, performing the subskills one at a time does not constitute reading. Reading can be said to take place only when the parts are put together in a smooth, integrated performance. Second, success in reading comes from practice over long periods of time, like skill in playing musical instruments. Indeed, it is a lifelong endeavor. Third, as with a musical score, there may be more than one interpretation of a text. The interpretation depends upon the background of the reader, the purpose for reading, and the context in which reading occurs. (p. 7)

In teaching children to read, we must remember Freire's point about the importance of knowledge of the world. We must consider the fact that people read and learn to read in different social and cultural settings. We must also remember that reading involves the orchestration of many different skills, and that proficiency can only be achieved through practice. We will emphasize throughout this book that reading and learning to read are acts performed in the world, or particular social settings, as well as acts performed in the individual's mind.

Reading may be defined as the process of constructing meaning from text.

SCHEMA THEORY AND THE FOUR ASPECTS OF READING

Much has been learned about the reading process by researchers investigating *schema theory* (e.g., Spiro, Bruce, and Brewer, 1980). Schema theory is a way of trying to explain how people store knowledge in their minds, how they use the knowledge they have, and how they acquire new knowledge. The term *schema* (the plural is *schemata*) refers to a "packet" or structure of knowledge in the human mind (Rumelhart, 1981).

The idea that there is nothing so practical as a good theory certainly applies to the teaching of reading. There should be a close, if not necessarily direct, connection between what we know about the process of reading and how we go about teaching children to read. In this section we discuss four aspects of the reading process as we can understand it from the perspective of schema theory. We can define reading as:

1. an active search for meaning
2. a constructive process
3. an application of different kinds of knowledge
4. a strategic process

To make the ideas being discussed more concrete, we include a short exercise illustrating each aspect.

Reading as an active search for meaning

Teachers should always remember that reading requires an orientation to meaning. First and foremost, reading should be seen as comprehension and a special form of reasoning, not word-calling or sounding out. This more scientifically valid view of reading as a search for meaning does not mean ignoring letters and words. Of course, they have to be identified. The identification of letters and words, however, is always subservient to the overall search for meaning. Even beginning readers need to be reminded and allowed to consider the larger meaning of the text.

As evident from the quotations below, this view that reading is a meaning-getting process is not a new one but has long been held by eminent scholars in the field:

Huey (1908): Reading is "thought-getting and thought manipulation."

Thorndike (1917): "Reading is reasoning."

Gray (1925): "Reading is a form of clear vigorous thinking."

Dewey (1938): Comprehension is "an effort after meaning." (from Mason, 1984a, p. 26)

EXERCISE

(1) Reread the paragraph above that begins, "Teachers should always remember . . ."

(2) Write in a sentence or two what you got from reading that paragraph.

(3) Now, answer the following questions:

(a) Were you aware of sounding out or stumbling over any of the words?

(b) Were you aware of thinking about the reasons we included this paragraph at this particular point? Refer to what you wrote in response to #2 above.

Let's consider your responses to questions 3a and 3b.

(3a) The chances are that you had no trouble with any of the individual words in the paragraph. In fact, you probably had so little trouble that you were scarcely aware of any particular words at all.

(3b) On the other hand, you probably were quite concerned with getting the overall meaning of the paragraph. If we succeeded in getting our message across, you probably noted that we would be talking about reading as a form of reasoning.

What we hope you have learned from this exercise is an awareness that, while words and letters are important in the process of reading, the whole point is to get meaning from text. Moving through the individual words is a means to this end.

What *is* new is that we are now beginning to understand the nature of the reasoning and sense-making people do when they read. In this view of reading, as an active search for meaning, we see the importance of the reader as a person. We realize that letters and words do not carry meaning and value in themselves, but take these on as they become the objects of the reader's attention. When we teach children to read, then, we should keep in mind that our job is basically one of helping them learn to use reasoning when dealing with text.

What do we mean when we say that reading is reasoning? To a large degree, we are referring to the importance of *inference.* Inference may be defined as the making of logical connections or the filling in of information from one's memory and experience. In an overview of research pointing to the importance of *inference,* Johnston (1983) writes:

> We do not consider readers to have comprehended something if they can give only a rote recall of the elements. We consider that readers have comprehended a text only when they have established logical connections among the ideas in the text and can express these in an alternate form. In this way, inferences are critical acts of comprehension, since they allow us to make various words meaningful, join together propositions and sentences, and fill in the missing chunks of information. (p. 7)

Making inferences itself, Johnston notes, is not a single type of skill. Rather, readers are required to make several different kinds of inferences. For example, not only must they infer the meaning of single words in context, they must also infer a larger framework for understanding the meaning of sentences and the text as a whole.

Here is an example of what we mean by making inferences while reading. Suppose you were to read the sentence, "John put a dime in his piggy bank." What you would probably infer is the following: A male person named John, most likely a child, owns a bank (probably three to twelve inches long, in the shape of a pig and made of metal or pottery) in which he is saving dimes and other coins.

Without ever thinking about it, we added a great deal to that one short sentence. We needed to make these additions through inference because without them we would not have had an adequate sense of meaning. Notice that we showed special knowledge in two areas. First, we used our knowledge of the reading process. We made inferences automatically because we know this to be a necessary part of reading. Second, we used cultural knowledge. By growing up in a certain culture, we acquired knowledge of children saving money in piggy banks.

According to the principles of schema theory, we were able to read with understanding because we already had in our minds the necessary schemata, or structures of knowledge, for the reading process and for saving money in piggy banks. This knowledge helped us to reason along the proper lines.

Reading as a constructive process

The second aspect we highlight is that of reading as a constructive process during which the reader makes meaningful connections among ideas in a text and to background knowledge. What does it mean to say that reading is a "constructive process"? Langer (1982) explains this idea in the following way:

Comprehension is not a simple text-based process in which readers piece together what the words, sentences, or paragraphs "say"—as if words themselves have some inherent meaning. Nor is it simply a concept-driven process in which readers begin with a global notion of what the text will convey and anticipate the larger meanings the text will convey. Rather, comprehension is a process which requires readers—real live readers with ideas and attitudes of their own—to interpret what the author is saying. (pp. 40–41)

Smith, Adams, and Schor (1978) showed how important it is for adults to be able to connect and integrate information as they read. Subjects in their study were first told to read and learn two sentences containing apparently unrelated facts. For example:

1. The banker broke the bottle.
2. The banker did not delay the trip.

Next, some of the subjects read and learned a sentence that allowed them to integrate all of the information. One example of such a sentence is:

3. The banker was chosen to christen the ship.

The other subjects were given a sentence which did not allow them to tie things together, such as:

4. The banker was asked to address the crowd.

The results of the study showed that people required less time to learn sentence 4 than sentence 3 and also remembered it better. The explanation for this finding is that sentences 1, 2, and 3 formed an integrated unit that readers

EXERCISE

(1) Place a card or a sheet of paper over the text below so that you will be able to read it just one sentence at a time. After you look at the first sentence, jot down on a sheet of paper what you think the text is about. Then read the second sentence and do the same. Then go on to the third sentence. (Passage and information about responses taken from Collins, Brown, & Larkin, 1980, p. 387.)

Text:

He plunked down $5 at the window.

She tried to give him $2.50, but he refused to take it.

So when they got inside, she bought him a large bag of popcorn.

(2) Think about your responses as you were reading.

(a) What was your first impression of what the text was about?

(b) If your impression changed as you read the second and third sentences, what triggered the change?

Let's consider your responses.

(2a) Some people think the man is at a racetrack window placing a bet, and many others see him at the window of a bank or theater. At any rate, the first sentence is fairly ambiguous.

(2b) Upon reading the second sentence, some people think that "she" refers to a cashier who is trying to give the man change. With this interpretation, it is somewhat puzzling when the man refuses the money. Upon reading the third sentence, most people arrive at the conclusion that the woman referred to in the second sentence is probably the man's date and that they are going to a movie. She wanted to pay for her own ticket but he wouldn't let her, and she then decided to use the money to buy him some popcorn.

The point we would like you to get from this exercise is that of the gradual shaping of meaning as the reader moves through the text. Text is often ambiguous. It does not "tell" us very much and can lend itself to different interpretations. Therefore, to comprehend at all, readers must actively work at developing a mental model of the text.

could relate to their own knowledge while sentences 1, 2, and 4 remained unintegrated and less meaningful.

Both Langer and Spiro (1980) point out that the text serves merely as a linguistic "blueprint" which readers must enrich with their own ideas, in this way creating their own meaning for the text. Langer adds:

> This is not to suggest that readers go off into an idiosyncratic world of fanciful meaning but that they alone have the power to create meaning—their meaning is closer to or further from the meaning that the author intended, but reader-generated nonetheless. (p. 41)

A related idea is that the construction of meaning does not occur spontaneously or in a perfectly straightforward way. Rather, the reader gradually constructs meaning from text through a trial-and-error process. This process is that of formulating hypotheses about the text, testing them, and then continuing or rejecting them (Spiro, Bruce, & Brewer, 1980).

During this process of generating and testing hypotheses, the reader appears to be constructing a mental model of the text. Collins, Brown, and Larkin (1980) suggest that the reader is trying to create an overall framework to fit the events and other information described. An initial model is constructed, then revised and evaluated. The authors refer to this process as one of "progressive refinement" in comprehending text.

As teachers we want to help our students learn to formulate and test their own hypotheses about text. In this process we will be less interested in whether answers are "right" or "wrong" than in the steps children follow in making and checking hypotheses. If their reasoning is sound, and their mental model of the text can account for the information presented, we may accept an unusual interpretation of the text. However, we might also acquaint the children with a more conventional interpretation of the text. In the foregoing example, some children might argue that the couple is going to a football game, where the same series of events could have occurred. If so, we would not reject their argument but might offer reasons for the more common movie interpretation.

Reading as an application of different kinds of knowledge

In discussing the third aspect of the reading process, we look at the different kinds of knowledge the reader must use in formulating and testing hypotheses about the text. We have seen that the reader must *construct* meaning from the text, which serves much like a blueprint. The act of reading with comprehension, then, requires the reader to use knowledge of the world as well as knowledge of text. He must draw upon information already in his mind, gained through life experiences, previous reading, and so on.

This means teachers should keep in mind the following two points: First, children cannot be expected to read with comprehension if they have no way of connecting the new information in the text to their prior or background knowledge (Adams & Bruce, 1982). Second, since no two readers will have had exactly the same life experiences, due to differences in culture and family circumstances, to name just two, teachers should expect differences in the ways students interpret text. Their interpretations may differ from the teacher's and from one another's.

A great deal of research has been conducted demonstrating how background knowledge (also referred to as prior knowledge, preexisting knowledge, knowledge of the world, or scriptal knowledge) influences reading comprehension. Background knowledge can affect comprehension in at least four different ways (Langer, 1982): (1) by influencing the way information is organized and stored in memory; (2) by influencing the type of information brought to mind when reading about a particular topic; (3) by influencing the associations made, due to personal experiences and background knowledge; and (4) by influencing the language or vocabulary applied because of the perspective brought to the task of reading.

EXERCISE

(1) To get some idea of just how powerful the effects of background knowledge can be, read the passage below (taken from Anderson, Reynolds, Schallert, & Goetz, 1977).

Rocky slowly got up from the mat, planning his escape. He hesitated a moment and thought. Things were not going well. What bothered him most was being held, especially since the charge against him had been weak. He considered his present situation. The lock that held him was strong but he thought he could break it. He knew, however, that his timing would have to be perfect. Rocky was aware that it was because of his early roughness that he had been penalized so severely—much too severely from his point of view. The situation was becoming frustrating; the pressure had been grinding on him for too long. He was being ridden unmercifully. Rocky was getting angry now. He felt he was ready to make his move. He knew that his success or failure would depend on what he did in the next few seconds.

(2) What do you think this passage is about?

(3) In the study by Anderson et al., two groups of subjects were asked to read this same passage. One was a group of students majoring in music, and one a group majoring in physical education. The passage was interpreted very differently by the two groups. The music majors thought they were reading about a jail break, while the physical education majors thought they were reading about a wrestling match.

If you look back, you will see that the passage lends itself equally well to both interpretations. Thus, the deciding factor was the subjects' background knowledge, which made it more likely they would see the passage from one perspective rather than the other. In your own case, which interpretation did you arrive at? What factors in your own experience do you think caused you to arrive at that particular interpretation?

We hope this exercise has helped you see the importance of background knowledge. Again, interpretation depends on what the reader brings to the text, and we can expect this to be different for different readers.

Of course, in addition to knowledge of the world, the reader must also apply knowledge of text. The text itself must be analyzed at different levels, from letters and words to its overall meaning (e.g., Rumelhart, 1976).

Another kind of knowledge the reader must apply is that of *text structure*, or knowledge of different types of text (more information on this kind of analysis is provided in Chapters 5, 6, and 7). Readers expect and look for different kinds of information based on their knowledge of the type of text they are reading. So, for example, at the beginning of a short story, they seek out information about the setting, because that is likely to be important to their comprehension of later events. When reading an editorial in the newspaper, they identify the stance being taken and the evidence used in support of it. Or, when reading a scientific article, they read carefully when the definition of an unfamiliar but important term is given.

The reader works to construct meaning from text by testing hypotheses using several different kinds of knowledge at once. We can imagine that there is a constant flow of information through the reader's mind, with information of one kind having to be coordinated with all the others. For example, the reader may guess that the text is about a wrestling match but still need visual evidence, at the level of letter and words, to support this idea. Only in this way can a coherent model of the text be developed. Thus, the reader is trying to adjust hypotheses about letters and words, and hypotheses about overall meaning, to be consistent with one another.

A practical implication here is that, when we teach children to read, we need to prepare them to deal with and coordinate different kinds of knowledge and information.

Reading as a strategic process

This fourth aspect is also consistent with our focus on the reader as a person who brings his or her own goals and unique store of background knowledge to the task of constructing meaning from text. When we say that reading is *strategic*, we mean that it can be adjusted depending on the reader's purposes at a certain time. Sometimes we will set purposes for students' reading, but we want them eventually to be able to read for purposes they find important and set for themselves. Mature readers do just that. They read for some reason, for example, to entertain themselves, keep up with current events, or learn how to use a new gadget. Having these different purposes might lead them to read in a somewhat different manner.

Reading as a strategic process includes the monitoring of ongoing comprehension activities to see if our purposes are being met (Brown, 1982). In addition to the evidence from our newspaper example above, consider the earlier exercise involving the passage about the couple going to the movie. In trying to make sense of that passage, you were probably aware of monitoring your own comprehension and making adjustments to your interpretation.

EXERCISE

(1) Reflect upon the habits you have for reading the newspaper. What do you usually do?

(2) Do you read the entire paper through, word for word, from start to finish? Or do you jump around, skipping some parts but not others? Of the parts you do read, do you give them all the same amount of attention? How do you treat some parts differently from others?

We guess that you do not read the paper through with equal attention from start to finish, but skim and skip around. You probably have a number of different purposes in mind, and you vary the way you read depending on those purposes. For example, when one of the authors read the paper recently, she just skimmed the front page, glancing at the headlines and deciding the stories were all too depressing to read after a hard day's work. She did stop to read a page 3 article about a possible teachers' strike. She then turned to the sports section, to read carefully articles about a couple of local teams. She made an effort to remember this information because she knew friends would be looking forward to discussing it the next day. Then she turned to the food section. She scanned the advertisement for the neighborhood supermarket and added a couple items to her shopping list.

What we hope you have gotten from this exercise is a sense, in daily activity, of how reading is used purposefully and flexibly.

In looking over the newspaper, this woman shows how adults use reading in a purposeful and flexible manner. She reads some articles carefully but skims quickly over others.

In contrast, young children often do not monitor their own comprehension processes while reading and seem blissfully unaware that information is not being put together in a sensible way. Small instances of this are often observed. For example, a first grader might read the title of a story as "Lucy Didn't Little," instead of "Lucy Didn't Listen." This might happen if the child is so busy trying to figure out the word on the basis of letter information that she fails to notice that the resulting phrase does not make sense.

Effective readers, unlike poor or beginning readers, are *aware* of what they are doing as they read, and of what they need to do, to meet their purposes. Awareness of one's own mental activity is referred to as *metacognition*. The practical implication here is that we want to help students develop an awareness of their own reading comprehension activities.

The idea that people generally read not as an end in itself, but to achieve some purpose, leads to our next key concept, that of reading as a social process.

KEY CONCEPT 2

Reading is a social process, one of the means people rely upon to communicate with one another and to make sense of their world.

THE IMPORTANCE OF READING IN DAILY LIFE

Research by Taylor (1983) shows what we mean when we say that reading is a social process. Judging that this social process had its roots in the family, Taylor set out to learn about young children's earliest experiences with literacy. She looked at six families, each with a child who was successfully learning to read and write. She found that the styles and values of literacy were transmitted to the children by their parents, and in turn were shaped by the personalities and preferences of the children themselves. The process of encouraging children's learning to read and write in the home turned out to be highly dynamic and flexible, with the parents preserving certain aspects of their own experiences (e.g., the reading aloud of storybooks) but deliberately changing others (e.g., making reading more important than it had been in the home when they were growing up).

Taylor discovered "that children learn to organize their environment through the use of print" (p. 54). This is one example:

Kathy was playing at Bonnie's house, and together they organized a club in which James was a member. Once again, print was used in many of the negotiations. Kathy and Bonnie designed membership forms which included the name, school, and birthdate of each member. Each member filled out the form and received a club pass on which his or her name was written. Kathy and Bonnie also wrote out the club rules. . . . (p. 46)

EXERCISE

(1) List three ways that you use reading and writing in connection with going to school.

(2) List three ways that you use reading and writing outside of school.

(3) Can you see any differences between the ways you use reading and writing in school and outside of it?

(4) How would your life in and out of school be different if you weren't able to read and write?

We find that many people think of reading and writing in school as a matter of taking notes during lectures, making notes on information read, and writing papers or answers to exam questions. Outside of school, what often comes to mind is leaving notes for family and friends, making shopping lists, reading mail, and reading books, the newspaper, or magazines for enjoyment. The two sets of lists are generally quite different.

In both cases, however, many of us find it difficult to imagine our lives without reading and writing. Participating in most school activities and going through some of our daily routines outside of school seem almost impossible without reading and writing.

Thus, when we speak of reading as a social process, we mean its central role in our daily lives. Literacy is often part and parcel of the way we carry out many activities.

Taylor observed that the children attended more to the *uses* of print in everyday life than to the print itself. That is, words and letters were not valued for their own sake but were seen as a means to an end. For example, the children used notes to communicate to their parents, just as their parents communicated to them through notes left on the refrigerator. Messages were also written to siblings and friends.

Reading and writing were ways of engaging in and making sense of everyday life. Children learned *before* they learned about the alphabet and the conventions of writing. As Taylor's work demonstrates, reading is part of the larger process of being literate and participating in a literate society.

We can think of reading as a social process involving different kinds of contexts. Smith, Carey, and Harste (1982) suggest the following three contexts:

Linguistic context is the written text per se, that which appears visually on the page.

Situational context . . . is the setting in which a reading-event occurs; it includes the linguistic text, the individuals involved (e.g., a student and a teacher), the location (e.g., in a classroom or at home), the expectations (e.g., that a recall test will be given over the material), and all such other factors impinging immediately on the event.

Cultural context is the social/political matrix in which the situation of reading has come about. (p. 22)

These abstract ideas can be made more concrete by considering an example. Many of us are familiar with elementary school reading lessons. The linguistic context is often a story in a basal reader. Besides the story, the situational context often includes ten or more students but just one teacher. The lesson takes place in a classroom, with other students working on assignments at their seats. Frequently, one child at a time is required to read part of the story aloud while the others follow along.

But how did these students come to be involved in lessons like this every day? To answer this question we must consider the cultural context. It includes such diverse factors as the value the children and their families attach to education, the need for children to be occupied while their parents are off at work, laws requiring children to be in school, and the way schools are organized into grade levels and classes.

Notice, as in Taylor's view, that the printed page itself, the linguistic context, is only one of the contexts or factors to be considered in the act of reading. Since reading is a social process and a form of communication, it is equally important to consider its larger situational and cultural contexts as well.

What it means to be a competent reader or to be literate may vary, depending on these broad contexts. For example, parents may encourage the young child to "read" a favorite storybook by retelling the events without actually repeating the words verbatim (Holdaway, 1979). If the child goes to school the next day and does the very same thing, however, he or she might be scolded by an unsympathetic teacher for "reading carelessly." This might happen because the parent is trying to encourage enjoyment of reading, while the teacher sees her goal as calling the child's attention to the details of words and letters.

Similarly, there is not just one way to learn to read or to become literate. This point is clearly established in the work of Scribner and Cole (1981), who studied literacy among the Vai in Liberia. The Vai are a traditional people who in the early nineteenth century invented a syllabic writing system to represent their own language. Scribner and Cole found that many Vai men could read and write using this script. Except for this high rate of native-language literacy, however, the Vai lived in virtually the same way as neighboring groups. One did not become literate in Vai by attending school or by becoming educated, in the sense of having to master a written body of knowledge. Obviously, a young person becoming literate in Vai goes through very different experiences from a young person becoming literate in English in a school in the United States.

There is an important practical implication stemming from the key concept of reading as a social process. As a social process, reading may have a different meaning for different people. Thus, teachers need to be alert to the overall meaning of the reading event to their students. Children have larger lives, outside the school, which may give the situational and cultural contexts of reading in the classroom a different definition from that assumed or intended by the teacher.

Young children, in particular, are best taught to read in situations compatible with those of their home culture. Au and Mason (1983), for example, investigated this issue with students of Polynesian-Hawaiian ancestry. Teachers who insisted that Hawaiian children speak one at a time in answering their questions had great difficulty in conducting effective reading lessons. On the other hand, teachers who allowed the children to cooperate or speak together in answering questions could conduct highly effective lessons.

Teachers who used this second style of interaction were teaching in a manner consistent with the rules for talk story, an important nonschool speech event for Hawaiian children. In talk story, speakers cooperate with one another in telling stories. Rather than one person telling the whole story, two or more speakers take turns, each narrating just a small part. Use of a cooperative talk-story style was important to the students, perhaps because it seems to reflect the value many Hawaiians attach to the performance and well-being of the group or family, as opposed to the individual.

In short, the effective teaching of reading depends on the teacher's taking a broad view of the contexts of literacy and learning to read. In the study by Au and Mason, for example, the text itself was not the problem at all. Rather, the barrier to effective instruction was found in the situational and cultural contexts.

KEY CONCEPT 3

Children can be seen to go through three broad phases in developing as readers.

THREE PHASES OF READING DEVELOPMENT

Reading is a complex process, and it takes most children considerable time to learn to read at the level of capable adult readers. The three broad phases children seem to go through in learning to read are:

(a) early reading
(b) formal beginning reading
(c) emerging mature reading

For many children the first phase seems to cover the ages up to about five (roughly until the middle or end of kindergarten), the second, the ages from about five to eight (roughly from the first through third grades), and the third, the ages from about eight to eleven (roughly from the fourth through sixth grades).

Teachers should be careful to view these ages and grade levels only as very general markers, because there are such wide differences among individual children. Also, they should be aware that children progress gradually from one phase to the next, so that there are no hard and fast lines marking off one phase from the next.

By reading the description of each of these phases, you should get a sense of the growth in children's reading ability across the elementary school grades. Within each phase we try to give you a holistic picture of children and their knowledge and experiences as readers. This knowledge and experience cannot be neatly placed in set categories, but for the sake of organizing the descriptions, we discuss typical experiences children may have with print, their awareness of reading, learning outcomes, and instructional implications.

Early reading

Experiences with print. Many children begin to learn to read and write at home (Mason, 1984a). A typical home literacy experience for many children at this period would be the kind of storybook reading described by Aulls (1982):

"Daddy . . . wake up . . . don't go to sleep now!" Tommy, age four, nudges his father as he is reading one of Tommy's favorite bedtime books. "Oh, Oh yes . . ." His father rubs his eyes and refocuses them on the page. Tommy's pudgy finger points to a word in the last line his father read. "Here, Daddy. You begin here." "Thank you, son.' . . . and an ocean tumbled by with a great boat for Max and he sailed off through night and day and in and out of weeks and almost over a year to where the wild things are.' "Tommy sighs and mumbles to himself, 'r-r-r-,' in anticipation of the best part of the next line. "... they roared their terrible roars and gnashed their terrible teeth and rolled their terrible eyes and showed their terrible claws till Max said 'BE STILL.'"   (p. 3)

This book, *Where the Wild Things Are* by Maurice Sendak (1963), has been read to Tommy many times before, Aulls notes, but Tommy is perfectly happy to hear it yet again. Tommy has started to show an interest in becoming a reader himself, as we can tell from his active participation.

Another typical experience for young children is seeing their parents use print, when reading for pleasure, as part of their jobs, or for such everyday purposes as making a shopping list (Taylor, 1983). The children studied by Taylor began at an early age to use print themselves. As mentioned earlier, an important purpose in these efforts was to communicate with their families, for example, by writing notes. Other home literacy activities may include reading or reciting an alphabet book, reading familiar words, watching *Sesame Street*, and recognizing signs and labels.

Awareness of reading. Asking children how they are learning to read or how they go about reading can be very informative. Even kindergarten children can tell you what they understand about reading. This information can show a teacher if lessons are having a positive effect. Mason, Stewart, and Dunning (in press) had kindergarten children from a rural school respond to these questions:

How are you learning to read at home?
How are you learning to read in school?
How might you teach someone else to read?
What does next year's kindergarten class need to know to learn to read?

For children in the stage of early reading development, a common literacy experience is hearing a parent read aloud. Somewhat older children in the stage of formal beginning reading also enjoy these events.

One child, for example, explained how she was learning as follows:

My Mom's helping me and my Dad's helping me and they're helping me sound it out because I don't know the *o*'s. I know "to" but the others I don't know. I sound them out.

About school, she said:

She gives us a book and we tell the word to her and we sound it. Well, we read some stuff in the book. We learn some words.

About how next year's kindergarten children ought to learn, she advised:

Try to read by yourself.
Read it with your mom.
Let your mother read and then you read.

This child has an awareness of reading as the process one uses when trying to figure out the words in books. She realizes that reading is something young children generally cannot do on their own. Like many children, she is learning to read through experiences both at home and at school.

Learning outcomes. Many children learn a great deal during this period. They recognize book reading as a pleasurable activity, one they can participate in and begin to take over. They are able to recognize signs and labels, as well as letters. In some cases, letters are being tied to their sounds and heard in words. All of these outcomes help to prepare children for the barrage of printed words and reading tasks that are introduced more formally in the first grade.

Instructional implications. Kindergarten and first grade teachers will want to build upon the foundation for literacy often laid in the home, or to provide basic literacy experiences for children who come to school without them. The key points to remember are that early reading often proceeds best with activities that capture children's interest, particularly the reading together of stories. Early reading activities should involve a constant exposure to many different uses of reading and writing in communicating with others. They should make use of print in the environment. Finally, they should give the child the opportunity develop a sense of the patterning of letters in words.

Formal beginning reading

Experiences with print. The typical home experiences of beginning readers are much like those of younger children, because many continue to participate in story reading with parents and siblings and to use writing to communicate with family and friends. But school experiences usually center on basal readers, workbooks, and trade books (all discussed in detail in Chapter 11), and some-times on their own writing or that of their classmates.

A typical school reading experience for many children is a guided discus-sion lesson on a basal reader story. Usually there is a brief teacher-led discus-sion before the story is read, and then the children read a few pages of the text. That part of the story is discussed, and the children go on to read the next few pages. Here is the start of a lesson observed in a typical third grade classroom. It shows a teacher trying to focus the children's attention on ideas in the story. The observation began just after the teacher had introduced the story:

At 1:20 everyone in the class had begun reading the same story. The teacher was sitting at a child's desk between two difficult-to-manage boys. At 1:25, eight chil-dren had finished and were quietly waiting. At 1:26, the teacher asked, "What does [the main character] think of all the excitement? What was the problem? Why did they think . . . ? What did he do at the beginning?" The teacher also pointed out the pictures to remind children of information from the story and then asked children to find information from the text: "Find the sentence that tells . . ." At 1:35, she told the children to see if a particular event had been planned in advance, by reading to the end of the story. At 1:39, eight children had finished and were waiting. At 1:44, she asked, "Do you think it was planned?" From 1:45 to 1:55 she told them to turn to particular pages of the story, inquiring about the main problem in the story, words, and illustrations.

Awareness of reading. Apart from guided discussion lessons, much beginning reading instruction tends to focus on word identification rather than comprehension or constructing meaning from text. Probably for this reason, beginning readers focus, or believe they should focus, on word identification and not on thinking about the meaning of the text.

Canney and Winograd (1979), for example, found that 77 percent of second graders described reading as identifying words, while another 5 percent said it involved knowing word meanings. Only 14 percent described reading as using text information or a book, while 5 percent described it as listening to the teacher.

This limited understanding of reading, as only identifying words rather than constructing meaning from text, is clearly shown in the responses below, given by three first graders. These children, all average readers, were asked to write about how they were learning to read. The reason they mentioned so many classroom rules was probably because it was only a month after the beginning of the school year.

Sound out the words and when you are reading a book you do not look around the room.

Pay attention to your teacher and do not talk when you are reading a book. You are supposed to be concentrating on your book.

Sound out a lot. Read. Listen. Pay attention.

As these responses show, children do not automatically come to understand that reading is the process of constructing meaning from text, or that the purpose of reading is to understand the text (Mason, Stewart, & Dunning, 1986).

Learning outcomes. By the end of this phase, many children can read stories silently and aloud and show an understanding of story events. They can learn from group lessons and many have become adept at answering teacher questions about their reading. Most children come to know hundreds of words by sight and are able to identify new words in sentence and story contexts. They are able to work independently for longer periods of time and are beginning to be able to do quite a bit of reading on their own.

Instructional implications. Like early reading, formal beginning reading proceeds best in a warm, positive environment, centered on activities the children find meaningful. Although we ask children during this phase to become more and more precise in deriving meaning from text and in dealing with words and letters, we always need to keep these demands in the proper perspective, that of the larger purposes of reading. Thus, the sound primary grade reading program covers comprehension along with word identification, and aims to help children expand and organize their knowledge of the uses of reading and writing.

Emerging mature reading

Experiences with print. By about the fourth grade, most children can read quite fluently. In the phase of emerging mature reading, they are expected to learn new information from reading the printed page. They read articles in social studies and science textbooks, as well as expository texts in their basal readers. Reading expository texts is not easy, since these texts often introduce new information, are organized differently from stories, and contain unfamiliar terms.

Before they begin reading, much of what children learn comes from their personal experiences. To become competent readers, however, they must be able to read to understand the experiences of others and to remember new ideas. In this process, they must learn to think critically in judging the quality and adequacy of new information. They should also be able to fit new information with what they already know.

Guided discussion of difficult text is given in some classes at these grade levels, but research indicates the need for much more teacher-guided comprehension discussion, of a much better quality (e.g., Mason & Osborn, 1982). To illustrate this point, here is an example of a fourth grade social studies lesson. It shows a teacher's attempt to help the students use what they already know to gain a better understanding of the text about to be read.

Teacher: What do you know already about Abraham Lincoln?

The children reply that he was famous, freed the slaves, was the sixteenth president, died in a little house, enjoyed reading, had children, etc.

Teacher: We'll stop there. We do know quite a bit. (She passes out books and a ditto sheet containing five questions.) Turn to page 94. This starts with Lincoln. Let's think about what we know about Lincoln and about places you've been on our field trips. Think about where Lincoln lived.

A child comments about a field trip to Springfield, Illinois.

Teacher: (Nods an acceptance of the child's response.) Look at your pictures. See New Salem, his home in Springfield. . . . today I only want you to read from page 94 to 100. I want you to look for answers to these questions. (Reads the questions on the ditto and explains what information she wants on each.) Are you ready to start? Good.

The children begin reading and some immediately pick up pencils to answer the first question. Others attend only to the text.

The teacher speaks briefly with the observer and then walks around the room helping individuals who have raised their hands to ask for help in understanding a question.

This teacher was able to conduct an orderly and well-paced lesson. However, while her questions were intended to lead the children to a clearer understanding of the subject, in actuality they merely touch on unsorted bits of information. Some of the children in the class probably retained very little of the information covered. To help the children learn and remember more about

Lincoln, the teacher could have planned her lesson around a number of important points she wanted the children to understand, such as the struggles of Lincoln's early years or the difficult decisions he had to make while president. She could then have asked questions to bring out these points, to help the children differentiate important from unimportant information and to see cause and effect relationships in Lincoln's life. Often, very carefully planned lessons are needed to prepare children to read and learn from expository text.

Awareness of reading. Canney and Winograd (1979) asked fourth and sixth graders the same questions about their perception of reading that they asked of second graders. These older children still gave many responses that described reading as identifying or working with words (62% of the responses from fourth graders, 57% of those from sixth graders). Some children stressed the importance of word meanings (14% in fourth grade and 29% in sixth grade). Only a few mentioned the importance of the meaning of the text (14% in each grade).

Thus, most children, even in the upper elementary grades, apparently are unaware that reading or learning to read has much to do with constructing meaning from text. Their lack of awareness of the main reason for reading mirrors the fact that most teachers spend little time providing instruction on text comprehension (Durkin, 1979; Mason & Osborn, 1982). Here, for example, are the responses of two sixth grade students who were asked to write about what would make children in their class better readers:

Put more words in syllables so they can pronounce the words a lot better.

Have the kids that are having trouble go up to the teacher and have them read a book and she will see what words he needs work on.

To have special workbooks and sheets that explains the words a lot better and to pronounce them.

By sounding out the words and by trying to make the accents.

By trying to take one hard word and practicing it over and over.

When one of these children, a very good reader, was later asked what helped *her* read better, two of her responses were then oriented to comprehension:

After I read a story, have comprehension questions.

I read in the morning. It helps me absorb better.

Learning outcomes. During this phase, most children develop some means of gaining new knowledge through reading. They are generally able to read well enough to entertain themselves with children's novels, adventure stories, magazines, and other printed materials they find interesting. They can follow simple written directions and so can use print to teach themselves to fix or make things. They are able to understand and make use of information in the signs and labels in their environment. In other words, they can use print for most school and home activities and have, in fact, become literate enough to use print in many of the same ways as adults.

Instructional implications. The effects of instruction during this phase can be significant, if teachers remember that most children will benefit greatly from lessons on text comprehension. Many children begin the phase understanding how to comprehend and interpret stories presenting rather familiar information. By the time they complete the sixth grade, they should be able to read and understand many nontechnical texts, use print to learn how to do things and to carry out routine activities, and read for pleasure. Children can be helped to develop in this way if they have the opportunity to receive direct and guided instruction on how to relate new information to their own knowledge and to critically evaluate text ideas.

At this point you should have a series of mental images giving you a sense of children's development as readers. In the first phase, that of early reading, reading in the home may be done for and around children at first, but they quickly start to become literate themselves. In the second phase, that of formal beginning reading, children's learning to read is being shaped by the school as well as the home. Now we recognize the roots of reading as we commonly think of it, calling for close and careful attention to text, to words, and to the letters within words. Children in this phase need to be given an awareness of reading as the process of constructing meaning from text, even as they are developing the ability to identify words. In the third phase, that of emerging mature reading, children should be "reading to learn," studying and dealing with unfamiliar material in an increasingly independent way. While their attention may still be focused on individual words, teachers can help them understand and remember the important information contained in texts.

GOALS OF THE CLASSROOM READING PROGRAM

Teachers want to prepare students to use literacy for a variety of purposes throughout their lives. These purposes can be placed in two general categories:

1. Recreational and aesthetic, involving reading for pleasure.
2. Functional, involving reading to meet the demands of everyday life, at work or in the context of the family or community.

Earlier, we discussed the key concept of reading as a social process, one of the ways people communicate with one another and make sense of their world. Mature readers are capable of using reading for a wide variety of purposes, according to many different patterns. For this reason, teachers want to give students the opportunity to develop fully as readers, while being sensitive to their individual tastes and preferences. Thus, the elementary school reading program should be broad in scope, exposing students to many of the ways reading can be useful and enjoyable.

When we think of reading in this broad, multipurpose sense, we see that reading instruction should not be limited simply to use of a commercial program for only a short period each day. We need to call children's attention to the many, many uses of reading within the school and community, to everything from print on the cereal boxes they may see on the table, to the street signs they pass on their way to school, to the teacher's sending notes to the office, to the librarian's reading stories aloud to them, and so on throughout the day. During their elementary school years, we want to give students a view of reading as an integral part of life in a literate society.

We mentioned recreational and aesthetic goals first because one of the best ways to motivate children not already eager to learn to read is by treating them to good literature. Once students have experienced the joys of reading, the teacher's job is made much easier. If in the elementary school children begin to read for the sheer pleasure of reading, they have started to develop a habit that can be a source of enjoyment throughout their lives.

Functional goals are those related to using reading on the job or in the home and community for the tasks of everyday life. Reading on the job may entail everything from scanning memos, to close analysis of technical and scientific articles, to checking bills of sale. In the home family members leave notes for one another on the refrigerator, read the newspaper, sort through mail, and write checks. Thus, in the classroom reading program we want to prepare students to tackle many of these tasks, large and small, simple and complex.

Of course, students' achievement of these recreational and functional goals cannot be the sole responsibility of their elementary school teachers. For one thing, many children receive a good start toward achieving these goals in the home, before they ever come to school. For another, their development of reading abilities will continue for a long period of time, through their secondary school and perhaps college careers. Still, the aim of the elementary school program is to lay a solid foundation for future learning in both broad areas.

In summary, the goals of the elementary school reading program are best thought of in very broad terms. The teaching of reading even from the very beginning, in kindergarten and first grade, should be guided by our vision of children as literate citizens of the future. Such a vision will encourage us to give students a wide variety of lessons and opportunities for exploration in learning to read. Our aim is to create a classroom program designed to show children the power and joy of reading, and to enable them to use reading for the purposes they choose.

SUMMARY

In the first key concept we defined reading as the process of constructing meaning from text. In doing so we looked at four aspects of reading as a psychological process. First, reading may be thought of as an active search for meaning, in the sense that the reader must reason and make inferences about text. Second, reading is a constructive process, one which requires the making and testing of hypotheses about text. Third, reading involves the application of different kinds of knowledge, of the real world and of the properties of text. Fourth, reading is a strategic process, being adjusted according to the reader's purposes.

In the second key concept we pointed out that reading is a social process, one of our principal means of communication. Three different contexts for literacy were identified: that provided by the text, by the social situation, and by the larger culture and society. We looked at how reading and writing are a natural part of some children's home experiences. We also considered how reading may have different meanings in different cultures, and, similarly, how culture may have a powerful influence on learning to read.

In the third key concept we described the three broad phases of development children seem to move through in learning to read during the elementary school years. These are the phases of early reading, of formal beginning reading, and of emerging mature reading. Children often have different experiences with print in each phase. As a result, there are changes in their reading proficiency and awareness of reading. Teachers need to be aware of these changes and of how to tailor instruction to meet children's needs at each phase.

Finally, in the fourth key concept we set out the goals of the elementary school program. To prepare students for lifelong literacy, teachers need to help children learn to read both for enjoyment and to meet the demands of everyday life.

BIBLIOGRAPHY

REFERENCES

Adams, M., & Bruce, B. C. (1982). Background knowledge and reading comprehension. In J. A. Langer & M. T. Smith-Burke (Eds.), *Reader meets author/Bridging the gap: A psycholinguistic and sociolinguistic perspective.* Newark, DE: International Reading Association.

Anderson, R. C., Hiebert, E., Scott, J., & Wilkinson, I. (1985). *Becoming a nation of readers.* Urbana, IL: University of Illinois, Center for the Study of Reading.

Anderson, R. C., Reynolds, R. E., Schallert, D. L., & Goetz, E. T. (1977). Frameworks for comprehending discourse. *American Educational Research Journal, 14* (4), 367–381.

Au, K. H., & Mason, J. M. (1983). Cultural congruence in classroom participation structures: Achieving a balance of rights. *Discourse Processes, 6* (2), 145-167.

Aulls, M. W. (1982). *Developing readers in today's elementary school.* Boston: Allyn & Bacon.

Brown, A. L. (1982). Learning how to learn from reading. In J. A. Langer & M. T. Smith-Burke (Eds.), *Reader meets author/Bridging the gap: A psycholinguistic and sociolinguistic perspective.* Newark, DE: International Reading Association.

Canney, G., & Winograd, P. (1979). *Schemata for reading and reading comprehension performance* (Tech. Rep. No. 120). Urbana, IL: University of Illinois, Center for the Study of Reading.

Collins, A., Brown, J. S., & Larkin, K. M. (1980). Inference in text understanding. In R. J. Spiro, B. C. Bruce, & W. F. Brewer (Eds.), *Theoretical issues in reading comprehension.* Hillsdale, NJ: Erlbaum.

Durkin, D. (1979). What classroom observations reveal about reading comprehension instruction. *Reading Research Quarterly, 14,* 481-533.

Freire, P. (1985). Reading the world and reading the word: An interview with Paulo Freire. *Language Arts, 62* (1), 15-21.

Holdaway, D. (1979). *The foundations of literacy.* Sydney, Australia: Ashton-Scholastic.

Johnston, P. H. (1983). *Reading comprehension assessment: A cognitive basis.* Newark, DE: International Reading Association.

Langer, J. A. (1982). The reading process. In A. Berger & H. A. Robinson (Eds.), *Secondary school reading: What research reveals for classroom practice.* Urbana, IL: National Conference on Research in English and ERIC Clearinghouse on Reading and Communication Skills.

Mason, J., & the staff of the Center for the Study of Reading (1984a). A schema-theoretic view of the reading process as a basis for comprehension instruction. In G. G. Duffy, L. R. Roehler, & J. M. Mason (Eds.), *Comprehension instruction: Perspectives and suggestions.* New York: Longman.

Mason, J. (1984b). *Acquisition of knowledge about reading in the preschool period: An update and extension* (Tech. Rep. No. 318). Urbana, IL: University of Illinois, Center for the Study of Reading.

Mason, J., & Osborn, J. (1982). *When do children begin "reading to learn": A survey of classroom reading instruction practices in grades two through five* (Tech. Rep. No. 261). Urbana, IL: University of Illinois, Center for the Study of Reading.

Mason, J., Stewart, J., & Dunning, D. (1986). Measuring early reading: A window into kindergarten children's understanding. In T. E. Raphael (Ed.), *School-based contexts of literacy.* New York: Random House.

Rumelhart, D. E. (1976). *Toward an interactive model of reading* (Tech. Rep. No. 56). San Diego, CA: Center for Human Information Processing, University of California.

Rumelhart, D. E. (1981). Schemata: The building blocks of cognition. In J. T. Guthrie (Ed.), *Comprehension and teaching: Research reviews.* Newark, DE: International Reading Association.

Scribner, S., & Cole, M. (1981). *The psychology of literacy.* Cambridge, MA: Harvard University Press.

Smith, E., Adams, N., & Schorr, D. (1978). Fact retrieval and the paradox of inference. *Cognitive Psychology, 10,* 438-474.

Smith, S. L., Carey, R. F., & Harste, J. C. (1982). The contexts of reading. In A. Berger & H. A. Robinson (Eds.), *Secondary school reading: What research reveals for classroom practice.* Urbana, IL: National Conference on Research in English and ERIC Clearinghouse on Reading and Communication Skills.

Spiro, R. J. (1980). Constructive processes in prose comprehension and recall. In R. J. Spiro, B. C. Bruce, & W. F. Brewer (Eds.), *Theoretical issues in reading comprehension*. Hillsdale, NJ: Erlbaum.

Spiro, R. J., Bruce, B. C., & Brewer, W. F. (Eds.) (1980). *Theoretical issues in reading comprehension*. Hillsdale, NJ: Erlbaum.

Taylor, D. (1983). *Family literacy: Young children learning to read and write*. Exeter, NH: Heinemann.

CHILDREN'S BOOK CITED

Sendak, M. (1963). *Where the wild things are*. New York: Harper & Row.

FURTHER READINGS

Clay, M. M. (1979). *Reading: The patterning of complex behaviour*. Auckland, New Zealand: Heinemann.

Greaney, V., & Neuman, S. Young people's views of the functions of reading: A cross-cultural perspective. *Reading Teacher, 39*, 158–163.

Purves, A. C., & Niles, O., Eds. (1984). *Becoming readers in a complex society*. Eighty-third yearbook of the National Society for the Study of Education, Part I. Chicago: University of Chicago Press.

Taylor, D. (1982). Children's social use of print. *Reading Teacher, 36* (2), 144–148.

Teale, W. (1982). Toward a theory of how children learn to read and write naturally. *Language Arts, 59*, 555–570.

Vaughan, J. (1983). One child's query about reading instruction. *Language Arts, 60*, 987–990.

CHAPTER 2

Reading in Kindergarten

The first time I asked Wally if he wanted to write a story he looked surprised. "You didn't teach me how to write yet," he said.

"You just tell *me* the story, Wally. I'll write the words."

"What should I tell about?"

"You like dinosaurs. You could tell about dinosaurs."

He dictated this story.

The dinosaur smashed down the city and the people got mad and put him in jail.

"Is that the end?" I asked. "Did he get out?"

He promised he would be good so they let him go home and his mother was waiting.

We acted out the story immediately for one reason—I felt sorry for Wally. He had been on the time-out chair twice that day, and his sadness stayed with me. I wanted to do something nice for him, and I was sure it would please him if we acted out his story.

It made Wally very happy, and a flurry of story writing began that continued and grew all year. The boys dictated as many stories as the girls, and we acted out each story the day it was written if we could.

Before, we had never acted out these stories. We had dramatized every other kind of printed word—fairy tales, storybooks, poems, songs—but it had always seemed enough just to write the children's words. Obviously it was not; the words did not sufficiently represent the action, which needed to be shared. For this alone, the children would give up play time, as it was a true extension of play.

(Paley, 1981, pp. 11-12)

OVERVIEW

We begin this chapter by looking at the importance of early experiences with reading. Many, but not all children, enter school with some knowledge of the functions and forms of literacy. Thus, the kindergarten teacher's aim should be to broaden children's understanding of literacy by building upon their existing knowledge and experiences. We turn then to a discussion of the importance in kindergarten of attending both to the child's social and academic development. The next topic addressed is that of giving children a wide range of different experiences with reading and writing, so they will come to understand the many ways that literacy can be useful. We emphasize the importance of starting reading instruction with material familiar to the children. Finally, we look at ways that children can be involved in reasoning actively with text.

The key concepts in this chapter are the following:

Key Concept #1: Learning to read in kindergarten proceeds best in a warm, positive classroom environment, allowing the child time to become familiar with classroom settings and routines.

Key Concept #2: Early reading instruction should be multifaceted in reflecting the many different uses of reading and writing in the family and community.

Key Concept #3: Early reading instruction should be meaningful, beginning with familiar information and building on the children's background knowledge and language.

Key Concept #4: Early reading instruction should require the child to participate actively, engaging and developing the ability to reason and to make inferences.

PERSPECTIVE

EARLY EXPERIENCES WITH READING

To introduce the issues involved in early reading, we would like you to reflect back on your own experiences. What do you remember about learning to read? Do you remember any favorite books that you could (or thought you could) read before you went to first grade? Do you remember writing or printing letters? Do you recall being able to identify any signs or labels? Many people *do* recall learning to read before going to school. For example, here are the memories of eight college students:

We had boxes of books at home because I had an uncle who was a publisher. My Mom taught me to read them because she didn't want me to grow up with a foreign accent (she was born in a European country). I remember picking out books without pictures to read and it made me feel grown up.

I remember being at my grandparents' house and going through my mother's early reader and then feeling that I got it—I knew how to read.

I had little Golden Books that I would memorize and say that I could read. I tried to sound things out using the letters in my name.

My Mom was a first grade teacher and she brought home the Dick and Jane books and taught me to read them before I went to school.

We told stories in our home and did a lot of storytelling with younger brothers and sisters. I don't think that I read before school.

I had Dr. Seuss books and I listened to story records.

On Sunday all of us kids were given a section of the newspaper and my father would have us do things like circle all the a's that we could find.

I didn't read before going to school but when I was seven I taught my three-year-old sister to read using valentines. I remember even shuffling the cards so that she had to figure the words out instead of just memorizing where they were in the set.

Were your own experiences like any of these? In any case, these memories indicate the importance of attending to young children's early attempts to read or write and of encouraging an interest in stories and print from any source. The roots of literacy are widespread and young children are often learning about reading *before* they enter kindergarten, as we observed also in Chapter 1.

Many preschool children have considerable knowledge about reading before they begin reading books. Some begin by writing (Bissex, 1980). Many know how to orient a book and use the proper left-to-right sequence (Clay, 1979). As Ferreiro and Teberosky (1982) show, they begin to understand what print is for and to distinguish it from picture information. They learn to

EXERCISE

Are you in contact with any preschool children now? If so, try to find out what they know about reading. Can they hold a book right-side up, turn its pages, and tell you what it's about? Can they print or recognize their name? Do they know what STOP says? Can they spell CAT? If you were to hand them pictured advertisements of cereal, toothpaste, soaps, or soft drinks, would they be able to tell you what the large print said? If you wrote down a story they dictated to you, would they be able to read it back to you? Many four- and five-year-olds can do these things correctly, or partially correctly.

distinguish signs and labels (Harste, Woodward, and Burke, 1984; Mason, 1980). Some are taught by parents (Soderbergh, 1977). However, you will find some children entering kindergarten having had no introduction to books, not even alphabet books. Fortunately, you can help them learn that they have adequate language and problem-solving skills to understand a wide range of topics, particularly concepts about reading and writing. A literacy-laden classroom environment offers children the chance to gain confidence in their capacities to do school tasks and to begin distinguishing oral from written language. With their curiosity about reading and an interest in figuring out how to learn, they can easily extend what they already know. If you are a kindergarten teacher you will have the opportunity to build on these strengths and enthusiasms.

Kindergarten is generally thought to be the appropriate place to begin informal reading instruction and to foster literacy development. But not all schools endorse this view, and not all children attend kindergarten. In either of these situations, the first grade teacher will also find the key concepts and activities in this chapter very important. This same material should also be kept in mind by primary grade teachers working with children with special needs (e.g., those from homes where they have been less exposed to reading and writing, and those who are slower to learn).

While teacher sensitivity and good judgment are important at every grade, they are particularly vital in developing a kindergarten classroom reading program. For one thing, basal and other commercial programs are generally weakest at this level. For another, there is a wide range of different opinions about what constitutes a sound kindergarten reading program. We recommend that you sample from the many readable texts listed in the references at the end of this chapter for additional ideas about how to introduce and extend literacy.

KEY CONCEPT 1

> Learning to read in kindergarten proceeds best in a warm, positive environment, allowing the child time to become familiar with classroom settings and routines.

SOCIAL ENVIRONMENT FOR LEARNING TO READ

In Chapter 1 we pointed out that reading is a social process which can be thought to involve different contexts (Smith, Carey, & Harste, 1982), including *situational context*, or the setting for a reading event. Expanding on this general idea, Bloome (1983) explained that, while we usually think of reading in terms of the relationship between the author and the reader, we should see it as a broader social process, "an activity by which people orient themselves to each other, communicate ideas and emotions, control others, control themselves, acquire status or social position, acquire access to social rewards and privileges, and engage in various types of social interaction." (p. 165) He points out that reading events involve not only working with the text, but "establishing social relationships, social positioning, and group formation and membership."

Bruner (1984) emphasizes the teacher's role in promoting text-related social relationships with an example from a Headstart class discussion about the story, *Little Red Riding Hood.* He reports that the teacher helped the children relate their experiences to the text section about the wolf dressed as Grandmother who said he was going to eat the little girl:

The teacher was clever enough to ask the children how the story *should* have gone at that point. "She shoulda killed the wolf!" was the response. The teacher asked, "And then what?" And then there *was* a good discussion—not great, but good for 4-year-olds. It was not quite about the text, but at least it was about different ways in which a scenario (or was it life?) should have turned out. (p. 197)

We emphasize that the teacher needs to help children understand how written text is related to their lives. Kindergarten children, who generally are less able than older students to tie their social experiences to written texts, need extensive opportunities to talk about and dramatize their thoughts. This idea is consistent with Paley's recommendation quoted at the beginning of the chapter. It means that you need to provide ways for children to act out their own ideas and the ideas they find in stories. Through the social structures you set up, reading, writing, and story listening can all lead children to integrate text information with their own ideas.

FOSTERING LANGUAGE INTERACTIONS

How soon we introduce reading and writing activities depends on the children's previous language and book experiences. What they already know comes from home or preschool opportunities to talk about language and words (Olson, 1984) and stories (Goldfield & Snow, 1984; Snow & Ninio, in press). For children who have had few of these opportunities, it may be best to highlight oral language activities while school adjustment is taking place. The main reading-related activities might be the following:

1. Listening to and talking about stories.
2. Rehearing and reciting stories in books.
3. Discussing favorite words, signs, and labels.
4. Talking about pictures children have drawn.

For other children, reading and writing may already be so familiar that they can early on become the focus of the kindergarten program. However, listening to stories and discussion of pictures and stories should be present to some degree right from the start.

As often and as soon as possible, we want to let children know when they are making progress in learning to read, measured only against their *own* starting points. For example, children who have not had much reading or writing experience might pick up a book and "tell" us the story, but not in the exact words of the text, or they might print a phrase but misspell every word. We quickly show our appreciation for their efforts. They are showing an *approximation* to (or movement toward) skilled reading or writing which they were not capable of before. We do not correct or punish them because, while they are not yet reading or writing in an adult way, they are trying out new ways of constructing meaning with print. We like the way Holdaway (1979) puts this idea:

The environment is secure and supportive, providing help on call and being absolutely free from any threat associated with the learning of the task.   (p. 23)

GENERAL GUIDELINES FOR WORKING WITH KINDERGARTEN CHILDREN

The kindergarten program should strike a balance, with the teacher providing direction to the children but not being overly demanding. Here are some ways you can capture this balance:

1. Establish simple-to-follow rules for classroom behavior and explain them clearly to the children. Briefly discuss with children the reasons it makes sense to have these rules.

2. Find ways to make group activities pleasant. Many teachers, for example, make sure that each small group has enough space and time for completing projects. They remind the children when time for an activity is almost up, but then find a way to allow slower children to finish, without embarrassing them or keeping everyone else waiting.

3. When activities are hard for children to carry out on their own, make sure you introduce them slowly and model the appropriate behavior for them. Provide the activity several times a week, but offer it for short periods of time at first. For example, sustained silent reading is likely to be difficult for children unless you make it a regular routine and begin with brief sessions. Don't worry if it doesn't work the first time. Try it again. You might sit with the children, for example, reading silently along with them, thus modeling the desired behavior.

4. To strengthen home-school connections for children, use time-honored activities such as "sharing time" and "show and tell." These give the children the opportunity to talk about their personal interests and important home events. Encourage the children to express their ideas, regardless of whether they are speaking perfect Standard English or a dialect, or sometimes using words from another language. You will, however, model the Standard English forms in your

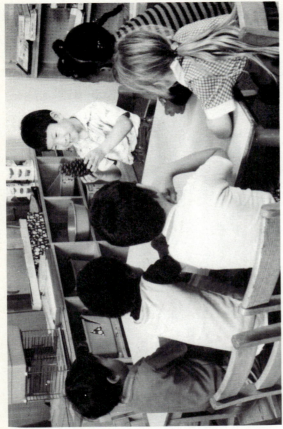

Show-and-tell time provides an opportunity for kindergarten children to use their language to describe, explain, relay significant personal events, and tell stories.

responses to the children. As you listen, you will learn about their oral language abilities and their knowledge of the world. The more you know about the children, the better you will be able to link reading activities to what they already know, thus building upon their strengths.

5. To strengthen home-school connections for parents, regularly send home a newsletter describing past and future classroom events. Include samples of children's pictures and writing, and describe particularly successful lessons or activities. Make the newsletter even more useful to parents by describing in detail an activity they might enjoy carrying out with their child at home. Parents might also appreciate listings of books they can borrow from the library and read to their child.

6. When providing formal instruction, introduce the children gradually to school rules for participating in lessons. For example, don't at first require kindergarten children to respond to your questions by raising their hands and answering one at a time. Instead, direct your questions to the group as a whole and let several individuals respond, or let the children respond in a chorus. Then repeat the correct answer, or a number of appropriate responses, for the whole group to hear. Eventually you can ask that responding occur in a one-at-a-time pattern. Again, this is the idea of allowing the children to approach a goal through approximation.

7. Use child-directed activity periods to teach children how to work without supervision. Help them learn where to find the materials

they need, how to carry a task to completion, and how to use their time constructively when they have finished one thing and are ready to move onto another. Developing good work habits is important, because once children are able to work independently for at least short periods of time, you will be able to work with individuals or with small groups on more challenging reading and writing activities.

8. Because the school is the first step in socialization beyond the family, kindergarten teachers must behave somewhat like parents, as well as like the teachers of older children. Help children begin to function away from their families, learning about the social rules, norms, and values of the world outside their homes. Be sure this includes a comfortable classroom environment. Ideally, this environment serves as a bridge between children's home experiences and the more demanding program of instruction they will usually encounter in the first grade.

In this section we have been concerned primarily with ways of creating a social environment supportive of children's learning to read. We turn now to other key concepts leading to specific ways of teaching reading and helping children to become literate.

KEY CONCEPT 2

Early reading instruction should be multifaceted in reflecting the many different uses of reading and writing in the family and community.

THE MANY FUNCTIONS OF LITERACY

We want children's early reading instruction to be multifaceted, in keeping with what we know about the variety of purposes for which adults read. We do not want to give young children a misleading view of reading, although we obviously do not expect them to understand all of its many aspects. Reading instruction should not focus exclusively on phonics, vocabulary, and grammar, or on letter names and letter sounds, or on a small selection of familiar words. Remember that the goal is comprehension, an understanding of text and of how it relates to self and society.

Bruner (1984) explains that, while children intending to be readers must master some elements of letter-sound correspondence, a more important factor is the following:

Reading requires that language be understood outside of its immediate context . . . [Young children want to learn to read because] it is a way into worlds unheard of and undreamed, the worlds of Maurice Sendak and Dr. Seuss, of Snow

White and E. B. White, even of the comics and the television advertisements. (pp. 195–196)

Consider how many different yet important activities might take place in a multifaceted program. There is story reading to encourage listening comprehension and literary appreciation. The teacher and children discuss the story, and the children use story language and ideas in their own early attempts at writing. Children act out the texts they create, refining and extending their language in the process. The teacher writes messages to children on the chalkboard or sometimes hands notes to individuals. They write back and may begin to send and receive letters through a classroom mail system. The teacher creates a "store" in a corner of the classroom and the children make signs and lists of goods and prices. The teacher introduces a word rhyming game for children to play and expand on. And so on. There seems to be no limit to the number of activities a kindergarten teacher can use to acquaint children with books and other reading materials, with writing and ways to use written information, and with oral language and ways to express ideas.

In any event, purpose and meaning (*functions* of literacy) are the principal focus of early reading instruction, providing the larger framework for children's learning about the details of words and letters (*forms* of literacy) and procedures for reading and writing (*conventions* of literacy). Knowledge of words and letters grows naturally and rapidly from meaningful and interesting classroom activities (Mason, 1984).

INSTRUCTIONAL GUIDELINES AND ACTIVITIES

We discuss below ways of developing kindergarten children's literacy which we think emphasize the multifaceted nature of reading and its different functions. These ideas concern (1) book reading, (2) writing, (3) letter sounds, and (4) classroom routines. Notice in each section how the function and purpose, whether self-expression or communication, is highlighted for children first, before the form or the conventions.

Reading, rereading, and reciting stories in books

As a kindergarten teacher, you will want to spend a lot of time reading and rereading stories to your students. Your goals for doing so include the following:

1. To introduce children to fine stories and poems.
2. To show children how stories are read.
3. To help children begin to "read" on their own.

Reading stories to children. The reading aloud of storybooks to children is an important activity in kindergarten. Snow and Ninio (in press) explain how story reading sessions teach young children the following:

Books are for reading, not for manipulating.
In book reading, the book is in control; the reader is led.
Pictures are not things but representations of things.
Pictures are for naming.
Pictures, though static, can represent events.
Book events occur outside real time.
Books constitute an autonomous fictional world.

Storybook reading will be a more effective learning experience if it is followed by discussion or if you coach children to retell the story. Morrow (1984) found that the story retellings of kindergarten children improved when the teacher helped them to focus on the structural elements of the story:

If children could not begin, it was suggested that they start with "Once upon a time," or "Once there was." Next children were encouraged to introduce the characters and to describe the time and place of the story. Then they were asked to tell the main character's problem or what the main character wanted to do in the story. Next, the children were asked to tell how the main character tried to solve his or her problem and how it was solved. Finally, children were prompted to put the ending on the story. (p. 96)

Discussion helps to foster not only an understanding of stories but also children's listening comprehension and oral language. Analyzing stories helps them see how authors convey ideas in a written form and how written language is different from or similar to their own oral language. Helping children verbalize about the fictional world can also get them excited about reading.

Developing children's language. Gambrell and Sokolski (1983) recommend the use of picture storybooks, read aloud to children to stimulate oral language development. They suggest using Caldecott Award-winning books because their illustrations have a high "picture/language potency." You can evaluate picture books for their potency. Look for books with large and colorful pictures of many different things, actions, and people. Then follow these suggestions for using picture books to foster oral language development:

1. Show children the illustrations in a book before you read it and ask them what they think will happen.
2. Model how to study storybook pictures. As you read to the children, point out how the pictures helped you understand the story. Encourage them to look at the pictures as they tell the story to themselves.
3. After reading a storybook aloud to children, have the children take turns telling the story as you show the pictures.
4. Encourage children to work in pairs looking at a book and telling each other the story.

5. Arrange a time for children to use the illustrations as aids in dramatizing the story.

6. Encourage children to tape record their version of the story.

Modeling reading. Think for a moment about all the things you know to do when you read a book. You know, for example, which side is up, how to find the first page, in what order to read the words, sentences, and pages, how to use the table of contents, and how to guess about the content of a book from its title. Sometimes you even know a little about the author. In addition, you know when you do or do not understand a text and what to do when you do not. Children must acquire all of this knowledge and more in order to read, and they learn much more quickly if adults model the act of reading for them.

To help children learn more, on some occasions when you read to them, point out parts of the book or describe your actions. You could say, "Here's the name or title of the book" (point to the title); "Here's the beginning of the story"; "Here's the first word"; "This is the way we read" (run your finger from left to right under a line of print); "Now we read the next page" (turn the page or let the child know that you've read the left page and will now read the one on the right); "This is the end." On other occasions, especially when there are a few words to a page, you can put your finger under each word as you read aloud. Kindergarten children are likely to use these words and mimic these actions as they look at books. They will understand the terms (e.g., *word*, *title*, *beginning*) you use and also start attending to the words in books and sweeping their eyes in the correct direction over lines of print.

Rereading stories. Rereading favorite stories can help children acquire conventions for reading books, as described above, and can also give them a feeling of confidence about reading stories. Specifically, rereading offers the opportunity for them to develop the following types of understanding:

1. Particular information appears on each page. Each story has its own unchanging wording and one reads (says) precisely those words.

2. Connected text is orderly and predictable. For example, one begins with the left-hand page and then goes to the right-hand one. Words can be pointed to and identified, and a given printed word always denotes the same spoken word. Breaks in thought and speech are marked by spaces, commas, or periods.

3. Stories usually start in a certain way (e.g., "Once upon a time"), and the characters often run into a problem, but then there is some sort of climax or resolution.

Here are a set of guidelines (based on those in McCormick & Mason, 1984) used successfully by teachers and parents to help children begin to read easy books:

1. Talk about the main idea in the book you are about to read. You might say, "Here's a book we will read. Look at the title on the front

cover. It says, ———. ———. What do you think this book will be about?"

2. Read the story to the children. Be dramatic or enthusiastic, emphasizing important words on each page. Hold the pages so that the pictures and words are clearly visible to the children. Pause in your reading and let them interrupt to talk about the pictures or story. Sometimes put your finger under the important words as you read. Discuss the story with them when you have finished reading it.

3. Have the children help you read the story. You could say, "Now you can help me read it," or "Let's read it together." Begin reading but hesitate occasionally so that the children say some of the words before you do. If children say the wrong words, simply go ahead and read the text aloud correctly, without commenting on their errors.

4. Help the children read the story alone. Go through the story several times, giving them more and more to read on their own until they can "read" or recite it all by themselves. Then allow individuals or small groups to take turns reading a page. Be enthusiastic about their progress.

5. Encourage the children to read books often. Books you have read aloud to them come to have a special significance because of the warm, positive environment of the story-reading experience. Keep these and other books in a place where the children can easily reach them. Let them show off their accomplishments by encouraging them to read to, and help, one another read.

With daily story reading in kindergarten, the teacher captures children's imagination as she introduces them to book language and the topics of childhood.

Shared book experience. Holdaway (1979) describes a way to teach children to read or recite familiar stories, songs, and rhymes. First, make a "big book" by enlarging the print of each story page so that it can be seen from about 15 feet. One way is to make transparencies of the pages and show them on an overhead projector. He suggests that you begin by using a familiar tale with a strong and repetitive storyline, such as *The Three Billy-Goats Gruff* and *The Gingerbread Man*. These stories are introduced and read several times. Children are encouraged to say the words along with the teacher. When the half hour sessions are running successfully, you can begin to ask children to predict what will happen, to figure out what words will appear, and to find and analyze words into parts.

Using caption books. To teach reading to young children, Burris and Lantz (1983) recommend the use of picture books that contain short language captions closely related to the pictures. These books have a limited range of vocabulary and simple and often repetitive sentence structures and are appropriate for rereading and shared book experiences. Moreover, they can easily be created by the teacher. Here are some of their suggestions:

1. Create a book called, *I can smell*. On each page place a scratch-and-smell sticker, a picture of the object and the sentence, "I can smell a _____." Stickers can be obtained for food and other "smelly" items.

2. Create a book called, *Where are we?* Take photographs of each child as he or she is involved in school or neighborhood activities (or have photos donated by parents). On each page, place a single photograph along with a sentence describing it.

3. Create other books called, for example, *Animals We Like, Colors, Shapes*, or *Our Senses*. Have children select the items to be pictured and labeled. Place one picture and a brief caption on each page.

Learning about authors. Highlight a favorite children's author for a week. In this activity, the children hear three stories written by the same author and, on the last two days, they discuss similarities and differences among the three stories. The purpose of this activity is to give children a sense of the author as a person with a certain vision of the world, be it humorous, melancholy, or whimsical, expressed by the creation of storylines, perhaps involving the same characters, in a distinctive style of writing. The idea here is to strengthen and give more continuity to connections among reader, text, and author than is possible with the reading of a single storybook.

Here are just a few of the authors whose stories many kindergarten children enjoy (recommended by Sutherland & Arbuthnot, 1986; refer to that volume for specific titles and the names of other authors): Martha Alexander, Aliki, Edward Ardizzone, Ludwig Bemelmans, Tomie dePaola, Ezra Keats, Leo Lionni, Maurice Sendak, and Charlotte Zolotow. Other authors may also be suggested to you when the children bring books from home, or when they are particularly charmed by other storybooks you read to them.

Day 1. Begin with a brief word about the author. Read the first storybook to the children. As you read, have the children predict what will happen, discuss the character's problem and how it might be solved, and help them understand how the character attempted to deal with the problem. Alternatively, you may follow the suggestion described earlier by Morrow (p. 36) or use the directed-listening-thinking approach described near the end of the chapter. Refer also to Chapter 6 for other ideas about drawing out children's responses to literature.

Day 2. Tell the children that they will be hearing a second story by the same author. Read the new storybook and encourage discussion and responding as during Day 1. Then ask them to talk about how the two stories were both similar and different. Help them start to see what we mean when we say an author has a certain style.

Day 3. Read a third story by the same author and go through the same basic procedure as during Day 2. Have the children compare and evaluate all three stories.

Day 4. Lead a discussion about the similarities among the three stories. From that help children identify some of the author's interests, particular point of view, or use of language. Then have children talk about parts of the stories they really like. Reread those sections and write parts of them out, each on the bottom of a large sheet of paper.

Day 5. Review what the children suggested you write out and then have them draw illustrations to go with favorite sections. Put these on the bulletin board for a week and then organize the clearest examples into a book for the children to read. Put the author's name and picture, if available, on the front. If the children go to the library, remind them that they might like to look for other books by the author.

Learning about topics. To study a topic, use a similar approach. Pick a favorite social studies or science topic and construct a five-day series of lessons around it. Try to select something children will find meaningful and interesting. This activity is designed to give the children a sense of how authors give information about a topic. Besides showing children how books present factual information, it helps them learn about new concepts and extends their knowledge of familiar ones.

Here are some examples of possible social studies topics: forms of transportation, holidays, the family, and staying healthy. Possible science topics include: growing plants, wild animals, pets, and the weather.

Day 1. Lead children in a discussion about what they know about the topic, why it is important, and what they want to learn about it. Write their questions on large sheets of paper, one question to a page, to be referred to on the following days.

Day 2. Read a book about the topic to the children. Lead a discussion about the information learned, and have them help you summarize the information, particularly as it applies to the questions they raised on the first day.

Any information obtained should be written on the sheets of paper below the questions.

Day 3. Read a second book about the topic. Lead a discussion about the new information learned and again help the children summarize it. Then help the children begin to relate and integrate information from both books. More information relevant to the questions can be added to the paper.

Day 4. Help the children make a simple semantic map of the information, including both their background knowledge and the new knowledge presented in the two texts. (Semantic mapping is discussed in detail in Chapter 4.)

Day 5. Have the children choose a question/answer sheet and draw pictures about it. Help them organize the pictures to create a class book with the semantic map at the beginning and the illustrated question/answer pages following. If children go to the library, encourage them to find other books on the topic.

Writing

Reading and writing are closely related and at times inseparable, especially in the experiences of young children. A number of authors describe this relationship, focusing on the young child's understanding (Bissex, 1980; Sulzby, in press; Taylor, 1983; Temple, Nathan, & Burris, 1984). For a more extensive discussion of writing, see Chapter 8. When we speak here of writing we are referring to the process of putting one's thoughts into print, not to tracing letters or copying. Here are some ways kindergarten experiences with writing can further literacy development:

1. Writing helps children to see more clearly some of the uses of print—recording important information, communicating with others, and organizing ideas.
2. As a creative activity, writing helps children to arrange their thoughts and learn how to express their ideas more formally and precisely.
3. Children become more familiar with the properties of written language when they struggle to translate their own oral language into print.
4. Writing provides practice in printing, spelling, and work recognition.

Art activities lead naturally to writing because children can merge drawing with printing a few letters or letterlike forms, and eventually words (for more information on this point, see Clay, 1975).

Most children usually have their own notions about what they want to draw or paint, but you should be on the lookout for those who seem stymied. A short conversation about recent events at home or at school generally is all it takes to get them started. At times, you may wish to give the group a specific topic. For example, following a field trip to the zoo, children could draw pictures about what they saw or did.

In addition, you can ask children to label their pictures, or you can write out their descriptions for them. If you do the latter, be sure to print the letters clearly and say the words as you write. Ask children to read the words out loud to you. In this way, children can see how their language can be written down and spelled. Display good examples on the bulletin board.

Another approach, which can be used if children have begun to print, is to show an interesting photograph and ask them to label it with a word or phrase. When children have discussed possible captions, place the picture at the writing table so that they can write out their own captions. Because you are interested in having them express their ideas, do not cross out or criticize their misspellings. They will gradually shift to a standard spelling, but to help them, you can reprint the standard spelling below theirs. Post the photograph and all captions on a bulletin board. Later, using the photograph as the cover page, put the captions together in a book. This can be placed alongside storybooks in the classroom, and the children can help one another read it.

Developing knowledge of letter sounds through language games

These activities give children who already have considerable knowledge of the functions of print the opportunity both to use language playfully and to extend their knowledge of the alphabet and letter sounds. Here the alphabet becomes

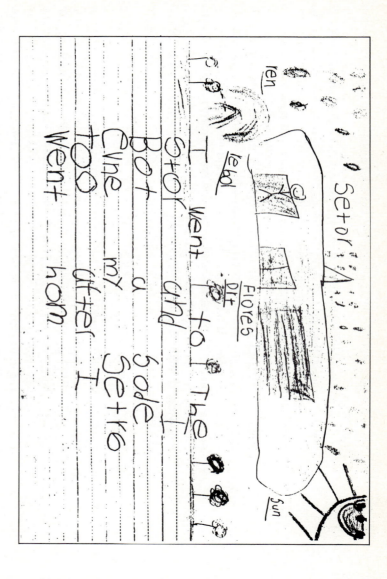

the basis for imaginative games. Different themes are used, and the children are encouraged to come up with alliterative phrases and sentences. One could, for example, construct a book around the theme of animals going aboard Noah's ark:

Arthur, the absolutely, awful alligator.
Betsy, the big, beautiful bear.
Clara, the clamoring, crabby cat.

Or have children help make a book around the theme of traveling:

A asked for an airplane and an automobile.
B and his friends bought a boat, a bicycle, a bus, a buggy, and a bobsled.
C couldn't carry a car and a canoe, a cart and a camel.

Or construct a book around the theme of an apple pie (adapted from an old English rhyme):

A asked for an apple pie.
B bought it for A.
C called for it.
D dove for it.

Bringing literacy into classroom routines

In most kindergartens the day begins with "opening exercises," often including discussions of the weather and the date. While teachers often use picture symbols for rain, sun, and clouds, words can be used just as well. Children can also learn to recognize the names of the months and days of the week, especially on the basis of initial letters. Many teachers also have pocket charts, with the names of the children who will serve as monitors or helpers. Different activities in the schedule can be shown on other charts with a combination of words and clock pictures.

Signs and labels provide a bridge from the outside world to the classroom. Many items and places in the classroom can be labeled, just as buildings, stores, and food products are labeled. Labels can be put on shelves showing the location for art and writing materials in parts of the room (for example, the library corner), and on furniture that children use (for example, their chairs).

You can ask children to copy or take from magazines or food products signs and labels that they want to read. Have them describe the word, where it was found, what they think it says, and why it was written. The child who brought in the word can draw a picture to accompany it. When the class has collected a set of related words (e.g., on traffic signs, neighborhood stores, or favorite foods), a book can be put together using the words and accompanying pictures.

A similar approach is for you or a parent to photograph neighborhood signs from restaurants, public buildings, the park, the school, and the street. Be sure the photograph includes part of the setting so that there are cues about the sign's location. Glue each photograph on one side of a card and rewrite the sign word at the bottom on the other side. Children can use the cards to play a naming game, using either the picture side or the word-only side.

Information about special events can also be communicated to the children in writing. For example, the teacher might write on the board: "Today is Sandra's birthday. We will eat birthday cake at 11 o'clock." The children's job, with as little help from the teacher as possible, would be to decipher the message.

If songs are part of the opening exercises, the words to a song can be written on a large piece of posterboard. Put each phrase or sentence on a separate line to help children see where the pauses occur. You can point to each word as the children sing. Later the words could be placed on a smaller card, with other songs and rhymes the children have learned, for a class songbook.

Our purpose in giving you these examples is to illustrate how an effective teacher uses every chance to show children how reading and writing can be useful and to encourage them to relate reading concepts to their own language and experiences.

KEY CONCEPT 3

Early reading instruction should be meaningful, beginning with familiar information and building on the children's background knowledge and language.

BEGINNING WITH MEANINGFUL INFORMATION

As you know from Chapter 1, reading is not simple and straightforward, although for adults it has become automatic. Reading depends a great deal on the individual reader's knowledge and experiences. If this is true for skilled readers, imagine the challenge reading poses to a kindergarten child and how large a role must be played by background knowledge.

As a starting point, consider in general that people can only learn something new by connecting it with what they already know. This idea is explored by Adams and Bruce (1982):

So very much of what we learn, we learn through language. Certainly most of our formal education is acquired through language. These observations seem almost too common to set in print. Yet they turn from banal to deeply paradoxical with the realization that we can only learn through language that which we, in some sense, already know. That is, through language, novel concepts can only be communicated in the form of novel combinations of familiar concepts.   (p. 2)

In applying this idea to teaching kindergarten children to read, we should begin by building on the knowledge and experiences they bring with them when they come to school. Consider what children are likely to know, so you can make those connections in early reading instruction.

What children already know

First of all, as we mentioned earlier, many children have already developed some *understanding of literacy* in the home. While what they know varies considerably, this usually includes knowledge of books, book language, and words (particularly sign and label words in the environment), and letter names. Learning to read will proceed in the kindergarten year if you give children the opportunity to build on their initial understanding of literacy.

Second, whether or not the children already have an understanding of books and printed words, they will almost invariably have strengths in *oral language*. They will have learned about communicating through speech and the power of words. Of course, spoken and written language differ in many ways (see, for example, Rubin, 1980). Furthermore, we frequently see kindergarten classrooms with children from a variety of language backgrounds. For example, a single big city classroom may have some children whose first language is Spanish, some whose first language is Chinese, some who are bilingual in Spanish and English or in Chinese and English, and some who speak a dialect of English. The important point to keep in mind is that all of these children have already learned to express themselves through language. This is quite an intellectual accomplishment in itself. Learning to read can proceed if you make connections to the children's existing strengths in spoken language, helping them develop their ability to analyze language (Olson, 1984). In short, your goal is to enable children to draw connections between oral and written language, to talk about both kinds of language, and to treat language as an object of study.

In addition, children have a great deal of *knowledge of the world*. As with knowledge of literacy and language, exactly what they know can vary tremendously. This may be a function of cultural background, which gives some children special knowledge of customs or of other countries; of family circumstances, which gives some children knowledge of eating in restaurants, going to the supermarket, and catching the train; or of the child's own interests, which may have led to an understanding of certain animals or plants. All teachers are occasionally surprised by the extent of children's knowledge of the world. This knowledge will affect their understanding and memory of information heard or read. Learning to read can proceed if you make connections to what children already know about the world so they can make their own interpretations.

INSTRUCTIONAL GUIDELINES AND ACTIVITIES

The activities that follow deal with information that is already meaningful to the children.

Finding familiar words and print in the environment

Early reading lessons ought to begin with the use of familiar and meaningful materials. However, it was once believed that the most effective way for children to learn words was to drill them on word cards containing the Dolch words or some other set of very common words. It was also thought that having pictures with the words distracted the child and made it harder to learn the words. To the contrary, Mason (1980) found that preschool children who associated each word with a picture learned more words than did those who were taught to pay attention to the first letter. Rash, Johnson, and Gleadow (1984) showed that children learned words more quickly when they were in meaningful sentences than in a word list. These studies buttress observations by Clay (1979) and arguments by Goodman (1965) that printed words ought to be personally meaningful or introduced in a meaningful context. The suggestions below for teaching kindergarten children words follow that recommendation.

Children's names. Begin the school year by teaching children to recognize their own names. It's a good idea to check with parents about how the child is to be addressed (some go by a nickname, some by a middle name because their first name is the same as that of a relative, and so on). Print children's names on cards and put these above storage places or at their desks or table spaces. Have another set of cards to hold up, to see if the children are learning to recognize their names, and use the cards often. For example, the cards can be shown one at a time, with the children going out to recess or to get a snack as soon as they see their names. The cards can be used in other classroom routines, for example, in listing special helpers. To call roll, you can hold up the cards one at a time and ask if the person is there. Then, before the semester is over, many children will recognize not only their own names but also those of their classmates.

Label and sign activities. Many items and places in the classroom can be labeled. Play games using cards with these label words. For example, give the children each a card and have them find the matching label, wherever it is in the room. Have them tell you what the word is. Labels can also be obtained by the children from cereal boxes, candy bars, soap, toothpaste, wrappers on clothing, or pictures from magazines and newspapers.

To develop familiarity with signs and their functions, take children in groups of about five for walks around the school building. Stop in front of a sign and ask the children the following questions:

1. What does that sign say? Usually someone will know and say it. If not, ask what they think its purpose is and then help them to figure out the words, as in Step 2 below. An EXIT sign is ideal for beginning this activity because it is common, uncomplicated, and likely to be prominently located.

2. Can you read that word or those words? Put your hand under the word you want them to name and move your hand from left to right. Then give each child an opportunity to read.

3. Why is that word there? What does it mean? Elicit answers about its use or function.

4. Are there any other signs like this around here? Encourage children to explain why there is only one PRINCIPAL'S OFFICE but several EXIT signs. See if anyone can lead the group to another EXIT sign.

5. Copy sign words onto tagboard. Say the words and then name each letter as you form it to help the children remember the word. At first use the same letter case as that in the real sign, but later transcribe the words in lower case.

6. Put copies of the signs at a word-learning table for review by the children. When a child forgets what one of the words says, a quick trip down the hall will usually be enough to spur recall. Later children can print the words themselves or copy them to label their drawings.

Keep track of the signs noticed by the children and added to the collection. Eventually, there will be enough for a classroom book called "Signs in My School."

Personal sets of words. In addition to printed signs and labels, words for common objects are likely to be familiar to many kindergarten children or at least meaningful, and so not too difficult to learn in printed form. Examples are names of animals (especially cat and dog) or vehicles (e.g., car, truck), beverage and food words, and words for important people (Mom, Dad, a brother or sister, a close friend).

An excellent approach to word learning is to encourage children to tell you new words they would *like* to learn (see Ashton-Warner, 1963, for a vivid account of a teacher's experiences with this method). You can print each at the bottom of a card with a space for children to draw a picture that helps to depict the word. Then, put the word alone on the reverse side of the card. Each child's set of words can be placed in a *word box* and added to a list in his or her own folder. When the children have a free moment they can look at their words and read them aloud. Later they can sort them (for example, putting all words starting with *B* together, looking for all the words containing an *E*), and refer to them when they are writing and want to know how a word is spelled.

Secret messages. The communication of "secret messages" is also a good way to get children to attend to words. Cards can be constructed issuing directives for a group game, with the teacher saying that she is sending a "secret message" to the class, a certain group of children, or individuals. The children's job is to figure out the message and do what it says. This activity helps the children become familiar with verbs and function words. For example, after the children have learned to recognize labels for parts of the room, you can teach them about five to ten action verbs (e.g., sit, touch, walk, run, hop, skip, roll, jump, stop, crawl). Write phrase cards with these words (e.g., sit on the floor, touch the wall, walk to the door). Later, make the messages more complicated. Cards might say, for example, "Make a big circle on the floor," "Walk to the rug to hear a new story," or "Hop to the door to go outdoors."

Using children's language for reading

The term *language experience approach* or *LEA* (Allen, 1976) is used in a number of slightly different ways. We describe below an approach that relies first on children's expressing ideas orally, in their own words. The phrases and sentences they generate become the "text" used for encouraging reading development. The language experience approach is a powerful way to help children see that thoughts expressed orally can be written down and given a permanent form for all to see. This helps children develop a sense of "authorship" of the text (Ringler & Weber, 1984).

LEA can be used with the whole class, with smaller groups of children, and with individuals. In each case, the same three basic steps are followed (adapted from Hall, 1976 and Ringler & Weber, 1984).

Step 1: Oral language, or having the children express their thoughts. Your first task is to stimulate a lively discussion focused on a particular topic. Therefore, you want to make sure the children have something interesting and exciting to talk about. If the children are helping you set up an aquarium or a cage for a rabbit, observing tadpoles grow and change or a caterpillar spin a cocoon, these and similar experiences are sure to generate a lot of talk. Making sandwiches, baking cookies, carving pumpkins, and other high interest activities with a definite sequence of steps offer excellent prospects. Field trips, school programs, and other special events, such as a classroom visit by a friendly policeman, can also stimulate an animated exchange of ideas. It's best to start with direct experiences like these, but later pictures and storybooks can also be used.

Ask the children open-ended questions, requiring lengthy answers, and try not to ask any more questions than necessary to keep the conversation flowing but also well-focused. Encourage the children to explain exactly what they mean. However, don't correct them if they speak in dialect forms or use words imprecisely. Instead, paraphrase and extend their responses in Standard English and supply more precise vocabulary. Create a warm, accepting environment for the free communication of ideas, and try to draw shyer children into the discussion.

Step 2: Writing or recording the children's ideas. When you feel that the children have developed a sense of the important aspects of the experience, you are ready to begin writing down their ideas. Many teachers write with a black felt marking pen on chart paper tacked to the wall. Write down what the children say without correcting them, unless you feel the message will be ambiguous or unclear. If so, try to have the children rephrase the idea on their own. By taking care in these matters, you ensure that the language and ideas written down remain the children's own.

As you write, say each word, and sometimes even say each of the letters. After a time, you can make remarks about the conventions of writing, such as that each sentence is started with a capital letter and ended with a period.

Language experience charts should be short and memorable, often no more than six or seven sentences. After the chart has been composed, discuss with the children what an appropriate title might be, and write the title at the top. If you are working with a small group of children, you can write their names into the story or at the bottom of the chart. Here is an example of some statements that a small group of kindergarten children might have dictated after discussing pets. In this case, the teacher began each statement by naming the child. At another time, she might have left out "_____ said" and ended with the statement, "This was written by Jane, Paul, Marianne, and Vera."

Our Pets

Jane said, "I like my fuzzy wuzzy kitten."

Paul said, "I'm going to get a big dog soon."

Marianne said, "My mother says I can have a puppy."

Vera said, "We can't have pets in our building."

Step 3: Reading and working with the chart. When the chart has been completed, have the children read it together (with help from you if necessary), and then perhaps call on individuals to read the whole story (if it's very short) or the sentence each composed. Sentences can be read in order and then out of order, as you point to the words for the children. Observe whether or not the children show great interest in the text. Only those charts which hold their attention should be used for follow-up activities.

If ideas in the chart represent a sequence, the sentences can be written on long strips of tagboard, and the children can practice reading the sentences and putting them in order. You may ask the children if they want to add any words from the chart to their word boxes. Post the charts around the room and encourage the children to practice reading them and referring to them if they want to know how to spell a word. Finally, when too many charts start to accumulate, let each child have a turn to take a chart home.

Relating letter sounds to alphabet knowledge

Kindergarten children vary in their knowledge of letters, some coming to school being able to name all the letters and others only a few or none at all (McCormick & Mason, 1981). The traditional method for introducing letters has been to teach children to recite the alphabet and to name and print the letters. We recommend that you have kindergarten children recognize and print letters and also begin to associate consonants (but not vowels) with their principal sound.

You can teach children to recognize and print letters by introducing upper and lower case letters one at a time, and by giving the children many opportunities to print letters and to play games using letters. Have them, for example, make an alphabet book, sign their name on their work, label their pictures, and dictate and copy their favorite words.

Teaching the children to associate consonants with their sounds requires more carefully orchestrated instruction. Beginning instruction in letter-sound relationships can follow two different approaches. In one, the children learn to associate letters with sounds before they learn letter names (the SRA Distar program, for example, uses this approach). In the other, children are taught letter names and then are made aware that most letter names suggest their principal sounds (e.g., the letter *t* is named "tee," you hear its sound when you say its name, and it goes with words like *tall, terrible, tiny*). Both approaches seem to work, but we prefer the latter, simply because many children enter kindergarten already knowing the names of some of the letters.

The general approach is to focus on one new letter for a few days. Begin with consonants that are easy to hear and say (e.g., *b, t, s, m*), taking care when you teach *c* because its name often misleads children into assuming that its sound is /s/. Teach *w, h, y,* and *x* later because the names of these letters do not help children know their sounds. You might follow some of these ideas:

1. Feature one letter each week. Give children a page with the letter written clearly in upper and lower case and with ample space for them to draw one or more pictures. Help them think of two or three key words that represent common objects, such as *B* for ball or bike, *C* for cake or coat, *D* for dog or desk, *F* for fish or finger, etc. Have them draw pictures of the objects that stand for the letter. If they can, have them label their pictures.

2. Play games with the sound of the letter. For example, have children think of many different words that begin with the letter, and write these words on the blackboard. Or say three words and ask them which ones begin with the letter. If they have no difficulty with the initial letter sound, then you can have them work with words with the letter sound at the end. Use one-syllable words for these games because most children are not yet able to distinguish syllables from separate words. You might end the session with a short story or poem that features the letter.

3. Use children's key words to help them remember a letter's sound. Write out other words on the board that have the same initial sound and help children figure out how to read them. Let children copy and illustrate some of the words. Alternatively, children can search magazines and catalogues and copy or cut out words or pictures of objects that begin with the letter.

4. Have children select their best picture examples of objects that begin with the letter for a class poster or bulletin board display.

5. Have children describe their illustrated letter-words and talk about how the letter can be heard in their words and pictures. Encourage them to construct phrases that use these words, such as, "bouncing the big ball." This activity could be expanded to sentences, such as, "Bertha is bouncing the big ball," and then made into a book that children read to each other.

Almost all kindergarten children can benefit from an exposure to letter name and letter sound associations. Some, however, might not know all the letter names and consonant sounds until they are in the first grade, and may not learn vowel sounds until even later.

First, remember that we are working with the forms of literacy when dealing with letters and sounds, and that the learning of forms should not be emphasized over an understanding of why letters and words are important, that is, the functions of literacy. Thus, there can be no hard-and-fast rule about when letter sound learning is introduced, or when children should be expected to know all of the initial consonant sounds, short vowel sounds, and so on. Second, keep in mind that letter sound learning is just one of many aspects of learning to read, and that there are many other beneficial reading activities (such as those presented elsewhere in this chapter) to be used with children who do not seem to be benefiting from letter sound instruction.

KEY CONCEPT 4

Early reading instruction should require the child to participate actively, engaging and developing the ability to reason and to make inferences.

ACTIVE PARTICIPATION IN REASONING ABOUT TEXT

In Chapter 1 we spoke of reading as a special form of reasoning involving the making of inferences about text. Although we cannot expect kindergarten children to duplicate the sense-making activities of a mature reader, we can start them on the path toward skilled reading by encouraging reasoning and inferencing about text. As we described in the second key concept, you can help children develop their reasoning and expressive abilities through discussion of ideas from stories and from classroom events. Your aim is to give children the proper frame of mind to see reading as a process that requires asking probing questions, listening to others' ideas, and actively constructing meaning from text. You will want them to make "an effort after meaning." And, as Holdaway (1979) reminds us, you will look for every approximation, or step in the right direction, and give positive recognition to children's efforts.

Directed listening-thinking activity

Much of the same kind of reasoning with stories seems to be involved in both listening comprehension and reading comprehension (Crowell & Au, 1981). To lay the foundation for having the children make sense later of stories they read themselves, we first give them the experience of using their reasoning abilities with stories read aloud to them. The purpose of the directed listening-thinking activity (DLTA), a procedure developed by Stauffer (1980) and modified in work by Anderson, Mason, and Shirey (1984), is to foster attention to text meaning.

Specifically, it encourages the children to make predictions and then to attend to the text to see if their predictions are verified. This is an excellent method to encourage active participation and making sense of text.

The procedure can be used either with a story or informational book. We recommend using both types of books so children develop the ability to comprehend different text structures.

Working with a storybook

Planning.　Choose a story with a good plot or storyline. Begin with familiar stories where a series of parallel events occur (for example, a version of *Goldilocks and the Three Bears*). Less familiar stories with more surprising or less predictable plots can be used later. Read the story through and select several natural stopping places. For example, with the Goldilocks story, stop when she finds the bears' house, when she notices the porridge, the chairs, and the beds. At each point ask, "What *might* Goldilocks do now?" Encourage a variety of plausible answers because understanding of a story comes in thinking of possible outcomes, not merely guessing the one chosen by the author.

Reading the story.　If possible, place the children in a semicircle and work with no more than eight at a time. Show them the illustration on the book cover and read the title. Ask what the story might be about, encouraging everyone to give one idea. Go quickly around the circle accepting all responses, including repetitions and wrong answers. Read the story aloud, showing each page. At the first stopping place, ask one or two children to summarize what was learned so far. Rephrase or elaborate if their answers are vague or brief. Then ask everyone to predict what might happen next, going in order around the circle so that each has a chance to present an idea. In this way you have fast-paced responses and involvement by all the children. Repeat this same two-question process when you come to each stopping place.

Discussing the story.　Here your goal is for children to give accurate restatements of the whole story and explanations of its most important dimension, particularly of its applicability to their own lives. Begin the discussion by asking children, "What happened in the story? What happened first?" Solicit one or two answers or continue until you obtain an accurate response. Then ask what happened next. If children have forgotten, show them the pictures again in order. Continue until you have a complete retelling. Now go back through the story to have children explain the important story concepts such as the problem, how the main character tried to solve the problem, how it was resolved, and what lesson the author wanted to teach children think and talk about the story. Alternatively, have them act out the story, dramatizing the principal incidents.

After the children have had several experiences with DLTA lessons, you can talk to them about their story thinking and reasoning. Discuss with them why predictions help them understand the story and how the discussions give an added understanding of the important story ideas.

Working with an informational book

The primary difference between using a story and using an informational book is the focus. Here you will emphasize the book's topic, one that your children are studying. Before you introduce the book, review with them what they already know about the topic. Pictures and actual objects can be used to help them remember what they know. List on the board what they know about the topic and discuss with them what else they would like to know. Then show the book cover and ask them what they think they will learn about the topic from this book. When you ask for predictions, be sure to allow each child to give one idea.

Progress through the book by reading short sections and stopping at natural breaks for children to restate what was learned so far and to predict what they next expect to hear. Since they are dependent upon their memory of what you read and what they see in the illustrations, don't read too much of the book at one time. Continue the reading on another day if you notice that they are having difficulty restating what they just heard or predicting what they will hear next.

When you have finished reading for the day, lead them in a discussion summarizing the important points covered, especially with reference to the original list of things they wanted to learn. When you have finished reading the whole book, review all the important concepts. Help the children understand that the book did not necessarily cover all the information they wanted to know. Be sure to help them relate what they learned to what they knew before. Sometimes this can be carried out by having children draw pictures about the information.

As with the DLTA storybook procedure, you can later discuss with the children the process you are taking them through in reasoning about informational text.

SUMMARY

We began by looking at the nature of young children's early experiences with reading. Although these vary from child to child, many enter kindergarten already knowing quite a bit about reading and writing. For these children, we advised that you be sure to build upon home literacy experiences. For others, who may come to school without such a foundation, we reminded you to focus first on developing the children's understanding of the many functions of literacy.

In the first key concept we discussed the importance of creating a warm, positive environment for learning in the kindergarten classroom. Both the social and academic contexts need to be considered. In the second key concept we looked at ways of acquainting young children with the many different uses of reading and writing in the family and community. Among activities recommended to bring out the many functions of literacy, were reading storybooks aloud, encouraging the children to write, and bringing literacy into classroom routines.

The idea that early reading instruction should use familiar information and build on children's existing knowledge was stressed in the third key concept. All children come to school with strengths in oral language and with knowledge of the world, although they may differ in their understandings of literacy. The language experience approach and activities with environmental signs and labels were highlighted as being consistent with this key concept.

Finally, in the fourth key concept we pointed out ways of involving children in reasoning with text through directed listening-thinking activities. Throughout this chapter, we emphasized that kindergarten teachers must see that their students learn first about the functions of literacy, before being asked to work at the level of forms (words, letters, and sounds) or conventions (procedures for reading).

BIBLIOGRAPHY

REFERENCES

Adams, M., & Bruce, B. C. (1982). Background knowledge and reading comprehension. In J. A. Langer & M. T. Smith-Burke (Eds.), *Reader meets author/Bridging the gap: A psycholinguistic and sociolinguistic perspective.* Newark, DE: International Reading Association.

Allen, R. V. (1976). *Language experience in communication.* Boston: Houghton Mifflin.

Anderson, R., Mason, J., & Shirey, L. (1984). The reading group: An experimental investigation of a labyrinth. *Reading Research Quarterly, 20,* 6–38.

Ashton-Warner, S. (1963). *Teacher.* New York: Simon & Schuster.

Bissex, G. (1980) *GNYS AT WRK: A child learns to write and read.* Cambridge, MA: Harvard University Press.

Bloome, D. (1983). Reading as a social process. In B. Hutson (Ed.), *Advances in reading/language research.* Greenwich, CT: Jai Press.

Bruner, J. (1984). Language, mind, and reading. In H. Goelman, A. Oberg, & F. Smith (Eds.), *Awakening to literacy.* Portsmouth, NH: Heinemann.

Burris, N., & Lantz, K. (1983). Caption books in the classroom. *Reading Teacher, 36,* 872–875.

Clay, M. (1975). *What did I write? Beginning writing behavior.* Portsmouth, NH: Heinemann.

Clay, M. (1979). *Reading: The patterning of complex behavior.* 2nd ed. Portsmouth, NH: Heinemann.

Crowell, D. C., & Au, K. H. (1981). A scale of questions to guide comprehension instruction. *Reading Teacher, 34* (4), 389-393.

Ferreiro, E., & Teberosky, A. (1982). *Literacy before schooling.* Portsmouth, NH: Heinemann.

Gambrell, L., & Sokolski, C. (1983). Picture potency: Use Caldecott Award books to develop children's language. *Reading Teacher, 36,* 868-871.

Goldfield, B., & Snow, C. (1984). Reading books with children: The mechanics of parental influence on children's reading achievement. In J. Flood (Ed.), *Understanding reading comprehension.* Newark, DE: International Reading Association.

Goodman, K. (1965). A linguistic study of cues and miscues in reading. *Elementary English, 42,* 639-642.

Hall, M. A. (1976). *Teaching reading as a language experience.* Columbus, Ohio: Charles E. Merrill.

Harste, J., Woodward, V., & Burke, C. (1984). *Language stories and literacy lessons.* Portsmouth, NH: Heinemann.

Holdaway, D. (1979). *The foundations of literacy.* Sydney, Australia: Ashton Scholastic (distributed in the United States by Heinemann).

Mason, J. (1980). When do children begin to read: An exploration of four-year-old children's letter and word reading competencies. *Reading Research Quarterly, 15,* 203-227.

Mason, J. (1984). Early reading from a developmental perspective. In P. D. Pearson (Ed.), *Handbook of reading research.* New York: Longman.

McCormick C., & Mason, J. (1981). What happens to kindergarten children's knowledge about reading after a summer vacation? *Reading Teacher, 35,* 164-172.

McCormick C., & Mason, J. (1984). *Intervention procedures for increasing preschool children's interest in and knowledge about reading* (Tech. Rep. No. 312) Urbana, IL: University of Illinois, Center for the Study of Reading.

Morrow, L. (1984). Effects of story retelling on young children's comprehension and sense of story structure. In J. Niles & L. Harris (Eds.), *Changing perspectives on research in reading/language processing and instruction.* Rochester, NY: National Reading Conference.

Olson, D. (1984). "See! Jumping!" Some oral language antecedents of literacy. In H. Goelman, A. Oberg, & F. Smith (Eds.), *Awakening to literacy.* Portsmouth, NH: Heinemann.

Paley, V. (1981). *Wally's children.* Cambridge, MA: Harvard University Press.

Rash, J., Johnson, T., & Gleadow, N. (1984). Acquisition and retention of written words by kindergarten children under varying learning conditions. *Reading Research Quarterly, 19,* 452-460.

Ringler, L. H., & Weber, C. K. (1984). *A language-thinking approach to reading: Diagnosis and teaching.* San Diego, CA: Harcourt Brace Jovanovich.

Rubin, A. (1980). Comprehension processes in oral and written language. In R. Spiro, B. C. Bruce, & W. F. Brewer (Eds.), *Theoretical issues in reading comprehension.* Hillsdale, NJ: Erlbaum.

Smith, S. L., Carey, R. F., & Harste, J. C. (1982). The contexts of reading. In A. Berger & H. A. Robinson (Eds.), *Secondary school reading: What research reveals for classroom practice.* Urbana, IL: National Conference on Research in English and ERIC Clearinghouse on Reading and Communication Skills.

Snow, C., & Ninio, A. (in press). The contribution of reading books with children to their linguistic and cognitive development. In W. Teale & E. Sulzby (Eds.), *Emergent literacy: Writing and reading.* Norwood, NJ: Ablex.

Soderbergh, R. (1977). *Reading in early childhood: A linguistic study of a preschool child's gradual acquisition of reading ability*. Washington, DC: Georgetown University Press.

Stauffer, R. G. (1980). *The language-experience approach to the teaching of reading*. 2nd ed. New York: Harper & Row.

Sulzby, E. (in press). Writing and reading as signs of oral and written language organization in the young child. In W. Teale & E. Sulzby (Eds.), *Emergent literacy: Writing and reading*. Norwood, NJ: Ablex.

Sutherland, Z., & Arbuthnot, M. H. (1986). *Children and books*. 7th ed. Glenview, IL: Scott, Foresman.

Taylor, D. (1983). *Family literacy: Young children learning to read and write*. Portsmouth, NH: Heinemann.

Temple, C., Nathan, R., & Burris, N. (1984). *The beginnings of writing*. Boston: Allyn & Bacon.

FURTHER READINGS

Dyson, A. (1984). *Emerging literacy in school contexts: Toward defining the gap between school curriculum and child mind*. Athens, GA: University of Georgia.

Goelman, H., Oberg, A., & Smith, F. (1984). *Awakening to literacy*. Portsmouth, NH: Heinemann.

Graves, D. (1981). In R. Walshe (Ed.), *Donald Graves in Australia: Children want to write . . .* Rosebery, NSW, Australia: Bridge Printery.

Heath, S. B. (1983). *Ways with words: Language, life and work in communities and classrooms*. New York: Cambridge University Press.

Jensen, J. (1984). *Composing and comprehending*. Urbana, IL: National Council of Teachers of English.

Read, C. (1971). Pre-school children's knowledge of English phonology. *Harvard Educational Review, 41*, 1-34.

Teale, W., & Sulzby, E. Eds. (in press). *Emergent literacy: Writing and reading*. Norwood, NJ: Ablex.

Wells, G. (1981). *Learning through interactions: The study of language development*. New York: Cambridge University Press.

CHAPTER 3

Teaching Word Identification Skills

Word recognition is the foundation of the reading process. To be sure, there is much more to reading than word recognition. The reader who would understand an aphorism, such as the following, must do much more than recognize 11 words.

A woman needs a man like a fish needs a bicycle.

He must, among other things, discern that MAN is a noun, not a verb, and that it is the object of the verb NEEDS, not the subject of that verb; he must, in short, discover the grammatical relations among the words in order to arrive at the meaning of the sentence. If he is to appreciate that meaning, he must draw upon his knowledge of men and women, fishes and bicycles. And if he is to understand its significance, he must integrate it into the discourse of which it is a part.

But before any of this can be done, those 11 words must be recognized. The reader must see that the sentence contains MAN, not FAN or MAT, and NEEDS, not FEEDS or NEARS, or the sentence will be misunderstood.

It behooves the students of reading, then, to understand something of word recognition. (Gough, 1984, p. 225)

OVERVIEW

In this chapter we present ways you can help children develop strategies to identify words, first in their oral vocabularies, with meanings they already know, and later with relatively unknown words. We begin by looking at how skilled readers proceed through text and at the relationship between word identification and reading comprehension. We then discuss the five different word identification strategies children can be taught. These have to do either with knowing words by sight or being able to analyze words using letter sounds, syllables, morphemes, and context. After going over methods for teaching students all five strategies, we show how you can assist students in using the strategies effectively, in combination with one another. Teaching students to use a combination of strategies is a necessary step toward helping them gain independence in word identification.

The key concepts in this chapter are:

Key Concept #1: Printed words are best remembered at first if they are meaningful and important to the child.

Key Concept #2: Children should learn word identification skills which help them use knowledge of letter-sound relationships.

Key Concept #3: Children should learn word identification skills which help them use knowledge of syllables.

Key Concept #4: Children should learn word identification skills which help them use knowledge of morphemes, the smallest meaning-bearing parts of words.

Key Concept #5: Children should learn word identification skills which help them use knowledge of context.

Key Concept #6: Children should learn that word identification is a problem-solving process, requiring the use of a combination of strategies.

PERSPECTIVE

HOW THE MIND DIRECTS THE EYES

Reading is the process of constructing meaning from text. Thus, word identification is important not as an end in itself, but because, by becoming effortless, it enables the reader to focus on comprehension. When skilled readers read, the eyes are not moving on their own but are being carefully directed by the mind, in its search for meaning. As McConkie (1984) puts it:

Recent research leads to a view of the reader as actively engaged in attending to the text in response to the needs of the comprehension processes. The task is to comprehend the message; the goal of the perceptual system is to provide the visual information needed to keep this mental activity moving smoothly. Apparently this comprehension process proceeds on a word-by-word basis with the individual words perceived and having their effect on the mind. . . . How long the eyes remain in a location, and how far they move next, are determined by the needs of comprehension processes and the control of the eyes seems to be both precise and delicate. (p. 20)

We have known since Huey (1908) that our eyes move in *saccades* or jumps across the page, making brief *fixations* or stops of about one quarter of a second. According to McConkie (1984), even though it seems when we read that our eyes are almost always moving, in reality they are moving only about 10 percent of the time. We do not pick up information during saccades but only when a fixation is made. We also know that the reader's mind has planned where the next fixation will be before the eyes begin their next jump. These and other findings make it clear that mature reading is a carefully controlled process rather than a hit-or-miss affair, involving well organized and efficient movements of the eyes to predetermined locations in the text.

Relationship between rapid word identification and comprehension

Being skilled at anything requires *automaticity,* or the ability to perform parts of the total process quickly, without thinking about them. Thus, proficient reading requires the ability to identify words very quickly (LaBerge & Samuels, 1976) so that attention can be placed on comprehension. Beginning readers who develop automaticity in word identification are better able to comprehend text (Perfetti & Hogaboam, 1975; Lesgold, Resnick, & Hammond, 1985).

Does this mean that children's reading comprehension will improve if they are taught to read a set of words very quickly? It has not turned out to be that simple. While children must develop their word recognition skill to the point where it requires little conscious attention, the best approach does not appear to be reading lists of words. Recognizing words should not be a mindless activity because, as we emphasized in Chapter 1, reading requires the child to become an active, strategic thinker, a problem-solver. This is difficult to achieve if children are not taught to figure out how words are pronounced within a text context. Teaching children letter-sound rules will not be sufficient either. It appears that skilled readers do not apply letter-to-sound rules when confronted with unknown words but look for similarities to words they know (Stanovich, 1980).

Children must learn to process not only letters and words, but also phrases and sentences. This information must be integrated with their background knowledge so that the text being read makes sense. Since our goal is to enable children to derive meaning from text, effective word recognition instruction must pull in and relate words to the sentence and larger text context.

In short, we cannot conclude either that good word identification produces good comprehension, or vice versa, that good comprehension produces good word identification. Instead, in children learning to read as well as in proficient readers, word identification and comprehension processes are best viewed as supporting one another.

Implications for reading instruction

What do these research findings mean for instruction? They mean that the most sensible course in teaching beginning reading is *balanced* or *simultaneous* instruction (Resnick, 1979) of comprehension and word identification. While, depending on the children's need, teachers may wish at some points to emphasize either instruction in comprehension or in word identification, they must always strive to integrate one with the other and achieve a balance between the two.

Different ways of identifying words

You are probably familiar with at least two different ways of identifying words:

1. by sight (instantly, because the reader is already familiar with that particular pattern of letters);
2. by letter sounds (or *phonemes*, the distinguishable speech sounds in words).

Research indicates that there are at least three more ways used by proficient readers:

3. by *letter cluster pattern* or syllables (letter groups that are likely to appear together);
4. by *morphemes* (the smallest meaning-bearing parts of words);
5. by *context clues* (using surrounding words and the overall meaning of the phrase, sentence, or larger text unit).

Efficient word identification appears to depend on using a *combination of strategies* (Cunningham, 1975–76; K. Smith, 1977). This implies that teaching children only one or two strategies will not help them to identify words efficiently. Instead, children should learn to use all five ways of identifying words. In this chapter, we discuss each of the ways of identifying words listed above and describe activities you can use to help children learn to use them.

Most of the material in this chapter will be relevant to teachers working with children in the phases of reading development we call *formal beginning reading* and *emerging mature reading*, but not *early reading*. Many children move into the formal beginning reading phase late in kindergarten or early in first grade.

As you study these key concepts, keep in mind that instruction in word identification proceeds most rapidly if the children already have an intuitive understanding of some patterning of letters and sounds in words. This means that they can hear and think of rhyming words and words that begin with the same sound. Instruction in word identification is best seen as applying these intuitively understood word analysis skills to other words fitting the same pattern. You will find it much easier to teach the regularities if the children have had a chance to begin to notice them on their own.

KEY CONCEPT 1

Printed words are best remembered at first if they are meaningful and important to the child.

BEGINNING WITH A SIGHT WORD APPROACH

This approach follows from one of the key concepts central to Chapter 2: early reading instruction should be meaningful, building on young children's background knowledge and experiences. As Durkin (1983) points out, high interest and familiar words, representing people or things children know, are easily learned by a sight word approach. Learning words by sight means simply memorizing them as wholes, without giving attention to their letter sounds.

Having children first learn perhaps fifty or so words by sight lays the foundation for their systematic learning of word identification skills. It helps children establish a connection between print and meaning (Ehri & Wilce, 1985; Mason, 1980). The experience and understanding they gain in learning these words provides a basis for noticing and remembering letter patterns (McCaughey, Juola, Schadler, & Ward, 1980).

Another reason for starting with a sight or *whole word* method is that none of our four other ways of identifying words can be applied to common English words with irregular spelling patterns, such as *was*, *are*, and *said*. A certain number of words have to be learned by a sight method anyway. Finally, a sight method allows children to do some reading of connected text almost immediately. This gives them the opportunity to get a sense of what it means to be a reader working to construct meaning from text and, as McCormick and Mason (1984) found, it can foster an interest in reading.

With which words should you begin?

Teachers' decisions about the words children will learn by sight can be based on just three criteria: (1) the children's interests, (2) word meaningfulness, and (3) word frequency. Notice that word length is not an issue, because short words are not always easier for children to learn than long ones. If the children's sight words vary in length, they will appear different and so be somewhat easier to identify. For example, Mason (1980) found that preschool children remembered *elephant* best, even though it was the longest of the five words they had been taught.

High interest words.   In the section on personal sets of words in Chapter 2, we made some suggestions about the kinds of words likely to be of the greatest interest to young children. This includes names of classmates, environmental print words, and words for things children want to learn about.

Meaningful words. There are many, many words children will find *meaningful.* Meaningful words are those that stand for something children already know. They include nouns representing objects or people (*house, fireman*); often used adjectives for size, shape, color, or number (*big, round, red, three*); and certain verbs of action (*jump, run*). Children find it easier to identify these meaningful words than words that represent more abstract ideas (Mason, 1977a).

Because of their importance and familiarity to children, we can expect high interest and meaningful words to be learned fairly rapidly by sight. Knowing these words by sight will give children confidence in their reading abilities and probably some intuitive understanding of the patterning of letters in words and of letter sounds. However, high interest and meaningful words usually do not occur very frequently in the texts children are likely to read. Thus, reading these words by sight will not be of much help with the important task of reading connected text.

High frequency words. Knowing *high frequency words* by sight will help children with the reading of connected text. There are 100 or so words used so often that they make up about 50 percent of most texts (Carroll, Davies, & Richman, 1971). The problem is that these words do not carry much meaning in and of themselves and therefore tend to be very uninteresting and difficult to convey to children. Furthermore, with many being irregularly spelled (e.g., *are, one, was*), there are few good examples to help children learn regular letter-sound patterns.

Figure 3.1 contains a list of the 200 most frequently used words, as determined by Carroll et al. Some people refer to these as "glue" words, because they hold the text together, and others speak of them as the "mortar" for the "brick wall" of text. While these are not elegant phrases, they certainly make clear how useful it is for children to be able to identify these words by sight. As we will see, these phrases also provide a clue about how these words can be taught by sight.

INSTRUCTIONAL ACTIVITIES

Above all, make sure children understand something of the meaning of the words they are learning by sight. The more interesting, important, and meaningful the words are, the more likely they are to remember them. One school district (Urbana, IL) puts out a booklet of 200 high frequency words for children to use as they write stories. Other ways to help children learn words by sight were presented in Chapter 2. These include story rereading, writing, bringing literacy into classroom routines, sign and label activities, personal sets of words, secret messages, and language experience stories.

FIGURE 3.1   200 Most Frequently Occurring Words

1. the	31. but	61. into	91. long	121. also	151. great	181. sound
2. of	32. what	62. has	92. little	122. around	152. tell	182. below
3. and	33. all	63. more	93. very	123. another	153. men	183. saw
4. a	34. were	64. her	94. after	124. came	154. say	184. something
5. to	35. when	65. two	95. words	125. come	155. small	185. thought
6. in	36. we	66. like	96. called	126. work	156. every	186. both
7. is	37. there	67. him	97. just	127. three	157. found	187. few
8. you	38. can	68. see	98. where	128. word	158. still	188. those
9. that	39. an	69. time	99. most	129. must	159. between	189. always
10. it	40. your	70. could	100. know	130. because	160. name	190. looked
11. he	41. which	71. no	101. get	131. does	161. should	191. show
12. for	42. their	72. make	102. through	132. part	162. Mr.	192. large
13. was	43. said	73. than	103. back	133. even	163. home	193. often
14. on	44. if	74. first	104. much	134. place	164. big	194. together
15. are	45. do	75. been	105. before	135. well	165. give	195. asked
16. as	46. will	76. its	106. go	136. such	166. air	196. house
17. with	47. each	77. who	107. good	137. here	167. line	197. don't
18. his	48. about	78. now	108. new	138. take	168. set	198. world
19. they	49. how	79. people	109. write	139. why	169. own	199. going
20. at	50. up	80. my	110. our	140. things	170. under	200. want
21. be	51. out	81. made	111. used	141. help	171. read	
22. this	52. them	82. over	112. me	142. put	172. last	
23. from	53. then	83. did	113. man	143. years	173. never	
24. I	54. she	84. down	114. too	144. different	174. us	
25. have	55. many	85. only	115. any	145. away	175. left	
26. or	56. some	86. way	116. day	146. again	176. end	
27. by	57. so	87. find	117. same	147. off	177. along	
28. one	58. these	88. use	118. right	148. went	178. while	
29. had	59. would	89. may	119. look	149. old	179. might	
30. not	60. other	90. water	120. think	150. number	180. next	

Excerpt from "Rank List" from *Word Frequency Book*. Copyright © 1971 by American Heritage Publishing Co., Inc. Reprinted with permission.

Contrasting high frequency words

When the opportunity arises to teach high frequency words, present the "bricks" along with the "mortar." That is, begin by showing the high frequency words in meaningful phrases or sentences made up of concrete nouns, adjectives, and action verbs. Something of the meaning of high frequency words can be given to the children by contrasting them. For example, one morning a first grade teacher wrote the following "morning message" to her class:

Linda brought her pets to school today.

One is a boy rabbit and his name is Timmy.

The other is a girl rabbit and her name is Tammy.

After the children had figured out her message, the teacher wrote:

```
His name is Timmy.

Her name is Tammy.
```

She asked the children to read both sentences, and some referred back to the message to read them correctly. She then discussed with the children differences between words in the two sentences (*his* and *her*; *Timmy* and *Tammy*).

This example shows how you can make up your own exercises to teach high frequency words such as *is* and *her* in a meaningful context, and have children notice differences in the spelling of words.

Using predictable materials

In the following activity, developed by Bridge, Winograd, and Haley (1983), books with highly predictable or structured language were used to help children learn sight words. Lessons with these materials were found to be more effective than those conducted with a preprimer from a basal reader series.

You might start with the patterned books used in the Bridge et al. study: *Brown Bear, Brown Bear, What Do You See?, Fire, Fire, Said Mrs. McGuire, The Haunted House,* and *Up the Down Escalator,* all by Bill Martin; and *Jimmy Has Lost His Cap, Where Can It Be?* and *The Elephant's Wish* by Bruno Munari.

Bridge et al. list the following steps for using each patterned book. You will need to prepare in advance a large chart with the text of the book, sentence strips, and individual word cards. If the children are working with a basal reader, you can select words which appear in both the structured language books and the basal. The same basic steps listed below can also be used with a language experience chart.

Step 1. Read the book aloud to the group. Then read it again, this time encouraging the children to try to predict what comes next. Let the children take turns reading the book in a chorus.

Step 2. Read the story from the chart with the children. Give children the sentence strips, which they try to place under the corresponding lines on the chart. Then give them the individual word cards, also to be placed under the matching words in the chart.

Step 3. Have the children read aloud in a chorus the whole story from the chart. Place the individual word cards in random order at the bottom of the chart. Have the children match the word cards to the words on the chart.

KEY CONCEPT 2

Children should learn word identification skills which help them use knowledge of letter-sound relationships.

LETTER-SOUND RELATIONSHIPS

Phonics instruction involves teaching children to use the alphabetic principles of our language and knowledge of letter-sound relationships. In our second word identification strategy we are helping children learn to associate letters with the *phonemes* or basic speech sounds of English. The purpose of phonics instruction is to help children "break" the alphabetic code and become self-reliant in working out the pronunciations of words.

But the correspondence between letters and sounds in English is less regular than in some other languages, and the number of rules for representing the correspondences is too large to be completely taught. That means that a great many words children will try to read cannot be sounded out letter by letter. (For discussion of this point, see Cunningham, 1975–76, or F. Smith, 1978.) While a letter-sound analysis will be useful, it cannot be the exclusive strategy used to identify words.

This point helps to put phonics in proper perspective. In general, only teach or encourage beginning readers to use phonics on words already in their oral vocabulary. When they see such words in the context of a phrase or sentence, they will usually only have to use a slight bit of knowledge about letter-sound relationships to figure them out. Emerging mature readers, however, will occasionally be confronted with words that are not in their oral vocabulary, so teach them to make flexible use of context and word analysis strategies.

INSTRUCTIONAL GUIDELINES

We recommend that you teach children strategies for analyzing words into phonemes and relating letters to sounds through methods that lead them to a problem-solving orientation. Try to follow these three guidelines:

1. Make your instruction simple. Teach regular and easily distinguished phonetic principles. Teach beginning readers the most common sound for each consonant and help them distinguish these sounds in different positions in the word (initial, final, and then in the middle) and in different combinations (in initial or final consonant blends). For example, teach them *b* as /b/ in *ball, rub, rubber, brown,* and *blow.*

2. Help them realize early on that letters sometimes have more than one sound and that there are variations to the regular rule. For example, while you teach that *c* usually makes a /k/ sound, present the idea that it occasionally has a different sound (you might show them *city*). Later, when teaching the long *a* sound for *ai*, show them that most words containing *ai* (e.g., *pain, laid, mail, bait,* but not *said*), have the same sound.

3. Use reading materials that exemplify the phonetic principle you are teaching. For example, you can find poems or stories that feature words beginning with the consonant you are teaching. Later, when you teach short vowels, look for stories that contain many consonant-short vowel-consonant (CVC) words.

Letter-sound and letter-cluster-to-sound patterns

Your aim in phonics instruction is to give children the greatest amount of useful knowledge in the shortest amount of teaching time. You want children to apply the patterns to words they have not seen in print before. This means that you should teach patterns consistent with the letter-sound relationship shown in the largest set of words.

Fortunately, linguists have analyzed our language to uncover these generalizable *major patterns*. For consonants, we focus on their major sounds as single letters and pairs. For vowels, we focus on their major sounds in *clusters* of letters (e.g., *ade*) or syllables. We present the major patterns, consonant-influenced patterns, and minor patterns for vowels.

Major patterns are the most common letter-sound relationships. They occur frequently enough to be useful in word identification and are the principal phonics patterns. You can emphasize major patterns for both consonants and vowels by using familiar, representative words. For example, you might teach the major pattern sounds for *c* and *ch* with words such as *cat* and *coat, chair* and *chin*. You could teach the short *a* sound with words such as *cat, ham,* and *man*.

Consonant-influenced vowel patterns are those in which the vowel sound is changed by the preceding consonant (*w*) or the one following (such as *r, l*). Because these patterns do not occur as often as major vowel patterns, you need not cover them as systematically. On occasions when children have failed to read such words correctly, call their attention to the pattern. For example, if children missed the word *ball*, you could present the *all* pattern, and remind them that *all, tall,* and *fall* have the same ending sounds.

Minor patterns consist of words whose proper pronunciation will not be revealed by using knowledge of usual letter-sound relationships. Some are words borrowed from other languages (e.g., *cello*), others represent unchanged, archaic spelling patterns (e.g., *could*), and others show regular word endings of morphemic patterns (e.g., the *c* in *musician*). These words should be treated as exceptions for beginning readers and taught as sight words.

FIGURE 3.2 Consonant-Sound Patterns

Major and Minor Examples	Major Patterns in Initial and Final Positions	Minor Pattern Examples	Consonant Digraphs	Major Patterns	Minor Pattern Examples
b	bat cab	climb	ch	child march kitchen	ache choir school
c	cat	city cellar cello muscle	ck	black	
d	dot pad	handkerchief helped	dg	edge	
f	fan cuff	of	gh	high night	laugh spaghetti ghost
g	gate big	gem gnat sign garage	ph	phone graph	
h	hat	honest	sh	shop dish	
j	jaw	Juanita	th	think this cloth with	asthma thyme
k	kite	knight	wh	where	who
l	lamp	would colonel			
m	man ham				
n	nest pen				
p	pot cap	corps pneumonia			
q	queen				
r	run tar				
s	sat pass	boys sugar aisle			
t	ten pet	depot			
v	valentine				
w	war row	answer			
x	xylophone box				
y	yellow penny				
z	zebra buzz				

In Figure 3.2 we list major and minor patterns for single consonants as well as for *digraphs* (consonant pairs with one sound). Figure 3.3 (see p. 72) displays pattern information for vowels. Here, many of the vowel pattern examples are arranged into *phonograms* (sets of rhyming words). Both tables highlight words which might be encountered in texts written for elementary school students.

Before going further, complete the exercise below to see which kind of letter-sound information is more likely to be useful to children, information about consonants or information about vowels.

EXERCISE

Look at the paragraph below:

(1) On a separate piece of paper, write down as many of the words in the paragraph as you can figure out.

(2) While you do this, observe what type of letter was deleted from the words.

(3) Try to guess what the implications of this exercise are for teaching children letter-sound relationships.

- s--n l--rn-d t- kn-w th-s fl-w-r b-tt-r. -n th- l-ttl- pr-nc-'s pl-n-t th- fl-w-rs h-d -lw-ys b--n v-ry s-mpl-. Th-y h-d -nly -n- r-ng -f p-t-ls; th-y t--k -p n- r--m -t -ll; th-y w-r- - tr--bl- t- n-b-dy. -n- m-rn-ng th-y w--ld -pp--r -n th- gr-ss, -nd by n-ght th-y w--ld h-v- f-d-d p--c-f-lly -w-y. -u- o-e -ay, --o- a -ee- -o-- --o- -0 o-e -e- --e-e, a -e- --o-e- -a- -o-e u-; -n- --e -i--e -i-e -a- -a--e- -e-y --o-e-yo-e- -i- --a-- --ou- --i-- -a- -o--i-e a y-o-e- -a- --o-e- -a- --ou- o- -i- --a-e-. l--i---, you- -ee, -a-e -a- -a- -e- -i- o- -ao-a-.

The paragraph is from *The Little Prince* by Antoine de Saint Exupéry (1943, p. 31):

I soon learned to know this flower better. On the little prince's planet the flowers had always been very simple. They had only one ring of petals; they took up no room at all; they were a trouble to nobody. One morning they would appear in the grass, and by night they would have faded peacefully away. But one day, from a seed blown from no one knew where, a new flower had come up; and the little prince had watched very closely over this small sprout which was not like any other small sprouts on his planet. It might, you see, have been a new kind of baobab.

(1) While you may not have figured out all of the words in either the first or the second part of the paragraph, you almost certainly had better luck with the first than with the second.

(2) All of the vowels were deleted in the first half, all of the consonants in the second (although we left the y's in both).

(3) You may have concluded, correctly, that teaching children consonant letter-sound relationships will give them more information about unknown words than teaching them vowel letter-sound relationships. Obviously, however, it's best to know something about both.

Guidelines for teaching consonants

Consonant-sound relationships are quite consistent. For this reason, and also because beginning readers will find them to be much more useful than vowels in identifying words (K. Smith, 1977), teach consonants before vowels.

Most consonants are associated with only one or two major sounds, and the name of the letter gives children a clue to their most common sound. These should be taught first:

| b | d | f | j | k | l | m |
| n | p | r | s | t | v | z |

We have no evidence that teaching these consonant sounds in any particular order is better than any other. Therefore, start with those which occur as the first letter in a number of the children's sight words, seem more common in general, and are quite distinctive. *S* is often a good first choice. Many teachers find it easier not to teach one after another the sounds of letters that look much alike to the young child (e.g., *b*, *d*, and *p*; *m* and *n*).

The major sound associated with some consonants tends to be more difficult for children to learn because the letter name does not serve as a good clue. Teach these later:

| c | g | h | w |

Children usually learn to notice and hear the letter-sound relationships of single consonants in the *initial* position (e.g., *mat*), that is, at the beginning of a word. Therefore, first teach letter-sound relationships with single consonants in the initial position. Second, help children understand that the same letter-sound relationships may help them figure out how a word ends (i.e., teach single consonants in the *final* position; e.g., *jam*). Third, help children recognize that the letter may also be found in the *medial* position, or in the middle of a word (e.g., *camel*).

After they know single consonants, children should be able to figure out consonant *blends*. These are pairs (or sometimes trios) of consonants that quite frequently occur together. Each letter in the blend retains its own sound, so the two letter sounds can be thought to "blend" together. The most frequent blends at the beginning of words contain a consonant followed by an *r* or *l*.

Begin by introducing blends that occur in the initial position. If the blend occurs in other positions, this can be pointed out later. You usually do not need to teach more than one or two blends before children realize how two consonant sounds are merged together. Again, begin with the blends occurring in the children's sight words.

Here are two-letter blends often found at the beginning of common words:

bl	cl	fl	gl	pl	sl
br	cr	dr	fr	gr	pr	tr
st	sk

After blends, cover consonant *digraphs*. Digraphs are combinations of two letters, such as *th*, which together are pronounced as one sound. They are different from blends in that the separate sounds usually associated with each letter cannot be heard. Consonant digraphs you need to teach are the following;

| ch | sh | ph | th | wh | gh |

With respect to the *wh* pattern, in many communities today no distinction is made between the pronunciation of *wh* and *w*. You can teach whatever fits local pronunciation.

Point out to the children that these digraphs or pairs of letters have their own special sound. To help them remember to treat digraphs as a unit, you could join the two letters with a cursive stroke, (for example, *ch*).

Guidelines for teaching vowels

Vowel-sound relationships are much less consistent than consonant sounds. (Some individual vowels can be associated with 20 or more sounds!) However, most vowel sounds can be predicted within their *syllable* environment. When a single vowel is supported on either side by a consonant, it typically has a short sound (e.g., *pat*). When there is no second consonant or when the second consonant is followed by a silent *e*, the vowel typically has a long sound (e.g., *pane*). When the second consonant is an *r* or *l*, the vowel has a predictably different sound (e.g., *part, pall*). Finally when there are two vowels together (e.g., *pain, peak*), another set of patterns is evident.

Although we do not advise you to teach in a formal way all of these relationships, *you* as the teacher will need to understand the pattern regularities so that you can decide how best to help children. For this purpose, it is helpful to look at Mason's (1973, 1977b) analysis of one-syllable words, based on work by Venezky (1970). This analysis places vowel patterns into three types of clusters.

Consonant-vowel-consonant (CVC) clusters. The major vowel pattern for this cluster is a short sound. Examples are *cat* and *pet*. The same basic pattern applies to words beginning with blends, for example, *crib* and *grab*. Words beginning or ending with digraphs, for example, *chop* and *much*, also fit the pattern. Consonant-influenced patterns, which are listed along with the major patterns in Figure 3.3, have other sounds, (for example, *star* or *fight*).

FIGURE 3.3   Vowel-Sound Clusters

	Major Patterns (Presented as Phonograms)	Consonant-influenced Patterns	Minor Patterns (Examples)
Consonant-Vowel-Consonant (CVC) Clusters:			
a	bad, dad, glad cat, sat, fat back, sack, tack bag, rag, tag can, ran, man cap, map, tap ash, cash, mash last, fast, mast band, strand, land	star, far, car, call, tall, wall bank, sank, thank bang, hang, sang	what was wand war
e	bed, led, red set, met, get less, mess, chess pen, hen, ten send, bend, end nest, best, rest neck, deck, peck bent, sent, tent	her fern	
i	bin, pin, tin chip, tip, lip bit, fit, hit dip, rip, skip dish, fish, wish sick, pick, tick ink, think, mink	sir hill, mill, bill mind, kind, rind fight, tight, light child, mid	pint sign
o	hop, chop, drop pot, got, hot clock, dock, rock	for roll, toll, troll most, post, ghost cold, hold, told song, long, gong	clothes off won worn
u	mug, bug, rug sun, fun, run duck, truck, luck junk, sunk, trunk	fur hurt dull, hull, skull	pull truth
Consonant-Vowel-Consonant-Silent E (CV and CVCe) Clusters:			
a/e	ate, gate, skate gave, cave, save cake, bake, lake plane, cane, mane same, lame, tame	care, bare, dare tale, pale, sale	have are dance
e/e	he, me, we these	here were there	fence
i/e	fine, mine, nine bike, like, hike hide, wide, slide	tire, fire, hire pile, smile, file	give since

FIGURE 3.3 *Vowel-Sound Clusters* (continued)

	Major Patterns (Presented as Phonograms)	Consonant-influenced Patterns	Minor Patterns (Examples)
o/e	go woke, choke, joke bone, tone, phone	core, bore, tore pole, hole, sole	love once come lose
u/e	use, muse, fuse blue, true, sue	sure, pure, cure nurse, purse	

Consonant-Vowel-Vowel-Consonant (CVVC) Clusters:

	Major Patterns (Presented as Phonograms)	Consonant-influenced Patterns	Minor Patterns (Examples)
ai, ay	say, day, hay train, brain, pain	air, hair, chair jail, hail, mail	said plaid
au, aw	law, saw, thaw draw, claw, paw	haul, maul crawl, bawl	laugh
ea	tea, sea, pea peach, teach, each leave, weave, heave	dear, fear, sear earn, learn bear, tear, pear deal, peal, heal	great break
	bread, dead, head		been
ee	bee, tree, see peep, deep, keep feet, beet, meet	cheer, sneer, seer heel, eel, feel	
ei, ey	they, hey, grey vein, rein weigh, neigh	their, heir veil	key weird seize
eu, ew	new, grew, few		sew
ie	die, lie, pie		
	chief, grief, thief	tier, pier field	friend
oa	boat, coat, oat boast, toast, roast	boar, roar, soar goal, coal	broad
oi, oy	boy, toy, joy join, coin, loin	choir boil, toil, soil	
oo	too, coo, moo room, loom, boom goose, moose, loose	door pool	brooch book flood
	book, look, took		
ou, ow	cow, now, sow found, sound, mound mouse, house	flour howl	
	blow, crow, flow dough, though	course	group could
ui	fruit, suit	build	suite

Consonant-vowel (CV) or consonant-vowel-consonant-silent e (CVCe) clusters. Here the major pattern is that the vowel has a long sound. Examples include *me, made, tripe, he,* and *shine.* Again, the presence of certain consonants following the vowel changes the sound, as in *care* and *here.*

Consonant-vowel-vowel-consonant (CVVC) clusters. There are many patterns here, each vowel pair having its own rule. Note, however, that most vowel pairs, with the exception of *ie, ea, ou,* have only one major pattern.

Rely on the concepts of major patterns, consonant-influenced patterns, and minor patterns to help children understand how to recognize different patterns. To teach the major pattern clusters, show children a set of examples (you can use Figure 3.3), discuss with them how the words are alike (ending pattern) and different (initial letters), and have them generate other examples. A complete sample lesson is presented in the instructional activities section.

Should you teach children phonics terms?

At this point you might be wondering whether it helps children to know terms such as *consonant, vowel, blend, digraph,* and so on. Since your end goal is to have children *apply* phonics to the reading of connected text, the most sensible course is to introduce as few terms as possible. Some concepts can be described to children in simple, nontechnical words and phrases. When teaching the major pattern clusters, for example, you can refer to *word parts* or *chunks.*

Tovey (1980) conducted an interesting study on this point. He found that most children do not know the definitions of phonics terms. Surprisingly, the second through fourth graders he tested could not even say what a consonant was, despite the fact that this term had been introduced in the first grade and used repeatedly in every grade after that. Even though they could not define any phonics terms, the children could still *apply* phonics. Learning to use phonics is apparently easier than learning what phonics terms mean. Also, the ability to use phonics does *not* depend on knowing definitions for the terms. Tovey concluded that children are better taught phonics through the use of examples, rather than with definitions.

In short, you should be familiar with the technical terms used above. But since your goal is to help students apply the pattern concepts so as to derive meaning from text, you need not have students memorize these terms.

INSTRUCTIONAL ACTIVITIES

Described below are activities designed to help children become familiar with the sounds associated with different letters and letter clusters. All build from the idea that children can learn word identification skills through active reasoning or problem-solving, rather than just rote memorization.

Using patterned books to highlight consonant sounds

Introduce kindergarten and first grade children to beginning consonant sounds by using books like those in the *Kinder Owl* and *Little Owl* series, as K. Smith (1977) recommends. These are books which feature characters like "Big Billy Bear" in stories written to emphasize a particular initial consonant sound.

Stage 1.   Introducing the book. (1) Show the children the book and read its title to them. Have them react to a picture in the book. (2) Read the book aloud to the children, pausing to hear their reactions to it. (3) After the book has been read, have the children discuss the ideas in it. (4) Then have them read it with you. This may be all you want to do for a first lesson.

Stage 2.   Familiarizing the children with the book. (1) Show the children the book again and see how much they remember about it. (2) Help them to read as much of it as they can, starting sentences and phrases and seeing if they can finish them.

Repeat this procedure on several days, if necessary, until you feel they are very familiar with the book. Make sure that they are continuing to enjoy the experience.

Stage 3.   Pointing out letter-sound relationships. (1) Write on the board or on chart paper a sentence or two from the book, choosing those which highlight the initial consonant sound you are targeting. (2) Have the children try to figure out what the sentence says, and then have them take turns reading it. Place your hand under the words as they read them. (3) From the sentence, write the words beginning with the same initial consonant sound in a short list, and see if the children can read them. (4) Ask them if they can see something similar about the words. When they point out that all begin with the same letter, help them understand that the letter signals that the words all start with the same sound. Try to assist the children in discovering this pattern for themselves, rather than lecturing to them about it.

Use this activity with a number of different books, trying to select those which are interesting and use words familiar to the children.

Teaching children to apply knowledge of similar words

This activity derives from the following recommendation by Tovey (1980):

Instruction which requires children to deal constantly with abstract or technical language related to phonics does not warrant the time and effort often expended. This time might better be spent reading. Then, when word recognition problems are encountered, children could be shown or helped to discover known words containing the same sound-symbol relationship(s) as the unknown word. For example, if the unrecognized word were *knight,* the child could be shown *know, knee* and *knife* and *light, might,* and *right* in order to discover the relationship(s) in question. This eliminates talk about silent letters and long vowels.   (pp. 436–437)

As implied above, the best phonics lessons are often those which occur when children are facing an immediate problem in word identification, that is, when they are reading a selection in a basal reader, a storybook, or other connected text. This is a *teachable moment*, a unique opportunity for student learning, when you can use the procedure outlined by Tovey. You can do this if you have prepared children to analyze words into familiar patterns. Here are stages to move the children toward independence in using this strategy:

Stage 1. Write on the board words the children already know that begin with the same letter and sound as the unknown word. Then write words with the same ending. (At a very early stage, you will want to introduce children to the concept that words with the same ending often *rhyme* with one another.) Encourage them to use a problem-solving strategy to read the words.

Stage 2. When the children have had a number of Stage 1 experiences, have them suggest words they know beginning with the same letter or letters as the unknown word, and write these on the board. Then, have them suggest words they know with the same ending. Again, encourage them to put the sounds together.

Stage 3. Finally, when children encounter unknown words that fit a major pattern, encourage them to use the strategy of comparison with words with similar beginning and ending letters or a similar letter cluster.

Teaching phonics with phonograms

Ringler and Weber (1984) present a general teaching plan for phonics based on the use of phonograms, rhyming words spelled with the same ending. They give the following rationale:

> Rhyming words are ideal for teaching phonic analysis because they incorporate letter clusters or phonograms familiar to the learner. A goal of this instruction is to focus learners' attention on the written features of words they already know auditorily. (p. 134)

Examples of phonograms are listed in Figure 3.3 according to the type of cluster (e.g., *bad, dad, glad, sad, mad, tad, lad, fad*). We recommend that you use the following steps to introduce some of the major patterns as phonograms, beginning with CVC clusters.

Planning. Select the specific phonogram for instruction based on diagnostic information (for example, teach a phonogram the children encountered while reading and were not yet familiar with). Choose the words you will use. For example, if the phonogram is *-op*, you might choose *hop* and *drop* from Figure 3.3, adding others likely to be familiar to the children, such as *stop, mop, top, pop,* and *cop*.

Introduction. To call children's attention to the phonogram, have them listen to a poem or play a word or rhyming game. For example, you might make up silly phrases such as "Pop, the cop, stops the hopper." Or have children try to think of phrases including rhyming words, such as *the fat cat* or *the cat on the mat*.

The teacher acquaints children with the -ed phonogram by using familiar rhyming words from labeled pictures and stories.

Learning the letter-sound relationship. Pronounce a series of words (e.g., *pep, pop, pot*). Have the children respond when they hear a word with the phonogram being taught. Then write the words on the board and have the children read them aloud. Emphasize the phonogram by having the children underline or circle it in each word. Help the children to notice that all the words containing the phonogram have a common ending but different initial letters and beginning sounds.

Substitution. Have the children substitute different initial letters/sounds to form other words with the targeted phonogram (e.g., *pop→top, drop, stop*). Begin with words known by sight or familiar in meaning and move on to having the children try to identify new words independently.

Application. Find or prepare texts of various lengths (sentences, paragraphs, poems, stories) containing the targeted phonogram. Have the children first do some oral reading so you can see if the word identification strategy is being applied in context. Follow up with practice in more natural silent reading activities.

KEY CONCEPT 3

Children should learn word identification skills which help them use knowledge of syllables.

LETTER CLUSTER PATTERNS AND SYLLABLES

The third strategy involves the use of *letter clusters*, groups of letters commonly found together within syllables. Some of these letter patterns are identical to the major and minor pattern clusters described in the last key concept or to the meaning-related word chunks discussed in the next one. Proficient readers use knowledge of letter clusters (Adams, 1978, 1980), affixes, and analogous words (Glushko, 1979) to identify unknown words.

Good readers are easily able to break long words into CVC, CV, and CVC clusters and to separate *affixes* or additions from the *root* or base word. They also work by analogy using words they already know to aid them in pronouncing unknown words (Cunningham, 1975–76). For example, good readers are likely to pronounce the make-believe word, *prespander,* similarly. They might separate the affixes (*pre-, -er*) and focus on the middle of the word, working by analogy to see *and* and pronouncing it with the *sp* to rhyme with *hand.* At the heart of this process of identifying longer words is an approach for separating word parts into recognizable and pronounceable chunks. Finding the dictionary-defined syllables is not the goal. Rather, the purpose is to break multisyllable words into chunks that can be pronounced in an approximately correct way.

Cunningham (1975–76) suggests that good readers go through the following process:

1. Good readers search through their memory of similar words and compare the unknown to the known.
2. They segment unfamiliar words into chunks of the largest manageable units.
3. They compare the chunks to known words, phonograms, or familiar letter clusters, looking for recognizable patterns.
4. If the word is in the readers' oral or listening vocabulary, it can then be recognized.
5. If the word is not known in other ways, readers form and use their own rules for analyzing unknown words and comparing or contrasting the known with the unknown.

The following five guidelines for breaking words into chunks are based on an amalgamation of the work of Adams (1980), Glushko (1979), and Cunningham (1975–76). They suggest a way to help children begin to use more systematic approaches when they are confronted with unknown, multisyllablic words.

EXERCISE

To understand how readers use a word and word-part comparison process for identifying words, cover up the right column below and try to pronounce the unfamiliar words listed on the left. Then look at the correct pronunciation on the right. You will probably notice that most of your pronunciations depended on identifying familiar word chunks and one-syllable patterns.

diffuseporous	/dif-ūs-pōr-əs/
peripatetic	/per-ə-pə-tet-ik/
spalpeen	/spal-pēn/
teratogenesis	/ter-ə-tə-jen-ə-səs/
utriculus	/yu-trik-yə-ləs/
bladdernose	/blad-ər-nōz/
barbet	/bär-bət/

1. Look for and block off any prefixes or suffixes and concentrate on the rest of the word. For example, for practice, have children cover with their finger the prefixes on such words as *enclosure, conformation,* and *prepackage.*

2. See if part of the word looks like a known word. For example, they ought to find *clos(e), form,* and *pack* in the words above. You could also have them find words or word parts they know, for example, in *horsepower, command, badminton,* and *bamboozle.* They should try to pronounce the rest of the word after picking out the part they know. Then they can listen to see if their pronunciation is close to that of a word they have heard before.

3. If the first two steps do not result in a correct pronunciation, children can look after the first vowel for two adjacent consonants that are not consonant digraphs. They will usually find that a break between syllables comes between two consonants. They then have a CVC or VC cluster that they can pronounce. You can give them words similar to these for practice: *cab-bage, ap-ple, pic-ture, blan-ket, car-pet, mir-ror, el-bow, fin-ger, can-dy, bab-ble, bad-lands.*

4. If there is only one consonant after the first vowel, and the word seems to be two syllables long, they should make a syllable break before that second consonant. They then have an initial CV, V, or CVV pattern that they can recognize. This can be practiced on words such as: *ba-by, na-ture, bou-quet, boo-ty, bi-son, o-ver, o-men, ma-ple, fau-cet, la-tex,* and *bea-con.* However, if the word appears to be more than two syllables long, because of the presence of three or more groups of vowels, then they should make a syllable break after the second consonant, as in: *pop-u-lar, tel-e-vise, doc-u-ment,* and *pres-i-dent.*

5. If there are three or more consonants in the middle of the word, the break between syllables is usually where there is a low association between adjacent letters. For example, the letter pair *kb* seldom appears together and so is a natural place for a syllable break, as in *back-bite*. Other examples include: *back-ground*, *back-lash*, *bald-head*, and *bank-rupt*. Often, this guideline is unnecessary because there is a recognizable small word in the large word to cue the syllable break. Therefore, this fifth guideline can probably be left untaught.

A reasonable way to go about acquainting children with syllabication is to use teachable moments, as we recommended earlier. Help them mark off the affixes and find recognizable word chunks and letter clusters. If the word is still not recognized, it can be broken into syllables according to one of the rules. Of course, you will need to familiarize the children with the procedure by showing them how it works on words already in their oral vocabulary. This will make it easier for them to see the logic of using the strategy with unknown words.

Children should learn word identification skills which help them use knowledge of morphemes, the smallest meaning-bearing parts of words.

MORPHEMES

With this and the next key concept we shift our focus somewhat, turning to strategies having less to do with sounds and more to do with meaning- bearing parts of words and with connected text. As you know, words can often be divided into smaller, meaningful units. For example, the word *oversights* can be divided into three smaller units, *over-*, *sight*, and *-s*. Such meaning-bearing units, the smallest we can find within words, are called *morphemes*. The strategy based on using morphemes to identify words and determine their meaning is often called *structural analysis*.

The *sight* part of the word *oversights* is generally referred to as the root word. The *over-* part of it is a kind of *affix* which changes the meaning of the root word (prefixes and suffixes are both types of affixes). The *-s* part of the word is an *inflection* which does not change the basic meaning of the word but, in this case, makes it a plural. Other common inflections signal possession (child, child's), change the person or tense of a verb (hint, hints, hinted, or hinting), or allow comparison (high, higher, highest).

The morphemic or structural analysis strategy can be used as well in working out the identification of *compound words*, those made up of two root words, such as *gingerbread* or *rainbow*. It can also be applied to *contractions* such as *I'm* and *can't*.

Teaching children to identify morphemes is an important strategy for word identification and for discovering word meanings. But it is not a strategy easily used in all cases. Here are just three common problems children are likely to encounter. First, some morphemes are "hidden" by affixes (e.g., the morpheme *-ate* in *accusation* or in *lavatory*). Second, the same meaning can be expressed by several different morphemes. There are, for example, different morphemes to express the idea of a person who performs a certain action: *-er*, as in *tester*; *-or* as in *operator*; *-ar*, as in *liar*; *-ant*, as in *immigrant*; and *-ard*, as in *drunkard*. Finally, the boundaries between morphemes are not necessarily the same as the boundaries between syllables (e.g., *pre-* is the first syllable in *preview* but not in *premise*).

INSTRUCTIONAL GUIDELINES

Obviously, morphemic analysis is extremely complex. Thus, as with letter-sound instruction and syllabication, our purpose cannot be to teach a complete set of rules. Our goal is, first, to provide children with some guidelines that can be applied to many of the words they read, and second, to teach them to use these guidelines flexibly.

Because research has not supported the effectiveness of instruction on morphemic or structural analysis (Johnson & Baumann, 1984), you need to rely on more general, overarching instructional principles. Begin with concepts that are most meaningful to children, provide guidelines that focus on the most representative patterns, and use examples that they will see in their reading materials. Condry (1979) describes instruction in morphemes that uses these principles. You should select the patterns to teach from those listed below after looking over the stories children are to read. Choose patterns that appear frequently in their reading materials.

1. Inflections are usually understood before affixes. Teach children to recognize and know the meanings of common inflections first.

Here are the more common inflections:

-ed	-s	-ing	-er	-est

Here are the more common prefixes:

ad-	en-	per-	super-
be-	ex-	pre-	sur-
com- (con, col)	in-	pro-	trans-
de-	inter-	re-	un-
dis-	ob-	sub-	

Here are the more common suffixes:

-age	-ary	-ic	-ment
-al	-ate	-ion	-ness
-ance	-ence	-ist	-our
-ant	-ent	-ity	-ure
-an			-y

2. Knowledge of affixes is acquired gradually, on the basis of meaningfulness. Teach children affixes using words in their oral vocabulary. Then apply the concept to words that appear in their stories and content area texts.

3. Rule-consistent affixes, those that always alter the meanings of words in the same way, are easier to learn than those that are not rule-consistent. Teach children rule-consistent affixes first, pointing out to them how the meaning of the root word is changed in a predictable way. Nearly every affix carries several slightly different meanings, however, so you will need to look up the dictionary definitions of each before teaching them. For example, in *Webster's New Collegiate Dictionary* (1980), *ad-* means "to, toward" or "near, adjacent." *Com-* (or alternative forms *con-, col-*) means "with, together." *De-* indicates "opposite of" or one of five other meanings. It will be easier for children to learn *ad-* or *com-* than *de-* because these affixes have fewer different meanings and so are more predictable.

As with all other types of word identification strategies, most instruction in morphemic analysis should take place around the children's reading of connected text. The point here is not merely for the children to be able to identify words but for them to discover their meanings. For this purpose, children should be given the opportunity to use the context provided by the phrase, sentence, or passage in which the word to be analyzed is found, since these contexts often provide many valuable clues to meaning. There is little point in teaching morphemic analysis on words taken out of context, because this just makes the task artificial and more difficult.

INSTRUCTIONAL ACTIVITIES

Notice how children are taught to analyze the structure of words placed in sentences rather than in isolation. As with earlier activities, these too involve children in a reasoning or problem-solving approach to word identification.

Using words in text previously read

This activity can be used to introduce children to virtually any new type of morphemic analysis. Use text children have read, because they will be familiar with the words and so will be better able to see the logic behind the new type of analysis.

Step 1.   Locate a word in a previously read text which contains the type of morpheme being targeted. Write the entire sentence on the board, underlining the sample word containing the targeted morpheme. See if the children can read the sentence.

Step 2.   Tell the children you are going to show them something interesting about the sample word. See if the children can tell you what the word means and/or divide the word into parts on their own. If they can do neither, show them first how the word can be segmented and then see if they can tell you what the different parts mean. If not, explain to them how you would work out the word's meaning from these parts, as well as from the sentence in which it was found.

Step 3.   Have the children go through the text looking for other examples of the same type of morpheme. (Of course, you will have checked in advance to make sure there are plenty to be found!) Have them write out each word, divide it into parts, and circle the targeted type of morpheme. Have them discuss how they would work out the meanings of these words, both from analysis of morphemes and from the context provided by surrounding words.

At a later time you might wish to provide the children with short passages which include unfamiliar words containing the targeted morpheme. This will give them a chance to try the strategy out in earnest.

Word reductions and expansions

This activity is adapted from one successfully tried out with second graders by Condry (1979), as well as another developed by Floriani (1979) for use with remedial readers. The steps below can be used to give any group of children a sense of how root words are built upon to form other words.

Step 1.   Begin with a set of root words or words containing inflections and affixes the children already know by sight. Place the words in sentences. For example, you could have children find the root word in the context of sentences such as these:

Bill is the *owner* of this bicycle.

Tammy and Terry have an *argument* every day.

Or you could have children add affixes to the root word to complete sentences such as these:

Bill used to own this bicycle. He was its ————.

Tammy and Terry always argue. They have an ———— every day.

Step 2. Have the children discuss how the new words and their meanings are different from the originals.

Step 3. Discuss with them how the "taking apart" strategy they use when trying to identify and work out the meanings of unfamiliar words is related to the "putting together" strategy they used to make up the longer words.

Other suggestions. Condry found that it was easier for children to find the root word than to find the affix or inflection, and for children to learn suffixes and inflections than prefixes. This suggests that children probably should first be taught to pick out the root word. They can later be taught to spot word endings (suffixes and inflections), and then to identify prefixes.

Floriani (p. 156) recommends teaching according to the order shown below. In following this approach, the teacher begins with inflections but then introduces a mixture of prefixes and suffixes.

Level 1: s, ed, d, ing

Level 2: y, ies, ly, es, er

Level 3: un, re, est, en, ful

Level 4: ex, pre, be, dis, in, ion, tion, sion, cian, ous, ness, ture, ment, ish, less

CONTEXT CLUES

Proficient readers rely upon the context provided by surrounding words to help them identify target words. They recognize words more quickly in the context of a sentence than out of it (Tulving & Gold, 1963). For example, the word *avalanche* can be recognized faster when seen in the sentence, "The skiers were buried alive by the sudden avalanche," than when seen in isolation.

In related work with children, Perfetti, Golden, and Hogaboam (1979) found that better readers were faster at identifying words in all contexts and were more accurate at predicting the next word in a story. Thus, good readers are highly efficient at identifying words in context and are able to use context to anticipate words.

INSTRUCTIONAL GUIDELINES

As with morphemes, we do not know much about the effectiveness of teaching children to use context or how it can best be taught (Johnson & Baumann, 1984). Again, however, we can rely on logic and common sense. Here are some ideas about context which we find reasonable.

Teach both the use of *general context* and *local context* (Durkin, 1983). The two can be distinguished in the following way:

General context refers to the main topic in the article, chapter, or book being read. General context is helpful in word recognition because the ideas provide a basis for expectations of certain words to come. An article on the weaving process, for example, leads a reader who knows about that craft to expect such words as *hettles, loom, shuttle, weft,* and *warp.* The reader who expects those words is in a better position to identify them.

Local contexts are connected, meaningful phrases, clauses, or sentences. Local context provides an expectation for particular words as well as the ordering of ideas. For example, if you read, "When the girl came home from school . . ." you would expect the pronoun *she* or the name of another person who may begin to talk to the girl.

When you teach children to use general context clues to figure out particular words, have them scan the text before reading, look back at the title and introduction, or recall the topic, setting, or main purpose of the passage. When you teach the use of local context clues, have children think about the focus of the sentence, what kind of word belongs in the place of the unknown word, or what word could go in that place to make the sentence meaningful.

Ringler and Weber (1984) provide another useful set of distinctions. They divide context clues into four categories:

1. *Typographical clues.* These include parentheses, dashes, commas, and sometimes quotation marks around a word. They signal that the author might have provided a definition or synonym for a word. For example, a text might read, *"Ballast,* which is a heavy substance put in a ship to keep it steady, was used . . ."

2. *Pictorial and graphic clues.* These include pictures, diagrams, maps, charts, tables, and graphs. These probably do not help with the identification of individual words, but they do add to general context.

3. *Syntactic clues.* These allow the reader to use knowledge of English grammar to determine whether the word is likely to be a noun, verb, or adjective. For example, with the following sentence, the reader can

assume that the unknown word is a noun: "The *barnacle* clung tightly to the ship's bottom."

4. *Semantic clues.* These allow the reader to use knowledge of word meanings, and are considered by Ringler and Weber to be the most helpful kind of context clue. Types of semantic clues include:

(a) Synonyms, as in "The woman's *babushka*, a kerchief, kept her head warm."

(b) Definitions, categories, or examples as in, "The *azalea*, a type of flowering plant, blooms in the spring."

(c) Antonyms, comparisons, or contrasts. The unknown word is often set off in comparison to a more common word as in, "*Barley*, not wheat, is what these people eat."

(d) Summary clues (used in putting together text information that usually has been described earlier), such as, "Thus, an ability to make a fine sauce for any kind of meat or vegetable is a sign of a *gourmet* cook."

(e) Inferences (used in inferring meaning through text and back-ground knowledge). Several inferences are needed, for example, to figure out that a balalaika is probably a Russian musical instru-ment in the following sentence: "The Russians sang to the sound of the *balalaika* until the early hours of the morning."

INSTRUCTIONAL ACTIVITY

Using the cloze procedure with passages

The standard way of teaching children to attend to context clues is through use of the *cloze* procedure. The general idea with this procedure is to delete all or part of the word you want the children to identify. By removing all or part of the word, you prevent children from relying exclusively on a sight, phonetic, syllabic, or morphemic strategy. Thus, they are forced to attend to the context provided by surrounding words. Replacing, for example, any of the underlined words in the sentences above with a blank would force children to pay more attention to the surrounding context clues.

Using the cloze procedure with passages is a practical means of helping children learn to use general context, as they would when reading a story, informational article, or other text. The use of general context requires chil-dren to look beyond a single sentence, perhaps to think about two or more sentences or the larger context.

Valmont (1983) gives the following guidelines for use of the cloze procedure with passages:

1. Generally, do not delete words from either the first or last sentence of the passage.

2. Be clear about your reasons for deleting a word. Although when the cloze procedure is used for testing, words are deleted at regular intervals (e.g., a blank replaces every seventh word), this same technique should not be used for instructional purposes.

Steps 3, 4, and 5 are designed to help the students experience success in using context.

3. Especially while introducing the use of context, delete words most students will be able to guess correctly through applying knowledge of passage meaning.

4. In the early stages also try to delete words used over and over again in the passage. Delete them for the first time only after they have already appeared several times.

5. In general, only delete words in the students' oral vocabulary, those representing concepts familiar to them.

6. In the early stages delete categories of words, such as nouns, verbs, adjectives and adverbs, for which the children will be able to generate many different possibilities. In later stages, when more precision is being sought, delete other categories of words, such as prepositions, where fewer alternatives can be suggested.

7. If you want to give students more within-sentence context, or make the task easier, delete words at the end of the sentence.

8. If you want students to practice using context clues coming after the deleted word, remove words from the beginning of the sentence.

Valmont concludes with the important reminder that teachers spend time discussing alternative answers with students. This reinforces the idea that cloze activities are meant to show word identification as a problem-solving process. Encourage children to give their reasons, even if their answers seem rather peculiar to you. After all, it is perfectly possible to arrive at the wrong answer for a good reason, or for that matter, at the right answer for a poor reason. As Valmont suggests, attend to the thinking process reflected in the answer, rather than just to the answer itself. Help the children recognize the importance of self-correction and of checking their own responses to see if they make sense.

KEY CONCEPT 6

Children should learn that word identification is a problem-solving process, requiring the use of a combination of strategies.

IMPORTANCE OF LEARNING TO APPLY A COMBINATION OF STRATEGIES

You have now been introduced to five strategies for identifying words: (1) sight, (2) letter sounds, (3) syllables, (4) morphemes, and (5) context. Five strategies were presented because each has limitations, in and of itself, and is to some extent dependent on the others. As mentioned earlier, no one strategy can serve as a complete and efficient means of identifying words.

Part of the reason for this situation lies in the very nature of our language. Written English is redundant, with overlap between each layer of information and the next. To make full use of this redundancy, efficient word identification is always a matter of using strategies in coordination with one another. Therefore, you can seldom decide what sound a vowel has unless you look at the letters around it. (For example, the letter *a* has a different sound in *sham* and *shame*.) This means that a letter-sound strategy must be supplemented with letter-cluster analysis. Consider another example. One of the things you might do in trying to break a complicated word into syllables is to look for a root word within it (for example, in *recaptured*, you notice the root word *capture*). This means that the strategies of syllables and morphemes are related to one another.

Helping students learn to *apply* a combination of strategies while reading is at once the most important and most neglected aspect of instruction in word identification. To make the best use of all the text information available, readers need to have command of a combination of strategies. They can then orchestrate the use of whichever strategies allow a rapid and sensible process-ing of the information, giving the best "fit" with background knowledge of the topic and the evolving "mental model" of the text.

Thus, it would not be enough to teach children to use each of the five individual strategies. We need to go further, to help them learn to apply the strategies in combination with one another, while actually reading. We will now give you a sense of the relative usefulness of the various strategies, and of how to help children apply a combination of strategies for efficient word identification.

Identifying words using multiple strategies

The idea underlying the combination of strategies is that the child should be taught a general approach to word identification, useful across a wide variety of situations. Crowell (1980) refers to a *hierarchy* of strategies. By this she means that children should learn to apply strategies that are most efficient for the situation, beginning with those that take the least amount of time and, if they fail, then trying more time-consuming strategies. In other words, you will be teaching children to identify words quickly, by means that will detract least from comprehension.

The approach below combines the ideas of K. Smith (1977), Crowell (1980), and Cunningham (1975–76). For the sake of simplicity, think of the strategies as falling into three larger categories: sight, context, and individual word analysis. This last category covers analysis by the strategies of letter-sounds and letter clusters, syllables, and morphemes. Now, think of helping your beginning readers focus principally on the first four steps listed below (sight, context, letter-sounds, and letter clusters). Help emerging mature readers, who read more complicated and unknown words, to use all six steps. Your goal is to help all children use a problem-solving approach to achieve independence in word identification.

1. *Sight:* If the children know the word by sight, there is no further problem. If, however, the word is unfamiliar but they recognize a familiar word in part of the word, they should try to see if it seems to fit.

2. *Context:* If the word is not known by sight or analogy to a sight word, the children read to the end of the sentence, or perhaps a little further. They try to imagine what word would go there and make the sentence more meaningful, and look again for a familiar word within the unknown word that fits the context.

3. *Word analysis, initial letters:* If the word is not known from context, the children look at the initial letter (or letters if the word starts with a consonant blend or digraph) and combine letter-sound analysis with context.

4. *Word analysis, ending letter cluster:* If still unsure about the word, the children look at its final set of letters for a phonogram that they know. They should pronounce this, adding the beginning of the word, and see if it fits with the context. This step combines letter-cluster-to-sound analysis and context.

5. *Word analysis, morphemes:* If context plus letter clusters have not yielded the answer, the children should try to separate the root from prefixes, suffixes, or inflections. They should pronounce these, try to put them together, and then determine whether the product fits the context. This step combines morphemic and letter cluster analysis with context.

6. *Word analysis, syllables:* As a last resort, they break the word into syllables and try pronouncing each one. Again each pronunciation should be checked against context clues.

Applying multiple strategies: an example

Although each of these strategies has been reviewed, let's look at them now from a slightly different angle, trying to understand how they fit together in combination, as a whole. Consider the following example:

Suppose that the child is reading a story about the circus and comes to the following sentence:

The horses galloped into the ring.

How would we want the child to go about quickly identifying the words in this sentence, with the least disruption to the search for meaning?

As mentioned earlier, the most efficient strategy is simply to know words by sight. *Sight words* are those the child can identify instantly and automatically, seemingly without having to do any kind of conscious analysis. If the child knows the word by sight, then he or she doesn't need to try any of the other strategies. In this case, let's assume that the child knows all the words by sight except *galloped* and that the word does not look like any that he or she knows.

This brings us to the second strategy, the use of *context*. As discussed earlier, this means the application of semantic and syntactic knowledge, as well as background knowledge about the passage topic. This knowledge is used to determine what words might *make sense* in that particular spot. In this case, if we were encouraging the child to use context alone, we would turn to the chalkboard and rewrite the sentence in the following way:

The horses _____ into the ring.

We come then to the third kind of strategy, *word analysis*. We might then add the letter *g* to the sentence in the following way:

The horses g _____ into the ring.

Now we ask the child to name words which would fit in that context. The child will almost certainly realize that the missing word describes how the horses got into the ring, and so may make guesses like the following: *ran, trotted, walked, galloped.* Notice that context alone will lead to a set of possible answers but not necessarily to the exact word itself.

Recalling the list generated earlier, the child will now be able to see that the word is *galloped.*

Suppose, however, that the word had been *cantered* instead. Now the children would still be unable to guess the word. They can look for similar words or for small words that they know. They might think of *can't, can* or *ant.* With these clues, they put together *canter* and then *cantered.* They now remember hearing that word before, in the context of a horse's running and so realize its meaning as well.

With our sample sentence, if the word *cantered* had been even more difficult, we could have had the children analyze the word in other ways. For example, we could have had them separate the inflection *-ed* from the rest of the word. Then we could have asked them to divide *canter* into syllables (between the two middle consonants, as one of the guidelines suggests) and try to pronounce each one. These activities might have value at some other time, in focusing the children's attention on the usefulness of morphemic analysis and syllabication, but in this instance they were not needed.

Turning now to emerging mature readers, suppose fifth graders are reading a science text that is explaining flip-type switches. A sentence therein is:

Instead of pieces of hard metal, liquid mercury is used to make the connection on these switches.

Suppose the word *mercury* is unknown. In looking at it children think of no familiar smaller words and do not find the context particularly helpful. However, they notice that the ending pattern, *cury*, is somewhat familiar and might rhyme with *hurry*. Another familiar syllable is noticed, *mer*, which reminds them of *her*. They then remember that a proper syllable division is between two consonants. They try to say these two parts of the word, *mer-ker-ē* and see if it fits in the context. Some recall that mercury is a liquid and is sometimes used not only in thermometers but also in switches. A discussion follows about what mercury is and how it can operate an electric switch, because several children have little knowledge about this. Now, word identification becomes embedded in the role of understanding concepts.

Remember, the idea in teaching children to use a combination of strategies is to help them identify words by the most efficient means available. Overall, the most effective method of developing word identification skills probably is to encourage children to read for meaning and to use context in combination with a plausible guess about what the word or part of the word could be.

Labeled picture books provide a particularly effective opportunity to teach children multiple word recognition strategies.

Following that, with one-syllable words, they can use the first letter and ending pattern. With multisyllable words they can look for familiar words, or word chunks within the word, separating the root from an affix or breaking the word into approximately correct syllables.

Using teachable moments

In general, you will want to use the teachable moment approach to walk children through the procedures described above. In other words when, in their reading, they encounter an unfamiliar word, you will give them a quick lesson in using the combination of strategies. At other times, you will not want to break the flow of comprehension activity to work on word identification, and you will just tell the students what the word is. In these instances you may want to jot down the unfamiliar word and where it first occurred in the text. Then, after reading of the passage has been completed, give a short lesson to show students what they could have done to identify it on their own, going through the combination of strategies procedure outlined above.

SUMMARY

The teaching of word identification is an important part of the beginning reading program, because the ability to identify words rapidly and to read with comprehension are closely linked. But being able to read words quickly does not automatically make one a good reader, able to read with understanding. Thus, instruction in word identification should aim to have children take on word recognition as a problem-solving process, and should be balanced with comprehension instruction.

In the first key concept we discussed the first method that children can use to identify words, which is simply to know them by sight. To increase the number of words children know by sight, it is important to begin with high interest and meaningful words. In the second key concept we provided guidelines and activities for teaching children to use knowledge of letter-sound relationships. We introduced the concepts of major patterns, minor patterns, and consonant-influenced vowel patterns. These concepts help us see which letter-sound relationships to emphasize in instruction. In the third key concept we looked at how children could be taught to use letter clusters and the patterning of syllables to identify multisyllable words.

In the fourth key concept we turned to the strategy of using morphemic or structural analysis. Suggestions were made about the order and methods to be used to teach inflections and affixes. The fifth key concept dealt with teaching children to use context to identify words. Different types of context were discussed, and the cloze procedure was presented as a way of teaching children to make use of context clues.

Finally, we discussed under the sixth key concept how no one strategy is sufficient in and of itself to identify all words. Thus, we emphasized the importance of leading children toward independence in word identification through a combination of strategies. We concluded by presenting a problem-solving procedure children can learn, so they will be able to recognize words in an efficient manner. Throughout this chapter we emphasized the importance of providing instruction in word identification, not as an end in itself, but within the broader framework of reading for meaning.

BIBLIOGRAPHY

REFERENCES

Adams, M. (1978). *Models of word recognition* (Tech. Rep. No. 107). Urbana, IL: University of Illinois, Center for the Study of Reading.

Adams, M. (1980). *What good is orthographic redundancy?* (Tech. Rep. No. 192). Urbana, IL: University of Illinois, Center for the Study of Reading.

Bridge, C. A., Winograd, P. N., & Haley, D. (1983). Using predictable materials vs. preprimers to teach beginning sight words. *Reading Teacher, 36* (9), 884–891.

Carroll, J. B., Davies, P., & Richman, B. (1971). *Word frequency book.* Boston: Houghton Mifflin; and New York: American Heritage.

Condry, S. (1979). *A developmental study of processes of word derivation in elementary school children and their relation to reading.* Unpublished doctoral dissertation. Ithaca, NY: Cornell University.

Crowell, D. C. (1980). *Kamehameha Reading Objective System.* Honolulu, Hawaii: Kamehameha Schools.

Cunningham, P. (1975–76). Investigating a synthesized theory of mediated word recognition. *Reading Research Quarterly, 11,* 127–143.

Durkin, D. (1983). *Teaching them to read.* Boston: Allyn & Bacon.

Ehri, L., & Wilce, L. (1985). Movement into reading: Is the first stage of printed word learning visual or phonetic? *Reading Research Quarterly, 20,* 163–179.

Floriani, B. P. (1979). Word expansions for multiplying sight vocabulary. *Reading Teacher, 33* (2) 155-157.

Glushko, R. (1979). The organization and activation of orthographic knowledge in reading aloud. *Journal of Experimental Psychology: Human Perception and Performance, 5,* 674–691.

Gough, P. (1984). Word recognition. In P. D. Pearson (Ed.), *Handbook of reading research.* New York: Longman.

Huey, E. B. (1908). *The psychology and pedagogy of reading.* New York: Macmillan.

Johnson, D., & Baumann, J. (1984). Word recognition. In P. D. Pearson (Ed.), *Handbook of reading research.* New York: Longman.

LaBerge, D., & Samuels, S. J. (1976). Toward a theory of automatic information processing in reading. In H. Singer and R. B. Ruddell (Eds.), *Theoretical models and processes of reading.* Newark, DE: International Reading Association.

Lesgold, A., Resnick, L., & Hammond, K. (1985). Learning to read: A longitudinal study of word skill development in two curricula. In T. G. Waller & G. E. MacKinnon (Eds.), *Reading research: Advances in theory and practice*, Vol. 4. New York: Academic Press.

Mason (Lucas), J. (1973). A stage processing model of reading for elementary school pupils. Unpublished doctoral dissertation, Stanford University.

Mason, J. (1977a). Questioning the notion of independent processing stages in reading. *Journal of Educational Psychology, 69*, 288–297.

Mason, J. (1977b). Refining phonics for teaching reading. *Reading Teacher, 31*, 197–201.

Mason, J. (1980). When do children begin to read? An exploration of four year old children's letter and word reading competencies. *Reading Research Quarterly, 15*, 203–227.

Mason, J. (1984). Early reading from a developmental perspective. In P. D. Pearson (Ed.), *Handbook of reading research*. New York: Longman.

McCaughey, M. W., Juola, J. F., Schadler, M., & Ward, N. J. (1980). Whole-word units are used before orthographic knowledge in perceptual development. *Journal of Experimental Child Psychology, 30*, 411–421.

McConkie, G. (1984). The reader's perceptual processes. In G. G. Duffy, L. R. Roehler, & J. M. Mason (Eds.), *Comprehension instruction: Perspectives and suggestions*. New York: Longman.

McCormick, C., & Mason, J. (1984). *Intervention procedures for increasing preschool children's interest in and knowledge about reading* (Tech. Rep. No. 312). Urbana, IL: University of Illinois, Center for the Study of Reading.

Perfetti, C., Golden, S., & Hogaboam, T. (1979). Reading skill and the identification of words in discourse context. *Memory and Cognition, 7*, 273–282.

Perfetti, C. A., & Hogaboam, T. (1975). The relationship between single word decoding and reading comprehension skill. *Journal of Educational Psychology, 67* (4), 461–469.

Resnick, L. B. (1979). Theories and prescriptions for early reading instruction. In L. B. Resnick & P. A. Weaver (Eds.), *Theory and practice of early reading*. Vol. 2. Hillsdale, NJ: Lawrence Erlbaum Associates.

Ringler, L., & Weber, C. (1984). *A language-thinking approach to reading*. New York: Harcourt Brace Jovanovich.

Smith, F. (1978). *Understanding reading*. 2nd Ed. New York: Holt, Rinehart and Winston.

Smith, K. J. (1977). Efficiency in beginning reading: Possible effects on later comprehension. In S. Wanat (Ed.), *Language and reading comprehension*. Arlington, VA: Center for Applied Linguistics.

Stanovich, K. (1980). Toward an interactive-compensatory model of individual differences in the development of reading fluency. *Reading Research Quarterly, 16*, 32–71.

Tovey, D. R. (1980). Children's grasp of phonics terms vs. sound-symbol relationships. *Reading Teacher, 33* (4), 431–437.

Tulving, E., & Gold, C. (1963). Stimulus information and contextual information as determinants of tachistoscopic recognition of words. *Journal of Experimental Psychology, 66*, 319–327.

Valmont, W. J. (1983). Cloze deletion patterns: How deletions are made makes a big difference. *Reading Teacher, 37* (2), 172–175.

Venezky, R. (1970). *The structure of English orthography*. The Hague: Mouton.

Webster's (1964) *New World Dictionary of the American Language*. College Edition. New York: World Publishing Co.

CHILDREN'S BOOKS CITED

Martin, Bill (1967). *Brown Bear, Brown Bear, What Do You See?* New York: Holt, Rinehart and Winston.

Martin, Bill (1970). *Fire, Fire, Said Mrs. McGuire.* New York: Holt, Rinehart and Winston.

Martin, Bill (1970). *The Haunted House.* New York: Holt, Rinehart and Winston.

Martin, Bill (1970). *Up the Down Escalator.* New York: Holt, Rinehart and Winston.

Martin, Bill (1971). *Little Owl Books.* New York: Holt, Rinehart and Winston.

Martin, Bill (1971). *Kinder Owl Books.* New York: Holt, Rinehart and Winston.

Munari, Bruno (1980). *Jimmy Has Lost His Cap, Where Can It Be?* New York: Philomel.

Munari, Bruno (1980). *The Elephant's Wish.* New York: Philomel.

FURTHER READINGS

Biemiller, A. The development of the use of graphic and contextual information as children learn to read. *Reading Research Quarterly, 6,* 75-96.

Brown, B. (1981). Enrich your reading program with personal words. *Reading Teacher, 35,* 40-43.

Calfee, R., & Piontkowski, D. (1981). The reading diary: Acquisition of decoding. *Reading Research Quarterly, 16,* 346-373.

Ceprano, M. A. (1981). A review of selected research on methods of teaching sight words. *Reading Teacher, 35,* 314-322.

Cunningham, P. (1979). A compare/contrast theory of mediated word identification. *Reading Teacher, 31,* 774-78.

Frenzel, N. (1978). Children need a multipronged attack in word recognition. *Reading Teacher, 31,* 627-31.

Mosenthal, P., Walmsley, S., & Allington, R. (1978). Word recognition reconsidered: Toward a multi-context model. *Visible Language, 12,* 448-468.

Smith E. E., & Kleiman, G. M. (1979). Word recognition: Theoretical issues and instructural hints. In L. B. Resnick, & P. A. Weaver (Eds.), *Theory and practice of early reading.* Vol. 2. Hillsdale, NJ: Lawrence Erlbaum Associates.

Venezky, R. (1967). English orthography: Its graphical structure and its relation to sound. *Reading Research Quarterly, 2,* 75-106.

CHAPTER 4

Teaching Vocabulary and Word Meanings

Our language is calorie-rich. We are a nation unafraid of borrowing. We have never penalized our citizens in any way (as have the French, for example), for using words from another nation. In our adoption of foreign terms, as was said of Shakespeare, we invade like conquerors. There is much children can learn about the nature of language through reading.

Importance of imagination.   Since language itself is fluid, chameleon-like, and has an unlimited potential for change and growth, children can be helped to see that imagination (what Jan Carew (1974) has called "the third gift") is the most important element in talking about our language.

Delight and magic of words.   Helping children realize the delight and the magic of words should be one of our foremost goals as language arts and reading teachers. If we can accomplish this, then many children will become "word gatherers," as was the title character in Leo Lionni's (1973) charming book *Frederick.*

Influence of words on all of us.   Children also should become aware of the influence that words have upon all of us. We want our youngsters to be like Patricia Hubbell's Word Woman, who carries words with her in a jar, threading them to stars when she wants to travel (1958). We want them to be able to create, to soar and fly with language.   (Pilon, 1984, p. 231)

OVERVIEW

In this chapter we focus primarily on the learning of new words, those which are not in children's oral vocabulary, whose meanings are not yet known. We discuss the role that vocabulary plays in reading for meaning. We point out that having a good vocabulary helps one read with understanding. However, doing a lot of reading can itself be a way of increasing vocabulary.

Especially for younger children, we stress the importance of oral language and concept development. We consider the teaching of words related by topic and students' learning of new meanings for words already known in some other sense (for example, the child may already know about a freshwater *spring* but not about a bed *spring*). Throughout the chapter we emphasize two themes: The first has to do with the role of context in helping children work out new word meanings. The second has to do with teaching children strategies they can use to learn new words and their definitions on their own.

Our discussion is organized around the following four key concepts:

Key Concept #1: Oral vocabulary development should be emphasized for children in the early reading phase as well as for those in the phase of formal beginning reading.

Key Concept #2: Children can learn the meanings of many new words if they are related by topic and presented in meaningful contexts.

Key Concept #3: Children need to understand that words may have more than one meaning and that they can learn these different meanings from written context.

Key Concept #4: Children need effective strategies to learn the meanings of new words, including the ability to identify familiar roots and affixes and to apply the concept of definition.

PERSPECTIVE

THE KNOWLEDGE HYPOTHESIS

We consider a person's *vocabulary* to consist of words which have some personal meaning. That is, the words are understood when read in context and used appropriately when spoken or written, even though the individual may not know the dictionary-style definition for them. An important part of becoming a proficient reader is increasing one's vocabulary by learning to identify new words and understand them in context. This process does not require a person to be able to recite the definitions of all these words.

We have known for a long time of the close relationship between vocabulary, or knowledge of word meanings, and reading comprehension (e.g., Davis, 1944; Thurston, 1946). A plausible explanation of the relationship between vocabulary and reading comprehension is stated in the *knowledge hypothesis* (Mezynski, 1983). According to this hypothesis, a word in a reader's vocabulary indicates that he or she has knowledge, not only of that word, but of related words and concepts as well. This sum of knowledge, represented or indexed by vocabulary, is what enables the reader better to comprehend the text.

For example, the reader familiar with such terms as *ultrasonics, electrostatic transducer,* and *capacitor* is one who knows something about the field of electronics. Such a reader, in contrast to others who know little or nothing of this field, would have no trouble comprehending an article about how to build an ultrasonic ranging system. Thus, the knowledge hypothesis fits with previous discussions in this textbook of the importance of background knowledge to text comprehension.

While the knowledge hypothesis helps account for the way vocabulary contributes to reading ability, it is also important to realize that reading itself can improve vocabulary (Ingham, 1981; Nagy, Herman, & Anderson, 1985). Competent readers have the ability to pick up new words and their meanings from text. That is, they have learned to learn the meanings of new words through reading. The exercise on page 99 will help you understand this idea.

As you can see, the relationship between vocabulary and reading comprehension works in both directions. Knowledge of word meanings contributes to one's ability to understand text. However, being able to read well also enables one to learn the meaning of new words.

The practical implication of this perspective is that we should have two major goals for vocabulary instruction. First, we want children to have the opportunity to learn the meanings of new words directly, through independent reading and from instruction. Second, we want them to learn to derive the meanings of new words to be able to figure out the meanings of words in context. This involves teaching them *strategies* for working out meanings of new words while they read.

KEY CONCEPT 1

Oral vocabulary development should be emphasized for children in the early reading phase as well as for those in the phase of formal beginning reading.

LANGUAGE AND CONCEPT DEVELOPMENT

This key concept is based on the idea that teachers need to attend to young children's *language development*. This is important because children entering kindergarten and first grade may differ greatly in their ability to use language to express their thoughts, including the number of different words they can use and understand. Language development in turn is tied to *concept development* and learning of new ideas. Knowledge of language and concepts is critical to the child's learning to read.

Remember that at this point most children will be learning a great deal from direct experience and not very much from books or lectures. Some children will have had a wide range of experiences and will have learned many new words on these occasions. Others will have had many experiences but not necessarily learned all the words to describe objects, their qualities, and situations. For all, however, the learning of new words and refinement in the understanding of word meanings continues through the elementary school years and into adulthood (Ringler & Weber, 1984).

Younger children, unlike older children and adults, can be expected to have difficulty dealing with words as objects in and of themselves. Thus, the

EXERCISE

(1) Read through the passage below and try to get a general idea of what it is about.

In seasonal allergy ("hay fever"), the specific source of the patient's trouble can often be identified by careful history-taking. Skin testing and *in vitro* immunologic tests can often be utilized to provide definitive evidence; these measures are appropriate only when an allergen such as dog dander must be identified to assist in environmental treatment or when immunotherapy is being considered. . . . In patients with year-round allergic symptoms, differentiation from nonallergic rhinitis may be more difficult. Indirect evidence for an allergic etiology for nasal symptoms includes other manifestations of atopy . . . and a history of typical allergic rhinitis in one or both parents.   (Barker, Burton, & Zieve, 1982, pp. 175–176)

(2) On a sheet of paper, write down what you think the passage is about.

(3) By referring back to the passage, see if you can figure out at least partial answers to the following questions. Jot down these answers:

(a) What is a seasonal allergy?
(b) What is an *in vitro* immunologic test? Why would such a test be given?
(c) What is an allergen? Give an example of an allergen.
(d) What is nonallergic rhinitis?

Most of us would find the sample passage very difficult to understand. Yet we are still able to provide at least partial answers to several of the questions. Here is the reasoning that might be used in trying to answer the questions. As you read further, think about the reasoning that you did.

(a) Although many readers have not seen the words *seasonal* and *allergy* together before, they do know what each individual word means. It helps that the layman's term "hay fever" is given.

(b) Many readers have some sense of what a skin test would be and guess that an *in vitro* immunologic test may involve injections or something else besides just a scratch on the skin. They infer that such a test would be given to provide evidence that the person has a seasonal allergy.

(c) The word *allergen* resembles allergy, so many readers think it is probably the substance that causes the illness. Readers might not be certain of what dog dander is, but they know that it is an example of an allergen.

(d) Many readers know that *rhinitis* is probably a kind of medical problem, although they may still be uncertain about exactly what it is. They can guess that there must be at least two types of rhinitis, nonallergic and allergic, and that the first type is *not* related to seasonal allergies.

The purpose of this exercise was to give you a sense of the kinds of reasoning proficient readers use to figure out the meaning of unfamiliar words contained in the texts they read. Readers use the context provided by the passage as a whole and by surrounding words. They look for words and phrases they already understand, such as *hay fever*, and relate these to terms they are uncertain of. They use background knowledge. They analyze individual words (*allergen*, *nonallergic*). All of these are strategies we want children to learn to use, too.

learning of new vocabulary can better be accomplished by engaging children in activities and having them talk about their experiences. At these times new words can easily and naturally be introduced, used, and learned. For example, while the children are shaping objects out of clay, a teacher can extend their vocabulary by introducing terms such as *mold, pinch, fasten,* and *smooth.*

Obviously, when they first enter school, children are able to speak many more words than they are able to read. That is, their oral vocabulary will be much larger than their reading vocabulary, their store of sight words. As time goes on, though, there is a gradual shift, with reading vocabulary becoming equal in size to oral vocabulary and then usually becoming much larger. Most mature readers can read many more words than they hear or use in everyday conversation, even on topics where many technical terms or unusual words could be applied. Thus, the relationship between oral vocabulary and reading vocabulary changes over time. At first, words are spoken and then read. Later, words may be read and then spoken.

Because kindergarten and first grade children are far from making this shift, we want to emphasize the development of new concepts and oral vocabulary. For example, we can model the proper use of a new term, read stories with interesting words, and encourage children to express their ideas in a more complete and accurate form. But while we may show children the printed form of newly learned words, those whose meanings they may still be rather uncertain of, we do not expect those words to be added immediately to their reading vocabulary.

New concepts obtained here from a science field trip help children acquire the necessary background for vocabulary understanding.

Older children, those in second grade and above, may also benefit from lessons where oral language activities are used as a basis for developing vocabulary. While the focus would be on more technical terms, the same instructional guidelines described below could be applied for use with these students.

INSTRUCTIONAL GUIDELINES

Four teaching behaviors for developing children's language, and hence for increasing their oral vocabulary, are at the heart of the language development program of the Far West Laboratory for Educational Research and Development (Ward & Kelley, 1971; definitions, p. 4; examples, pp. 4, 15, 81, 82). These behaviors may be used both in formal, teacher-led lessons, as well as during informal interactions with children.

1. Expand the complexity, flexibility, and precision of language and thought. In expanding language ability, you will be helping children to put thoughts into complete sentences and to use words that accurately and precisely express meaning. For example:

Child: Bumpy cloth.
Teacher: Yes, the cloth feels bumpy; the fabric is rough.

2. Model new language patterns. In modeling a new language pattern, you will be introducing language to the children in context and, whenever possible, in conjunction with concrete objects. For example:

Teacher: (Modeling the use of terms of position, in this case *top, inside, under.* Color words are reviewed.) Today we are going to play a game with this box and these toy trucks. Each of us will have a truck. I'll begin with my red truck. I will place my truck on the top of the box. Now your turn. What color truck will you use? Where will you put your truck?

3. Elicit children's use of new language. In fostering the use of new language, you will be encouraging children to use various language patterns and words in their own speech. For example:

Teacher: Look at this pencil. What are all the things you can say about it?
Child: It's yellow.
Teacher: Yes. It's yellow. And it is long and thin. What is it made of?
Child: It has wood on it.
Teacher: Yes. It's made of wood and inside the wood is the lead. What do we use a pencil for?
Child: We write with it.
Teacher: Good answer. We use a pencil to write and draw on paper. What else do you see on the pencil?
Child: That thing there (points to eraser).

Teacher: Yes. It's called an eraser. What is it for?

Child: To 'rase on the paper.

Teacher: Good. We use the eraser to rub out some marks on the paper that we don't want.

4. *Provide specific praise for use of precise language.* In using specific praise to highlight improvements in the child's use of language, you will be reinforcing newly acquired skills.

Teacher: Mary, tell Sue where you would like her to place her yellow truck.

Child: She can put it under the box.

Teacher: Yes. Now tell *her* and use all the important words.

Child: Put the yellow truck under the box.

Teacher: That was a very good way to tell Sue what you wanted her to do. You said that she should put her yellow truck under the box.

These same kinds of teaching behaviors can also be used with older children during content area lessons to encourage the use of new terms. During a science lesson on the heart, for example, you might first expand children's responses by introducing more accurate terms such as *artery, vein, valve,* and *muscle.* You might then model the giving of more complete descriptions. Then, after the children have read or conducted an experiment, you would have them try to use the terms on their own, both in group discussion and in written reports.

INSTRUCTIONAL ACTIVITIES

Described below are three activities to support children's oral vocabulary development. All may be adapted for use with children at both the upper and lower grades.

Field trips and other opportunities for direct experience

Almost all kindergarten and first grade programs include opportunities for children to go on field trips, whether to visit the supermarket, the zoo, the fire station, or to see a play. Older children could visit an art or science museum or see an historical landmark. Use these opportunities to develop the children's language and increase their vocabularies.

Step 1. Before going on the field trip, have the children discuss what they expect to see. Make a list of their predictions, and during the discussion, use the methods for developing oral language listed above. Also use this pretrip discussion to introduce concepts to the children. For example, if the class is going to the supermarket, talk about the different types of food they are likely to see (dairy products, produce such as fruits and vegetables, meats). On a piece of chart paper, print the familiar as well as new words used in discussion. A similar procedure can be used for older children. For example, if they are going to an art museum, discuss and list names of artists whose work they will see. Different periods in the history of art and the techniques used to produce the works might also be discussed.

Step 2. During the field trip chat with the children about what they are seeing and whether their predictions are being confirmed. Have parents or other adults accompanying the group converse with the children in this same manner. Encourage the children to ask questions about what they are seeing. Point out how the concepts discussed earlier relate to what they are seeing. ("See, all the dairy products are together in this part of the store.") Older children can be allowed to move around independently after a preliminary orientation. They may be asked to use the new vocabulary in a variety of ways, such as when jotting down notes about different works of art.

Step 3. After the field trip, have the children talk about what they saw. Encourage them to use precise terms and point out the words used on the chart, or, if new words come up, add them to the list. The discussion can lead to a language experience chart, drawing, or, for older children, a written report showing appropriate use of the new terms.

Step 4. At later times, try to remember to use the new vocabulary when speaking to the children and encourage them to use the new words when appropriate occasions arise. ("We're having both milk and ice cream with our lunch today. Do you think there's anything similar about them, something that we learned from our trip to the supermarket?") For older children, new terms could be used when continuing studies in related areas. For example, if the students had learned the term *portrait*, they could be asked to discuss what they had learned about colonial times from having seen portraits painted at that time.

In-class activities, such as baking cookies, setting up an aquarium, or carrying out science experiments, can also be used as opportunities for increasing oral vocabulary. Begin with an introductory discussion in which you expand or modify children's responses by filling in more accurate terms. Then encourage children to use the new vocabulary while the activity is going on. Have older children use new vocabulary in their writing to describe what happened and what they learned. Throughout, remember to use new vocabulary yourself when speaking to the children and to encourage them to continue using the new terms.

Vocabulary development during the reading aloud of storybooks

New and different words can be introduced by reading stories aloud to children. Listening to you read aloud gives them the chance to hear new words in context. The steps to be followed are similar in principle to those used with field trips. They are readily adapted for use with older children, when chapters of a novel are read instead of storybooks.

Step 1. Before reading, encourage discussion of the story title and cover page. Tell the children the title of the book, or perhaps show them a picture, and invite predictions about what they expect to hear. Say, for example, "Here's a book called ————. What do you see on the cover? What do you think it'll be about?"

Step 2. Highlight new words and unusual expressions during reading. Encourage the children to repeat them. Signal the presence of new or unusual words by emphasizing or perhaps repeating the phrase or sentence as you read. Stop at certain points to have the children react to the text and pictures. When a child gives a well-phrased response, say, "Listen to the good way she said that" and repeat the child's words.

Step 3. Encourage children to express the new words and use precise language in the discussion after reading. When finished going through the book once, have the children go through it with you, page by page, and see if you can get them to use some of the new or unusual words in retelling or reacting to the text. You might say, "What was the little girl's problem? What did she say about it?"

Step 4. Remind children later of the new words and special language learned. In your postreading discussion, model and encourage use of the new words. This can all be done very naturally without making a particular fuss over the new words, taking them out of context, or explicitly defining them for the children. For example, the opportunity might come up to say, "I think you have the same problem as that little girl that we read about yesterday. What was it she said?"

Vocabulary, language, and prediction strategy

The vocabulary language, and prediction (VLP) strategy developed by Wood and Robinson (1983) is designed to meet two purposes: (1) to preteach vocabulary through oral language activities and (2) to reinforce knowledge of the new words through the making of predictions about the text. The VLP strategy may be used with basal reader selections as well as other types of text. With minor modifications, it can be used in lessons given to students in all elementary grades, to good as well as poor readers.

There are seven steps in the VLP strategy. Wood and Robinson illustrate these steps with sample exercises based on the words below, taken from a third grade basal reader selection:

Story words

typical	eighteen
woven	pupils
modern	language
reservation	spinning
mesa	weave
cattle	Jerry Begay
grazing	Navajo Indian
rough	Arizona
supply	

Vocabulary:

1. Examine the selection to be read and determine which words are important and which may cause the students difficulty. (The words may be underlined or listed in the basal reader guide, but teachers may want to emphasize some words not highlighted by the authors.)

2. Note the skill to be emphasized in the unit (for example, long vowel sounds) and determine other skills previously taught which may need review. Think of ways these skills can be associated with the vocabulary words.

3. Put these words on separate flash cards, indicating in one corner the page on which the word appears. (For whole class teaching, putting the words on the board would be more convenient.) Since preteaching all of the terms in a selection at once would be overwhelming for both student and teacher, this page numbering procedure allows teachers to emphasize only the words from the pages covered during that class period. The words can be stored in a file with the selection title on front.

4. Place the cards on a table in front of the students and explain that they will see these words in the reading selection. Then explain that the object is to point to the word that answers the question or fills in the blank.

Language:

5. Begin the oral language activities by asking questions about the structural and conceptual elements of each word. In addition to any skill areas emphasized in the instructional unit, questions can be asked in the following areas.

   Synonyms: Which word means the same as *students?* What is another name for a *group of cows?*

   Antonyms: Which word means the opposite of *old-fashioned?* I would rather feel a *soft* surface than a _____ surface.

   Categorization: Group all the words that have *something to do with animals.* What label can we give to these three words: *flower, tree, bush?*

   Homonyms: What is another way of spelling *mane* that means something entirely different?

   Context: People in some parts of our country and in other countries speak a different _____ than we do.

   Dictionary usage: Using your dictionaries, find the definition of *supply* that fits in this sentence—"Father bought a *supply* of food for our trip."

   Parts of speech: Which words show action? Which words name something?

   Structural analysis: Which words begin with *re* as in *restore?* Which words end like *examination?*

Prediction:

6. Once the students understand the vocabulary, ask them to use the words to predict what the story may be about, or, if part of the story has already been covered, to anticipate what might happen next. Prediction questions can be developed in specific areas to provide background information and lay the groundwork for the new knowledge. In this sense, the responses serve as student-generated purposes for reading.

   Characterization: Which words probably tell you about the main character?

   Setting: Which words tell where he or she lives?

   Mood or feeling: Do any words tell you about the mood of the story?

   Reality/fantasy: Do you think the story will be a fantasy or a realistic story? Use the words to support your answer.

   Events/outcomes: Which words give clues about the events in the story?

7. These predictions can be recorded on the board to be confirmed, rejected, or modified during the reading to correspond with the actual events in the selection. (Wood & Robinson, 1983, pp. 393–394)

THE IMPORTANCE OF CONTEXT IN THE LEARNING OF NEW WORDS

The presence of a meaningful *context* is extremely important to vocabulary learning. The context for a new word can be given by the situation and the topic being discussed, as well as by surrounding words, phrases, and sentences. Words taught in a situational context, or a spoken or written context, are likely to be learned more readily than words taught apart from such contexts (Jenkins & Dixon, 1983).

In fact, children learn the meanings of more words through reading them in context than through vocabulary instruction. Nagy, Herman, and Anderson (1985) demonstrated that children infer the meanings of about 3000 words a year. This means that although children learn some words from school instruction, they build their vocabulary more from encountering new words in text as they read.

It follows then that the amount of independent, nonschool reading a child does is a major factor in vocabulary growth. During the elementary school years, however, children appear to vary greatly in the amount of independent reading they do, and therefore in the amount of vocabulary they are acquiring.

For example, in a study of fifth graders, Fielding, Wilson, and Anderson (in press) found that 10 percent of the children did no out-of-school reading, and 50 percent read for an average of four minutes or less per day. Only 10 percent, the better readers, read for more than 25 minutes per day. By contrast, children watched television for an average of 130 minutes per day.

The implications of this research are clear. If we want to help children increase their vocabularies for the purpose of becoming competent, school-successful readers, we should try to motivate them to read for information and for pleasure outside the classroom. Most children could benefit from doing much more independent reading than they now do (for ways of motivating independent reading, see Chapter 13).

The need to encourage independent reading is further underscored by studies suggesting that reading comprehension probably cannot be directly improved simply by teaching children new words and their meanings. Attempts to improve reading comprehension by giving children vocabulary instruction have *not* often been successful (for a review, see Mezynski, 1983). In one of the few successful attempts, twenty minutes of class time was required for each word learned (Beck, Perfetti, & McKeown, 1982).

The sheer volume of words students apparently must learn is another reason for not relying on direct training alone. School books read by many students in grades one through twelve contain about 90,000 distinct words, according to Nagy and Anderson (1984). There is no way this number of words can be taught directly. The largest number ever reported taught was 1800 in one year, but it was on a specialized topic (Draper and Moeller, 1971).

In the past, many educators assumed that most word meanings were learned through instruction and so concluded that children should be taught the meanings of most new words before reading. Teachers are still advised in some basal programs to teach the meaning of all new vocabulary words before they begin having children read a selection. The logic behind this idea, the "preteaching of vocabulary," is that this knowledge will greatly improve children's ability to comprehend the text.

While preteaching vocabulary can be helpful to comprehension in some instances, such preteaching has to be done carefully and selectively. Particularly if the meanings of new words are taught out of context, preteaching is likely to have little or no effect on comprehension.

There is also a very good reason *not* to preteach all new vocabulary. Following this procedure may deny children the opportunity to practice working out the meanings of new words on their own, from the context of the passage.

Does this mean that direct instruction in word meanings should be abandoned? Certainly not. The meanings of some words can and should be taught directly. But classroom vocabulary instruction should be aimed at teaching children strategies for learning new words in sets, with all the words being related to the same topic.

The key is to build on the children's background knowledge of the topic, merging the learning of new word meanings with what they already know. The way to do this is to have the children engage in *active processing* of the new words. We concentrate on showing how they can understand and remember the new words by making connections to their background knowledge, and how the new words can be useful in expressing ideas more accurately.

INSTRUCTIONAL ACTIVITIES

The activities described below all can help children learn the meanings of many new words. In all cases the words are related by topic and made meaningful for children.

Teaching new words around a topic

The following approach is adapted from those developed by Draper and Moeller (1971) and Palincsar (1984). It works particularly well with texts on content area topics such as science and social studies. Technical terms in these texts are usually repeated regularly (Cohen & Steinberg, 1983), so the children have the opportunity to encounter them more than once. They are likely, then, to see how the text will be easier to read and the topic better understood if the terms are added to their vocabulary. The approach described below can easily be used with children from the third grade on up.

Step 1. Give a brief introduction to the topic, perhaps doing no more than naming it, if the children are likely to be quite familiar with it. Elicit from the children what they already know about the topic and have them predict the information to be presented in the first segment of text to be read.

For example, take the case of a sixth grade teacher presenting a lesson on the circulatory system. The lesson is centered around the second section in a health textbook chapter entitled "Your Body Systems at Work." The third page of this section of the chapter is shown in Figure 4.1.

The teacher began the lesson by asking the children what they knew about the circulatory system. The children did not know what the term *circulatory* meant, but when she told them it had to do with blood and the heart, they came up with many ideas, e.g., the heart pumps blood through the body, blood travels through blood vessels, people can have a condition known as high blood pressure. The teacher wrote these ideas on the chalkboard and told the children they would be reading to find out if these statements were true, and also to learn other things about the circulatory system.

Step 2. Have the children read the text segment silently. As they read, have them write on a separate sheet of paper the words with meanings they do not know or are unsure of. Use text segments of just a paragraph or two for younger children or if the text is on a difficult topic. Older children can be assigned longer segments to read on their own.

In the lesson on the circulatory system, the teacher had the children read the set of five pages silently. While reading, the children wrote down such

FIGURE 4.1 *Your Body Systems at Work*

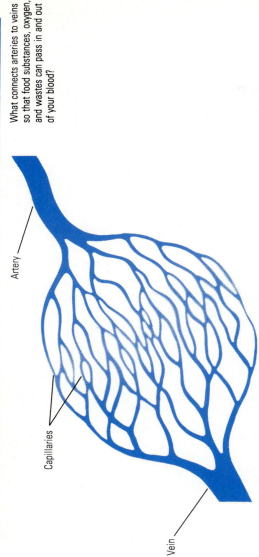

Artery

Capillaries

Vein

What connects arteries to veins so that food substances, oxygen, and wastes can pass in and out of your blood?

terms as *hemoglobin, antibodies,* and *platelets.* The teacher walked around the room and noted the terms that seemed to be puzzling them.

Step 3. Ask the children to give an oral summary of the text segment read. Work with the group to construct an accurate and concise summary from the different responses given. You may wish to write notes and then the final summary itself on the board.

In our sample lesson, the text was organized into seven shorter parts, signaled by subheadings. Each part covered a topic such as red blood cells, white blood cells, and the heart. The teacher had the children summarize the text orally as a group. That is, she first had them state in a few sentences what the entire section had been about. Then she had them give the important facts under each subheading.

Step 4. As the summary is being developed, problem words may also be written on the board. If convenient, group these words by subheadings. Although all words may be discussed, most of the time should be devoted to those related to the main idea (if any) of the text. Have children talk about the likely meaning of the words, and then have them return to the text to look at the sentence and paragraph contexts of some of the problem words. Help children work out the meanings from context in the ways mentioned in the third key concept in this chapter.

In the sample lesson, the children were asked while summarizing to note any problem words they had come across in that particular part of the text. Under the subheading of red blood cells, several of the children said they were

FIGURE 4.2   Original Semantic Map for Climate

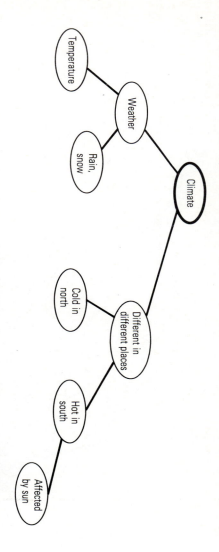

uncertain about the term *hemoglobin*. The teacher felt it was important for the children to understand this term so she had the children reread and then discuss the relevant section of the text.

Step 5. Clarify through discussion the context-supported definition of problem words or have the children consult a dictionary to find the appropriate definition. You might have them write the word and its definition in a diary of new words on that topic.

Step 6. Keep the special terms listed on the board or put them on a piece of chart paper to be displayed and referred to over the period of time the topic is being studied. Encourage the children to use the terms during discussion and in writing reports. When these terms reappear later, be sure the children notice them. If children do not spot them, call the terms to their attention. For example, in a later health lesson, the children read about diseases of the circulatory system, where they were called upon to apply their understanding of terms such as *artery*.

Semantic mapping

The purpose of this procedure, using a visual display of words, is to help children see relationships among the new words they are learning (see McNeil, 1984, for further discussion of semantic mapping). These words may fit together to describe a concept or process or to explain an idea or event. Semantic mapping works well if the words stem from a topic encompassing particular and technical vocabulary.

Before beginning the lesson, you will need to preview the text and make a list of the important terms the children will be reading, or should know, when studying the topic. For example, a third grade teacher might teach a social studies unit on the topic of climate. The terms taken from the textbook selection on that topic are likely to be *equator, climate, poles, globe*.

Step 1. Introduce the topic around which you want the children to form the semantic map. Write it at the top of the chalkboard and ask the children to give you words or phrases that they associate with the topic. As they do so, try to group their responses in categories. For example, Figure 4.2 shows the semantic map the teacher could have elicited for the topic, *climate*.

Step 2. When the children have no more to add, ask what further information about the topic they need to know to understand it. Write these questions on the board and then have them read the text, searching for this information. In our example, the children might have raised questions such as the following:

Why are some places in the world hot while others are cold?
What is the coldest place in the world?
Can people do anything to change the climate?

Step 3. After they have finished reading, have the children use the new terms to add to or correct items on the map. If the new words are used correctly, the mapping activity may end here. Otherwise, work with the children to reorganize the map to better illustrate relationships among the items. Also have them discuss answers to the questions they raised, although perhaps not all questions will have been covered in the text.

In our example, suppose the teacher first worked with the children to reorganize the map as shown in Figure 4.3. To make sure the children incorporated new terms into the map, the teacher listed them on the chalkboard and

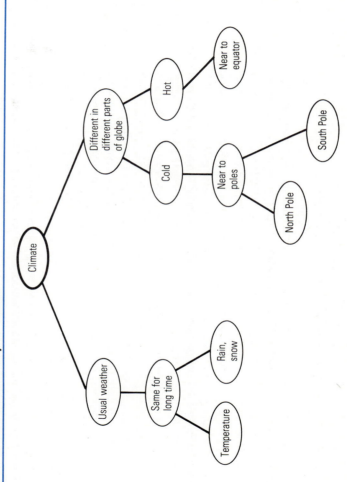

FIGURE 4.3 Revised Semantic Map for Climate

FIGURE 4.4   Semantic Map for Gas

Gas

Related to	Uses	Kinds	Properties
Molecular movement	Healing	Natural	Expands
Chemical changes	Illuminating	Acetylene	Fills space
States of matter	Purifying	Helium	No volume
Evaporation and condensation	Putting people to sleep	Chlorine	No shape

Table from *Reading Comprehension: New Directions for Classroom Practice* by John D. McNeil. Copyright © 1984 Scott, Foresman and Company, p. 11.

checked them off as they were included. Then she had the children discuss answers to the questions they had raised.

Step 4. For an independent seatwork assignment, you could have the children write a summary of the text using the key words from the semantic map. Children who have had some experience with teacher-led semantic mapping might be encouraged to try to develop maps on their own from material read independently. Maps generated by different children on the same text or topic could then be compared during group discussion. In the sample lesson, the teacher could have had the children work in groups of three to write a summary of the text using the key words and information in the semantic map.

Depending on the ability and background knowledge of the students, and the complexity of the topic or concept, the semantic map may either be very simple or quite elaborate. The map developed during the sample lesson was a very simple one. A much more elaborate semantic map for the concept of gas is shown in Figure 4.4 (McNeil, 1984, p. 11).

Semantic categories

A vocabulary learning program based on introducing words by semantic categories (meaningfully related collections) is described by Beck, McCaslin, and McKeown (1980; see also Beck & McKeown, 1983). The purpose of this program is to teach vocabulary well enough to enhance comprehension. It emphasizes the development of "word consciousness," with the aim of making students more aware of words in general. Grouping the words into meaningful sets helps students learn and remember subtle differences in word meanings.

The program was designed to give children an in-depth knowledge of word meanings through a carefully planned sequence of activities. It was successfully used with fourth graders who were presented with groups of eight to ten words, as listed in Figure 4.5 (Beck et al., 1980). The *people* category, for example, included such words as *accomplice, virtuoso, rival,* and *philanthropist.* Words were grouped in this way to allow the children to build relationships among them.

The children received a five-day cycle of instruction on each set of words.

Each day's lesson lasted about thirty minutes. The first couple of lessons were designed to be fairly easy, while the later lessons were more demanding. Each cycle covered a range of tasks, including defining, sentence generation, oral production, and games calling for rapid responding. The point of presenting students with a variety of tasks was to help them develop a rich understanding of the words and the ability to use them flexibly (for further details refer to Beck, McCaslin, & McKeown, 1980).

When introducing semantically related words, here are four activities you can try (adapted from Beck & McKeown, 1983):

Yays and boos. If a set of words has opposing dimensions, (e.g., *good/bad, together/apart*) have the children respond positively (with a yay) or negatively (with a boo) to each word in the set. For example, with the people category, they might "yay" someone who is a virtuoso but "boo" someone who is a tyrant. After each word is given a yay or a boo, have the children give reasons for responding as they did.

Pantomime. If the set of words can be acted out, read the children a story containing the words and have them pantomime the action associated with each word. For example, one of the sets of words used centered on the theme "how we move our legs." It included words such as *galumph, trudge,* and *meander.* The teacher read a story that used these words, and when each was mentioned, the children acted out that movement.

FIGURE 4.5   *Words Selected for Vocabulary Instruction by Cycle*

Cycle	Semantic Category	Words Taught
1	People	accomplice, virtuoso, rival, philanthropist, novice, hermit, tyrant, miser
2	What You Can Do With Your Arms	beckon, embrace, knead, flex, hurl, seize, nudge, filch, thrust
3	Eating	obese, glutton, devour, appetite, fast, wholesome, nutrition, famished, edible
4	Eyes	gape, spectator, binoculars, squint, focus, scrutinize, glimpse, inspector
5	Moods	cautious, jovial, glum, placid, indignant, enthusiastic, diligent, envious, impatient
6	How We Move Our Legs	stalk, galumph, vault, trudge, patrol, meander, strut, lurch, dash
7	Speaking	wail, chorus, proclaim, mention, banter, commend, berate, urge, retort
8	What People Can Be Like	frank, gregarious, independent, ambitious, impish, obstinate, vain, generous, stern
9	Ears	eavesdrop, rustle, audible, din, volume, melodious, serenade, shrill, commotion
10	More People	acquaintance, journalist, introvert, scholar, prophet, merchant, scapegoat, ancestors, extrovert
11	Working Together or Apart	feud, ally, foe, conspire, diplomat, compromise, pact, harmony
12	The Usual and the Unusual	typical, monotonous, obvious, habitual, unique, exotic, extraordinary, peculiar

Table from *The Rationale and Design of a Program to Teach Vocabulary to Fourth Grade Students* by Beck, McCaslin, and McKeown. Reprinted with permission of Isabel L. Beck.

Concept learning. This activity requires students to identify the critical features which differentiate a word from others with somewhat similar meanings. It also allows students to see ways in which some words are related in meaning. To do this, present the students with two possible uses of the target word. Have them select the one showing the correct use of the target word and then give reasons for their choice. Beck and McKeown (1983, p. 624) give the example of this pair of choices for the target word *beckon*: "a friend telling you over the telephone about her new puppy," or "a friend motioning you to come into her house to see her new puppy." The first choice, but not the second, gives the concept that to beckon someone you must be able to see the person and use a physical gesture to signal that person to come closer to you.

Context generating. Have the children imagine and then describe a situation involving each word in the category. For example, with the *people* category, you could have them tell what the person might do (e.g., an *accomplice* might drive a getaway car, while a *hermit* might be walking alone, and a *novice* would be in a driver education car). With the *ears* or *eyes* categories, you might have the children talk about and then perform an action for the target word. For example, they can act out what people do when they *gape*, *squint*, and *scrutinize*.

USING TEXT CONTEXT TO DETERMINE THE MEANING OF WORDS

Many words are *polysemous*, having more than one meaning. For example, you may use a *plane* to smooth a piece of wood, but this would not be the same kind of *plane* as the one you boarded to go on a trip. To get a sense of just how many of the words in children's stories may be polysemous, complete the exercise on the following page.

Because so many words are polysemous, we should help children realize that words are not fixed in meaning. They should understand that the same word can take on a number of different meanings, depending on the context in which it appears. The instructional implication here is that we need to give children a flexible and open attitude toward word meanings, so they will be able to recognize the less common meanings taken on by words whose primary meanings they already know.

The polysemy of words can add to children's comprehension problems. According to Mason, Kniseley, and Kendall (1981), this happens especially when an uncommon meaning of the word must be known to understand the text. Consider, for example, the following sentence:

Sally *pitched* the guitar too high for the singer.

*Students discuss ideas
for a semantic map being
drawn to show
relationships among new
vocbulary words.*

Many fifth graders thought this sentence meant that Sally had made an error in throwing the guitar! They did not consider that *pitch* could mean *tune*.

We can conclude, then, that children do not necessarily attend to context enough as a way of selecting the proper meaning of a polysemous word. They often assume that the primary or more common meaning is the one intended,

---

EXERCISE

(1) Read through the text below, taken from a second grade reader. (Fife, 1973, p. 164):

The Little Park

Peter, Jill, and Ben saw the new sign.
FOR SALE LAST EMPTY GROUND IN TOWN.
"But this is where we play," said Peter. "It's not empty. Little things live here."
"I see a rabbit," Jill said.
"Look at the bees around the flowers," said Ben.
The children saw a grasshopper. A raccoon ran to its hiding place. A bird flew to its nest.
"Bugs and ants live in this log," Jill said. "People don't know. They say this land is empty."

(2) Now go through the text word by word, circling each one that could have at least one other meaning in a somewhat different context. For example, *park* could refer to what we do with a car, or to a place outdoors with trees and grass.

(3) How many polysemous words did you find? We circled nineteen, and even then we weren't sure we had found them all!

INSTRUCTIONAL GUIDELINES

Your students might well be unaware of the different ways that new meanings of familiar words can be learned from written context. Here are some you can point out to them. (Other ways of categorizing context clues were described in Chapter 3.)

Usage. Students can figure out less common meanings of words from the *topic of the passage* and associated ideas. Have them try to develop an understanding of new meanings for old words by constructing sentences showing these new meanings. Remind them to write sentences using the word in the same sense it has in the passage being studied. For example, if the passage is about one-celled organisms, students should not think of a jail cell.

Synonym or antonym. Students can become aware that, for some words, there is a synonym or antonym that can be used to express a meaning nearly the same or directly opposite. By trying to substitute synonyms or antonyms in the text, they can check to see if they are gaining a sense of what the new word means. For example, suppose the target word is *recess* in the sentence, "The plant was *growing* in a recess of the rock." The students could check their understanding by trying to substitute other words for *recess* (which they may know only as the break time in school), such as *hole* or *cavity.*

Function. Students can be led to use this method when a word is defined in context in terms of a use or a process. Many verbs are defined in context in this way. For example, students probably know *mold* as a *growth* on old food. But if they see the sentence, "The children molded the clay into animals," they will probably realize that this use of *mold* denotes a process of shaping, forming, or kneading.

Example. Students can also be shown how to look for new meanings from written context when a particular instance or a typical description is given. Meanings of nouns can be recognized in this way. For example, the less common meaning of the word *game* could be inferred if deer or moose were mentioned.

The practical implication here is that teachers need to help children develop an awareness that many, if not most, words carry several meanings. Encourage children to take a *self-monitoring* or *critical thinking* approach when reading to avoid being fooled or confused when knowledge of an uncommon or unexpected word meaning is called for.

even when the context of the sentence provides clues that a secondary meaning is correct.

INSTRUCTIONAL ACTIVITIES

The following two activities can be used to develop children's awareness of, and ability to deal with, polysemous words.

Context (or GLURK) training with polysemous words

The purpose of this activity, which was developed by Kendall and Mason (1980) for fourth graders, is to help children attend to context so that they will select the proper meaning of a polysemous word. Examples of polysemous words found in basal readers are listed in Figure 4.6. You can use these words or words like them for the following activity. This activity can probably be used with children from the second grade on up.

As a first step, have children work with sentences in which the polysemous word is replaced with the nonsense word, GLURK. The sentences you construct should be tapping a less common meaning for the word being replaced by GLURK. For example, the following could be written on the board:

The dog can GLURK after the stick.

John's knees GLURKED from carrying the heavy weight.

Have the children discuss what GLURK might mean in each sentence and also what it could *not* mean. They might think of "jump" or "run" for the first sentence and "broke" or "hurt" for the second. Then replace GLURK with *bound* in the first sentence and with *buckled* in the second. Have the children

FIGURE 4.6 Polysemous Words Found in Basal Readers

Listing of words with two or more different meanings found in *The Sun that Warms* (grade 4 text), *On the Edge* (grade 5 text), and *To Turn a Stone* (grade 6 text), all from Ginn 360.

anchor	are	bank	bat	batter
bay	band	beat	bill	bite
blow	beam	boom	bore	bound
bow	bond	brush	buckle	burst
cane	brake	chain	charge	court
crack	cast	chain	cuff	drive
fancy	crest	fell	firm	game
grave	heel	hem	hide	hitch
iron	jam	kick	lap	lick
match	mate	pass	pay	pipe
pit	plain	plate	pitch	press
print	quarter	race	racket	rail
recess	record	rent	ride	row
rush	scale	scrape	seal	skirt
snap	spare	spark	spring	spur
staff	stall	steel	stem	stitch
stock	strain	strike	swell	switch
tack	tackle	tag	tender	thumb
tongue	tramp	wake	watch	wolf

try to improve on the meanings they inferred from context. They should now be able to avoid thinking of *bound* only as "tied" and of *buckle* only as "part of a belt." Lead a discussion about how words carry more than one meaning and how context can be used to reveal new and different meanings.

After the children have had a number of experiences with context training and can easily work through exercises such as the one described above, show them how this strategy can be applied in actual reading conditions. For this purpose, take sentences containing less common meanings of polysemous words from the texts they are reading, e.g., "The water *ran* down the glass." Write these sentences on the chalkboard but do *not* substitute GLURK for the polysemous words. See if the children can use context, as well as other clues, to identify the polysemous word and to decide on its proper meaning. Point out to the children how context training may help them read many different kinds of material with better understanding.

Dictionary hunt for polysemous words

The purpose of this activity is to make children aware of just how many words are polysemous. You can use it with older children who have already had other experiences with figuring out the meanings of words from context and with GLURK or an equivalent type of training.

Break students into teams of two or three with one dictionary per team. Have the teams find polysemous words unrelated in meaning (such as *bank, bat, bow, box*). Have them list each word and write sentences for two of its alternate meanings.

STRATEGIES FOR WORKING OUT WORD MEANINGS

In this section we look at ways of helping children become independent in learning meanings of new words. We focus on giving children strategies for working out the meanings of new words while they read. As Schwartz and Raphael (1985) point out, teacher-directed vocabulary activities generally have children learn the words present in a particular text. These activities are not likely to help children acquire strategies they can use later when they encounter words with unknown meanings. Yet the ability to learn the meanings of new words while reading is an important part of becoming a competent reader, especially for the purposes of dealing with content area texts, such as those in science and social studies.

INSTRUCTIONAL ACTIVITIES

We describe two kinds of strategies you can teach to move children toward independence in vocabulary learning: applying knowledge of familiar roots and affixes and applying the concept of definition.

Applying knowledge of familiar roots and affixes

Rationale. This strategy has students determine whether a new word is *related in meaning* to any words they already know. (This approach may be contrasted with that introduced in Chapter 3, in which students looked at words related by letter cluster patterns.) From a knowledge of affixes, root words, and how compound words are formed, children can have some idea of a word's meaning. They can check their initial hypotheses about it by considering the context provided by the surrounding sentence or passage.

We estimate from the findings of Nagy and Anderson (1984) that, for each root word, children who employ this strategy can probably work out the meanings of about seven new words. This includes about four words formed with regular or irregular inflections, and about three words formed with affixes or as compounds. As you can see, a child who could learn seven new words for each root word known has a great advantage in dealing with school reading material.

In teaching this strategy, we can begin by familiarizing students with the concept of the *word family.* Word families consist of words so closely related in meaning that they seem very similar, as we see in the following pairs:

senselessly	senseless
washcloth	wash
elfin	elf
litigant	litigate
gunner	gun
everyday	every
theorist	theory

As mature readers we are able to distinguish word pairs like those above from others which, while similar in spelling, would not be taught as part of the same word family. For example:

inlay	lay
hookworm	hook
fender	fend
apartment	apart
prefix	fix
misgiving	give

In other words, a word family includes words whose meanings could be predicted or derived from knowledge of the root word.

For instructional purposes, teachers can think of a word family as all those words derived from the same root and related in meaning. For example, the word family of *drive* would include the forms *driver, driver's, driving, drives, drove, driven,* etc. It would also include *overdrive* and *driveway.* Thus, in the *drive* word family we have words created through regular and irregular inflections, as well as compounding.

Our aim, then, is to enable children to make the connection between root words already known and the obvious variations formed from inflections and affixes.

Familiarizing children with inflections and comparatives

As we advised in Chapter 3, inflections ought to be introduced before affixes, simply because inflected forms often have meanings closer to that of the root word, follow fewer different patterns, and occur more frequently in elementary school texts. You can provide systematic instruction in inflected forms from about the second grade on, although Hanson (1966) found that first graders were able to benefit from instruction on these patterns.

Children can be taught about three kinds of inflections: those having to do with plurals, verb tense, and comparison. In each case, let the children know that most words follow the rule, but that a few will be exceptions. The regular patterns and some sample exceptions are as follows:

Plurals

-s		-es		exceptions
boys		grasses		women
girls		dishes		children
pets				mice

Tense

-ed			exceptions
planted	(two syllables)		saw
plowed	(one syllable)		went
walked	(one syllable, /t/ sound)		did
			was
			swept
			heard
			rode
			swam
			flew

Comparison

-er/-est	exceptions
longer/longest	better/best
finer/finest	
prettier/prettiest	

Here is a sample instructional sequence for developing children's awareness of plural forms. You can easily adapt this sequence to work on other inflections.

Step 1. Lead the children to induce the rule from words they know. For example, to teach plurals you might begin by asking, "What do you say when you want to talk about more than one girl?" "More than one boy?" "More than one cat?" Include primarily words the children know by sight.

Step 2. As the children come up with responses, write the singular and plural forms in columns.

girl   girls
boy   boys
cat   cats

Allow the children to come up with pairs of their own.

Step 3. If examples following different rules (e.g., -*es* rather than just -*s*) or irregular forms (e.g., *mouse, mice*) are generated, write them in a separate set of columns.

Step 4. Ask the children if they see a pattern in each plural column. They will be able to see how an -*s* or -*es* was added. If some irregular forms have been introduced, cue them to come up with others (e.g., "We say one man, but two _____"). Point out to the children that plurals can be formed in different ways, although there are some very common patterns.

Step 5. Keep the lists on the board for a week or so and encourage the children to add other examples of each pattern (or of an irregular form). They might be asked to look for these patterns in the materials they read that week (but only after comprehension activities with these materials have already taken place). Because many examples are likely to be found, you then have the opportunity to point out how useful it is to be able to read plural forms.

Introducing common prefixes and suffixes

Included in Chapter 3 (pp. 81–82) was a list of common affixes. Choose from the list a prefix or suffix that has appeared in some of the words the children already know. You will need to use a slightly different set of steps because, unlike inflections and comparatives, most affixes do not have alternative forms. The steps are shown below, using the prefix *un-* as an example:

Step 1. Put a short list of familiar words in a column on the blackboard or chart paper.

unhappy
unhealthy
unclean

Step 2. Have the children explain how the words are alike and then see if they can think of other examples.

Step 3. Have the children think about how the meaning of the words has been changed by that addition. Have them generate the rule that explains how the prefix changed the meaning.

Step 4. Keep the list posted and encourage the children to add to it. They can add words they think of or come across during their reading. If you begin with common affixes, many will be added to the list and you can point out how knowing the affix can be useful in working out the meanings of all of these words. Save the lists for use in the activity discussed below.

At some point the children may come up with exceptions, words that look like they should fit the pattern but in fact do not. For example, *uncle*, *unite*, and *under* seem to begin with the prefix *un-* but do not. In others, such as *untie* or *uncover*, the prefix *un-* is present but takes on somewhat different meanings. On these occasions you have the opportunity to give children more informa- tion about the kinds of words which do and do not have affixes and to show that certain affixes have more than one meaning. New lists could be started for other meanings noticed by the children, for example, in this case where the prefix *un-* is added to verbs (e.g., *untie*, *undo*, *uncork*).

Promoting a general understanding of prefixes and suffixes

Try to develop this more general understanding after the children have be- come familiar with a number of prefixes and suffixes, presented as described above.

Stage 1. Put up several lists of words with either prefixes or suffixes. Review with the children how the affix systematically changes the meanings of the words. For each affix, add one or two new examples and see if the children can work out the meanings of these new words. If they have trouble, put the words into sentence contexts. Discuss with the children how knowledge of prefixes and suffixes can be useful in working out word meanings.

Stage 2. Later on, take the children further, by introducing new words with *both* prefixes and suffixes. See if the children can find the root words and identify the affixes. Then see if they can work out the meanings from seeing the words in sentences.

Stage 3. Still later, help the children combine knowledge of affixes with the use of context. Show them how combining these two strategies will generally give a better indication of what the word means than either strategy alone. Sentences should again be taken from materials the children are reading, so they can see the direct relevance of using this combination of strategies to their everyday reading.

Concept of definition procedure

Rationale. Since one of our goals is to help students become independent in learning new words while reading, it may be important to make sure they have a good *concept of definition*, as Schwartz and Raphael (1985) suggest. These investigators point out that, when encountering a word they don't understand, skilled readers have the ability to work out a definition by using context and

FIGURE 4.7   *Structure of a Word Map*

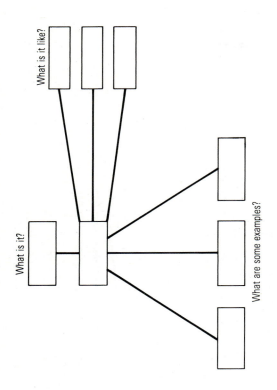

combining new information with existing background knowledge. Giving students the ability to do the same could contribute to their becoming much better readers.

How can teachers help children develop a concept of definition? According to Schwartz and Raphael, children often first need help in learning about the type of information needed to define a word. Second, they need to know how the information should be organized.

The approach proposed by Schwartz and Raphael centers on the use of simple word maps, adapted from those described by Pearson and Johnson (1978). To construct an adequate word map, students need to bring together three pieces of information:

1. The class of which the concept is a part: What is it?
2. The properties that distinguish the concept from others in the same class: What is it like?
3. Examples of the concept: What are some examples?

The structure of a word map is shown in Figure 4.7 (from Schwartz and Raphael). Presented in Figure 4.8 is a completed word map for the concept of *sandwich*. In the concept of definition procedure developed by Schwartz and Raphael, students teach themselves new word meanings by understanding three categories of information that comprise a definition. Students can learn the strategy in a sequence of four lessons, as described below (adapted from Schwartz & Raphael, 1985). The procedure was tested with fourth and fifth graders and can easily be used with students in any of the upper elementary grades.

FIGURE 4.8　Completed Word Map for Sandwich

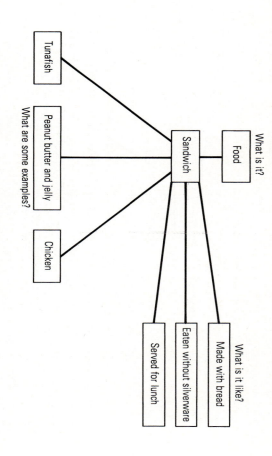

First day: preparation. Before teaching the lesson, choose three or more concepts the children already know to use as examples in a categorization task showing the components of a definition. For each concept, prepare a list of information including the concept class, at least three properties, and at least three examples. Sample lists of two concepts, *soup* and *clown*, are shown below.

SOUP

chicken noodle
served with sandwiches
tastes good
is a liquid
cream of mushroom
eat it with a spoon
served before the main dish at dinner
vegetable noodle
made from milk sometimes
served in a bowl

CLOWN

wears a lot of makeup
Bozo
a person
works in a circus
does funny things
wears bright colored clothes
likes children
rodeo clown
Oopsy
has a large fake red nose

Conducting the lesson. Begin by giving children explicit information about the purpose of the procedure and what they will be doing. Discuss with them how knowing the meanings of words helps with understanding material being read. Explain to them that the procedure they will be learning will enable them to judge whether they know the meaning of a particular word. Introduce the children to the structure of a word map (see Figure 4.7).

Draw this structure on the chalkboard, putting the labels *What Is It?* above, *Examples* below, and *What Is It Like?* to one side. This gives you a place to list the information for class, examples, and properties. Tell the children that this is a kind of picture which shows three things we generally know when we have a really good understanding of a word. Tell them that they will be learning what these three things are by completing word maps for a number of words they already know.

Have the children work from the lists prepared earlier. Ask them to place the information from the list for each word into the three categories in the word map. Here, for example, is an exchange between a teacher and students which occurred when the children were trying to categorize the information for the word *computer*:

T: To answer the question, "What is it?" you need a very general word. This is a word that would answer the question, "What is it?" for many different words. Look on your list under the word *computer*. Can you find a very general word that answers the question, "What is it?" It could answer the question for lawn mower, or dishwasher, or pencil sharpener, as well as computer.

S: Machine.

T: That certainly is very general, and it does answer the question, "What is it?" Now we'll talk about the question, "What is it like?" The answer to this question gives details about the word being studied. For example, the details for computer are descriptions of what computers are like. These descriptions tell things about computers and how they are different from other machines like lawn mowers, pencil sharpeners, or dishwashers. Can you find any?

S: Has a keyboard.

S: Can play games on it.

S: Has a screen to read from.

T: Yes, those are properties of computer; they answer the question, "What is it like?" To answer the last question, "What are some examples?" check the list again. Do you see any examples of computers?

S: Apple IIc.

S: IBM PC.

S: It isn't on the list, but there is the TRS-80 computer.

T: Excellent. You used information from the list, and also from your own experiences. (Schwartz & Raphael, 1985, pp. 201–202)

After you have worked through a number of examples with the children, have them try to map and write definitions for some words on their own. They can begin by using words from the lists already prepared. Have them map a word of their own choice using background knowledge to complete the map. Then have them write a definition for the word they just mapped. Here is an example of a definition a student might have written after mapping the word clown:

A clown is a person who entertains you. He wears a lot of makeup and does funny things. He usually works in a circus. Some examples are Bozo and Oopsy and a rodeo clown.

Second day: preparation. Look for a number of passages where information about the target word is presented in the surrounding context. Try to locate passages which give "complete contexts," that is, those providing the class three properties and three examples. Content area textbooks may be a good source of passages, although you may have to modify them to make them more complete. An example of a complete context is shown below:

CROPS

Have you ever been to a farm? Have you ever seen a farmer work with his crops? Crops come from seeds planted by the farmer early in the spring. The farmer takes care of his seeds all spring and summer long. Early in the fall, crops are harvested and taken to market. At the market they are sold to people like you and me. Farmers can plant different kinds of crops. Some plant potatoes. Some plant onions. Some plant corn and tomatoes. Fresh crops sure taste good!

Once the children understand the approach, emphasize that it is not necessary to have exactly three properties or three examples. Let them know that some words have less than three properties or three examples and that more ideas important to an understanding of the word can often be included.

Conducting the lesson. Let the children know that the purpose of the lesson is to teach them to locate in passages the information needed for a definition. Work through several sample passages with the children. Tell them what the target word is and ask them to mark the information to be put in the word map. Have them transfer the information to the map, then generate either oral or written definitions.

Third day: preparation. This time look for a number of passages when the context is less complete. These "partial context" passages will not give all of the information students need to complete a map and arrive at a definition for the target word. An example of a passage providing only partial context is shown below:

ENVIRONMENT

You hear a lot these days about our environment, but what exactly is it? We hear a lot of talk about a clean environment. Many parts of our environment need cleaning. The better our environment, the happier we can be.

Conducting the lesson. Begin by letting the students know that passages will not always provide all the information they need to define a word adequately. Have them work through a passage as in the second lesson and identify the additional information needed. At this point the students may realize on their own that the missing information may be found in dictionaries and encyclopedias or in other books. If not, lead them to this conclusion. Encourage the children to use other references to complete their maps and definitions for the target words. Also, if they are not applying their own background knowledge, remind them to do so.

Fourth day: preparation. Again select a number of passages with only partial context. For each target word, make up an incomplete definition, e.g., one which lacks one of the three kinds of information or presents fewer than three properties or examples. A sample is shown below:

ASTRONAUT

The space shuttle is in space again, this time with five astronauts on board. What an exciting job to have! I'll bet people like John Glenn and Sally Ride really enjoy their work.

Definition: Astronauts enjoy their work. Examples of astronauts are Sally Ride and John Glenn.

———— This is a complete definition.
———— This is not a complete definition. Things to add are:

Conducting the lesson. Tell the students that the purpose of this lesson is to have them try to write down word definitions, incorporating all three kinds of information, but without necessarily mapping it first. Ask the children to think about the parts of the map and to try to put the information together in their minds.

Present the partial context passages and incomplete definitions and ask the students to see if the definitions are complete. Tell them that they should write in the missing information for definitions they find to be incomplete. Discuss with the students the kinds of thinking they are using to decide what is missing from the definitions and where they might find the information needed.

SUMMARY

We opened this chapter by discussing the knowledge hypothesis and the two-way relationship between vocabulary and reading ability: Having a good vocabulary enables readers read with understanding, and reading for understanding enables readers to learn the meaning of new words. In the first key concept we brought out the importance of oral vocabulary development for children in the early stages of learning to read. We also showed how oral language can be used to help children learn the meanings of new words, as in the vocabulary language prediction activity.

The second key concept covered a major principle of effective vocabulary instruction, that of teaching words related by topic and presented in context. The idea is not to teach words in isolation but in sets children will find meaningful. This approach allows children to make connections among new terms and between new terms and their background knowledge.

In the third key concept we looked at ways of teaching children to deal with polysemous words, those with multiple meanings. Finally, we introduced under the fourth key concept two strategies children can be taught for gaining independence in the learning of vocabulary. The first strategy involves the use of roots and affixes to analyze words. The second has to do with developing a concept of definition.

Research suggests that the meanings of most words are not learned through direct instruction, but are probably acquired through independent reading. While this finding points to the importance of encouraging out-of-school reading, it does not mean that we should abandon the practice of teaching vocabulary. But rather than having students memorize the meanings of particular words, we want to focus on helping them develop effective strategies for learning new words in context. Giving students the ability to learn new word meanings on their own is an important goal of the classroom reading program.

BIBLIOGRAPHY

REFERENCES

Beck, I. L., McCaslin, E. S., & McKeown, M. G. (1980). *The rationale and design of a program to teach vocabulary to fourth-grade students.* Pittsburgh: Learning Research and Development Center, University of Pittsburgh.

Beck, I. L., Perfetti, C., & McKeown, M. (1982). The effects of long-term vocabulary instruction on lexical access and reading comprehension. *Reading Research Quarterly, 74,* 506–621.

Beck, I. L., & McKeown, M. G. (1983). Learning words well—A program to enhance vocabulary and comprehension. *Reading Teacher, 36* (7), 622–625.

Carew, J. (1974). *The third gift.* Boston: Little, Brown & Co.

Cohen, S. A. & Steinberg, J. E. (1983). Effects of three types of vocabulary on readability of intermediate grade science textbooks: An application of Finn's transfer feature theory. *Reading Research Quarterly, 19* (1), 86–101.

Davis, F. (1944). Fundamental factors of comprehension in reading. *Psychometrika, 9,* 186–197.

Draper, A. G., & Moeller, G. H. (1971). We think with words (therefore, to improve thinking, teach vocabulary) *Phi Delta Kappan, 52,* 482–484.

Fielding, L., Wilson, P., & Anderson, R. C. (in press). A new focus on free reading: The role of trade-books in reading instruction. In T. E. Raphael (Ed.), *Contexts of school-based literacy.* New York: Random House.

Hanson, I. (1966). First grade children work with variant word endings. *Reading Teacher, 19,* 505–507.

Ingham, J. (1981). *Books and reading development.* Portsmouth, NH: Heinemann.

Jenkins, J. R., & Dixon, R. (1983). Vocabulary learning. *Contemporary Psychology, 8,* 237–260.

Kendall, J., & Mason, J. (1980). *Comprehension of polysemous words.* Paper presented at the American Education Research Association Annual Meeting.

Mason, J. M., Kniseley, E., & Kendall, J. (1981). Effects of polysemous words on sentence comprehension. *Reading Research Quarterly, 15,* 49–65.

McNeil, J. D. (1984). *Reading comprehension: New directions for classroom practice.* Glenview, IL: Scott, Foresman.

Mezynski, K. (1983). Issues concerning the acquisition of knowledge: Effects of vocabulary training on reading comprehension. *Review of Educational Research, 53,* 253–279.

Nagy, W. E., & Anderson, R. C. (1984). How many words are there in printed school English? *Reading Research Quarterly, 19,* 304–330.

Nagy, W. E., Herman, P., & Anderson, R. C. (1985). Learning words from context. *Reading Research Quarterly, 20,* 233–253.

Palincsar, A. W. (1984). The quest for meaning from expository text: A teacher-guided journey. In G. G. Duffy, L. R. Roehler, & J. Mason (Eds.), *Comprehension instruction: Perspectives and suggestions.* New York: Longman.

Pearson, P. D., & Johnson, D. D. (1978). *Teaching reading comprehension.* New York: Holt, Rinehart & Winston.

Pilon, A. B. (1984). Reading to learn about the nature of language. In A. Harris & E. Sipay (Eds.), *Readings on reading instruction.* New York: Longman.

Ringler, L. H., & Weber, C. K. (1984). *A language-thinking approach to reading.* New York: Harcourt Brace Jovanovich.

Schwartz, R. M., & Raphael, T. E. (1985). Concept of definition: A key to improving students' vocabulary. *Reading Teacher, 39* (2), 198-205.

Thurston, L. (1946). A note on the reanalysis of Davis' reading tests. *Psychometrika, 11,* 185–188.

Ward, B. A., & Kelley, M. A. (1971). *Developing children's oral language, Minicourse 2, Teachers' handbook.* Beverly Hills, CA: Far West Laboratory for Educational Research and Development and Macmillian Educational Services.

Wood, K. D., & Robinson, N. (1983). Vocabulary, language, and prediction: A prereading strategy. *Reading Teacher, 36* (4), 392-395.

CHILDREN'S BOOKS CITED

Fife, D. *The little park* (1973). Niles, IL: Albert Whitman & Co.

Hubbell, P. (1958). *Catch me a wind.* New York: Atheneum.

Lionni, L. (1973). *Frederick.* New York: Knopf/Pantheon.

SAMPLE PASSAGE FROM MEDICAL TEXTBOOK

Barker, L. R., Burton, J. R., & Zieve, P. D. (1982). *Principles of ambulatory medicine.* Baltimore: Williams & Wilkins.

FURTHER READINGS

Deighton, L. (1959). *Vocabulary development in the classroom.* New York: Teachers College, Columbia University.

McKeown, M., Beck, I., Omanson, R., & Perfetti, C. (1983). The effects of long-term vocabulary instruction on reading comprehension: A replication. *Journal of Reading Behavior, 15,* 3–18.

Pearson, P. D., & Johnson, D. D. (1978). *Teaching reading vocabulary.* New York: Holt, Rinehart & Winston.

Samuels, S. J. (1979). How the mind works when reading: Describing elephants no one has ever seen. In L. B. Resnick & P. A. Weaver (Eds.), *Theory and practice of early reading.* Vol. 1. Hillsdale, NJ: Lawrence Erlbaum Associates.

CHAPTER 5

Teaching Reading Comprehension:
General Considerations

If we suggest that someone should read a particular book we obviously intend that he should comprehend it. It would be redundant to the point of rudeness to say we wanted him to read *and* comprehend the book. But on the other hand it would be quite reasonable for the person to reply "Well, I've already read the book but I couldn't comprehend it." We could not object that the person has not read the book just because he did not comprehend it. We might suggest that he read the book again but not that he read it for the first time. So the word "reading" may sometimes entail "comprehension" and sometimes not, and any dispute about whether reading does or does not necessarily entail comprehension is a dispute about language, not about the nature of reading.
(Smith, 1979, p. 102)

OVERVIEW

Having presented you in earlier chapters with a view of the process of reading and details about how some of its pieces need to be taught, we now move into the main thrust of reading instruction. One purpose of this chapter is to provide more information about the process of reading comprehension, as it is seen in mature readers and in children still learning to read. A second purpose is to present guidelines and activities for teaching comprehension effectively. We discuss how teachers should gradually lead students to independence in comprehension, helping them learn to monitor their own thinking while reading. To accomplish this, teachers should be able to conduct well-organized lessons, to involve students in discussions, and to use effective questioning techniques. A theme developed throughout the chapter is that teachers should emphasize the comprehension process, or strategies students can use in understanding text.

The key concepts in this chapter are:

Key Concept #1: The teacher should help students learn to oversee their own reading comprehension processes, so they will be able to repair failures to understand the message of the text.

Key Concept #2: Reading comprehension lessons should be carried out following an orderly framework, usually involving prereading, guided reading, and postreading activities.

Key Concept #3: To provide effective comprehension instruction, the teacher should know how to conduct discussions which actively engage students.

Key Concept #4: The teacher should know how to use questioning effectively, as well as how to teach students to ask questions themselves.

PERSPECTIVE

A CLOSE LOOK AT THE COMPREHENSION PROCESS

On the surface, comprehension of text seems to be simply a matter of (1) paying close attention to the text, and (2) knowing how to decode all the words in it. In fact, no matter how carefully the reader pays attention to the text, or how easy it is for him to say all the words in it, he may still fail to understand its message. The exercise on page 132 is designed to help make this idea clear. *What we are trying to illustrate with this short exercise is that difficulties in comprehending text cannot be explained simply in terms of unfamiliar or "hard" words. Similarly, comprehension success cannot be explained in terms of an ability to decode all the words.* There is much more to it. In this and the next two chapters, we will give you more information about *reading as the process of constructing meaning from text.*

IMPORTANCE OF BACKGROUND KNOWLEDGE

As we will see in the exercise, readers do not passively take in information as they read. They actively *construct* a meaning, among other things supplementing text information with their own background knowledge, identifying important ideas, organizing information to be remembered, making connections among text ideas, and monitoring the success of their comprehension efforts.

Anderson and Pearson (1984) review a large body of research supporting the idea that an important aspect of reading is to fill in text gaps with inferences drawn from one's own background knowledge. Texts never present a complete picture and would be unacceptably boring if they did. Imagine, for example, how dull the passage below would be if all the trivial steps Mrs. White went through to get ready to go shopping were written in. Because we could easily infer this information (such as the fact that she probably had to open the door to get outside), there is no need for it to be written. Authors expect readers to fill in minor gaps from their own background experience and so focus their writing instead on important or unusual events. In the passage below, take notice not only of what we are told but also of what has been left out:

> One day Mrs. White was going to the market. She put some fruit in a basket. She put on her hat. She walked down the road.   (*Mrs. White's Hat*, 1978, p. 52)

The reader learns that Mrs. White carries some fruit, (Is she going to sell it or is that her lunch?) puts on her hat, (Now, why did the author bother to tell us that rather than that she put on her shoes, coat, or dress?) and walks down

EXERCISE

(1) Read the short passages below:

Passage 1: When you're ready to start your plass, make sure the gik is in the right position and the trad has been set. Only then turn the stip to the START position. While in START, the zud will crank until you release the stip. The stip returns to ON which is the normal running position.

Passage 2: To raise your jib, attach the jib tack to the U-bolt on the bow. Tie a painter to the U-bolt and then shackle the jib head to the jib halyard. Now hoist the jib, with the crew pulling forward on the forestay, and engage the stop on the halyard wire in the skyhook.

(2) Did you experience difficulty comprehending these passages? What, if anything, made the first one hard for you to understand? What contributed to the difficulty of the second?

Both passages were taken from operating manuals. The main difference between the two passages is that key words in the first were replaced with pseudowords such as *gik* and *trad*, while the other used real words. The texts are similar in that both describe real world events. However, the event described in the first, starting a car, is probably more familiar to most people than that described in the second, getting ready to sail.

(3) Try rereading the passages. You will probably find that the events in the first fall into place while those in the second remain as mysterious as ever. This is because your prior knowledge of the first topic is now assisting your comprehension. But if you lack prior knowledge about sailing, you will still find the second nearly incomprehensible. Even if we were to give you the dictionary definitions of *jib, painter, halyard,* etc., the second text would continue to be difficult because, unless you have sailed, you lack important knowledge about the concepts. Why do you need a jib—or do you? What part of the jib do you hoist? And so on.

the road. (It sounds as though she has no car and lives in the country or a small town rather than the city. Will that turn out to be true?) As experienced readers we assume that the author had good reasons for including certain information, that which we will need to know as we read on, and omitting other information, that which is unimportant. Holding these assumptions, we begin to ask ourselves questions, and this makes the story more interesting.

Prior knowledge not only helps children make inferences about text, it also helps them to learn and remember what they read. For example, Marr and Gromley (1982) showed that prior knowledge of a topic helped fourth grade students remember information from passages they read. Hayes and Tierney (1982) found that prior knowledge of sports and baseball helped high school students interpret and recall texts about cricket matches, itself a topic they knew little of.

Children can learn to use prior knowledge to help them remember text information. This was confirmed in a study by Stein and Bransford (1979), who asked fifth graders to try to remember sentences such as:

The kind man bought the milk.
The short man used the broom.
The funny man liked the ring.
The hungry man purchased the tie.

As presented, these sentences are not easy to remember, because there is no obvious relationship between the characteristics of the people (e.g., being short or funny) and their actions (e.g., using a broom or liking a ring). However, when the children were taught to elaborate on the sentences so that all the words were tied together in an understandable way (e.g., the kind man was buying milk for hungry children), they had no difficulty remembering the information.

Key areas of background knowledge

Two areas of background knowledge seem particularly important for successful reading comprehension: (1) knowledge of text structure, and (2) knowledge of the topic of the text.

Text structure.   Readers need knowledge of the *global* or overall organization of various types of text. Think, for example, how different our expectations are, once we know that we will be reading a novel, versus a short story, versus a poem, versus an essay, versus a report. We have expectations about length, type of language, and, given a title, about content. We expect the ideas in a poem to be presented and organized much differently from ideas in a report. Having all this prior knowledge of text structure at a global level allows comprehension to proceed much more efficiently and effectively.

Children need to be given the same opportunity to develop those expectations. They need to read a variety of kinds of texts and to discuss various text structures in reading lessons and the functions served by different structures.

We also need knowledge of text structure at a *local* level, or the level at which phrases and sentences are combined (Halliday & Hasan, 1976). Comprehension is boosted if we can see the links among text ideas at this level. For example, we use our knowledge of conjunctions such as *and*, *because*, and *or* to learn whether one idea is to be added to another, whether one event caused another, or whether one condition alters another. Children need to learn how these and other devices help readers keep track of information within a text. Instructional activities for both global and local text structures are presented in Chapters 6 and 7; the use of global and local context is discussed in Chapter 4.

Text topic. Prior knowledge about the topic of the text is important for successful reading comprehension because, as we noted earlier, readers have to fill in gaps in text. Readers construct possible interpretations—hypotheses—and then search the text *and their own background knowledge about the topic* for pieces of evidence which support or contradict their hypotheses. Having an adequate amount of prior knowledge about the topic is essential to the formation and evaluation of hypotheses to guide reading comprehension.

The instructional implication here is that teachers should attend to whether children have the necessary background knowledge of the text topic. If not, knowledge of the topic may have to be taught. Specific methods for doing this are presented in Chapter 7.

Changes in comprehension ability as children get older

The ability to comprehend text develops gradually over time. For example, testing 8- to 18-year olds, Brown and Smiley (1977) found older students better able than younger ones to distinguish important from unimportant text ideas. The older children, but not the younger ones, also knew how to study selectively, spending their time reviewing important rather than unimportant information. All students, however, recalled the most important information better than the least important.

Older children not only know better how to study text, they also have a sense of what makes text easier or more difficult to understand and remember. Danner (1976) gave children in grades 2, 4, and 6 passages with either well-organized or randomly ordered sentences. All children remembered the well-organized passages better, but only the sixth graders could explain which passages were more difficult and why. The sixth graders were also the only ones who knew that topic sentences, and not other less important ones, would help them remember the rest of the text.

Younger children do not necessarily realize that there are different ways of going about reading a text, that reading activity can and should be adjusted depending on one's purpose. Forrest and Waller (1979) had children in grades 3 and 6 read stories (a) for fun, (b) to make up a title, (c) to skim for just one piece of information, and (d) to study. They found that only the sixth graders varied their approaches to the text for these different purposes.

Another difference between younger and older children has to do with their ability to monitor and repair their own comprehension. If they become aware that they are failing to understand a text, younger children do not know what to do so they will understand it (Myers & Paris, 1978).

As you can see, being able to comprehend and remember text involves complex strategies which take years to develop. Reading comprehension does not come automatically but is learned over time. Strategies for understanding and learning from text, like those described above, are what we need to teach.

EMPHASIZING PROCESS IN INSTRUCTION

Effective comprehension instruction targets the *process* of constructing meaning from text, rather than the product (i.e., the correct interpretation of a particular text). Collins and Smith (1980) suggest that one way of getting a sense of the processes involved in comprehension is to look at possible reasons for comprehension failure. A comprehension failure, a problem with understanding the message of the text, might come about because the reader:

1. Encounters an unfamiliar word or a word that doesn't make sense in the context;
2. Cannot see the proper relationship between one sentence and another. The interpretation of one sentence conflicts with that of another; there are no or several possible connections between the sentences;
3. Cannot see how the whole text fits together. The point of the whole text, or some part of it, is missed, such as the significance of a certain episode or the motivations of certain characters.

Below, we suggest how you might teach students to remedy these failures. Note that the idea is to work on general strategies that will be useful not just for the text being read but for other texts as well.

1. Instead of teaching just the word missed, provide instruction on the use of context clues to identify new words.
2. Instead of telling the relationship between the sentences, ask students leading questions and have them work out the relationship. Then discuss with them the reasons why the relationship was difficult to work out, including the possibility that more background knowledge was needed.
3. Instead of summarizing the text for them, again ask leading questions and have the students work out an overall interpretation. Teach them to use a visual representation of text ideas, such as a diagram, map, or outline, to make relationships among episodes easier to see.

The teacher should help students learn to oversee their own reading comprehension processes, so they will be able to repair failures to understand the message of the text.

KEY CONCEPT 1

COMPREHENSION STRATEGIES USED BY MATURE READERS

What strategies do you use when you read? While readers may have general strategies for reading, they may also have certain strategies they use only when reading narratives or fiction, and others they use only when reading exposition or nonfiction. Think about how you prepare for reading and what you do while reading. Below are responses given by undergraduates who were preparing to be elementary school teachers. These responses give you an idea of the wide variety of comprehension strategies mature readers use.

Here are responses showing students' strategies for getting ready to read:

1. Find or construct an environment—place and time—that is conducive to learning and concentrating.
2. Go over the table of contents to determine how the chapter fits with the rest of the textbook.
3. Create hypotheses or make predictions about the text content to be expected, and then read to confirm or disconfirm these predictions.
4. On the basis of knowledge about the author, try to infer his or her intent, asking, for example, "What would this author probably say or believe about this topic?"

These responses show students' strategies for monitoring their comprehension:

1. Write down the major topics in the margin of the page and then underline parts of the paragraph that explain the topics.
2. Read a section of the text and mentally review it; check for understanding before continuing.
3. Question a concept that does not fit into one's own framework. Then reread and, if possible, resolve the discrepancy.
4. Paraphrase the author's words in "plain English," in one's own words.

Students reported using these strategies when they failed to comprehend the text:

1. Reread to identify the paragraph or sentence not understood.
2. Read ahead and look for clarifying information.
3. Look elsewhere for another presentation of the same information (e.g., summaries or introductions, illustrations or graphs).

Finally, here are strategies students used for identifying important information:

1. Notice the amount of space devoted to a particular topic in the text.
2. Notice how much emphasis the teacher places on the topic.
3. Look for the relevance of the topic to topics already known to be important.
4. Look for information important to career or personal interests.

These lists cover a wide variety of strategies for reading, and you can probably think of quite a few others. We see then that there are many strategies that children need to learn, both to be successful students and to use reading effectively while at home or at work.

METACOGNITION IN READING

There is a difference between having an understanding of a particular text and knowing about the strategies used to arrive at that understanding. Knowledge of one's own comprehension strategies, or the processes being used to comprehend text, is referred to as the *metacognitive* aspect of reading (Brown, 1979; Palincsar, 1984). The term *metacognitive* itself has to do with awareness of one's own thought processes. Metacognition in reading' thus concerns readers' awareness of their own thinking as they are trying to comprehend the text.

One way that mature readers show metacognition in reading is by monitoring their own comprehension of text. *Comprehension monitoring*, or keeping track of how well one is understanding the text, can be thought to have two different aspects, "knowing about comprehending" and "knowing how to comprehend" (Wagoner, 1983). Wagoner suggests that knowing about comprehending involves readers' being able to recognize when they have failed to understand the message of the text. Mature readers have an awareness of this kind of breakdown. On the other hand, knowing how to comprehend involves the repair strategies readers use after recognizing the problem, to remedy the breakdown in comprehension.

As Baker and Brown (1984) point out, this kind of awareness and control of one's reading activity, or the ability to monitor one's own comprehension, is highly important. Children may actually have the strategies needed but not know when to use them. Thus, teachers should make sure that instruction targets metacognitive activities central to reading, including clarifying the purposes for reading, identifying the important elements in a message, checking to see if learning is taking place, and taking corrective action when failures in comprehension are detected.

Coping with comprehension failure

Part of being an expert reader is knowing how to deal with comprehension failure. Readers, whether novice or expert, regularly fail to comprehend, at least in part. We all come across unfamiliar words, read a sentence and feel unsure about what the author intended, or miss the point and lose track of what is important in a text. Children need to learn to cope with these comprehension failures. That is, they must first notice that their comprehension has failed and then diagnose the problem and figure out what to do about it. This is what an expert reader does:

A good reader proceeds smoothly and quickly as long as his understanding of the material is complete. But as soon as he senses that he has missed an idea, that the track has been lost, he brings smooth progress to a grinding halt. Advancing more slowly, he seeks clarification in the subsequent material, examining it for the light it can throw on the earlier trouble spot. If still dissatisfied with his grasp, he returns to the point where the difficulty began and rereads the section more carefully. He probes and analyzes phrases and sentences for their exact meaning; he tries to visualize abstruse descriptions; and through a series of approximations, deductions, and corrections he translates scientific and technical terms into concrete examples. (Whimbey, 1975, p. 91)

Collins and Smith (1980) suggest that expert readers repair comprehension failures by resorting first to solutions that are the least disruptive to their ongoing reading activity. Moving from least to most disruptive, these solutions might be:

1. ignore the problem and continue reading
2. suspend judgment
3. form a tentative hypothesis, using text information
4. reread the current sentence
5. reread the previous context
6. go to an expert source.

In working with children, we want to be sure that they develop different methods for dealing with comprehension failure and that they learn to try the less disruptive strategies first.

INSTRUCTIONAL GUIDELINES

Fitzgerald (1983) suggests the following guidelines for giving children an awareness of their own comprehension activities:

1. Use explicit instruction to teach children strategies to use when comprehension goes awry. Don't rely entirely on spontaneous opportunities to teach.

2. Use self-control training. That is, discuss the objectives or reasons for the lessons you do with the children, and be sure they are aware that they should apply the strategies when they are reading independently.

3. For training lessons, use materials of moderate difficulty so that some miscomprehension can occur. If materials are too easy, complete or nearly complete understanding is probable. If materials are too hard, little or no comprehension can occur.

4. Provide necessary background knowledge before reading so that the children can use appropriate comprehension strategies. Students can't use metacomprehension strategies if they lack the information from which to construct meaning.

5. Teach students that taking risks and making guesses is good. Students who will guess are more likely to recognize the importance of making an effort to understand the text, that is, they are more likely to use intervention strategies when miscomprehension occurs. For example, demonstrate that good intervention strategies may still result in miscomprehension and point out that many texts can have a variety of interpretations. (Fitzgerald, 1983, p. 251)

INSTRUCTIONAL ACTIVITY

Here is one of the activities Fitzgerald recommends for improving comprehension monitoring, an important aspect of metacognition in reading.

Modeling comprehension monitoring

Discuss with the children the importance of active thinking while reading. Mention both the importance of checking on understanding and generating hypotheses about the text. Read part of a text out loud and, as you proceed, comment on your mental activity. That is, mention the hypotheses you have about the text, revisions you make to your original hypotheses, anything that strikes you as unclear, and so on.

Start lists on the board with the headings "Know" and "Don't Know." Pause every few sentences to add notes to the lists of what you know and don't know. Explain to the children that you are using the lists to keep track of information in the text.

Conduct follow-up lessons so you can gradually involve the children. The first time, essentially repeat the first lesson but have the children provide the hypotheses and information for the lists. The second time, have the students work in pairs and take turns thinking aloud while reading. Third, have the children practice the technique on their own.

Other activities for encouraging comprehension monitoring and other aspects of metacognition in reading are described in Chapter 6.

KEY CONCEPT 2

Reading comprehension lessons should be carried out following an orderly framework, usually involving prereading, guided reading, and postreading activities.

USING A LESSON FRAMEWORK

In developing students' comprehension ability through guided discussion, you should follow a *lesson framework* likely to prove effective (refer to Chapter 11 for information on the directed reading activity, the lesson framework typically recommended in the teacher's guides of basal reader programs). According to Cunningham, Moore, Cunningham, and Moore (1983), the teacher will generally wish to follow a sequence incorporating these basic steps:

Step 1. Activate or develop background knowledge necessary for understanding the text.

Step 2. Set purposes for reading (i.e., identify information to be searched for, questions to be answered, predictions to be verified).

Step 3. Have students read for these purposes.

Step 4. Have students show in some way (i.e., by answering questions, summarizing, reading relevant information aloud) whether they have met the purposes.

Step 5. Give students feedback about their comprehension performance (i.e., let them know if their reasoning was sound and if their responses were right, wrong, or perhaps incomplete).

The lesson frameworks below are specific approaches for incorporating these steps. Both include a prereading, guided reading, and postreading component. These frameworks may be used when comprehension instruction takes the form of guided discussion of a particular text. They should be distinguished from methods for the direct instruction of particular comprehension skills and strategies, such as comprehension monitoring, which was discussed in the first key concept.

Experience-text-relationship method (ETR)

The purpose of this method (Au, 1979) is to give students a general approach to text comprehension, bringing out the importance of background knowledge. Basically, lessons involve the teacher's leading the children in the discussion of text and text-related topics. At the same time, the teacher models for the children the process an expert reader goes through in trying to construct meaning from text. Through repeated experience in ETR lessons, the children should be able to use this overall approach independently. This method works well with basal reader stories and is particularly useful in working with primary grade children.

With this method more than one lesson, and perhaps even four or five lessons of twenty minutes or so, are required to complete the reading of most basal reader selections. Obviously, this amount of time should only be spent on stories with a strong theme and interesting plot, which provide suitable material for in-depth discussion.

Planning.   Preview the story and identify its central theme, topic, and/or important or interesting points you want the children to grasp. Decide in what way the central theme or points might be made relevant to the children's background experiences. Of course, this requires knowledge of your students as well as of the text. Suppose that the story is about a boy who wants to buy a guitar so he can "make music." You might decide to begin the lesson by asking the children if they know of ways to "make music."

Experience or E phase.   Begin the lesson by finding out what background experiences the children have had related to the theme or topic of the text. In our example, the teacher asked if the children knew what the term "make music" meant. They spoke of being at parties where people sang and played musical instruments.

From this general beginning, move the discussion closer to the story about to be read. Show the children a picture or tell them the title of the story and invite speculation about it. In this case the teacher told the children the title of the story, "Jasper Makes Music," and asked what they thought it would be about. They made predictions about the kind of musical instrument Jasper might want, how he could go about getting it, what kind of music he wanted to play, and so on.

With relevant background knowledge having been activated and predictions about the story made, have the children read a portion of the story silently. Remind them of their predictions and set other purposes as well, for example, having them identify the setting, characters, and problem presented in the text.

Text or T phase.   When the children have finished reading, reopen the discussion by having them talk about their predictions, whether or not they were confirmed by the text, and discuss other information covered in the purposes set for reading. Then have the children make predictions about the section of text to be read next, setting additional purposes as appropriate, to call their attention to important text information. Alternate periods of silent reading and discussion in this manner until the whole story has been read and discussed.

Relationship or R phase.   When the story has been completed, be sure to ask questions relating text information to background knowledge and experiences. For example, ask the children what they would have done if they had been in the main character's shoes. Or ask the children if they have ever faced a problem like that of the main character. (In the case of Jasper, ask if they have ever wanted something their parents said they could not have, because it was too expensive.) In other words, you want to pose questions which help them make the connection between text ideas and their own lives. This helps encourage a deeper, more active processing of text during the postreading phase.

Directed reading-thinking activity (DRTA)

Stauffer's (1969) Directed Reading-Thinking Activity encourages active involvement with text by having students generate hypotheses about text and then check on the accuracy of their predictions. The DRTA can be used with virtually any kind of reading material, selections in content area textbooks as well as in basal readers. As Spiegel (1981) points out, it is especially useful when students already have the necessary vocabulary and background knowledge. In practice, there are many variations to the basic DRTA concept. Here is the one we prefer:

Step 1. Tell the children the title of the selection or show them an illustration. On the basis of this information, have them make predictions about the story. If an informational text is being used, an alternative is to have them tell what they already know about the topic. Write predictions and other ideas on the board.

Step 2. Pointing out to the children that they will be reading to see if the text verifies the information on the board, have them read a portion of the text silently.

Step 3. Reopen the discussion by having the children go down the list of predictions and ideas on the board, telling which were verified. Point out to the children that there are several possibilities. The idea could be:

1. Verified by the text (in which case, you can have a child read the relevant sentence aloud);
2. Disproved by the text (again, a child might read the relevant sentence aloud);
3. Only partially verified or disproved, with more information being required to make a definite decision about whether the idea is right or wrong;
4. Shown to be only partially right or wrong, but definitely requiring revision on the basis of text information;
5. Not mentioned.

Items in the list are rewritten, marked as true, crossed off if false, and so on. New hypotheses may also be added. Thus, the list should become a running record of important text information.

Step 4. Alternate periods of silent reading and discussion until the whole text has been read. Older children who have participated in this procedure before may be asked to copy the original list from the board and directed to read and then revise the list on their own, for seatwork. In all cases, emphasize the quality of the reasoning students are doing, rather than just the correctness of their initial hypotheses. Point out how the process of mentally generating and revising hypotheses is something that should always be done while reading.

THREE-PHASE SEQUENCE FOR ORGANIZING LESSONS

Teachers can think of comprehension instruction in terms of a three-phase sequence: *prereading, guided reading,* and *postreading.* Each phase serves a different function. Prereading gives children background knowledge, if necessary, and orients them to the text. Guided reading enables them to track text ideas. Postreading helps them remember text information.

Guidelines for improving children's comprehension ability during the prereading, guided reading, or postreading phases of instruction are presented below. Many of the ideas come from the extensive review of methods for teaching reading comprehension prepared by Tierney and Cunningham (1984).

Prereading instructional guidelines

We mentioned earlier the importance of students' knowledge of text structure and topics. Instructional activities to provide knowledge in these areas generally are best presented during the prereading phase. Prereading activities can also help students learn to focus their attention on important information, set purposes for reading, and take an active interest in the text. All can be seen as forms of *advance organizers* (Ausubel, 1968) which help the reader know in advance what to look for in the text.

One way to prepare students to read with understanding, for a particular purpose, is to tell them what they should be learning, a practice usually called "setting purposes for reading," according to Tierney and Cunningham (1984). These authors suggest the following guidelines for stating objectives:

1. If you know in particular what you want your students to learn from reading the text, stating prereading objectives is a good idea. While students might in any event grasp the most important points in the text, stating objectives makes it more likely they will also recall certain details.

2. If you want your students to learn everything in the text or to develop a general familiarity with the ideas, do *not* state prereading objectives. This is because objectives tend to focus attention and your stating objectives might cause students to skip over information.

Guided reading instructional guidelines

Guided reading activities are those which occur during the time in which the children are reading. These activities serve two primary purposes (Tierney & Cunningham, 1984): (1) they make text material more accessible to readers and (2) they improve ability to comprehend text. Perhaps the most common guided reading activity is teacher questioning about text just read. Because of its importance and widespread use, questioning is covered in detail under the last key concept in this chapter.

When thinking of guided reading activities, the first issue that comes to many teachers' minds is whether to have the children read silently or aloud. Reading silently is much to be preferred, except under special circumstances. Reading aloud might occur if:

1. your purpose is to check word identification abilities, not comprehension,
2. you want the child to provide evidence from the text to support a
   point he or she has made during discussion,
3. you are preparing the children to perform in a play.

Otherwise, if you are working on comprehension, try to have the children read silently. An exception may be made for children at the very beginning stages of learning to read who may need to hear themselves saying the words.

A second issue is whether the teacher should have the children read the text in its entirety or break it into sections to be read. The answer here depends on your purposes for the lesson and on the difficulty of the text. For example, if your purpose is have the children read for enjoyment, and you know the text will be quite easy for them, they can be assigned to read it all at once. That is, after a brief introductory discussion, the children read the whole text independently and then participate in a postreading discussion.

On the other hand, if your purpose is to have the children analyze the text closely, and you know the text will probably be difficult for them, you will want them to read it in short sections. Look for natural breaks in the text and have the children read up to each break. Stop for a brief discussion of the informa-tion just read, to be sure they have grasped it. When working with primary grade students, the segments of text children read before discussion periods may be quite short, perhaps only a paragraph or a page or two.

Postreading instructional guidelines

Postreading activities occur after children have completed their reading of the text. The purpose of postreading activities is to help children remember important information, or through reflection to understand the text better.

Giving students *feedback* (i.e., telling them how well they have answered questions about the text) can improve learning (Tierney & Cunningham, 1984). Here are points to keep in mind:

1. Feedback need not be immediate to be effective. Thus, even if you cannot give feedback to students right away, you should try to speak to them later.

2. Feedback following an incorrect response may be particularly beneficial to the student. Such feedback should be stated clearly but without discouraging the child from responding again. One way of striking this balance is first to say something positive about the child's answer and then give the criticism. You might say, for example, "Your answer makes sense because you and I might feel that way. But think about the story. Why do you think Jasper's parents felt the way they did?"

3. As shown above, teacher feedback probably should go beyond just saying whether the answer is right or wrong. It should extend to helping students to work out the correct answer, perhaps providing background knowledge or explaining why the answer was wrong.

KEY CONCEPT 3

To provide effective comprehension instruction, the teacher should know how to conduct discussions which actively engage students.

ENGAGING STUDENTS IN DISCUSSIONS

We focus on discussions because of our interest in promoting students' active involvement in lessons. When discussion focuses on text or text-related topics, the teacher has the chance to strengthen aspects of the students' reading comprehension ability. By encouraging students to give responses, the teacher gains information about the kinds of comprehension activities students can carry out on their own and the ones they need help with. Here are some guidelines to consider when conducting discussions:

1. Aim for a balance between teacher talk and student talk. Create numerous opportunities for students to respond.

For a discussion to be successful in improving students' comprehension ability, there must be a *balance between teacher talk and student talk.* If the teacher does most of the talking, there will be little opportunity for the give-and-take required to further comprehension development.

2. In general, elicit responses from students instead of telling them the answer. When an incorrect answer is given, help the student to work out the correct response.

Research by Au and Kawakami (1984) suggests that effective teachers consistently try to draw answers from children during comprehension discussions. They almost never tell the answer, instead pushing the children to come up with the right answer themselves. They do, however, ask leading questions which make it possible for the children eventually to succeed. That is, they do not simply repeat their original question. Instead, they paraphrase it or break it into two or more easier questions for the children to answer. Then they help the children put the pieces together to answer the original, more difficult question. At a deeper level, these effective teachers are not just concerned with right and wrong answers but with guiding children through a process of sound reasoning about text ideas.

EXERCISE

(1) The next time you give a reading or other lesson to a group of students, make a tape recording of it.

(2) Play the tape back and, using a stopwatch, try to determine about how much time you spent talking versus how much time you allowed the children to talk. There may be times when both you and the children were talking at once, and these should be counted as "overlapping speech." Include in the "silence" category time spent in silent reading or writing. Time for the four categories of teacher speaking, students speaking, overlapping speech, and silence should add up to the total number of minutes in the lesson.

Teacher speaking:	_____ minutes
Students speaking:	_____ minutes
Overlapping speech:	_____ minutes
Silence:	_____ minutes
Total lesson time:	_____ minutes

(3) Consider the results of your analysis. A good goal is to aim for a 50-50 split, with half of the speaking time given to teacher talk and half to student talk. Many teachers find that they are doing almost all of the talking (75% of the time or more!).

(4) Play the tape again, and this time see if you can count the number of opportunities you created for the children to speak. Generally, these will be times when you asked a question and then allowed the children to answer it. Also included in this count would be times when you allowed the children to ask their own questions.

Opportunities for children to speak: _____

(5) Consider the results of this analysis. Do you feel, in view of the time spent, that you gave the children enough opportunities to respond, comment, or ask questions? The number might vary depending on the quality of the opportunities provided for the children. Fewer opportunities might be given if the children were providing lengthy answers. More opportunities should be given, however, if the children are giving short answers of just a word or a phrase.

(6) In future lessons, see if you can increase the amount of time you allow the students to speak. See also if you can create more opportunities for the students to respond.

EXERCISE

(1) Using the same lesson tape, try to identify all the times when the students gave an incorrect or incomplete answer to your questions.

(2) In each instance, identify your reaction. Note whether you helped the child work out the answer, had another child answer instead, told the answer, asked another question, and so on. List each of your different reactions and how many times it occurred.

(3) Consider this analysis. In what way might each of your reactions help the students learn? In what way might each tend to prevent the students from learning? What, if anything, do you think you might try to do differently?

Effective teachers tend to ask challenging questions, so it is not uncommon for their students to answer incorrectly. In fact, according to Au and Kawakami, about one out of every five lead-off questions asked may be too difficult for the children to answer correctly on their own. On these occasions, however, the teacher helps them work out the answer, in the manner described above.

While there is no particular teacher response that will work in all instances, here is a procedure you can try to follow when you ask a difficult question which the children are unable to answer correctly. The idea behind using this procedure is that you will be encouraging the children to do as much of the thinking as they can.

1. Begin by paraphrasing the question. If you used difficult vocabulary, try to substitute terms the children would be more likely to know. For example, suppose your original question was, "What was Annie's predicament?" You might rephrase your original question as, "What problem was Annie facing?" and tell the children that a predicament is the same as a problem.

2. If this does not work, have the children review the text or background information required to answer. In this case you might ask, "What just happened in the story? Why was everyone in Annie's family so upset?" Keep asking these more specific questions until the information has been covered.

3. Finally, pose your original question again. If necessary, point out to the children how the specific text or background information just discussed should be used in answering your original question. In this case you might say, "Now who can use the points we just discussed, about what grandmother told the family, to answer my question. What was Annie's predicament?"

4. When a child comes up with the correct response, paraphrase it for the group. This allows all of the children to see the elements in a complete and appropriate response. Repeating children's answers also signals that you have recognized their thought and effort.

Working with a small reading group allows this teacher to respond instantly to individual questions about the text.

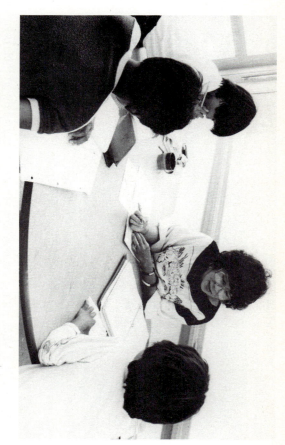

3. *Be aware of the different ways that you can manage talk during discussions. Use methods which involve all students, being careful to use an interactional style which shows respect for the values of the students' culture.*

Most of us tend to be unaware as we teach of the way that we are managing talk during discussions. Yet as we teach we decide what students must do to get a turn to speak, which students will win turns, and what they may talk about. These procedures can have a profound effect on how much students learn during lessons.

To understand this subject, consider the importance of the rules for three types of behavior: speaking, listening, and turntaking (Shultz, Erickson, & Florio, 1982). People from all cultures have unwritten rules for these behaviors. These rules have to do with beliefs about the proper behavior to be shown in face-to-face discussions. While we are not generally aware of these rules, even for our own culture, we act upon them all the time. They affect what we do and how we judge the behavior of others.

These unstated cultural rules operate in classrooms, just as they do in other settings. In classroom discussions one of the common rules is that the teacher sets the topic. That is, he or she determines what will be talked about. Usually, the teacher sets the topic by asking a question. Another common rule, this one affecting turntaking, is that the children do not call out the answer but raise their hands. This signals to the teacher that they want to answer. The teacher then chooses one of the children to speak. Usually, a further rule is that no other child but the one called on may speak. After that child answers, the teacher may evaluate the response given, call on another child to answer, or ask another question.

Meanwhile, the usual rule for listening is that all of the children keep their eyes on the teacher, or perhaps look at the child chosen to answer. They are not supposed to look around the room or at other listeners.

This pattern for organizing discussion (see Mehan, 1979) is outlined below:

Pattern #1

Teacher asks question
One child answers
Teacher evaluates child's answer

While you will probably use this pattern quite often, you should be aware of other patterns that may be equally or perhaps more effective for achieving comprehension goals. Four other patterns are outlined below. Think about when you might try them. Remember, of course, to announce to the children any changes in the rules for participation.

Here is a pattern useful if you are working with a small group, want to give many children the chance to answer, and are after a range of different responses.

Pattern #2

Teacher asks a question (often an opinion or open-ended one)
Children are allowed to respond if they have something to say (several may be speaking at the same time)
Teacher repeats the highest-quality student responses for the benefit of the group

This pattern can be used if the teacher wants to pick up the pace with an activity involving all of the children. Children who are having difficulty responding can still join in with the group, without the fear of being embarrassed.

Pattern #3

Teacher asks a question (requiring a very short answer)
Children respond in a chorus
Teacher gives group feedback

In encouraging children to contribute more, and so to take as much responsibility as they can for the comprehension discussion, you might use the next two patterns.

Pattern #4

Teacher invites or allows children to introduce a text-related topic for discussion, or to pose a question for the group to address
One or more children propose topics or questions
Teacher leads group discussion of topics or questions

Pattern #5

Teacher asks an open-ended question
One child answers
Second child reacts to first child's answer
Third child reacts to second child's answer
Children continue to discuss one another's answers
Teacher summarizes or gives feedback to group

Research in classrooms with culturally different children suggests that there may be a negative effect on learning to read if the teacher conducts discussion using a pattern uncomfortable for the children. For example, in research with Hawaiian children, Au and Mason (1981) found the children paid more attention to the text and gave better answers if discussion generally followed pattern #2 instead of pattern #1. As mentioned in Chapter 1, this was because pattern #2 was closer to the rules for speaking, listening, and turntaking the children followed outside of the classroom in an event called "talk story." The rules in talk story reflected the values of Hawaiian culture, including an emphasis on group rather than individual achievement (for other examples of this idea, refer to Chapter 9).

KEY CONCEPT 4

The teacher should know how to use questioning effectively, as well as how to teach students to ask questions themselves.

EFFECTIVE TEACHER QUESTIONING

There are two main ways teacher questioning can be effective in improving children's comprehension ability. First, teacher questions can call the child's attention to important or interesting text information. By highlighting the information, teacher questions can make it more likely the child will actively process that part of the text, and thus learn and remember it.

Second, teacher questions can serve as a way of "walking the child through" the comprehension process used by an expert reader (Au, 1984). This can happen if the teacher uses questioning as a way of guiding student thinking. An example was shown in the ETR method. In this method teacher questions first help the child activate relevant background knowledge. Then teacher questions call the child's attention to important ideas in the text. Finally, they prod the child to draw relationships between his or her own background knowledge and text ideas.

When using questioning in either of these ways, it helps to have an idea of how to categorize or think about the different questions you might use. Pearson and Johnson (1978) suggest that a question may be placed into one of

During large group discussions, children in this class raise their hands and wait to be called on before responding, following Pattern #1.

three categories, depending on the source of information the reader will need to use to answer it (sample text and questions from Wixson, 1983, p. 288):

1. The answer to a *text explicit* (TE) question is explicitly stated in the text. Such a question can almost be answered just by quoting from the text. Often, the answer is contained in a single sentence.

Text: The wheel fell off the car. The car crashed into a tree.

TE question: What fell off the car?

Text explicit questions covering low level details appear to be the type of question teachers ask most frequently (e.g., Guszak, 1967).

2. The answer to a *text implicit* (TI) question is implicitly present in the text. That is, the answer is hinted at or can be inferred from the text, but is not stated directly. Often the reader must integrate information from several sentences, paragraphs, or even larger portions of the text.

TI question: Why did the car crash into a tree?

3. The answer to a *script implicit* (SI) question comes from the reader's background knowledge (also called scriptal knowledge), not from the text.

SI question: Why did the wheel fall off the car?

The Pearson and Johnson taxonomy of questions is more consistent with our current understanding of the reading/thinking process than other well-known category systems. The idea here is that, if we are interested in improving children's comprehension ability, there is not much point in looking at questions in and of themselves. Instead, we need to look at the interaction of the reader and his background knowledge with the text and the question.

Other category systems for questions typically have been based on the assumption that literal, detail, or text-based questions requiring a value judgment are always) the easiest to answer, while questions requiring a value judgment are among the most difficult (e.g., Barrett, 1976; Bloom, 1956). These systems may be useful in helping the teacher reflect upon the variety of questions it is possible to ask. The following system is a good example (Burns, Roe, & Ross, 1984, p. 203):

1. Main idea—ask the children to identify the central theme of the selection;

2. Detail—ask for bits of information conveyed by the material;

3. Vocabulary—ask for the meanings of words used in the selection;

4. Sequence—require knowledge of events in their order of occurrence;

5. Inference—ask for information that is implied but not directly stated in the material;

6. Evaluation—ask for judgments about the material;

7. Creative response—ask the children to go beyond the material and create new ideas based on the ideas they have read.

In a study with second graders, Crowell and Au (1981) validated a scale of questions for reading comprehension. Moving from easiest to most difficult, the types of questions are (adapted from p. 390):

1. Association—calls for any detail from the story.

   Example: "What was this story about?"
   Standard for correct answer: Any information from the story.

2. Categorization—calls for a simple categorization plus justification, i.e., classifying a story character in a stereotypic manner and telling why this classification is appropriate.

   Example: "Did you like Anna Marie? Why (or why not)?"
   Standard for correct answer: Use of story information to justify classification.

3. Seriation—calls for drawing relationships among details, such as cause and effect or the sequence of events.

   Example: "What happened first? What happened next? Then what happened?"
   Standard for correct answer: Presentation of any three events in the correct order, but not necessarily a complete summary of major events.

4. Integration—calls for combining various story elements into a coherent structure not necessarily present in the text itself, including summarizing the story or giving the main idea.

Example: "What was the problem in this story?" followed by a parallel question related to the specific story such as, "What problem did Nino have?"

Standard for correct answer: Interpretation plus supporting reasons.

5. Extension—calls for applying understanding of the story beyond the boundaries of the immediate story structure, i.e., finding connections to other stories or events, changing opinions on the basis of new information, showing imagination, but with story content as a starting point.

Example: "Tell me another way this story could have ended."

Standard for correct answer: A plausible alternate ending, drawing upon story information in a reasonable manner but clearly different from the actual ending.

Redfield and Rousseau (1981), in an analysis synthesizing the results of twenty studies, conclude that gains in achievement can be expected when teachers use more "higher cognitive" questions. "Higher cognitive" questions are those which require students mentally to manipulate pieces of information, arrive at an answer, and then explain the reasoning behind it. "Lower cognitive" questions, on the other hand, require the student to recall the material verbatim or to recognize material previously covered.

Some guidelines for effective questioning which can be derived from recent research are in the following section.

ASKING QUESTIONS ABOUT EXACTLY WHAT YOU WANT CHILDREN TO LEARN

Studies by Wixson (1983) suggest that questioning can have a powerful effect on children's learning from text. In the first study fifth grade children were asked to read an informational passage and then answer six questions, all of one type: Text Explicit, Text Implicit, or Script Implicit. After a week, the children were asked to recall the passage. The children's recalls clearly were closely related to the types of questions they had answered. Children who had answered Text Explicit questions tended to remember parts of the text word for word; those who answered Text Implicit questions made more text-based inferences; and those who answered Script Implicit questions made more knowledge-based inferences.

In her second study Wixson demonstrated similar results for information at three different levels of importance. If children were asked questions about the most important information, that was what they remembered. If they were asked about the next most important, or the least important level of information, that was what they remembered.

Wixson's findings suggest that, if used correctly, questions can be powerful aids to teaching. She gives the following suggestions (adapted from pp. 292-293):

1. If you want your students to read for information, making few inferences, ask *text explicit* questions. This would include situations where your students are reading directions, recipes, or other material where an exact procedure is to be followed.
2. If you want your students to integrate ideas within the text, as would generally be the case for a selection from a content area textbook, ask *text implicit* questions. These encourage the students to pull together ideas spread across various parts of the text.
3. If you want your students to interpret text information in the light of their own background knowledge, for example in the reading of stories or news articles, ask *script implicit* questions.
4. Finally, if there is information you think is important for your students to remember, ask questions about it.

HELPING CHILDREN LEARN TO IDENTIFY THE SOURCES OF INFORMATION NEEDED TO ANSWER QUESTIONS

Students' ability to answer comprehension questions can be improved if they understand about the three question-answer relationships or QARs (Raphael, 1982) which can be derived from the Pearson and Johnson taxonomy. Raphael suggests the following labels be taught:

For text explicit: "Right there." The answer is "right there" in the text.

For text implicit: "Think and search." To come up with the answer the reader has to "think and search" through the text.

For script implicit: "On my own." The answer must come from the reader's head. It cannot be gotten from the text alone.

INSTRUCTIONAL ACTIVITY

Raphael has found QAR training to improve the question-answering ability of elementary children from the second grade on up. Systematic training may not be needed by older children (fifth and sixth graders); it may be enough just to tell them about the three QARs.

QAR training

Raphael (1982) suggests that four principles be followed in QAR training: "Give immediate feedback, progress from shorter to longer texts, build independence by guiding students from group to independent activities, and provide transition from the easier task of recognizing an answer to the more difficult task of creating a response from more than one source of information." (p. 187)

Lesson 1: Introduce the idea of QARs. To help focus the discussion, an overhead transparency or a handout can be made giving the information in Figure 5.1 (Raphael, 1982, p. 188). Discuss with the children how knowing about QARs will help them answer questions correctly. Go over each of the three QARs and teach children the labels.

Go into Stage 1 practice. Have the children read a two or three sentence passage with three accompanying questions and answers, identified for each QAR category, as shown in the figure. Have them discuss why each question belongs in that particular category.

Go into Stage 2 practice. Use the same type of passage, this time with only the questions and answers, as seen in the figure. Again have the children discuss the material, this time also identifying the QAR for each question.

Go into Stage 3 practice. Use the same type of passage, this time with only the questions, as shown in the figure. This time have the children decide on the QAR for each question and then write out their answer.

Lesson 2: Use passages of 75 to 150 words with three to five questions for each, at least one from each category. Begin by reviewing the purpose of the

---

FIGURE 5.1   **Three Kinds of Questions**

Where is the answer found?

Type 1

Type 2

Type 3

Right There

The answer is in the story, easy to find. The words used to make the question and the words that make the answer are Right There, in the same sentence.

Think and Search

The answer is in the story, but a little harder to find. You would never find the words in the question and words in the answer in the same sentence, but would have to Think and Search for the answer.

On My Own

The answer won't be told by words in the story. You must find the answer in your head. Think: "I have to answer this question On My Own, the story won't be much help."

"Three Kinds of Questions" from "Question Answering Strategies for Children" by Taffy E. Raphael, November 1982 in *The Reading Teacher.* Reprinted with permission of Taffy E. Raphael and the International Reading Association.

activity and the three QARs. Have students work through the first passage as a group, then complete the second individually. Pause for discussion when they are finished. Have the children complete the other passages on their own, while you circulate and provide them with feedback.

Be prepared to look for two things: whether students have identified the correct QAR and whether they have arrived at the correct answer. These are two different tasks, and you want to be sure students are able to do both.

Lesson 3: Use a longer passage, closer in length to the material the children would normally be reading. Divide the passage into about four sections, each followed by six questions, two for each QAR category. Begin with a short review and then have the children work through the first section. After discussion, have them complete the other three sections on their own. Circulate among the students and provide feedback.

Lesson 4: Use material the children are currently reading, such as a basal reader story or selection from a content area textbook. Have them read through the material and then answer a set of questions, several from each QAR category (questions in the basal reader teacher's guide may be appropriate for this purpose). Have the students first identify the QAR and then write the answer to the question.

Maintenance: With children at the fourth grade and below, you may wish to have a regular review of QARs, giving the children a short passage every couple of weeks for practice. Raphael and Wonnacott (1985) worked with teachers who developed a maintenance activity involving student "lawyers." The lawyer names the type of QAR represented by a particular question and then gives an explanation to defend his reasoning. If other students disagree they present their arguments, and the lawyer presents counterarguments. This is a good way to help students verbalize and examine their own thinking.

Teachers working with first and second graders may wish to begin by introducing only two types of QAR, "in my book" and "in my head" (Raphael, personal communication). Later, when the children understand these two, the category of "in my book" may be expanded into "right there" and "think and search." In a similar fashion, the category of "in my head" may later be divided into "on my own" and "author and me."

The "on my own" category is reserved for questions that can be answered more from background knowledge alone, such as, "Have you ever had to be brave and think of a clever solution to a problem?" Raphael points out that this type of question often occurs during the experience phase of ETR lessons.

"Author and me" questions are those where the child must read the text and then answer a question such as "How might the story have ended differently?" Raphael points out that these questions, along with "think and search" ones, generally occur during the relationship phase of ETR lessons. By keeping these points in mind, teachers can integrate QAR training with on-going comprehension instruction in the ETR method.

TEACHING STUDENTS TO ASK QUESTIONS

Teaching students to ask their own questions, instead of continuing to answer teacher-posed questions, is a good way of moving them toward greater independence in reading comprehension. To be able to ask questions, students must be actively thinking about and working with the text. In asking their own prequestions, that is, questions about material not yet read, students decide what the selection might be about and what they might want to learn from it. This gives students the chance to set their own purposes for reading. In asking their own postquestions, those about material just read, students decide what important or interesting information was covered. This helps them learn and remember what they read.

INSTRUCTIONAL GUIDELINES

In teaching students to ask questions, Singer (1978) suggests teachers use these approaches.

Teaching active comprehension

1. *Modeling behavior.* When asking questions, be aware that you are modeling for students the kind of questions to be asked when reading a certain type of text, whether a story, a chapter from a science textbook, or a news article. For example, suppose that the children are going to read a magazine article about an endangered species, the bald eagle. The teacher might begin by saying, "One question I have is, where do bald eagles live? Another question I would like to have answered is, what has caused them to become endangered?"

2. *Phase-out/phase-in strategy.* This is Singer's label for the method teachers should use to shift questioning over to students. Once having modeled the proper kind of questioning, you should have the students try to ask their own questions. According to Singer, there should be a gradual movement away from teacher questioning and toward student questioning. This may be in the same lesson, or in another lesson based on a similar type of material or perhaps covering the same topic.

3. *Active comprehension.* Singer defines active comprehension as a continuous process that should go on before, during, and after reading. Thus, you should have students ask both prequestions and postquestions. He also emphasizes the overall long-term value of teaching students to ask their own questions:

INSTRUCTIONAL ACTIVITIES

The purpose of teaching students to formulate their own questions is not just for attaining the goal of having students select and retain information, although this goal will be achieved in active comprehension, but also to teach students a process of reading and learning from text which emphasizes the reader's purposes and the dynamic interaction between the reader and the printed page, including selective attention to those aspects of text that are relevant to satisfying students' curiosity.   (p. 904)

Singer suggests the following methods for teaching active comprehension (adapted from Singer, 1978, p. 905):

Questioning to elicit questions

Ask students questions to stimulate them to ask questions, instead of giving you an answer. For example, if working with kindergarten children, show them an intriguing picture from a storybook (Singer uses the example of a picture showing a boy on a bicycle, a girl on roller skates, and a boy on a wagon, all about to collide at an intersection). Instead of asking a question such as, "What do you think will happen?" ask the children, "What would you like to find out about this picture?" Expect a wide variety of questions to be posed, and accept those about details as well as about the main problem. Encourage the children to listen to and try to answer one another's questions.

In reading the storybook aloud to the children, have them think about whether their questions were answered and if so, what they learned. Also have them give a critical evaluation of the author's solution to the problem.

This procedure might also be used with a basal reader story. In this case, the children would read the text themselves. You might wish to look at the questions in the teacher's guide, but Singer suggests you do this simply to get ideas.

Students' taking the teacher's role

Have the children take turns serving as the teacher. For example, tell the children the title of the story and ask if they can think of what you, the teacher, might ask them about it. If necessary, model a question to get the group started. Have the children give responses to one another's questions. Then have them read the first part of the text. Again ask them to pretend to be the teacher and suggest questions others in the group might try to answer. For more information about this kind of reciprocal teaching procedure, see Chapter 7.

Team question-asking

With students in the fourth grade and above, you can divide the class into two groups. Choose one student in each group to be the recorder, to write on the board all the questions generated by the members of his or her team. Have the students work with the title and first paragraph of the text. Invite the teams to compete to see which can generate more questions about just this portion of the text.

After the lists of questions have been generated, you might then have each group reduce its list to just the five or so questions it thinks best. Ask the students why they selected those questions and eliminated others. Then have them read the rest of the text and write answers to their own questions.

SUMMARY

We began this chapter by giving you a closer look at reading comprehension, highlighting the importance of background knowledge to understanding text. We also cited evidence to show how children's comprehension ability develops gradually over the elementary school years and beyond.

Under the first key concept we gave you an idea of the strategies used by expert readers, stressing the importance of helping children develop these same strategies. We also discussed the role of metacognition in reading, especially comprehension monitoring.

In the second key concept we discussed the importance of conducting comprehension lessons following carefully constructed lesson frameworks. The experience-text-relationship (ETR) and directed reading-thinking activity (DRTA) were presented as examples of frameworks. Reading comprehension lessons generally have three phases: prereading, guided reading, and postreading. The functions served by each type of phase, and guidelines for effective instruction in each, were presented.

In the third key concept we brought out the importance of actively involving students in reading comprehension discussions. This requires achieving a balance between teacher talk and student talk and the drawing out, rather than telling, of answers. Different patterns for structuring discussion were described.

Questioning was the topic of the fourth key concept. Different ways of categorizing questions were discussed, along with ways of using questions effectively. We suggested that children will be better able to answer questions if they know about question-answer relationships (QARs). We also stressed the importance of active comprehension and having students learn to pose and answer questions they themselves generate. Over time, students should be led to comprehend text with less and less help from the teacher, since the purpose of comprehension instruction is to give students the ability to construct meaning from text on their own.

BIBLIOGRAPHY

REFERENCES

Anderson, R., & Pearson, P. D. (1984). A schema-theoretic view of basic processes in reading comprehension. In P. D. Pearson (Ed.), *Handbook of reading research*. New York: Longman.

Au, K. H. (1979). Using the experience-text-relationship method with minority children. *Reading Teacher, 32* (6), 677-679.

Au, K. H. (1984). Principles of instruction in the KEEP reading lessons. Honolulu, HI: Kamehameha Schools.

Au, K. H., & Kawakami, A. J. (1984). Vygotskian perspectives on discussion processes in small group reading lessons. In P. L. Peterson, L. C. Wilkinson, & M. Hallinan (Eds.), *The social context of instruction: Group organization and group processes*. New York: Academic Press.

Au, K. H., & Kawakami, A. J. (in press). The influence of the social organization of instruction on children's text comprehension ability. In T. E. Raphael (Ed.), *The contexts of school-based literacy*. New York: Random House.

Au, K. H., & Mason, J. M. (1981). Social organizational factors in learning to read: The balance of rights hypothesis. *Reading Research Quarterly, 17* (1), 115-152.

Ausubel, D. P. (1968). *Educational psychology: A cognitive view*. New York: Holt, Rinehart & Winston.

Baker, L., & Brown, A. (1984). Cognitive skills and reading. In P. D. Pearson (Ed.), *Handbook of reading research*. New York: Longman.

Barrett, T. (1976). Taxonomy of reading comprehension. In R. Smith & T. Barrett (Eds.), *Teaching reading in the middle grades*. Reading, MA: Addison-Wesley.

Bloom, B. S. (1956). *Taxonomy of educational objectives: The classification of educational goals. Handbook 1: Cognitive domain*. New York: David McKay.

Brown, A. L. (1979). Reflections on metacognition: Discussant's comments. Paper presented at the Society for Research in Child Development, San Francisco, March 1979 (cited in Palincsar, 1984).

Brown, A. L., & Smiley, S. S. (1977). Rating the importance of structural units of prose passages: A problem of metacognitive development. *Child Development, 48*, 1-8.

Burns, P. C., Roe, B. D., & Ross, E. P. (1984). *Teaching reading in today's elementary schools*. 3rd ed. Boston: Houghton Mifflin.

Canney, G., & Winograd, P. (1979). *Schemata for reading and reading comprehension performance* (Tech. Rep. No. 120). Urbana, IL: University of Illinois, Center for the Study of Reading.

Collins, A., & Smith E. (1980). *Teaching the process of reading comprehension* (Tech. Rep. No. 182). Urbana, IL: University of Illinois, Center for the Study of Reading.

Crowell, D. C., & Au, K. H. (1981). A scale of questions to guide comprehension instruction. *Reading Teacher, 34* (4), 389-393.

Cunningham, P. M., Moore, S. A., Cunningham, J. W., & Moore, D. W. (1983). *Reading in elementary classrooms: Strategies and observations*. New York: Longman.

Danner, F. W. (1976). Children's understanding of intersentence organization in the recall of short descriptive passages. *Journal of Educational Psychology, 68*, 174-183.

Fitzgerald, J. (1983). Helping readers gain self-control over reading comprehension. *Reading Teacher, 37* (3), 249-253.

Forrest, D. L., & Waller, T. G. (1979). *Cognitive and metacognitive aspects of reading*. Paper presented at the meeting of the Society for Research in Child Development, San Francisco, March 1979.

Guszak, F. J. (1967). Teacher questions and levels of reading comprehension. In T. C. Barrett (Ed.), *The evaluation of children's reading achievement.* Newark, DE: International Reading Association.

Halliday, M., & Hasan, R. (1976). *Cohesion in English.* London: Longman.

Hays, D. A., & Tierney, R. J. (1982). Developing readers' knowledge through analogy. *Reading Research Quarterly, 17,* 256-280.

Marr, M., & Gromley, K. (1982). Children's recall of familiar and unfamiliar text. *Reading Research Quarterly, 18,* 89-104.

Mehan, H. (1979). *Learning lessons.* Cambridge, MA: Harvard University Press.

Myers, M., & Paris, S. (1978) Children's metacognitive knowledge about reading. *Journal of Educational Psychology, 70,* 680-690.

Palincsar, A. (1984). The quest for meaning from expository text: A teacher-guided journey. In G. Duffy, L. Roehler, & J. Mason (Eds.), *Comprehension instruction: Perspectives and suggestions.* New York: Longman.

Pearson, P. D., & Johnson, D. D. (1978). *Teaching reading comprehension.* New York: Holt, Rinehart & Winston.

Raphael, T. E. (1982). Question-answering strategies for children. *Reading Teacher, 36* (2), 186-190.

Raphael, T. E., & Wonnacott, C. A. (1985). Heightening fourth-grade students' sensitivity to sources of information for answering comprehension questions. *Reading Research Quarterly, 20* (3), 282-296.

Redfield, D. L., & Rousseau, E. W. (1981). A meta-analysis of experimental research on teacher questioning behavior. *Review of Educational Research, 51* (2), 237-245.

Shultz, J., Erickson, F., & Florio, S. (1982). Where's the floor? Aspects of the cultural organization of social relationships at home and at school. In P. Gilmore & A. Glatthorn (Eds.), *Children in and out of school.* Washington, DC: Center for Applied Linguistics.

Singer, H. (1978). Active comprehension: From answering to asking questions. *Reading Teacher, 31* (8), 901-908.

Smith, F. (1979). *Reading without nonsense.* New York: Teachers College Press.

Spiegel, D. L. (1981). Six alternatives to the Directed Reading Activity. *Reading Teacher, 34* (8), 914-920.

Stauffer, R. (1969). *Reading as a thinking process.* New York: Harper & Row.

Stein, B. S., & Bransford, J. D. (1979). Constraints on effective elaboration: Effects of precision and subject generation. *Journal of Verbal Learning and Verbal Behavior, 18,* 769-777.

Tierney, R. J., and Cunningham, J. W. (1984). Research on teaching reading comprehension. In P. D. Pearson (Ed.), *Handbook of reading research.* New York: Longman.

Tierney, R. J., & Pearson, P. D. (1983). Toward a composing model of reading. *Language Arts, 60,* 568-580.

Wagoner, S. A. (1983). Comprehension monitoring: What it is and what we know about it. *Reading Research Quarterly, 18* (3), 328-346.

Whimbey, A. (1975). *Intelligence can be taught.* New York: Dutton.

Wixson, K. (1983). Questions about a text: What you ask about is what children learn. *Reading Teacher, 37* (3), 287-293.

CHILDREN'S BOOK CITED

Taylor, P. (1978). Mrs. White's Hat. In L. G. Botko, J. K. Heryla, V. K. Klassen, & J. Manning (Eds.), *Dragon wings: Basics in reading.* Glenview, IL: Scott, Foresman.

FURTHER READINGS

Atwell, M. A., & Rhodes, L. K. (1984). Strategy lessons as alternatives to skills lessons in reading. *Journal of Reading, 27* (8), 700-705.

Babbs, P. J., & Moe, A. J. (1983). Metacognition: A key for independent learning from text. *Reading Teacher, 36* (4), 422- 426.

Duffy, G. G., Roehler, L. R., & Mason, J. (Eds.) (1983). *Comprehension instruction: Perspectives and suggestions.* New York: Longman.

Gambrell, L. B. (1980). Think-time: Implications for reading instruction. *Reading Teacher, 34* (2), 143-146.

McNeil, J. D. (1984). *Reading comprehension: New directions for classroom practice.* Glenview, IL: Scott, Foresman.

Paris, S. G., Oka, E. R., & DeBritto, A. M. (1983). Beyond decoding: Synthesis of research on reading comprehension. *Educational Leadership, 41* (2), 78-83.

Wilson, C. R. (1983). Teaching reading comprehension by connecting the known to the new. *Reading Teacher, 36* (4), 382-390.

Developing Children's Appreciation

of Literature and

Comprehension of Stories

From an interview with Mike, who had read *The High King* by Lloyd Alexander:

Interviewer: If you could be one of the characters from *The High King,* which would it be?

Mike: Either Gwydion or Taran. They seemed like the most noble. It seemed like they shared the same ideas I have.

(Mike described the friendship between Gwydion and Taran. "Close friends," he said, "go all out to help each other. They are loving, understanding, and selfless.")

Interviewer: Is it important to you in the books you read that there be some sort of good or noble idea?

Mike: Um-hmm. If you go to battle just because you feel like killing someone, that's just stupid.

Interviewer: What major point do you think Lloyd Alexander was trying to get across in this book?

Mike: I don't know. The point he got across to me was to care more about a million people, or three people, than one person—yourself.

(Cramer, 1984, p. 257)

OVERVIEW

In this chapter we stress the importance of helping children to appreciate literature, a central goal of the classroom reading program. Our focus is on the reading of fiction, with nonfiction being covered in the next chapter. Different types of children's literature are described, and ideas for introducing children to them are discussed.

We present three approaches to stories: the story structure approach, the literary criticism approach, and the social interaction approach. Instructional guidelines stemming from each approach are discussed. We reintroduce the

PERSPECTIVE

MOTIVATING CHILDREN TO READ ON THEIR OWN

There is a big difference between *being able* to read and *wanting* to read or *enjoying* reading. In this chapter we will look not only at ways of helping children develop the ability to comprehend fiction, but also at ways of helping them become motivated to read on their own.

Children who enjoy reading are those who have learned to become personally involved with text. Kindergarten children enjoy reading along with the teacher the words spoken by the Three Billy-Goats Gruff, lowering their voices when speaking the part of the biggest billy goat. They empathize with Ira, a little boy who is teased by his sister for wanting to take his teddy bear along when he goes to spend the night at Reggie's house. Older children laugh aloud at the antics of Pippi Longstocking and are moved by Wilbur the pig and his spider friend in *Charlotte's Web*. A child who is teased for being small or keeping to himself may be comforted by the story of *Crow Boy*.

This special interaction between the reader and the text might be thought to create what Dillon (1984, p. 227) calls "a unique aesthetic experience of knowing and feeling" and a form of "new life." To Rosenblatt (1978), this interaction results in the creation of a "poem."

To give children the opportunity to enjoy these experiences, and to help them acquire the habit of reading, teachers want to make sure that children become involved with good literature. Sutherland and Arbuthnot (1986) suggest that children's literature "consists of books that are not only read and

ideas of metacognition in reading and comprehension monitoring and show how they can be applied to the teaching of strategies for story comprehension. Procedures for planning and organizing story comprehension lessons are outlined, and two lesson frameworks designed to improve children's ability to understand stories are presented.

Chapter 6 is organized around the following key concepts:

Key Concept #1: The teacher should help children learn to appreciate books by encouraging them to respond to literature.

Key Concept #2: The teacher should help children understand the various elements of a story, including its structure, literary merits, and the nature of the social interaction between the author and reader.

Key Concept #3: The teacher should help children learn strategies for planning and monitoring their comprehension of stories, and encourage them to use these strategies independently.

Key Concept #4: The teacher should have a purpose for having students read a particular story, and should follow systematic procedures for planning and conducting story comprehension lessons.

enjoyed, but also that have been written for children and that meet high literary and artistic standards" (p. 5).

Niles (1984) suggests a number of ways that literature can help to promote a lifelong reading habit.

1. Books and stories can describe fantasies that help children stretch their imaginations.
2. They can introduce children to people with other ways of living.
3. They can present children's heritage in folk tales, myth, and history.
4. They can make children more curious about the natural world.
5. They can provide information about different careers and help children better understand the adult world.
6. They can help children deal with the problems of getting along with others, of growing up, of understanding oneself, and of being a responsible citizen.
7. They can be entertaining and provide lighthearted fun.

KEY CONCEPT 1

The teacher should help children learn to appreciate books by encouraging them to respond to literature.

DIMENSIONS OF RESPONSE TO LITERATURE

Benton (1984, p. 266) suggests that there are two important dimensions of response to literature, a "looking in," and a "positive effort at recollection." By looking in, readers become conscious of their own thought processes. By making an effort to recollect, readers interpret and reconstruct their experiences with the text. A child's response to literature is often readily observed by the teacher, but it may also be quite private and hidden. It may focus on connections between the life of story characters and the child's own life, or on the author's style.

The central point, according to Sutherland and Arbuthnot (1986), is the following:

Activities to encourage response to literature must grow naturally out of the reading, and different responses—in variety and quality—must be respected and nurtured. (p. 551)

GENRES OF CHILDREN'S LITERATURE

From the kindergarten year on, the teacher should give children the opportunity to respond to different types of literature. Children's literature may be divided into nine major forms or genres, according to Sutherland and Arbuthnot.

Drawing upon the work of these authors, we briefly describe the important characteristics of each genre. Instructional guidelines are presented for the genres many elementary teachers introduce to children.

1. picture books
2. folk tales
3. fables, myths, and epics
4. modern fantasy
5. poetry
6. modern fiction
7. historical fiction
8. biography
9. informational books

Picture books

Picture books play an important part in the classroom reading program in the primary grades, particularly in kindergarten. A key here is the quality of the illustrations and whether they can attract and hold children's attention. With picture books that tell a story, you might help children attend to the emotional responses of the characters and their problems. Sutherland and Arbuthnot point out that picture books of lasting value play up two themes: love or reassurance and achievement.

The Caldecott Medal is awarded each year to the illustrator of the most outstanding picture book. Caldecott award books young children especially enjoy include *Time of Wonder* by Robert McCloskey, *The Snowy Day* by Ezra Jack Keats, *Sam, Bangs, and Moonshine* by Evaline Ness, and *Sylvester and the Magic Pebble* by William Steig.

With Mother Goose, ABC, counting, and concept books you can point out the games that are played with language or illustrations. Read the books aloud to kindergarten and first grade students and then place them in the classroom library area. Encourage the children to read the books on their own or with other children. Many of these books will become classroom favorites, to be read aloud to the children several times.

Folk tales

Children are today the main audience for folk tales, which are part of a heritage based in oral tradition. According to Sutherland and Arbuthnot, qualities of folk tales children find appealing are that they are filled with action, convey a clear sense of right and wrong, often include rhyme and repetition, and end in a satisfying way.

Because most of these tales were meant to be told, rather than read silently, they lend themselves well to reading aloud, storytelling, puppetry, and creative dramatics. In any event, call the children's attention to interesting language (e.g., "And I'll huff and I'll puff and I'll blow your house down"), the recurring pattern in each episode (e.g., as in *Goldilocks and the Three Bears* or *The Three Little Pigs*), and what Sutherland and Arbuthnot term "the old verities that kindness and goodness will triumph over evil if they are backed by wisdom, wit, and courage" (p. 54). Excellent collections of the folk tales of many different groups are now available, and you may wish to introduce your students to folk tales from African, North American Indian, and Asian groups, as well as to American tall tales and traditional European tales.

Fables, myths, and epics

Fables, myths, and epics, like tales, have their source in folklore and are also important parts of the child's literary heritage. They are more moral in nature. Fables, such as those by Aesop, present straightforward, simple lessons. Myths often provided explanations for troubling or little understood aspects of the human condition, such as disease or the changing of the seasons. *Children of Odin* (Colum, 1962) is an example of a collection of myths written for children. Epics such as the *Iliad* and the *Odyssey* are usually cycles of tales describing the challenges faced by legendary heroes.

Both myths and epics can be highly complex and symbolic, but older children may find the stories both fascinating and inspiring. Very young children will usually only be interested in a simple version of the plot of these stories, but older children may be referred to versions which, while written in clear language, preserve interesting detail.

On his visit to the library, this boy checks to see if this is a book he will enjoy reading. Classroom experiences with books of different genres can help broaden children's reading choices.

Modern fantasy

According to Sutherland and Arbuthnot, fantasy "is the art form many modern writers have chosen to . . . lay out for children the realities of life—not in a physical or social sense, but in a psychological sense" (p. 226). Modern fantasy encompasses everything from Beatrix Potter's story of Peter Rabbit, to the elegant and elaborate novels of Lewis Carroll, J. R. R. Tolkien, Ursula Le Guin, and Madeleine L'Engle. These books, which present imaginary worlds and events which could not really happen, can appeal to children for the same reasons as folk tales, fables, myths, and epics. When reading such books, children experience a sense of adventure and escape and can come to understand different ways of approaching life's problems.

Books you feel the class as a whole will find appealing may be read aloud to the children, one chapter each day. A brief discussion, including reactions and predictions, may follow each day's reading. When the novel has been completed, interested children may be encouraged to read other works by the same author.

Basal readers contain much modern fantasy, often beginning with animal stories in the early grades and moving to excerpts from novels in the later ones. In the key concept after this one, we cover ways of improving children's comprehension of these and other stories.

Poetry

Poetry plays on emotions, triggers insight, and develops an appreciation for the beauty and power of language. Sutherland and Arbuthnot suggest that children enjoy the "singing quality" of poetry, its story elements, humor, and appeal to the senses. They provide an excellent listing of poets whose work is often enjoyed by children, ranging from Edward Lear to Myra Cohn Livingston. Here are the guidelines they suggest for the use of poetry:

Do read poetry aloud often.
Do provide a variety of poems in records, books, and tapes.
Do make several anthologies available to children.
Do select contemporary poetry as well as older material.
Do help children avoid sing-song reading aloud.
Do choose poems with comprehensive subject matter.
Do encourage the writing of poetry.
Do choose poems that have action or humor.
Do try choral readings. (p. 227)

Help children understand how the words create feelings and images to convey the author's message. Older children can begin to look closely at figurative language.

Modern fiction

This realistic form of fiction, according to Sutherland and Arbuthnot, introduces children to the lives of families past and present, to worlds similar to or very different from their own. While some modern fiction, such as mysteries, is written largely to entertain, other books explore deeper themes, such as being different or alone, and touch on controversial topics. An example of the former is *Encyclopedia Brown Saves the Day* by Donald Sobol (1970), while an example of the latter is *Julie of the Wolves* by Jean George (1972). In considering which of the vast array of books of this genre to introduce to the class or recommend to individual children, Sutherland and Arbuthnot propose these guidelines:

If these books center on children's basic needs; if they give them increased insight into their own personal problems and social relationships; if they show that people are more alike than different, more akin to each other than alien; if they convince young readers that they can do something about their lives—have fun and adventures and get things done without any magic other than their own earnest efforts—then they are worthwhile books. (p. 333)

Basal readers include many selections about children in real-life situations. These, too, offer opportunities to promote story comprehension.

Historical fiction

Historical fiction for children introduces characters, often children themselves, in an authentic setting of the past. According to Sutherland and Arbuthnot, such writing should show life in an accurate and honest way because children generally do not have the background knowledge to evaluate the material critically. Otherwise, much the same criteria can be used for selecting historical fiction as with other stories, and similar teaching methods can be applied.

The authors point out that in true historical fiction, the picture painted of the historical period is an integral part of helping the reader to understand the events in the story. This is likely to make the facts much more interesting to children. Because of this possibility, historical fiction can serve as a bridge to informational text, particularly in social studies. Point out to the children that there are ideas to be remembered as well as appreciated. Encourage them to seek out other books on the same historical period to verify information or to learn more. Help children to identify the important historical events in the story (for example, the Boston Tea Party in *Johnny Tremain*), to trace the story line, and to separate important ideas in the text from incidental details simply used to add a bit of color.

Biography

A good biography, or account of someone's life, will be historically accurate and treat its subject as an individual, not merely as the ideal or representative of a group. *Carry On, Mr. Bowditch* (Latham, 1955) is an example of an excellent biography written for children. Sutherland and Arbuthnot recommend that biography and historical fiction be used to reinforce one another, because

INSTRUCTIONAL ACTIVITIES

The activities below can be used to foster children's interest in a variety of literary genres. Refer to Chapter 13 for other ways of promoting interest in books and recreational reading.

Informational books

Informational books for children cover a huge number of topics, and books can be found to match the natural curiosity of every child to learn more about something. Examples of science books for children are *Benny's Animals* (Selsam, 1966) and *Evolution Goes On Every Day* (Patent, 1977). This genre is discussed further in Chapter 7.

Teachers might have students read about different people from the same era and then contrast their views and experiences. For example, for the Revolutionary War period, students could read biographies of an American patriot and a British loyalist.

Both give children a sense of what it was like to "be there" in another time and place.

Sharing books

Plan times for the children to share books. The important idea here is to let children see how reading can be a social experience, as well as one experienced alone. For example, set up occasions for discussions of favorite books. Children could take turns signing up to talk about a book they've just read and answer other children's questions about it.

Use this and other means to encourage children to recommend good books to other children. This creates a "community of readers" with classmates in a network to offer one another suggestions about what to read next (Hickman, 1984).

Books can also serve as a basis for oral interpretation, creative drama, art projects prepared by small groups, or games such as charades. For example, Cleary (1978) suggests the following five-day program for the sharing of plays:

Day 1: Students divide into small groups, select a play, and read it in its entirety.

Day 2: Within each group, students determine who will take each role and then rehearse by reading the parts aloud.

Day 3: Students rehearse the play, adding sound effects.

Day 4: Students tape record the plays, which may then be listened to by other students who read the same play.

Day 5: Groups may listen to their own tape recording or to those of other groups.

Other suggestions for working with plays, as well as a list of plays suitable for use with students in different grades, are given in Manna (1984).

Cleary also recommends the sharing of reading with another class of older or younger children. You could assign partners and have each read to the other. Cleary conducted a high school remedial reading program called the "super sport reading program." She had high school athletes who were poor readers practice reading easy books aloud in her reading resource room, then visit an elementary school to read and discuss the books with poor readers in the fourth and fifth grades. Each boy visited the other school four times, three times to read and the fourth to share poetry and help the younger children to write poetry. Both groups profited from the activity.

Another procedure is to send books home for students to share with family members. Younger children can take home books to read with their parents or older siblings, while older children might be encouraged to read to younger brothers and sisters.

Reading aloud to children

Read to the whole class every day so they will see that literature can be a source of pleasure. For young children, you could read well known fairy tales so they can understand how such stories are often constructed—from "once upon a time" to "and they lived happily ever after." Read them books with

These two boys reread a favorite book together. Sharing experiences with books shows children how reading can be a social, as well as individual, experience.

fanciful language so they hear how games are played with words. Read older children chapters from novels that will draw them out of a narrow world view. Let children know that you enjoy books and like to read.

Library corners and book floods

Create an inviting area in the classroom with pillows and a rug or perhaps a comfortable sofa. Flood this library corner with five to ten new books a week (Elley & Mangubhai, 1983). Read aloud all or just a small part of most of the books to the children, creating interest in books children might not have thought to pick up on their own. Encourage the children to seek out books of interest during free time or time allocated for recreational reading. Children then have the opportunity to read for enjoyment and practice, with no book reports required.

Sustained silent reading

Sustained silent reading (SSR), also referred to as uninterrupted sustained silent reading (USSR), is an activity giving students class time to read on their own. Its purpose is to encourage reading for pleasure, outside of the classroom as well, and to give students the chance to practice and apply reading skills. We recommend that sustained silent reading occur every day.

Levine (1984) suggests that the teacher follow these rules for sustained silent reading:

1. Have each student select his or her own book. Make sure there are plenty of books of different kinds available.
2. Have the students read silently for a set period of time. Begin with a short time, such as ten minutes, and then gradually extend the period, perhaps with older students to as much as forty minutes.
3. Spend the time reading yourself, and allow no interruptions. Set an example for the children by being a good role model, rather than using the time to grade papers or plan lessons.
4. Make sure the entire class is reading silently together.
5. Do not require reports or record-keeping, ask questions, or do anything which might discourage the reluctant reader.

Teachers working with kindergarten and first grade children, or with reluctant readers, may wish to use "booktime" (Hong, 1981) as a way of preparing the children for sustained silent reading. Hong offers the following suggestions, based on her experiences with a group of first graders: Include only five to seven children in the teacher-supervised booktime reading group. Have booktime occur at the same time every day, so that it becomes part of the children's routine. Begin with a period of five minutes or so and work up to a period of ten to fifteen minutes. Encourage each child to choose a different book, but allow pairs of children to read the same book together, if this arrangement seems likely to be more motivating. Let the children share ideas

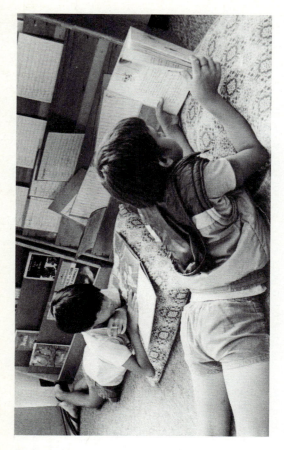

Children make themselves comfortable while reading in the classroom library corner. Shelves on the right hold sheets children use to keep records of their independent reading.

by speaking quietly to one another. At other times during the day, be sure to read aloud to the children, and to place the books read in an area where they are readily accessible.

Making the most of visits to the library

Prepare the children for visits to the school or community library so they will know how to use the time to find books they will enjoy reading. Discuss with the class as a whole, or with individuals, topics or types of books they might find interesting. With reluctant readers, you might begin by tying the reading of library books to their other interests, in computers, popular music, dancing, television shows, car racing, and so on.

The teacher should help children understand the various elements of a story, including its structure, literary merits, and the nature of the social interaction between the author and reader.

LEARNING TO ENVISION A STORY

What happens when we envision a story? From our own reading experiences we know that readers imagine that they are listening to the author speak or that they are one of the characters. Whether observing or taking a role, they become deeply involved in the plot, in the characters' plans, problems, and attempted solutions. They empathize with the characters, feeling joy, disappointment, love, anger, surprise, and resentment. They develop a closeness to the people, place, and time in the story, and come to know something about the author. It is this weaving of affect and ideas around the characters and plot that makes story reading a process of envisionment. This is the magic of reading stories that we hope all of our students will experience.

We present below three somewhat different ways of looking at the elements in stories. You will want to keep these elements in mind for the purpose of promoting reading comprehension and enjoyment of reading. This is because having knowledge of these elements may make it easier for children to comprehend and appreciate stories.

Story structure approach

What exactly is a story? While it is possible to come up with many different definitions, Stein and Policastro (1984) suggest that we think of good stories as those which involve some kind of *conflict* or problem and draw some kind of *emotional response*. In addition, many simple stories have the following *structure* or *grammar* (Stein & Nezworski, 1977):

Setting—The main character is introduced and the time and place of the story may be described.

Initiating event—Something happens which leads the character to think about trying to achieve some goal.

Internal response—The character has thoughts or feelings about the situation.

Attempt—The character takes action to reach his or her goal.

Consequence—There is some outcome, successful or not, because of the character's action.

Reaction—The character has thoughts or feelings about the course of action or goal.

In exploring further the basic idea that reading is the process of constructing meaning from text, we see that children learn gradually to comprehend more complicated stories as they move through the grades. Over this time they develop an increasingly refined concept of what a story is (e.g., Applebee, 1978) and an awareness of story structure (e.g., Stein & Glenn, 1979), as outlined above. In general, older children, in the fifth grade and above, seem better able to recall and retell stories which do not have a standard structure or do not present events in chronological order (Stein & Nezworski, 1977). This is because they already have considerable knowledge of story structure which they can use to help them understand and remember stories. They are also better able to remember the characters' internal responses and reactions than younger children, who tend to focus on the consequence alone (Stein & Glenn, 1979).

In short, story comprehension, like text comprehension in general, develops over time and can be improved through instruction.

INSTRUCTIONAL ACTIVITIES

As mentioned earlier, story structures or grammars are essentially outlines of the typical organization of many stories. Knowledge of story structures can be useful to teachers in two different ways. First, teachers can analyze the structure of a particular story and use the information for planning lessons based on that story. For example, such an analysis shows the teacher exactly how many episodes the story contains and how the text might be divided into sections for silent reading and discussion. Second, teachers can improve students' comprehension ability by teaching them about story structure. The activity below, as well as the central content story activity described at the end of this chapter, can be useful to teachers in both of these ways.

Teaching about story structure

Gordon and Braun (1983a) developed procedures to teach children about story structures. The purpose of this program was to improve children's ability to comprehend stories, as well as to write stories on their own, and it was used successfully with fifth graders (Gordon & Braun, 1983b).

Figure 6.1 (see p. 176) shows a simplified diagram for classroom use. This is an "ideal" story structure, one containing all elements in a straightforward order. Many actual stories will not contain all of these elements, and parts within each episode may occur in a different order from that shown. Folk tales, fairy tales, and fables, especially those in which a pattern of events is repeated, will lend themselves well to lessons on story structure.

Gordon and Braun (1983a) suggest the following steps (not presented here are four additional steps involving a transfer to writing):

1. Begin with an "ideal" story such as "The Owl and the Raven" to provide an overview of structure and to introduce story grammar terminology. Use a diagram of the story and fill in story information under each category as content is elicited from the children. . . Give the children copies of the diagram minus the story information. They then write the paraphrased story content on their own copies.

2. Set reading purposes by posing schema-related questions prior to having children read a story segment. Elicit responses to the question after the reading.

3. Use well organized stories initially and the inductive teaching approach. Have children first identify the major setting in each of three different stories, then the starter event of the first episode in each of three different stories, and so on, before trying to identify all story components in one section. Thus the structure element is held constant while story content is varied.

4. When children can associate story content with specific text structure categories on the diagrammed stories, begin asking the story-specific questions. Continue to expect paraphrased story content as answers.

FIGURE 6.1   Schematic Representation of Story Structure

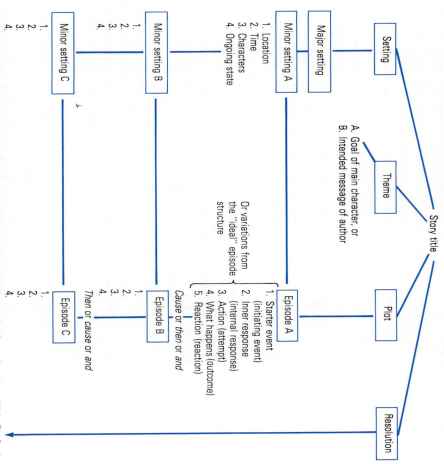

From "Using Story Schema as an Aid to Reading and Writing" by Christine Gordon and Carl Braun, November 1983 in *The Reading Teacher*. Reprinted with permission of the authors and the International Reading Association.

5. Gradually introduce less well organized narratives, so children will learn that not all stories are "ideal" in structure.

6. To help children handle structure variability, use the macrocloze technique on transparencies and individual structure sheets for less well organized stories. In macrocloze, some categories already contain story content; others are left blank for the children to complete.

7. Guide children to start asking their own schema-related or story-specific questions before reading. Have them read to find answers for their own oral or written questions. Knowledge of story grammar will serve as a framework on which to develop the prereading questions. (pp. 119-121)

Literary criticism approach

A second view of story elements is that which a literary critic might take. This view suggests concepts and terms children can be taught to enhance their understanding and appreciation of stories. Cullinan (1981) recommends, however, that the teacher keep to the following guidelines:

The literary concepts that a structuralist approach emphasizes can and should be taught to children, but only when they are ready to learn them—when they have a need to know and an experiential base upon which to anchor the concepts. Labels without concepts are detrimental to children's growth in the study of literature and often obscure the areas of study that need to be emphasized. Teachers aware of literary concepts *and* the levels of children's development can provide information and support when it is appropriate.   (p. 497)

The following list of major literary elements, proposed by Lukens (1982), should give you an idea of the concepts and terms to be introduced to your students, particularly those in the upper grades. A realistic approach is to teach children about a particular element only when it is especially important in the story they are reading. But over time, whether you are using books or basal reader stories, all of these elements can be touched upon.

1. *Character:* The person or, as is often the case with children's stories, the personified animal or object involved in the action of the story. You can teach children to learn about characters by reading about their actions, speech, and appearance, or the comments of other characters or the narrator. Children can also be introduced to the idea of *character development*, that the character may change over the course of the story.

2. *Plot:* The order of events in a story, showing the actions of the characters, and usually involving some kind of *conflict*. Children can be taught to look for a *sequence* of events and to identify the problem the characters face. You can also point out that the author may choose to present events in *chronological order* or with *flashbacks.*

3. *Setting:* The time and place of the story, usually described in some detail. Children can be taught to identify both. You can help them distinguish between stories in which the setting is merely a *backdrop* or relatively unimportant to the plot, or much more *integral* or important.

4. *Theme:* The idea that helps tie all other story elements together, that gives the story some overall meaning. Often, the theme is a truth about the human condition which the author wishes to convey. You can teach children to look for the theme of the story and point out to them that we often remember the theme after other details have been forgotten. Perhaps using the terms in parentheses, you can also teach them that themes may be *explicit* (obvious) or *implicit* (hidden or only suggested). There can also be *primary* (important or major) themes and *secondary* (less important or minor) themes. Teachers

should be aware, too, that certain stories written for children, such as some adventure or humorous works, do not necessarily have a theme.

5. *Point of view:* The perspective taken in the telling of the story. Teach children to recognize different points of view and how they can give a particular slant to the information presented. Sometimes one of the characters tells the story; this is the *first-person* point of view. At other times, the story is told from an *omniscient* or all-seeing point of view, which allows the writer to present the thoughts and feelings of several characters. There is also the *objective* point of view, where the writer concentrates simply on describing events, leaving interpretation to the reader.

6. *Style:* The author's use of words, how language is used to create an effect. As Lukens (1982) puts it, style is "*how* an author says something, as opposed to *what* he or she says" (p. 137). You can point out to your students examples of figurative language, hyperbole and understatement, puns and word play, and words and phrases with interesting or appealing sounds. With this approach your goal is to give them an appreciation for beautiful or effective use of language, and literary terms do not necessarily have to be used.

7. *Tone:* Use of style to convey the author's feeling about the subject of his or her writing. Teach children that tone has to do with the author's attitude toward the story and its readers and may reveal aspects of his or her personality. Help your students learn to recognize different kinds of tone, whether the story is light-hearted and humorous, gentle and warm, or grand and heroic.

Social interaction approach

The approach to stories developed by Bruce (1980) begins with the assumption that reading and writing are acts of communication. He points out that "an author and a reader are engaged in a social interaction which depends on their goals and their beliefs about the world and each other" (Bruce, 1981a, p. 273). In this approach, then, there are two different factors to be considered in understanding stories: (1) the relationship between the author and reader and (2) their goals and beliefs.

Relationship between the author and reader. There are many possible levels of social interaction between the author and the reader. First of all, the author may take various points of view, as was pointed out earlier. In doing so, he can make the story situation quite complex. To illustrate this point, Bruce (1981b) uses the example of Washington Irving's tale of Rip Van Winkle. Washington Irving is the *real author* of the story. But he assumes the role of a writer, the *implied author*, who in turn is presenting a text written by a historian named Diedrich Knickerbocker.

The reader, too, may take on different identities. For example, each of us is a *real reader* very different from the *implied reader* Washington Irving probably had in mind when he wrote about Rip Van Winkle. To take another example, in some cases the author may assign the implied reader a certain identity. For example, the story may be told in a letter addressed to a friend.

Goals and beliefs.   The goals and beliefs of real and implied authors, of real and implied readers, and of story characters also need to be understood. Bruce (1980) especially emphasizes the importance of the reader's knowledge of *plans* or intentions in understanding stories. For example, consider the story of *Annie and the Old One* (Miles, 1971). In this story, Annie's grandmother tells her family that she will return to Mother Earth when the rug that Annie's mother is weaving is taken from the loom. We can guess, although we are never told, that Annie gets herself into trouble at school because she wants to keep her mother from finishing the rug. Annie's action is part of her plan to keep her grandmother from dying. We can also guess at the author's plan in writing this story. The author seems to want us to understand, through Annie's experiences, the strength of the Navaho belief in the natural order.

Within this approach, the following three elements appear to be particularly important to children's story understanding:

1. Conflict
2. Inside view (information about a character's thoughts and feelings)
3. Point of view (that taken by the author)

Bruce (1984) found that basal reader stories were generally very different from those in tradebooks. For example, all the grade 1 through 3 stories in the basal series Bruce analyzed were written by authors who took the *objective* point of view. Tradebook stories, on the other hand, were more often written from a first-person or omniscient point of view, so that more information could be given both about the characters' thoughts and feelings and the author's opinions.

The practical implication of these findings is that, if you are working with basal readers, you should be sure to supplement their use with a rich variety of tradebooks. Working only with basal reader stories may not be the best means of preparing children to read books.

Guidelines for asking questions.   Whether working with stories in basal readers or tradebooks, and whether the children are reading the text on their own or hearing you read aloud to them, you will want to use questioning to help them cope with the elements the social interaction approach suggests will be difficult. For example, children probably need guidance in sorting out the different levels of social interaction between the author and reader. For this purpose teachers might ask questions to help students differentiate between the real author and the implied author of a literary work. Other questions might center on the students themselves as real readers, and whether they are the same as the implied readers the author probably had in mind.

The questions below are examples of those which teachers may ask to clarify children's thinking about conflict, inside view, and point of view. These questions may be asked within the ETR or other lesson frameworks (see Chapter 5) and should help students better deal with difficult story elements.

1. What is the problem in this story? (conflict)
2. What did X do? Why do you think X did that? What do you think X is going to do next? (character's goal or plan, inside view)
3. What would you do at this point if you were X? (inside view, reader's own point of view)
4. How do you think X felt when that happened? How do you think X felt when Y said or did that? (conflict, inside view)
5. Why do you think Y did that? Why didn't Y feel the same way that X did? (conflict, inside view of another character)
6. What was the theme of this story? What do you think the author was trying to tell us? (author's point of view)

STORY COMPREHENSION STRATEGIES

In Chapter 5 we discussed the comprehension strategies used by expert readers and the importance of *metacognition* in reading, awareness and control over one's own thinking, and of *comprehension monitoring*. We also emphasized the importance of helping children to become independent readers. We expand here upon those ideas and apply them to children's comprehension of stories. In particular, we emphasize the importance of teaching children to *plan* and *monitor* their own "efforts after meaning." Note that many of these points can also be applied to the strategies for comprehension of expository text introduced in Chapter 7.

In general, the strategy instruction you provide will have three parts:

Part 1—Teaching the children *why* the strategy is useful, or the purpose for learning it.

Part 2—Teaching them *how* to carry the strategy out.

Part 3—Teaching them *when* the strategy should be applied.

Part 3 is especially important. It involves what Paris, Lipson, and Wixson (1983) call *conditional knowledge*, or knowing when and why to apply various strategies. In other words, it isn't enough just to teach children the procedures or steps in a strategy, as in Part 2. This is because children rarely *generalize* or carry their use of a strategy over from one situation to another. For example, suppose that you have just taught your students the strategy of *skimming* (moving quickly through text). If you do nothing further, however, the chances are that they will never skim on their own, when you aren't there telling them to do so.

Here are general guidelines to be followed to ensure that story comprehension strategies will not only be learned but applied. An example of a story comprehension strategy is the experience-text-relationship method. Other story comprehension strategies involve application of knowledge of literary genres, story structure, literary elements, and character's plans and goals.

1. When the children have had experiences with various purposes for reading (e.g., to answer questions, to enjoy the story) and with various genres of literature (as described in Key Concept #1) discuss with them how their reading activity changes. Emphasize that the way we read depends both on our purpose and the nature of the text.

2. Explain and model the steps in the strategy, beginning with clear, simple examples that you prepared in advance.

3. Present more than one situation or text where the strategy would be helpful. This will help the children become aware of the conditions when the strategy can be applied, i.e., it will build up their conditional knowledge.

4. Provide lots of opportunities for practice, starting with easy examples.

5. Seek feedback from children about whether they understand how, when, and why to use the strategy. Allow time for the children to "think out loud" while trying to use the strategy, so mistakes can be corrected.

6. Have the children suggest times when they might use the strategy on their own. When these occasions arise, remind them to use the strategy.

Comprehension planning

Children need to plan how they are going to read before they begin reading, just as expert readers do. Expert readers generally know quite a bit about the nature or genre of the text they will be reading (e.g., modern fantasy, poetry, historical fiction). This knowledge helps them plan the way they will read because they know what the important information will be and how they can find it.

Suppose you were going to read a fable. You would expect it to have a moral at the end. You would expect the characters to be animals but with human characteristics. In effect, before you started reading, you would have directed yourself to identify the characters, their traits, and the plot, and to understand the moral.

As an expert reader, you would have gone through this planning process so quickly as to be unaware of doing any planning at all. Children do not automatically plan in this way, but their comprehension can be improved if they are taught to do so.

Help children plan their reading by reminding them to do the following:

1. Identify your purpose for reading. Why are you reading this story?
2. Identify the genre or type of story you are going to read.
3. Think about what you know about this genre or type of text, what makes it special, and what the important kinds of information are.

Part of planning may be looking for the name of the author, reading the title, and looking at the pictures. Or it could involve skimming the text itself, including seeing how long or difficult it is. Have the children try both of these. Or have them read the first few paragraphs or pages, then stop and reflect on the important elements. With more difficult texts, you can suggest what these might be, drawing from the story structure, literary, or social interaction approaches.

As with any kind of reading, another part of planning involves calling up background knowledge of the topic. This knowledge can come from personal, real life experiences, as well as from experience with similar reading material. For this purpose, Langer (1982) suggests asking the following three questions when working with a story:

"Tell me anything that comes to mind when . . ."

"What made you think of . . ."

"Based on our discussion, have you any new ideas about . . ."

Comprehension monitoring

While reading, expert readers often generate predictions about the problems, plans, and responses of story characters. Teaching children to make predictions, check them out, and then make new predictions, is a good way of helping them to monitor their own comprehension. Children who use this strategy become actively involved in thinking about the characters and what might happen to them.

Here is an approach we used successfully with reading groups in third and fourth grade classrooms. We broke the text into four to six parts (the breaks occurred after the setting had been presented and after each major episode or action). We then posed the question, "What might happen next?" to each child in the circle. We went around the circle quickly, in the same order each time.

Another approach is to teach the children to reflect on story events and ideas at regular intervals. Have them work at uncovering messages implicit in the text, those not stated directly. Encourage them to ask themselves questions such as those suggested by the social interaction approach to stories for getting at conflict, inside view, and point of view.

Two other activities for improving comprehension monitoring are the story structure procedure developed by Gordon and Braun, presented earlier, and Hansen's inference training procedure, described under the next key concept.

KEY CONCEPT 4

The teacher should have a purpose for having students read a particular story, and should follow systematic procedures for planning and conducting story comprehension lessons.

PLANNING STORY COMPREHENSION LESSONS

The eight-step procedure for planning story comprehension lessons presented below is adapted from the work of Mason (1983). This procedure builds upon the basic concepts introduced in Chapter 5, which were centered primarily around how teachers should organize lessons and interact with students during discussion. They extend these concepts by spelling out in more detail how teachers should go about preparing for lessons and follow-up activities.

Mason's planning approach, the two lesson frameworks presented at the end of this chapter, and the ETR and DRTA approaches described in Chapter 5, are all designed to provide teachers with stronger models for comprehension instruction than those generally provided in the teacher's guides of basal reader series. Guides may be a source of ideas but rarely provide the strong, systematic framework for comprehension instruction many children need.

Procedure for planning a story comprehension lesson

1. *Establish a lesson objective.* Be sure that you know why you are going to teach a lesson with this story and that you are able to explain to students why they are going to read it (e.g., for pleasure, to practice comprehension skills, to learn how to understand a story).

2. *Preview the text.* If you have not worked with this story before, you will almost certainly need to read it over several times. Identify the theme, as well as the other important story elements, using one of the three story approaches covered in Key Concept #2.

3. *Divide the text into segments for reading.* Locate the natural breaks in the story. For example, these might be after the setting, after the statement of the main character's problem, and after each attempt at resolving the problem. When working with younger children, or if the story is a difficult one, you will stop the children's reading at these breaks and use the time for discussing the story.

4. *Develop prereading questions.* Write down one or more questions you might ask to draw upon students' background knowledge, particularly that related to the theme of the story. These questions will be asked before the students begin reading.

5. *Develop retrospective guided reading questions.* For each segment of the story, write down one or more questions. These may be asked

after the students have read that segment. Design these questions to bring out the central theme, as well as to cover details involving the characters and plot.

6. *Develop predictive guided reading questions.* For each segment, also write down one question which will require the children to make predictions about the segment of text to be read next.

7. *Develop postreading questions.* These questions should be designed to foster synthesizing, interpreting, and evaluating of the text as a whole.

8. *Develop independent practice activities.* Think of at least one activity where the students can work with the story on their own, after the lesson is over. For example, younger students could draw a picture showing a scene from the story. Older students might write another episode for the story or think up a new adventure for the story's main character.

FRAMEWORKS FOR STORY COMPREHENSION LESSONS

These frameworks include prereading, guided reading, and postreading phases and can be used to organize a series of lessons based on the same story text. Besides giving children a thorough understanding of the story being read, they have the potential to improve children's overall ability to comprehend stories.

Inferential comprehension strategy

The purpose of this strategy is to improve children's ability to make inferences about text. Hansen (1981) initially tested this lesson framework with second graders, and later adapted it for use with poor readers in the fourth grade (Hansen & Hubbard, 1984; Hansen & Pearson, 1983). Basal reader stories were used, but other texts could easily be substituted. In this procedure, four lessons are needed for each story.

Planning. Preview the story and select three important ideas, or ideas that it might be difficult for the children to understand. Write two questions for each idea: (1) about aspects of the children's experience related to the idea, and (2) about a story-specific prediction.

Hansen (1981) gives this example of a pair of questions:

For example, in one story the isolated idea was that when people are embarrassed they break eye contact. In the story, Dick looked at his feet when a barber expressed displeasure about Dick's dog. The previous experience question was,

This teacher puts story events on a chart to help students keep track of important information. Students refer to the chart when discussing the text.

"What do you do when you feel embarrassed?" [The prediction question was] "In our story, Dick feels embarrassed when the barber asks him if Stanley is his dog. What do you think he will do?" (p. 667)

Day 1. Introduce new vocabulary words. The inferential comprehension strategy does not require any one way of doing this. For ideas, you may wish to refer to Chapter 4 or to the basal series teacher's guide.

Day 2. Using each of your three pairs of questions, discuss with the children background knowledge they might use to draw inferences about the story and have them come up with predictions. For each question asked, have the children write their individual response. Allow the children time to discuss and exchange ideas before having them write. Encourage a diversity of responses rather than pressing the children to reach agreement.

Day 3. Have the children read the story, following a normal guided reading procedure. That is, have the children read a portion of the story, then stop for discussion, read again, stop for discussion, and so on until the story is finished. At this point in her study, Hansen gave the children a worksheet with ten open-ended questions. You might use such a worksheet for seatwork to be completed on Days 3 and 4.

Day 4. Provide the children with instruction in word recognition. Again, no specific procedures are required as part of the inferential comprehension strategy, so you may wish to refer to Chapter 3 or the teacher's guide.

The inferential comprehension strategy, like the experience-text-relationship method and the directed reading-thinking activity, builds on children's background knowledge and encourages prediction. It differs from these other two lesson frameworks, however, in focusing specifically on children's ability to make inferences and to write out their responses.

Central story content lessons

Beck, Omanson, and McKeown (1982) developed and tested a reading lesson framework for use with basal reader stories, to highlight central story content for children and reduce potential comprehension problems. This framework recognizes the critical role of background knowledge and the importance of focusing children's attention on important, rather than unimportant, story information. The method used to identify important story information was based on use of a story map (Beck & McKeown, 1981; Omanson, 1982). Use of this lesson framework improved third graders' ability to recall information and answer questions about the story.

The four lesson components redesigned by Beck et al. are:

1. pre-story preparation
2. pre-SRU (silent reading unit) preparation
3. illustrations accompanying the text
4. post-SRU questions

We present below recommendations which are adaptations of the procedures used by Beck et al.

1. *Pre-story preparation*. When planning the lesson, identify the key concepts in the story. Design questions or activities to familiarize children with these concepts or, if they already know them, to call their attention to their importance. One of the stories used in the study by Beck et al. was entitled "The Raccoon and Mrs. McGinnis." Mrs. McGinnis' wish came true because of a series of coincidences. Thus, the concept of coincidence was targeted.

2. *Pre-SRU preparation*. This has to do with activities to prepare children for the story segment about to be read. Design these activities (usually, questions or explanations) to serve two purposes: first, to call children's attention to important events in the story segment to be read next; and second, to activate concepts covered in the pre-story preparation.

3. *Illustrations*. The important point about illustrations is that they should aid story comprehension. They can do this if they reinforce central story content, but not if they deal with minor details or conflict with the text. Examine the illustrations carefully and plan to call children's attention only to those which accurately depict central story content.

4. *Post SRU-questions*. These are intended to help the children "envision" the main events in the story. Design questions to target the main events and avoid asking questions on details irrelevant to the main events. Work out questions which cover events in the order of their occurrence in the story.

Figure 6.2 shows a sample story map and the post-SRU questions which grow logically from it. The story, "A Big Lunch for Father" (Marshall, 1983), is representative of those appearing in preprimers; reading textbooks often used

FIGURE 6.2 Story Map and Questions for "A Big Lunch for Father"

Central theme: The children set out to surprise Father, but they are the ones who get surprised instead, first because the picnic basket is empty, and second because Father gives them a "big lunch" of fish.

Problem: Amy and Sam have to take Father his lunch.

Questions: What did Mother ask Amy and Sam to do?
Who were the children going to surprise?

Episode #1: Amy and Sam stop for a swim and a frog takes some of the lunch.

Questions: What did Amy and Sam want to do?
What happened while they were swimming?

Episode #2: They stop to look at some pigs and a rooster takes some of the lunch.

Questions: What did they stop to look at?
What happened to the lunch?

Episode #3: They stop to take a nap and a fox takes some of the lunch.

Questions: What did Amy and Sam do next?
What happened while they were napping?

Episode #4: They find father, who is sitting on the pier fishing. Sam says, "Surprise, Father!" and the children hand him the picnic basket. But when Father looks inside it, he finds there is nothing there.

Questions: Where did Amy and Sam find Father?
What was he doing?
What did Sam say when he saw Father?
What problem did Father discover?
How did Amy and Sam feel then?

Resolution: Father has caught some fish which he suggests they eat for lunch instead.

Questions: What happened at the end of the story?
What did they eat instead?

Questions to get at the central theme:
Who was supposed to be surprised?
Who got surprised instead?
What two things happened to surprise the children?

with children in kindergarten and first grade. At the top of the figure are summary statements of the central theme, or the important idea a teacher might decide to develop, and the problem.

The story map helps the teacher to see appropriate pre-SRU questions for "A Big Lunch for Father." The theme has to do with surprises and the problem is that the children have to take their father his lunch. It would be logical, then, for the teacher to begin a lesson on this story by developing the concepts of running errands and of being surprised. Questions about running errands might include the following:

Do you ever run errands to help your mother and father?
What kinds of errands do you do?
Have you ever had trouble while running an errand?
What happened?

EXERCISE

The purpose of this exercise is to familiarize you with the use of story maps for planning lessons.

(1) Select a story which might be taught to a group of elementary school students. The story may be from a tradebook or from a basal reader.

(2) Begin by reading the story carefully. Identify the central theme or important idea you would like the students to grasp. Write this information in a box at the top of a sheet of paper, as shown in Figure 6.2. If you aren't certain about the central theme or important idea you want to develop, go on to Step 3.

(3) Identify one or more concepts to be brought out in the prereading or pre-SRU phase of the lesson, and write these below the central theme box. For examples, see the prereading questions developed for "A Big Lunch for Father."

(4) Make a map for the story along the lines of that shown in Figure 6.2. If this particular type of mapping doesn't fit your story, refer to the discussion of the story structure approach under Key Concept #2 for other ideas about mapping. Or develop your own variety of map. Remember that the main reason for mapping is to understand how the story is structured, not to force the story into a certain form of map.

If you have not yet written out the central theme or important idea, do so now.

(5) Develop at least one question for each item in your story map, as shown in Figure 6.2. Be sure to develop a set of questions to bring out the central theme.

(6) If you have the opportunity, use the story map and questions developed in this exercise as the basis for teaching a reading lesson to a group of students. Compare this lesson to others you have taught, when you did not use story mapping to aid in your planning. Did story mapping help you to teach story comprehension more effectively? If so, why do you think it helped?

Questions about surprises might include:

Have you ever been surprised?
What happened to surprise you?
Have you ever tried to surprise someone else?
Were you successful?

Episodes in the story and the resolution of the problem are shown in the other boxes in Figure 6.2. Questions appropriate for each part of the story are listed below the relevant boxes. The set of questions at the bottom of the figure is designed to allow the teacher to reinforce the children's understanding of the central theme.

Unlike the three lesson frameworks previously introduced, the central story content approach does not emphasize the making of predictions. It resembles the other frameworks, however, in building on children's background knowledge. Perhaps the outstanding feature of this approach is that it directs children's attention to important story information and so is likely to lead to their understanding the theme of the story.

You may have noticed that central story content lessons are much like experience-text-relationship (ETR) lessons. Pre-SRU questions are those which would generally occur during the experience phase of ETR lessons. Most post-SRU questions, those about particular episodes in the story, would occur during the text phase of ETR lessons. Finally, questions to reinforce children's understanding of the central theme would usually occur during the relationship phase of ETR lessons.

SUMMARY

We began this chapter by looking at the value of developing children's appreciation for literature, books, and stories. In the first key concept we discussed response to literature and nine genres of children's literature. We also suggested some ways that teachers might help develop children's appreciation and understanding of those genres.

In the second key concept we turned to ways that teachers can improve children's comprehension by helping them deal with the various elements in a story. Three different approaches to stories were covered (story structure, literary criticism, and social interaction) and elements important to each were identified. Instructional guidelines for helping children learn about these sets of elements were presented.

We covered in our third key concept strategies children should use for planning and monitoring their comprehension of stories. We reiterated the importance of helping children become independent in using any strategy. Finally, we discussed in our fourth key concept procedures teachers can use to plan story comprehension lessons. Two lesson frameworks, having to do with inference training and focusing on central story content, were described.

One of the themes developed in this chapter was that children should be given instruction that helps them comprehend stories. This in turn should contribute to their being able to read and understand books for their own enjoyment.

BIBLIOGRAPHY

REFERENCES

Applebee, A. N. (1978). *The child's concept of story: Ages two to seventeen.* Chicago: University of Chicago Press.

Beck, I. L., & McKeown, M. G. (1981). Developing questions that promote comprehension: The story map. *Language Arts, 58* (8), 913-918.

Beck, I. L., Omanson, R. C., & McKeown, M. G. (1982). An instructional redesign of reading lessons: Effects on comprehension. *Reading Research Quarterly, 17* (4), 462-481.

Benton, M. (1984). The methodology vacuum in teaching literature. *Language Arts, 61* (3), 265-275.

Bruce, B. C. (1980). Plans and social actions. In R. J. Spiro, B. C. Bruce, & W. F. Brewer (Eds.), *Theoretical issues in reading comprehension.* Hillsdale, NJ: Erlbaum.

Bruce, B. C. (1981a). A social interaction model of reading. *Discourse Processes, 4* (4), 273-311.

Bruce, B. (1981b). *Stories within stories* (Reading Education Rep. No. 29). Urbana, IL: University of Illinois, Center for the Study of Reading.

Bruce, B. (1984). A new point of view on children's stories. In R. C. Anderson, J. Osborn, & R. J. Tierney (Eds.), *Learning to read in American schools: Basal readers and content texts.* Hillsdale, NJ: Erlbaum.

Cleary, D. (1978). *Thinking Thursdays: Language arts in the reading lab.* Newark, DE: IRA.

Cramer, B. B. (1984). Bequest of wings: Three readers and special books. *Language Arts, 61* (3), 253-260.

Cullinan, B. E. (1981). *Literature and the child.* New York: Harcourt Brace Jovanovich.

Dillon, D. (1984). Editor's note. *Language Arts, 61* (3), 227.

Elley, W., & Mangubhai, F. (1983). The impact of reading on second language learning. *Reading Research Quarterly, 19,* 53-67.

Gordon, C., & Braun, C. (1983a). Using story schema as an aid to reading and writing. *Reading Teacher, 37,* 116-121.

Gordon, C., & Braun, C. (1983b). Teaching story schema: Metatextual aid to reading and writing. Paper presented at the Annual Meeting of the American Educational Research Association, Montreal.

Hansen, J. (1981). An inferential comprehension strategy for use with primary grade children. *Reading Teacher, 34,* 665-669.

Hansen, J., & Hubbard, R. (1984). Poor readers can draw inferences. *Reading Teacher, 37* (7), 586-589.

Hansen, J., & Pearson, P. D. (1983). An instructional study: Improving the inferential comprehension of fourth-grade good and poor readers. *Journal of Educational Psychology, 75* (6), 821-829.

Hickman, J. (1984). Research currents: Researching children's response to literature. *Language Arts, 61* (3), 278-284.

Hong, L. K. (1981). Modifying SSR for beginning readers. *Reading Teacher, 34* (8), 888-891.

Langer, J. (1982). Facilitating text processing: The elaboration of prior knowledge. In J. Langer & M. Smith-Burke (Eds.), *Reader meets author/bridging the gap: A psycholinguistic and sociolinguistic perspective.* Newark, DE: International Reading Association.

Levine, S. G. (1984). USSR—A necessary component in teaching reading. *Journal of Reading, 27* (5), 394-400.

Lukens, R. J. (1982). *A critical handbook of children's literature* (2nd ed.). Glenview, IL: Scott, Foresman.

Manna, A. L. (1984). Making language come alive through reading plays. *Reading Teacher, 37* (8), 712-717.

Mason, J. (1983). Lesson repair techniques for teaching comprehension. Paper presented at the Annual Meeting of the National Reading Conference, Austin, Texas.

Niles, O. (1984). Bringing books to children and children to books. In J. Baumann & D. Johnson (Eds.), *Reading instruction and the beginning teacher.* Minneapolis: Burgess.

Omanson, R. C. (1982). An analysis of narratives: Identifying central, supportive, and distracting content. *Discourse Processes, 5,* 119-224.

Paris, S., Lipson, M., & Wixson, K. (1983). Becoming a strategic reader. *Contemporary Educational Psychology, 8,* 293-316.

Rosenblatt, L. M. (1978). *The reader, the text, the poem: The transactional theory of the literary work.* Carbondale, IL: Southern Illinois University Press.

Stein, N., & Glenn, C. (1979). An analysis of story comprehension in elementary school children. In R. Freedle (Ed.), *New directions in discourse processing.* Vol. 2 in *Advances in discourse processes.* Norwood, NJ: Ablex.

Stein, N. L., & Nezworski, T. (1977). *The effects of organization and instructional set on story memory.* (Tech. Rep. No. 68.) Urbana, IL: University of Illinois, Center for the Study of Reading.

Stein, N. L., & Policastro, M. (1984). The concept of a story: A comparison between children's and teachers' viewpoints. In H. Mandl, N. L. Stein, & T. Trabasso (Eds.), *Learning and comprehension of text.* Hillsdale, NJ: Erlbaum.

Sutherland, Z., & Arbuthnot, M. H. (1986). *Children and books* (7th ed.). Glenview, IL: Scott, Foresman.

CHILDREN'S BOOKS CITED

Colum, P. (1962). *Children of Odin,* ill. by E. Sandoz. Houghton Mifflin.

Forbes, E. (1943). *Johnny Tremain,* ill. by L. Ward. Houghton Mifflin.

George, J. (1972). *Julie of the wolves,* ill. by J. Schoenherr. Harper & Row.

Keats, E. J. (1963). *The snowy day.* Viking.

Latham, J. (1955). *Carry on, Mr. Bowditch,* ill. by J. O. Cosgrave. Houghton Mifflin.

Lindgren, A. (1950). *Pippi Longstocking,* tr. by F. Lamborn, ill. by L. S. Glanzman. Viking.

Marshall, J. (1983). *A big lunch for father.* In W. K. Durr, J. M. Le Pere, J. J. Pikulski, & M. L. Alsin, *Boats.* Houghton Mifflin Reading Program, 1983.

McCloskey, R. (1958). *Time of wonder.* Viking.

Miles, M. (1971). *Annie and the Old One.* In W. K. Durr, J. M. Le Pere, & R. H. Brown, *Passports.* Houghton Mifflin Reading Program, 1976.

Ness, E. (1967). *Sam, Bangs & Moonshine.* Holt, Rinehart & Winston.

Patent, D. (1977). *Evolution goes on every day,* ill. by M. Kalmenoff. Holiday House.

Selsam, M. (1966). *Benny's animals, and how he put them in order,* ill. by A. Lobel. Harper & Row.

Sobol, D. (1970). *Encyclopedia Brown saves the day,* ill. by L. Shortall. Nelson.

Steig, W. (1969). *Sylvester and the magic pebble.* Windmill/Simon & Schuster.

Waber, B. (1972). *Ira sleeps over.* Houghton Mifflin.

White, E. B. (1952). *Charlotte's web,* ill. by G. Williams. Harper & Row.

Yashima, T. (1955). *Crow boy.* Viking.

FURTHER READINGS

Beach, R., & Appleman, D. (1984). Reading strategies for expository and literary text types. In A. C. Purves & O. Niles (Eds.), *Becoming readers in a complex society.* Eighty-third yearbook of the National Society for the Study of Education. Part I. Chicago: University of Chicago Press.

Golden, J. M. (1984). Children's concept of story in reading and writing. *Reading Teacher, 37* (7), 578-584.

Hill, S. E. (1985). Children's individual responses and literature conferences in the elementary school. *Reading Teacher, 38* (4), 382-386.

Moffett, J., & Wagner, B. J. (1983). *Student-centered language arts and reading, K-13: A handbook for teachers.* Third edition. Boston: Houghton Mifflin.

Pearson, P. D. (1982). Asking questions about stories. Ginn Occasional Papers, Writings in Reading and Language Arts, No. 15, Columbus, OH: Ginn.

Reutzel, D. R. (1985). Story maps improve comprehension. *Reading Teacher, 38* (4), 400-404.

CHAPTER 7

Developing Study Skills and Teaching

Comprehension of Expository Text

James D. Watson, twenty-four years old in the early 1950s, was knocking around the biological laboratories of the United States and Europe trying to figure out the structure of deoxyribonucleid acid, or DNA, the basic substance of life. In Copenhagen he came upon some writing by Linus Pauling. He read it and reread it. But he said, "Most of the language was above me." He could get only a general impression of Pauling's argument. He could not judge "whether it made sense." But he was sure "that it was written with style." One thing that caught his eye and stuck in his mind was Pauling's reference to something called an *a*-helix.

For Francis Crick, the Englishman with whom Watson worked on DNA, a crucial influence was his reading of *What Is Life?* by Erwin Schrödinger. This book, which introduced the idea that genes were essential parts of living cells, turned Crick from physics to biology and research at Cambridge University.

The *Double Helix* (1968) was unusually personal and uninhibited for a book on a scientific subject. In it Watson recalled the pell-mell search for the structure of DNA. His reading about the *a*-helix and Crick's reading on the genes as parts of living cells were basic in the search, in which they were joined by Maurice H. F. Wilkins. The three of them won the Nobel Prize in 1963 for their discovery, which had tremendous implications for future genetic research. The creation of new forms of life in the laboratory was brought closer by what they found.
(Castagna, 1982, p. 90)

OVERVIEW

In this chapter we stress the importance of helping children learn to study and remember information acquired through reading. Our focus will be on the reading of nonfiction, fiction having been covered in the previous chapter. We begin by presenting procedures the teacher can follow to plan and conduct effective content area reading lessons. We discuss the importance of making the purposes of these lessons clear to students and also describe activities for improving the comprehension of students at different levels of proficiency in working with expository text.

The different kinds of structures commonly found in expository text are discussed, along with methods teachers can use to familiarize students with them. We emphasize the importance of providing systematic instruction in study skills and of helping students know how to apply these skills to accomplish various tasks. A theme developed throughout the chapter is the importance of helping students reach the point where they can recognize the situations that call for the application of expository comprehension and study strategies and then carry these strategies out independently.

The key concepts in this chapter are:

Key Concept #1: The teacher should follow systematic procedures for planning and conducting content area reading lessons.

Key Concept #2: The teacher should make the purpose of lessons clear to children, helping them understand that the main reason for reading expository text is usually to learn and remember information.

Key Concept #3: The teacher should help children learn to deal with the different structures often found in expository texts.

Key Concept #4: The teacher should help children develop strategies for studying expository text.

PERSPECTIVE

EXPOSITORY AND CONTENT AREA TEXT

We will be using the term *expository* text to describe the kind of reading material usually written for the purpose of conveying factual information, explaining ideas, or presenting an argument. Another term for expository text is *informational* text. Expository text may be contrasted with narrative text or stories, which generally contain elements such as characters, a setting, and a plot, and are often written to reveal an aspect of human nature or to entertain. Thus, expository and narrative text generally differ both in purpose and structure.

Much of the writing in content area textbooks is expository in form, and so *content area* text is yet another term applied to this type of material. Most of the prose in textbooks for social studies, science, and health is indeed expository. The text in math books, however, generally is not, since it consists mostly of directions and word problems (for ways of helping students deal with word problems, refer to Charles, 1981; Le Blanc, 1982).

Out-of-school reading of expository text covers a wide range of types and topics. There are many informational books intended for children, including numerous award-winning books on natural and physical science topics. Other expository material written for children includes newspapers and magazines, discussed in Chapter 13.

As we might expect, children generally find expository text more difficult to comprehend than narrative. For example, the fourth graders studied by Alvermann and Boothby (1982) could distinguish between these two types of text and judged the expository selection to be more difficult. In fact, studies show that most readers seem to find it more difficult to comprehend expository than narrative texts (Kendall, Mason, & Hunter, 1980).

Importance of expository comprehension

By the time students are attending secondary school, the majority of the texts they are expected to deal with will be expository in nature, rather than narrative. Certainly, most reading in the workplace involves reading for specific information (e.g., Guthrie, 1984). This suggests that learning to comprehend and study expository text is at least as important as learning to comprehend and appreciate stories and literature. However, because the reading program in many classrooms centers on use of basal readers, which consist primarily of stories, teachers probably pay less attention than they should to helping children learn to comprehend expository text.

Teachers working with students in the fourth, fifth, and sixth grades generally are very aware of how important it is for their students to be able to read and comprehend expository text. In the conventional view, these are the grade levels when "reading to learn" begins to be emphasized over "learning to read." Typically, though, upper grade teachers find that many of their students have a great deal of difficulty reading and studying content area material. Part of the reason may be that the students have not had much previous experience with texts of this type.

Our view is that even kindergarten children can be given some experience with expository text; this would generally involve reading such material aloud to the children. Certainly, opportunities to work with expository text should be provided to first, second, and third grade students. By the time students are in the fourth grade and above, perhaps half or more of the reading instruction they receive should involve expository text.

Two means of increasing instructional time

How can we increase the amount of time spent in improving children's ability to comprehend expository text? There are two obvious approaches, and if possible the teacher will want to use both. The first approach is to build reading instruction into content area lessons. Particularly in mathematics, science, and social studies, much instruction often centers on work with textbooks. Lessons in reading comprehension can be developed to help the children learn more while working with these textbooks. These lessons do not have to increase the amount of time the teacher is devoting to these content areas. In addition, this approach has the added benefit of familiarizing children with the types of school situations in which their ability to comprehend and study expository text will most often be needed: content area classes.

If the teacher is having the children work with basal readers, the second course is to provide expository comprehension lessons with these materials. In many basal series, however, few expository selections are available in readers below the third grade level, and even upper grade readers contain more stories than expository texts. For example, an unpublished analysis we did of fourth grade readers from three widely used series indicated that 70 to 80 percent of the pages contained narrative text. Three percent to 7 percent covered study skills (short reports on how to read math, charts, directions, etc.), and 5 to 10 percent were informational but written in a narrative style (biographies, historical fiction, etc.). Only the remaining 10 to 16 percent of the pages were of expository text (articles on the natural and social sciences and sketches of people and places). These findings suggest that teachers will almost certainly find it necessary to teach reading comprehension lessons with expository materials from sources other than the basal.

With either approach, you generally will not want to rely on the content area textbook or basal reader selections alone. You will also want to hold reading lessons when the children work with other materials, such as articles from children's magazines, tradebooks, and the encyclopedia.

THE CONCURRENT PRESENTATION APPROACH

Because elementary students often have difficulty dealing both with the content and structure of expository text, teachers need to follow clearly organized plans for conducting content area lessons. The general approach to content area reading instruction we recommend involves *concurrent presentation of content and skills* (Moore & Readence, 1983; a similar approach is recommended by Gaskins, 1981). This approach is aimed at giving students knowledge of the topic as well as at giving them the necessary comprehension and study strategies, a point to be discussed further in Key Concept #2.

Moore and Readence note that there are three effective procedures for providing concurrent content and strategy instruction. These are *simulating, debriefing,* and *fading.*

Simulating is defined by Herber (1978) as a method of preparing students for a real experience by first taking them through a series of activities contrived to simulate that experience. Working with the specially contrived activities gives students the opportunity to practice the strategy they later will be encouraged to apply independently. According to Moore and Readence, simulating can involve first giving students rules for learning from text. After teaching the rules, the teacher has the students practice them with sample materials selected especially for that purpose. Then the students are asked to apply the rules in work with content area textbooks and other materials they normally use. Such a procedure might be used with the sequence for main idea comprehension developed by Baumann (1984; presented on pages 227–228).

Debriefing involves the teacher's asking students questions about their use of a particular strategy, such as the guided reading procedure (Manzo, 1975; presented on page 215). The purpose of debriefing is to have students introspect, to reflect upon the procedure itself and their thoughts while using it. Teacher questions during a GRP lesson might include the following:

How did you realize that some information was missing? How did you know some information was incorrect? How did you decide what seems to be the most important information? How did you decide what information supported the most important ideas? Might this be a useful means to help you read and learn from other text reading assignments?   (Moore & Readence, 1983, p. 400)

Fading is a process where the teacher at first provides a great deal of guidance when students are executing the strategy, and then gradually reduces the amount of guidance as students become better able to use the strategy on their own. This is the process seen in the reciprocal questioning procedure developed by Palincsar (1984; described on pages 211–213). At first the teacher must model the asking of questions. Later students are able to ask questions partly on their own, with some help from the teacher. Finally, they are able to ask questions with little or no teacher help.

In every content area reading lesson, plan to use one of these procedures. All have the advantage of actively engaging students in the lesson and making them aware of the purposes of instruction and of the steps involved in learning. A second advantage is that all are designed to move students toward independence in learning to comprehend and study expository text.

Organizing the concepts to be covered in content area lessons

In this section we look at how teachers should organize the content to be presented during content area lessons. Throughout this textbook we have emphasized the importance of background knowledge to reading, and that theme has particular significance here. In a sense, each lesson in a certain content area can be seen as building the background knowledge students will need for future learning in that area. In each of the content areas, your goal is to help your students develop a framework of concepts and facts, a broad and sound base of knowledge. Vocabulary is part of this knowledge, as pointed out in Chapter 4.

Systematic development of content area knowledge bases is an important instructional goal. Comprehension and learning of content area reading material can be improved by designing prereading activities to ensure that students have the necessary background knowledge (Pearson, Hansen, & Gordon, 1979; Stevens, 1982). Knowing in advance the topics and concepts that you want students to learn is an important step in the systematic building of content area knowledge bases. Here are some guidelines to follow in selecting and organizing the concepts you will be covering.

1. Become familiar with the topic. If working with an existing content area program, either textbook-based or involving other materials, take the time to familiarize yourself with all of the topics to be covered for your grade level. If possible, look also at the materials for the grade below and above to learn which of these topics are taught there.

Suppose, for example, that your grade 5 science text includes a section on light. If you were using the Laidlaw (1982) *New Exploring Science Green Book,* you would find no topics from fourth grade to build upon directly. The sixth grade text, however, builds on what you are going to teach and explains light as a form of energy.

2. Develop a plan for the units to be covered. Try to develop a plan including familiar topics or those directly related to important aspects of the children's own community. A unit will often take from two or three weeks to two months to complete. Try to link the new unit with other units. For example, the unit on light in the Laidlaw science text might be linked to the previous one on electricity or to the following one on living things.

3. Identify the concepts to be covered in the unit. Also identify the specific facts or examples to be presented with each concept. Decide whether your own knowledge is sufficient for teaching the unit, and if not, do background reading. In general, it is better to cover fewer concepts and facts more thoroughly, so they will be remembered by the children, than to cover a multitude superficially. If you look for concepts in the Laidlaw science book, for example, you would find a listing of eleven main ideas in the relevant chapter. One is, "You are able to see things when light bounces off these things and travels to your eyes" (p.189). You would select the most important concepts from this list and plan your lessons around them.

Many science concepts such as the one above are quite complex, so anticipate some difficult questions from the students, who might know as much about the subject as you do. Be sure you know enough to give an accurate response to likely questions. If students ask a question you can't answer, say, "I don't know but perhaps we can find out. How do you think we might do that?" Also anticipate teaching important vocabulary, for example, by following the concept of definition procedure described in Chapter 4. These occasions provide a natural opportunity for teaching children to use reference materials such as the dictionary or encyclopedia.

4. Focus on one or, at most, two new concepts each week. Make a list of points you wish to cover in the order you plan to cover them. Check to see that each point follows logically from the one before. You will do this to remind yourself to make explicit for the children the relationships among all the concepts and facts you will be covering. For example, there are five important interconnected concepts around the topic of reflected light in the Laidlaw text. You would want to teach them together and plan experiments and discussions around them.

5. *Study reading materials you plan to have the children use.* Evaluate whether the text adequately covers each concept, what information you will have to add from other sources, and what parts of the text you will want to stress or omit (an evaluation guide is found in Chapter 11). Also evaluate the usefulness of text aids such as headings, graphs, and illustrations. Find other books on the topic and put them in the classroom library for the children to read. The Laidlaw text, for example, provides a one paragraph explanation on the concept of being able to see by reflected light. You will need to expand this concept with illustrations, discussions, and experiments.

6. *Plan your lessons for the topic.* If working with the teacher's guide lesson for a textbook series, you may wish to modify the plan according to some of the recommendations in this chapter. In particular, you may wish to follow either the concept-text-application approach or the five phase instructional sequence.

FRAMEWORKS FOR EXPOSITORY COMPREHENSION LESSONS

Concept-text-application approach

The concept-text-application (CTA) approach developed by Wong and Au (1985) is a framework for organizing lessons to improve comprehension of expository text and can be used with students from the second grade on up. It takes students through prereading, guided reading, and postreading phases of instruction. The CTA approach incorporates many of the basic ideas developed by Herber (1978) and by Estes and Vaughan (1978); refer to these textbooks for a detailed treatment of content area reading issues, especially for upper elementary grade students.

Like Langer's (1981, 1984) PReP method, which has proven effective with students from the sixth grade and above, the CTA method is based on the idea that effective reading instruction starts by building on children's background knowledge. The approach is based on guided discussion and is best used with small groups. At least two 20 to 25 minute lessons are required to complete the reading of most expository selections, whether in a basal reader, content area textbook, or children's magazine.

The CTA method is designed to complement the ETR method for teaching comprehension of stories, as described in Chapter 5. It too incorporates three different phases. The concept assessment/development or C phase is a prereading discussion during which the teacher tries to find out what the stu-

FIGURE 7.1 *Do You Believe in Monsters?*

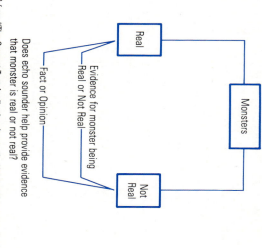

Does echo sounder help provide evidence
that monster is real or not real?

Fact or Opinion

Evidence for monster being
Real or Not Real

Real

Monsters

Not Real

Figures 1 and 2 [7.1 and 7.2] from "The Concept-Text-Application Approach: Helping Elementary Students Comprehend Text" by JoAnn Wong and Kathryn Hu-pei Au, March 1985, *The Reading Teacher*. Reprinted by permission of the authors and the International Reading Association.

dents already know about the topic of the text. Unfamiliar concepts and vocabulary necessary for understanding the text may be introduced during this phase. During the text or *T* phase purposes for reading are set and there is guided reading and discussion of the text. Finally, during the application or *A* phase, the teacher encourages the students to put to use the new information learned.

Planning. First, preview the text and identify the main idea or central theme you wish to focus on. If necessary, do some background reading on the topic. Second, reread the text and work out the visual structure to be developed with the children during the lesson. For example, Figure 7.1 shows the visual structure used by a teacher to plan a second grade lesson based on "The Monster of Loch Ness" (Shogren, 1978). When making up the structure, you may also wish to note vocabulary to be covered. Then plan the application or follow-up activity. In the example, the teacher decided to have the children conduct a survey of their classmates.

Concept assessment/development. Try to capture the children's interest at the very start of the lesson. In our example, the teacher generated a lot of discussion by asking the children if they believed in monsters. Then move on to more focused questions to identify key concepts and vocabulary unfamiliar to the children. For example, in this lesson the children had to be taught that *loch* was the Scottish word for lake.

Text. After assessing background knowledge and developing important concepts and vocabulary, move into guided reading of the text. Work with the children to set a purpose (usually, a question to be answered) for the reading of each segment. Have them read the segment and then discuss the information covered. Continue alternating periods of silent reading and discussion until the text has been completed.

After the first segment is discussed, lay out the framework for the visual structure. During each discussion period, continue to add to it. Figure 7.2 shows the visual structure completed in this manner for the lessons on the Loch Ness monster. The items in the structure were those mentioned by the children, and the lines were drawn after the children decided whether each item supported the view that the monster was "real" or "not real." The teacher used this visual structure to bring out the central theme, whether the monster was real.

When working with primary grade students, you may wish to teach useful vocabulary not present in the text. For example, over the course of the sample

FIGURE 7.2   *Completed Visual Structure on the Loch Ness Monster*

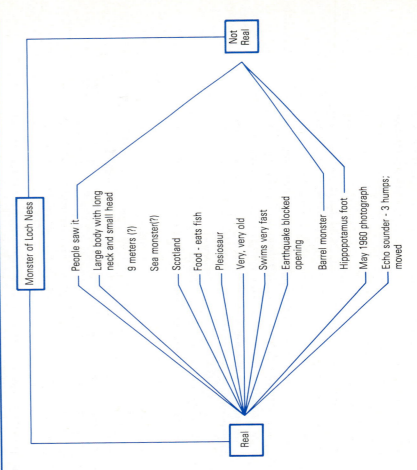

In the school library, students take notes for a group report. They will pool their information when they return to class.

lessons, the teacher introduced the terms *evidence, fact,* and *opinion,* all words not in the text.

Watch during the *T* phase for signs that you should help the children build up background knowledge and fit new text information with what has already been understood. For instance, in the sample series of lessons, the teacher found that the children did not understand how an echo sounder worked. She had to explain this to them because the text provided little information on this point. Then she led them to see how an echo sounder might be used to locate the monster.

Application.   Immediately after the entire text has been read, have the children try to summarize and synthesize the information. During this process, encourage them to refer to the visual structure. After the review, have the children engage in evaluative and divergent thinking. In this case, the children began on their own to debate the issue of whether the monster was real.

Finally, have the children engage in one or more follow-up activities. These may be very simple, taking perhaps only a half hour of class time, or more elaborate, stretching across several weeks. Possibilities include writing group or individual reports incorporating information from tradebooks and the encyclopedia, making a display or mural, or sharing information learned orally with the rest of the class. In our example, the children polled their classmates to see how many thought the Loch Ness monster was real. They then made a bar graph to display the results.

CTA lessons can easily be used as a springboard for SEARCH projects, described below. In this case, children highly interested in the topic continue to work on it.

SEARCH

The SEARCH method developed by Indrisano (1983) can be used to encourage students to pursue individual interests generated by content area reading. This is an important step in moving students toward independence in setting their own purposes for reading and study. The letters in SEARCH stand for the following:

Set goals
Explore sources and resources
Analyze and organize information
Refine and rehearse
Communicate with others
Help yourself to improve   (p. 2)

Indrisano sees the communication aspect of SEARCH, which encourages students to share their learning with other students and family members, as being especially important.

SEARCH draws upon the teacher's creativity, because the content and form of different projects depends on the interests of the students. Indrisano recommends beginning slowly, perhaps with just an individual student or a single team of two or three students. Have them aim to complete the SEARCH in less than a month. Gradually add other teams and reduce time for each SEARCH.

Here is an example of a SEARCH carried out by two fourth graders:

1. Set goals: After having read a story set in Boston, the students evidenced an interest in learning more about the city. They met with their teacher who helped them to understand how goals can be classified into *Knowing, Doing, Becoming* categories after having elicited examples of each type. The students then worked together on their goals in preparation for sharing them with the teacher in three days. With the teacher's help, these goals were established:

Knowing:
    What are the historic places in Boston?
          (Answering)
    How will we decide which places to visit?
          (Solving)

Doing:
    Talk to people who know about Boston.
          (Communicating)
    Look at pictures of Boston in books and magazines.
          (Observing)

Becoming:
    Learn about another place.
          (Learner)
    Find information to help us make decisions.
          (Researcher)

2. *Explore sources and resources:* Each "knowing" and "doing" goal was then listed at the top of a separate sheet of paper on which two columns were provided. The first was headed "Source," the second, "Information." The "becoming" goals were listed on a separate sheet. ["Becoming" goals are those which may be pursued in the future.]

With the teacher's guidance, students decided upon sources of information for each "knowing" and "doing" goal. . . . With any interview, pupils will find it beneficial to prepare questions in advance. This phase required one week and a half.

3. *Analyze and organize information:* When pupils are ready to record their information, they use the second column of the previously prepared sheet, matching information to source. This step requires them to record precise information rather than all the available data on the subject. For this first cycle, pupils were encouraged to take notes on separate sheets of paper and later to record the significant information on their charts. A useful time frame for this step was one week. Teachers need time to check student production as this phase is completed.

4. *Refine and rehearse.* Using whatever procedure the pupils find comfortable (e.g., outlining, organizing note cards according to goals), pupils survey their information and decide upon an audience and a mode of presentation. Given the type of data these students have gathered, they elected to share their information with the whole class. If they had wished, they could have devised a plan to create smaller groupings of the whole, to present the oral component via the tape recorder, or to share with a group of younger pupils.

These pupils were comfortable reporting to their classmates, but needed to be aware of the large group setting. So they arranged to make simple

This student is copying the final version of his report into a hardcover book he made himself. After he presents his report, other students will be able to read his book.

FIGURE 7.3 *Management of SEARCH*

Student (s) Cycle Topic	Sharing Date	Set Goals	Date	Explore Sources & Resources	Date	Analyze & Organize Information	Date	Refine and Rehearse	Date	Communicate with Others	Date	Help Yourself to Improve	Date

Chart, "Management of SEARCH," from *Independent Application of SEARCH in Reading and Language Arts* by Roselmina Indrisano, Number 12 of the GINN OCCASIONAL PAPERS. © Copyright 1983 by Ginn and Company. Used with permission.

overhead transparencies listing their questions and the names of the historic places they would describe. . . .

After their week of preparation and just before the sharing session, the pupils rehearsed their presentation with the teacher who helped them to keep within the twenty minute limit they had set.

5. *Communicate with others.* On a Friday afternoon, the time set aside for sharing, the pupils presented their SEARCH to the class with the aid of the overhead transparencies they had prepared. The report was oral and consistent with the question and answer format they had established when they set their "knowing" goals. . . .

6. *Help yourself to improve.* The final step is the creation of a plan for assessment. The range of possibilities includes self, peer, teacher, parent and/or visitor evaluation through the use of rating scales, checklists, comparison of product to goals, or analysis of tape-recorded presentation. For this first effort, self-evaluation was selected and a rating scale devised to guide the effort. Pupils simply listed their goals in the three areas: Knowing, Doing, and Becoming. They established three criteria: very good, good, needs improvement. After presentation, they met and completed the self-evaluation and later, shared it with the teacher who reminded them to keep the rating scale to use when setting goals for the next cycle. (Indrisano, 1983, pp. 5–7)

As more groups of students undertake a SEARCH, proper teacher management and monitoring becomes critical. Indrisano recommends that the teacher use a chart like that in Figure 7.3 (from Indrisano, p. 8). In the first column record the students' names, putting a bracket around those in the same team. "Cycle" refers to the number of the SEARCHes the student has already completed, and "topic" to the subject being explored. As noted above, the sharing date is set when the SEARCH starts, to ensure that students make steady progress through the various steps in the process. Keep notes and dates in the other columns, to remind yourself of what each team is doing.

Five phase instructional sequence

Roth, Smith, and Anderson (1984) propose the following five phase instructional sequence, adapted from Gagne (1970). This sequence was developed from studying science lessons given to fifth graders but can be applied to content area instruction for children at all grades. We have indicated where reading would usually be included in this sequence (refer also to Gaskins, 1981):

These steps demand that the teacher's role and strategies change as the students progress. The teacher acts as a facilitator, a diagnostician, or a director, depending on what is needed to keep students actively thinking. In each case, the teacher's verbal patterns are essential, particularly as they relate to student responses. (p. 288)

Preparation. Begin the instructional sequence by presenting an overview and background information for the unit. Make sure your overview leads students to realize that they have misconceptions or vague preconceptions about the topic. For example, in a study describing instruction of a unit on light reflections, Anderson and Smith (1984) found that students at first said that light helps people see by shining on objects or by making things brighter. While not completely wrong, these preconceptions were vague and interfered with the best explanation of the role played by reflected light. Included in the preparation for this unit were pictured representations of light rays from the sun bouncing from an object to a person's eyes. Questions about how light helps people see, with the correct answers below, were part of this display.

Roth, Smith, and Anderson stress the importance of getting students "mentally set for instruction" (p. 289) both by calling up relevant prior knowledge and providing necessary background information the students do not yet have.

Exploration. Help students explore the topic and become more aware of the ideas they already have. Activities that encourage students to explore their ideas include science experiments, open-ended discussions, opportunities for problem-solving, open-ended writing, and free reading. Tell students that the purpose of the activity is to let them express their own thoughts. Ask students challenging questions and otherwise encourage critical thinking. Your goal at this point, according to Roth, Smith, and Anderson, is to "create some internal mental conflict" (p. 289). Look for preconceptions and conflicts to be considered when you plan future lessons. With the unit on light, for example, activities could involve the use of differently textured surfaces and surfaces that differ in translucence. Light meters borrowed from photography buffs could be used to measure changes in reflected light.

Acquisition.   Having raised challenges for the students, you will now want to address the conceptual conflict directly. Discuss the conflict with the children and work with them to change their misconceptions. Present expository text from the content area textbook. Since some textbooks do not clearly present complex concepts, you should provide several sources or rewrite the important sections yourself. For the light unit, the text was rewritten by Roth, Smith, and Anderson. Be sure that the reading is prefaced with a discussion, during which time purposes for reading can be estalished. Also be sure that there is a follow-up discussion. Rereading of the text, or reading of other materials, may then occur.

At all times, structure the discussion carefully and keep explanations brief and understandable. During this step Roth, Smith, and Anderson believe the effective teacher:

1. Asks more closed questions.
2. Discourages divergent student comments.
3. Provides key explanations.
4. Models the desired thinking processes.
5. Emphasizes important points by frequent repetition of key concepts in new situations.
6. Carefully relates theories to observations.   (p. 289)

Straightening out misconceptions and building new content area knowledge is extremely demanding. You are trying to teach the students to see flaws in their own thinking as well as to fit the new concepts they must acquire into their knowledge framework. These goals cannot be accomplished merely by assigning reading in a content area textbook.

Practice/application.   To make sure that new knowledge is retained and new conceptual frameworks developed, give students ample opportunity to work with the ideas. Activities which permit practice and application include:

Recitation discussions where students practice talking about the ideas, with other students and the teacher providing corrective feedback;

Experiments and other hands-on activities that deal with new but related problems;

Small group problem-solving sessions;

Directed expository writing experiences that force students to explain the concepts in an applied situation;

Student creation of concept maps.   (p. 290)

Roth, Smith, and Anderson do not recommend using worksheets, which tend to provide only limited, perhaps overly structured work with the ideas. Instead, assist students as they discuss and try to apply the new concepts. For example, the unit on light reflection could be extended to photography or painting. Some students could read more technical reference materials. Others might write explanations for younger children.

Synthesis. Finally, help students synthesize new information for the purpose of ensuring that newly learned ideas are tied together and related to other concepts, and that a solid conceptual framework for future learning has been established. Use a visual structure to show the relationships of details to major concepts. Evaluate students' learning in more than one way. You can measure:

Accuracy in answering test questions.
Ability to explain the new concepts.
Ability to apply the new concepts.
Ability to construct a concept map of the interrelationships.

Roth, Smith, and Anderson emphasize the importance of striking a balance among the five phases. Their observations suggest that the acquisition phase, where the teacher actively directs students' learning, is often the most poorly executed phase of content area instruction. They caution teachers not to assume that students have learned the material simply because they have been assigned to read the text. To avoid this problem, they recommend that teachers see themselves as taking charge of students' concept learning, helping to rid them of ill-formed and vague preconceptions and to build a firmly structured conceptual framework of important new information.

PURPOSES FOR READING EXPOSITORY TEXTS

As adults, we may read expository texts for a variety of reasons, but we do so most often for the purpose of learning and remembering information. Adults at school or in the workplace read expository text to acquire new information, such as the concepts basic to an understanding of chemistry or the teaching of reading, the procedures for operating a new machine, the reasons for a change in company policy, and recent developments in politics or the economy. There generally are very good reasons for our learning and remembering. For example, in addition to the fact that you may be tested on the content presented in college classes and textbooks, this information might also be very important to your future career and job performance. For example, someone who is a teacher must know how to plan and conduct lessons, as well as about the content to be conveyed in lessons.

The purposes for reading expository text, then, are usually different from those for reading fiction or narratives, which often are read for recreation and enjoyment. This difference in purpose needs to be made clear to children.

As a teacher, you should first clarify in your own mind the purpose you have in teaching a reading lesson with a particular expository selection. There generally are two good reasons for having children work with such a selection. First, you could have children read an expository text because you feel it is important for them to learn and remember the information it presents. That is, there are facts to be learned, such as the countries that were colonized by England, or concepts that need to be understood, such as why colonies were later given up by England and other European countries.

Second, you could have the children read an expository text because you want them to learn and practice a certain reading comprehension strategy or study skill. That is, there are methods of understanding and remembering important facts and concepts to be learned. Of course, the most valued lessons will be those you teach for *both* of these reasons at the same time, as in the concurrent approach discussed earlier.

Stating purposes

Announcing the purpose at the very beginning of the lesson. The importance of this procedure has been discussed by Roehler and Duffy (1984). They found that few teachers ever remembered to make purpose-setting statements. When they did, however, the children not only remembered these statements, they also understood the text better and learned more from their reading. The teacher needs to tell students *what*, *why*, and *how* they are to learn. Here is an example of such a purpose-setting statement:

Today we are going to learn about how to tell apart the different kinds of clouds [the *what* information]. Why do you think it will be useful for you to tell apart the different kinds of clouds? [The teacher elicits the *why* information from the children, that identification of cloud patterns will help them predict some kinds of weather.] Now the way we will learn is first to read the next section of your science text. Then we'll set up small groups to observe the clouds over the next two weeks, record the weather each day, and find some other articles on the topic at the library [the *how* information].

Later, as the children learn about the purposes for reading text of different types and on different topics, encourage them to establish and state their own purposes for reading.

Stating the topic-related purpose for reading. If one of your purposes is to focus on the information in the text, which is valuable for its own sake, tell the children how learning the information will benefit them (the *why* information presented in the example above). Usually the information they are to learn is related in some obvious way to information they already know. For example, suppose that the lesson on clouds was preceded by a lesson on rain. In that case, help the children see the connections between new and prior knowledge. For example:

Do you remember what we learned about in our science lesson last Tuesday? [The teacher has the children recall that the last lesson was about rain and helps them to access possibly relevant prior knowledge.] What are some of the things we learned about rain? [The teacher elicits facts from the children.] Do you see any connection between that information and what we might be learning about clouds? [The teacher has the children identify how some of their background knowledge about rain might help them understand the new information, about clouds.]

Stating the strategy-related purpose for reading. Some of your lessons may be taught for the purpose of acquainting your students with a particular strategy for comprehending expository text. Such strategies include those for analyzing and critically evaluating information and monitoring their own understanding.

Sometimes the text being read will not contain information of much value in and of itself. You are using that particular text only to provide the opportunity for practicing the strategy. In this case, be sure to tell the children that the purpose of the lesson is to work on the strategy. Inform them that they should concentrate on the *procedure* being taught, rather than the topic. For example, suppose that the procedure is to identify the topic sentence. You could tell the children that the purpose is to learn how to find the one sentence that gives the reader an idea of what the entire paragraph is about. You could explain that identifying the topic sentence may help the reader in separating important from unimportant information.

Stating both kinds of purposes concurrently. Most often, if you are following the concurrent presentation approach to content area reading, you will tell your students that there will be two purposes for reading, one purpose to learn about the topic and the other to learn a strategy for reading for information. For example:

Now I would like you to open your science books to page 100. Remember that we will be reading to find out about the different kinds of clouds. First, we will be using headings to learn the names of the different kinds of clouds. Who can tell me one heading that gives the name of a kind of cloud? [The teacher calls the children's attentions to the headings, has them say what the headings are, and lists the headings on the board.] When you read, try to look for at least two facts under each of the headings. These facts will be information about what makes each type of cloud special. When you have finished reading, I will be asking you to tell me facts for each of these headings.

Later, after the children have provided the information for each type of cloud, the teacher can review the use of headings, discussing with the children how headings can be helpful in letting you know about the types of facts to be covered and how the text is organized.

INSTRUCTIONAL ACTIVITIES

The purpose of the activities below (reciprocal teaching, informed strategies for learning, ReQuest, and the guided reading procedure) is to help students learn and remember information about the topic of the text. Their value is both in encouraging students to engage actively in the process of constructing meaning from expository text and to become more aware of the strategies that will help them do this. Reciprocal teaching can be used with primary as well as upper grade students and provides a good starting point for students less experienced in working with expository text. The informed strategies for learning can be used to supplement virtually any expository comprehension activity.

ReQuest and the guided reading procedure are best used with students who already have some expertise in working with expository text but can still benefit from some systematic instruction. ReQuest differs from reciprocal teaching in that the teacher uses this procedure to initiate reading but does not lead students through the entire text. In the guided reading procedure the teacher offers the students even less help, since the students first read the text on their own, without any prereading discussion.

Reciprocal teaching

Palincsar (1984) describes a program of instruction shown to be effective in improving children's comprehension monitoring/fostering activities. The program targets these four activities: (1) self-questioning (asking main idea rather than detail questions), (2) summarizing, (3) predicting, and (4) evaluating (identifying and clarifying the meaning of difficult sections of the text). The basic procedure can be adapted for use with small groups of children from the first grade on up.

The method of instruction used for all four activities was *reciprocal teaching*. The teacher engages the children in discussion by first modeling an activity. Then the children try to engage in the same activity, with the teacher guiding their performance by providing corrective feedback.

In introducing the reciprocal teaching procedure, begin with a group discussion of why people might sometimes have difficulty understanding reading material. The children are likely to come up with responses such as "hard words." Follow this introductory discussion with instruction in each of the four comprehension monitoring/fostering activities. For example, teach your students some of the summarization rules presented in Chapter 8. Let your students know that these activities will help them focus their attention on the text and gain a better understanding of it. Finally, discuss the content areas, such as science and social studies, where these activities can be used, and how they can help with tasks such as writing reports and taking tests.

In Palincsar's study, the reciprocal teaching procedure was introduced in the following way:

Students were told that everyone in the group would take turns being teacher during the reading session. It was explained that whoever assumed the role of teacher was responsible for asking the group an important question, summarizing, predicting what might be discussed next in the passage, and sharing anything that he or she found unclear or confusing. The teacher was to call on someone to answer his or her question and was responsible for telling the student whether or not the answer was correct. In turn, the students who were not teaching that particular segment of the passage were to comment on the teacher's question(s) and statements and feel free to contribute to that segment. (Palincsar, 1984, p. 254)

After working for several days on the information above, have the students begin to follow this procedure. First, give the students an expository passage of about 1,500 words. Shorter passages would, of course, be given to younger students. If you are working with first and second graders, select passages to read aloud to them. If the passage is new to the children, have them make predictions based on the title. If they are already familiar with the passage, ask them to state the topic and the important points already learned.

Then, have the children read a paragraph or two. If the children are just being introduced to the reciprocal teaching procedure, let them know that you will be acting as the teacher for this text segment. If the children are already familiar with the procedure, choose a child to be the teacher.

After the segment has been read silently, ask an important question about it, or have the child teacher ask the questions. The teacher then summarizes and makes a prediction or clarification, if appropriate. If a child is serving as the teacher, Palincsar recommends providing the following kinds of assistance:

Prompting. "What question did you think a teacher might ask?"; Instruction, "Remember a summary is a shortened version, it doesn't include a lot of detail"; Modifying the activity, "If you're having a hard time thinking of a question, why don't you summarize first?" and by soliciting the help of the students, "Who can help us out with this one?" (pp. 254–255)

Invite the other members of the group to offer comments or additional information to supplement that presented by the child or adult teacher. Provide praise and feedback to the child teacher, using comments such as these:

"You asked that question well, it was very clear what information you wanted." "Excellent prediction, let's see if you're right." "That was interesting information. It was information that I would call detail in the passage. Can you tell us the most important information in that paragraph?" After this feedback, adult teachers modeled any activity they felt continued to need improvement: "A question I would have asked would be . . ." "I would summarize by saying . . ." "Did anyone else find this statement unclear?" (p. 255)

Palincsar reports that it takes most teachers about a week to feel comfortable with modeling the comprehension monitoring activities. She suggests that teachers practice with the materials they plan to use with the students. Teachers may also wonder if their students will really be able to engage in reciprocal teaching. To ensure that the first few lessons will be successful, Palincsar recommends that you select well-structured expository passages, clearly written and with headings. Be prepared to do a lot of modeling and to call on more capable students to act as models for less capable members of the group.

To get an idea of the kind of progress students can make through participation in the reciprocal teaching procedure, refer to Figure 7.4. These are

---

FIGURE 7.4 Reciprocal Teaching Procedure

Day 1:
S: What is found in the southeastern snakes, also the copperhead, rattlesnakes, vipers—they have. I'm not doing this right.
T: All right. Do you want to know about the pit vipers?
S: Yeah.
T: What would be a good question about the pit vipers that starts with the word "why"?
S: No response.
T: How about, "Why are the snakes called pit vipers?"
S: Why do they want to know that they called pit vipers?
T: Try it again.
S: Why do they, pit vipers in a pit?
T: How about, "Why do they call the snakes pit vipers?"
S: Why do they call the snakes pit vipers?
T: There you go. Good for you.

Day 4:
S: No question.
T: What's this paragraph about?
S: Spinner's mate. How do Spinner's mate . . . ?
T: That's good. Keep going.
S: How do Spinner's mate is much smaller than . . . how am I going to say that?
T: Take your time with it. You want to ask a question about Spinner's mate and what he does beginning with the word "how."
S: How do they spend most of his time sitting?
T: You're very close. The question would be, "How does Spinner's mate spend most of his time?" Now you ask it.
S: How does Spinner's mate spend most of his time?

Day 7:
S: How does the pressure from below push the mass of hot rock against the opening? Is that it?
T: Not quite. Start your question with "What happens when?"
S: What happens when the pressure from below pushes the mass of hot rock against the opening?
T: Good for you. Good job.

Day 11:
S: What is the most interesting of the insect-eating plants and where do the plants live at?
T: Two excellent questions! They are both clear and important questions. Ask us one at a time now.

Day 15:
S: Why do scientists come to the south pole to study?
T: Excellent question! That is what this paragraph is all about.

excerpts from the dialogue between a teacher and a student who was a very poor reader. Notice how much help the student required in the beginning, and how he gradually became able to ask questions with less and less help from the teacher.

Informed strategies for learning

Middle grade students can benefit from instruction to help them acquire "Informed Strategies for Learning" (Paris, Cross, & Lipson, 1984; Paris, in press). The purpose of this project is to help children learn and understand the uses of a variety of reading strategies. Although many of the texts used were expository, the basic approach is applicable to narratives, as well. Instruction is given to the whole class. The teacher first has the children discuss the concept and then gives them opportunities for independent practice.

There are three general guidelines for instruction. First, give the children instruction about what the strategy is, how it is performed, and when it should be used. Second, make the strategies public. That is, make visible to the children how one thinks when reading. For example, you could have the children discuss how they might go about monitoring their comprehension. Third, help the children become independent in their use of the strategies. As Paris states:

Teaching is more than telling; the information must be supplemented with a rationale for using strategies. This is where motivation blends with knowledge and where teaching and learning interact. The responsibility to use reading strategies must be shifted from teachers to students so that learning is self-regulated and not done merely for compliance or external rewards.

To improve strategy instruction, Paris recommends use of these techniques.

1. *Use metaphors on bulletin boards and during discussion.* Think of a way to describe the strategy so the students will learn and remember it. For example, Paris suggests trying these wordings:

Be a reading detective.
Plan your reading trip.
Round up your ideas.

2. *Conduct group dialogues.* Provide an outlet where the children can express confusion, state your ideas in their own words, or come up with new ideas of their own.

3. *Provide immediate opportunities for guided practice.* Build into each lesson some type of individual practice, or practice with peers. Always give the children a chance to try out the strategies introduced.

4. *Bridge to content areas.* Make sure to have the children use these strategies when working with content area materials, such as social studies and science textbooks. Help the children understand how the use of these strategies can make it easier for them to learn and remember content area information.

ReQuest procedure

According to Manzo (1969), the purpose of the ReQuest procedure is: "to improve the student's reading comprehension by providing an active learning situation for the development of questioning behaviors" (p. 123). Although Manzo originally used this procedure with individual children, we have adapted it for use with a small group. The teacher encourages the students to ask questions, guiding them through a number of sentences in the text. When it appears that they will be able to read the rest of the text with good comprehension, the teacher has them proceed independently.

1. Begin by explaining the procedure to the children in the following way:

The purpose of this lesson is to improve your understanding of what you read. We will each read silently the first sentence. Then we will take turns asking questions about the sentence and what it means. You will ask questions first, then I will ask questions. Try to ask the kind of questions a teacher might ask in the way a teacher might ask them.

You may ask me as many questions as you wish. When you are asking me questions I will close my book. . . . When I ask the questions you close your book. (p. 124)

Explain to the students that you will be trying your best to answer their questions, and that they will need to work hard to answer yours. Listeners may ask that a question be clarified or rephrased. The person answering the question should be prepared to state why he thinks his answer is correct (by referring back to the text, discussing his reasoning, etc.).

2. Have the students read the first sentence of the text. Then close your book. Select several students to ask questions, and try to answer them. If any particularly outstanding questions are asked, point out to the students why those questions are exemplary.

3. Have the students close their books and take your turn at asking them questions. At this point you are modeling questioning behavior for them.

4. Continue this same procedure with the next sentences in the first paragraph. Manzo does not recommend continuing the procedure beyond the third paragraph, because the idea is just to get the students started and then to let them continue on their own.

Guided reading procedure

The purpose of the guided reading procedure (GRP) developed by Manzo (1975) is to encourage students' ability in the following areas: (1) recall of text information, (2) recognition of inconsistencies or flaws in the text (for example, in the author's argument), (3) self-correction, and (4) organization of text ideas. The GRP can be used with upper elementary grade students who have the ability to read the expository material in the lesson independently. The GRP does not include an extensive prereading discussion, which may be a disadvantage for less capable students. As Manzo suggests, then, the procedure should not be used all the time, but perhaps once a week.

Ankney and McClurg (1981) tested the GRP in science and social studies lessons given to fifth and sixth graders. They recommend following Manzo's guideline of assigning passages about 500 words in length. In the textbooks they used, this was only about a page and a half. They found the GRP particularly useful when the text contained a heavy factual load. Students were enthusiastic about sharing the ideas they recalled from their reading and eager to go back and reread. The steps in the procedure are as follows:

1. A purpose is set for reading and the students are instructed to remember all that they can. When they finish reading, they close their books.
2. The teacher asks the class members to tell everything they can remember from the selection. This information is recorded on the chalkboard in whatever order and fashion it is remembered.
3. After the students have recalled all that they can, they will recognize there are some inconsistencies and material that was not remembered. At this point they are permitted to look in their books again and correct or add to the information recorded on the chalkboard.
4. Students are asked to organize the information they have compiled. This can be done in the form of a diagram, outline, or semantic web.
5. The teacher asks several synthesizing questions to aid in the transfer of learning. These questions are to help the students integrate new information with previously learned material.
6. A conventional teacher-made test (matching, multiple-choice, essay, true/false, unaided recall) is given to test the students' shorterm memory right after steps 1–5 have been completed.
7. Another form of the test given in step 6 is administered at a later date to assess medium or longterm memory.

(p. 682)

KEY CONCEPT 3

The teacher should help children learn to deal with the different structures often found in expository tests.

EXPOSITORY TEXT STRUCTURES

The term *structure* refers to the organization of ideas in the text, including the location of more or less important information and the means used to connect ideas to one another. While many simple stories follow a single structure or grammar, as described in Chapter 6, no one structure appears to be applicable to the majority of expository texts likely to be encountered by elementary school students. Familiarizing students with these different structures should improve their ability to comprehend expository texts (e.g., Taylor & Samuels, 1983), just as familiarizing them with story structure apparently improves their ability to comprehend narrative text.

Here are five kinds of structure commonly found in expository text written for elementary students (based on categories in Niles, 1965, and Meyer & Freedle, 1984).

Simple listing. In simple listings, the exact order in which information is presented is of little importance. Descriptions or definitions of objects, events or concepts often are given, along with examples. Here is an example of a simple listing:

Notice the lines of a globe that run across from left to right. They are called lines of latitude, and they form circles that run in the same direction as the equator. The smallest circles are near the north and south poles and the largest are near the equator. These lines measure how far north or south of the equator places are. [The text continues to define other terms.]

Ordered listing. The listing in texts with this structure follow a time sequence, spatial dimensions (e.g., left to right, top to bottom), operating procedures (e.g., the steps in operating a car), or other type of order. Here is an example:

The first Europeans to come to America settled along the Atlantic coast. They knew very little about the territory beyond the ocean. But soon after the American Revolution more people crossed the ocean. Families needed places to live and grow crops. Sometimes several families formed a small settlement, usually near a river or stream. As spaces for farming were taken, the frontier kept moving westward. Wilderness turned into settlements and settlements into towns.

Problem and solution. In this structure a problem is stated and its solution is then described. Here is the beginning of such a text:

Many people in the northern states wanted to end slavery but in the South they wanted to keep it. Northerners wanted Congress to pass a law ending slavery in all states, in the states that were being formed and in the South. [The text continues by describing how people worked to put an end to slavery.]

Cause and effect (or antecedent and consequence). One or more antecedents are described which lead to a result, effect, or conclusion. For example, the following text describes the cause and effect relationship between Europeans' needs for money and the discovery of America:

In Europe during the fifteenth century, many small kingdoms joined into large nations. These large nations began to fight with each other and they needed money for their soldiers. One way to get money was by trading. One of these new nations, Spain, was interested in trading with China and India. But the only route people knew about was around Africa. In 1492, Spain sent out a small fleet of three ships to find a new route to the East. They sailed across the Atlantic Ocean. Instead of finding China, the three ships discovered America.

Comparison and contrast. This structure is based on a description of similarities and differences, or statement of the pros and cons of two or more objects, approaches, concepts, or points of view. The following text, for example, began by describing the characteristics of globes. It then presented the following comparison:

Flat maps are often more useful than globes because you can see the whole world at one time. You can make maps of small parts of the world. For example, you could make a map of our state or city. These can't be shown on a *globe*. But a flat map distorts the real surface. Only a *globe* can show the rounded surface of our planet.

Effects of text structure on comprehension

According to Niles (1965), texts which list information are the most common, followed by those with a cause and effect structure, and then those with a comparison and contrast structure. The teacher will find, however, that many expository texts incorporate *several different* structures. That is, the first few paragraphs will follow one structure, and the next few another structure. Furthermore, the text often will not signal to the reader in advance that the structure or topic is about to shift.

The nature of a text's structure may affect children's ability to learn and remember information. The results of a study by Meyer and Freedle (1984) suggest that people find it most difficult to remember information in texts with a simple listing structure, and easiest to remember information in texts with a compare and contrast or a cause and effect structure.

Why should information in the simple listing structure, so common in the expository text written for children, be more difficult to learn and remember? In listings, important information is not usually separated from unimportant information, and headings highlighting different topics are not presented. Thus, this structure does not give people a convenient way of *chunking information*, that is, of organizing it into larger, meaningful units. Information "chunked" into such larger units is easier for people to remember than many individual little details.

Information in cause and effect structures is easier to remember because the cause statement is usually highlighted in the text and clearly tied to the effect statement and to supporting details. Similarly, in the compare and contrast structure, the ideas presented are consistently compared on a number of dimensions. Details can be organized according to these dimensions.

Unfortunately, much expository text written for children does not seem to be organized in a manner likely to make it easy to learn and remember information (Armbruster, 1984). For example, an analysis of second, fourth, sixth, and eighth grade social studies textbooks suggests that main idea statements are not all that common (Baumann & Serra, 1984). Only 27 percent of all short passages contained main idea statements. Findings like this suggest that children may often need to come up with a main idea on their own.

A number of studies provide evidence that children can be taught such special skills for comprehending expository text. For example, Bridge, Belmore, Moskow, Cohen, and Matthews (1984) were successful in increasing children's comprehension by getting them to pay more attention to the main idea. They had the children read 16 short paragraphs. The children were asked to note whether each paragraph contained a main idea statement. They were then asked to write a sentence stating what they remembered about the main idea of each paragraph. This task improved their comprehension of the information.

The ability to identify and make use of text structure is extremely important when reading to learn and remember information. Meyer, Brandt, and Bluth (1980), for example, found this ability to be the best predictor for recall of major details, better than vocabulary knowledge or even comprehension ability. If the text is not particularly well structured, then readers need to be able to impose their own structure on the text. This self generated structure makes it easier for readers to learn and remember text information.

Obviously, the points discussed above support one of the main themes of this textbook: Reading is a constructive process, one requiring the active involvement of the reader. As they read expository text, children should be searching out the key ideas or main thrust of each section. They should be asking themselves, "What's it all about?" "What is the author trying to tell me?" and "How has the author organized this explanation or argument?"

INSTRUCTIONAL ACTIVITIES

The following activities are aimed at giving children the ability to uncover the underlying structure of expository texts. They make the structure of the text evident to children, so they can see the kinds of information covered and how they are organized and presented.

Previewing

When previewing a book, have the children look at the title and author, date and place of publication, table of contents, and section and chapter titles. Have them talk about topics such as how the book is organized and the material to be covered in each section.

When previewing a chapter or shorter selection, have the children look at the title, headings, figures and tables, illustrations, and introductory and summary statements. Have them discuss the topics covered and the structure of the text.

Teaching students to identify and make use of text structures

The purpose of this procedure is to help children improve their comprehension of expository text by identifying and making use of its structure. The steps below are an adaptation of those developed by Niles (1965) for teaching high school students to organize factual material before writing. Our version can be used with fifth and sixth graders, and perhaps with some fourth graders.

Step 1. Discuss with the children why texts are structured in different ways. Introduce them to the five common structures and see if they understand the kinds of information which might be conveyed clearly through the use of each structure.

Step 2. Give the children a paragraph to skim. Have them identify its structure, and then have them reread the paragraph with this structure in mind. Discuss with the children how knowing about the structure might have improved their understanding of the idea in the paragraph.

Step 3. Repeat Step 2 but this time follow up by asking questions about the text. As the children provide answers, help them to see how knowledge of structures may make it easier for them to comprehend and remember the information.

Step 4. Have students search for signal words and expressions that often serve as cues for a particular text structure. Armbruster and Anderson (1982) identified the following signal words:

SIMPLE LISTING: for example, for instance, type of, kind of, such as, includes, example of, is a property of, is a feature of, is part of.
ORDERED LISTING: then, and then, before, after, next, follows, earlier, later, previously, prior, subsequently, precedes, first.
CAUSE AND EFFECT: brings about, results in, causes, affects, leads to, in order to, produces, therefore, because, since, as a result of, this is because, consequently.
COMPARISON AND CONTRAST: is similar to, like, in the same way, is different from, on the other hand, however, but, although, instead, yet, while.

Step 5. Since authors do not express their ideas with only one text structure, give students longer text sections so that they can begin to apply their knowledge to texts with a mixture of structures. As in Step 4, continue to point out to the children how using knowledge of text structures can lead to better comprehension of information read.

Informal analysis of text structures

When teaching a lesson with an expository text, point out to your students the kind of text structure used by the author, stating the appropriate label, such as *simple listing, cause and effect,* etc. If the text incorporates a number of different structures, identify each for the children. Have the children discuss why each section of the text appears to fit a certain text structure (e.g., the first two paragraphs covered the causes of the Civil War, while the next three paragraphs talked about the effects).

Use this procedure consistently during content area lessons. After a time, see if the children can tell you the text structure being used. Have them give reasons for their answers. If the text structure is not apparent, discuss with the children why this is so. For example, some texts may be variations of one of the common types, some may combine two or more types, and some may be so poorly structured that no type is apparent.

Pattern guides

Pattern guides are a variation of the *study guide* approach developed by Herber (1978). Olson and Longnion (1982) recommend pattern guides as a means of improving comprehension of expository text. Although developed for use with secondary students, simple pattern guides can be used with students in the fourth grade and above.

The pattern guide is extremely flexible. You can design pattern guides to focus students' attention on main ideas or on details, on information in one part of the text and not another. Thus, pattern guides can be applied to a range of tasks, from preparing to write an essay to taking a multiple-choice test. Pattern guides also enable you to familiarize students with the different structures found in expository text.

Here are the procedures for developing pattern guides (adapted from Olson & Longnion, 1982, pp. 737–738):

1. Identify the key concepts or information you want the students to learn. Usually, you will want to target just a few concepts, but have the students learn them thoroughly.

2. Read the text, marking the sections which cover your key concepts or information.

3. Identify the type of text structure the author used.

4. Think of how you can bring together (a) the key concepts or information, (b) text structure, and (c) reading comprehension skills. For example, the pattern guide shown in Figure 7.5 is based on a section of text on kinetic theory. The text is written with a cause and effect structure. The pattern guide is designed to have the students connect various causes with their effects.

5. Decide how much help to give the students. One area of help has to do with where the information is located. You can tell students the page and paragraph, the page number alone, or just the chapter.

Other examples of pattern guides, for a text with a compare and contrast structure and one with a list structure, are shown in Figure 7.6. The compare and contrast pattern guide gives students extra help in the form of hints about the content to be given in the answers. The list pattern guide gives extra help in the form of model answers. These show students the type of information to look for and the way to word their answers.

FIGURE 7.5   "Kinetic Theory"—Chapter 12

Cause/Effect

The kinetic theory explains the effects of heat and pressure on matter. Several ramifications of the theory are discussed in this chapter. Be alert to *causal relationships* as you read.

1. Gas exerts pressure on its container because
   A. p. 261, par. 1
   B. p. 261, par. 1

2. What causes pressure to be exerted in each arm of the manometer?
   A. p. 261–262
   B. _____

3. The effects of colliding molecules which have unequal kinetic energy is   p. 266

4. What causes the particles of a liquid to assume the shape of the container?
   p. 269, par. 1

Pattern guide created from *Chemistry, A Modern Course* (Smoot and Price, 1975)
From "Pattern Guides: A Workable Alternative for Content Teachers" by Mary W. Olson and Bonnie Longnion, May 1982 in the *Journal of Reading*. Reprinted with permission of the authors and the International Reading Association.

KEY CONCEPT 4

The teacher should help children develop strategies for studying expository text.

IMPORTANT ASPECTS OF STUDYING

Anderson and Armbruster (1982) define studying as reading with the requirement of having to perform some mental task or procedure, referred to as the *criterion task*. The criterion task might be taking a test, writing a report, or carrying out an experiment. Obviously, each type of criterion task places somewhat different demands on the student. This perspective helps us understand that we need to show students how certain study strategies can be useful in helping them meet the demands of different criterion tasks.

In order to study effectively, Anderson and Armbruster point out, students need knowledge of the criterion task. The more they know about what they

Once you have prepared the guide, go over with students what they will be studying and why. If the students have not worked with pattern guides before, go over the procedures for completing the guide, and perhaps work out the answer to the first question in a group discussion. After the guide has been completed, go over the correct answers with the students. Follow-up activities might include having the students rewrite the material in the guide in their own words, or read it over when preparing for a test.

FIGURE 7.6 *"The United States Divided"—Chapter 14*

Contrast/Compare

Using pages 264–265, you will contrast and compare the repercussions in the South and the North to the Supreme Court's decision in the Dred Scott case.

the South   the North

1. (Hint: newspapers)   1.

2. (Hint: Democratic Party)   2.

3.   3.

4.   4.

Pattern guide created from *The Adventures of the American People* (Graff and Krout, 1970)

have to learn and do, the better they are likely to perform. For example, if we have a list of the topics to be covered on a test, we will study those topics and ignore information on others. If we know that the test will require us to write essays, we might construct outlines for questions likely to be asked. On the other hand if we were going to take a multiple-choice test, we might just make a list of important facts.

The practical implication of this finding is that you should make sure your students have adequate knowledge of the criterion task. Tell them exactly what information you want them to learn. Also tell them how their learning will be evaluated.

According to Anderson and Armbruster, effective studying requires students to learn how to focus attention on the critical information and to think of a way to organize it, so that it can later be used. That is, students must be able to locate text segments that contain the important ideas and figure out how to remember them.

What makes information important also depends on the reader's purpose. For example, suppose that the reader is searching a newspaper article about activities at the state legislature in order to learn about the status of a certain bill. In this case the reader scans the article for the relevant paragraphs and then reads those very closely, ignoring information in the rest of the article. On the other hand, suppose that the reader is interested in gaining an overview of the major bills being considered by the legislature. In this case the reader skims the whole article, looking for the key pieces of legislation but making no effort to remember detailed information on any particular bill. Thus, the information important in the first case is no longer important, because the reader has a different purpose.

Students can be taught to look for signals in the text which may mark information important for different purposes. Identifying and knowing how to use these signals is a part of studying effectively. Among these signals are titles, headings, main idea statements, and key words. The study strategies listed below all involve use of these signals in one way or another.

Effective focusing techniques

Reading and study skills that can help students locate and focus on important information include the following:

Skimming and scanning. In skimming, students move quickly through the text, getting a sense of its content and structure. Skimming is similar to previewing, described earlier, where students are taught to use such signals as chapter titles. In scanning, students have a set purpose for reading and search quickly through the text to locate relevant information. In this case, key words might be an important signal.

Using references and test guides. After students know the topic to be studied, they often need to locate the information in textbooks, tradebooks, dictionaries, encyclopedias, newspapers, and magazines. To identify these sources, they should be able to use the card catalogue to find materials in a library. Once the source is located, students should be able to use other aids (such as a table of contents, index, headings, and guide words) to pinpoint the information sought. Some elementary students may learn to carry out computer searches.

Using visual aids. Students survey illustrations and photographs, graphs and other figures, tables, and maps. Students should be able to "read" or derive meaning from these visual aids, just as they do from text.

Effective study techniques

Anderson and Armbruster (1982) reviewed research on the following common studying techniques: underlining, note-taking, summarizing, student questioning, outlining, and representing text in diagrams. We present below a brief definition of each technique:

Underlining. Students draw a line under important text information, using such signals as topic sentences. *Highlighting* information with a marker is like underlining. According to Anderson and Armbruster, this technique can be effective because students have to make decisions about what to underline, and so presumably separate important from unimportant information. Check their choices of underlined material occasionally to determine if they are actually picking out important information, and watch for students who may have a tendency to "over-underline."

Note-taking. Students seek such signals as key words or phrases in the text, and jot them down or generate phrases on their own. This technique can be effective because it encourages students to reflect on the material when deciding what to write down. If students take notes on information important to the criterion task, this can be a good way of focusing attention properly. Look over their notes occasionally to see that they are learning to take down the information needed to accomplish the criterion task.

Summarizing. Students arrive at a condensed version of important text information, using such signals as summary statements (e.g., sentences beginning with phrases such as "in conclusion"). The summary may be stated verbally or written out. The key to effective use of summarizing is to make sure that the students actually reorder and reword text information, and that this kind of deeper processing of main ideas is required in the criterion task. For example, summarizing may not help with recall of details. For information about how to teach summarizing, refer to Chapter 8.

Student questioning. Students state or write down their own questions about the text. Students can be taught to generate certain kinds of questions, such as those about the main idea, and to look for different signals of importance, depending on the criterion task. This technique can be effective because it causes students to think about and work actively with the text.

Outlining. Students organize text information under major and minor headings, as described later in the hierarchical summary procedure, making use of such signals as subheadings. According to Anderson and Armbruster, most students need to be given careful instruction before they are able to outline text on their own. A problem may arise if students become preoccupied with the outline format itself and proceed to fill in information without really thinking very much about it. Instead, students should learn to use the outline format as a means for organizing and thinking more deeply about text information. Outlining can be very time-consuming. Thus, depending on the criterion task, it may not be the most efficient studying technique.

Representing text in diagrams. Students develop a diagram containing pieces of text information and showing the relationships among the various pieces. Concepts, vocabulary, main ideas, fact, and details can all be included. The diagram is often called a *structured overview* (Herber, 1978), a map, or a web. These diagrams are forms of *visual structures* or *visual displays*, but their purpose is only to show features of the text. They do not include what students already know about the subject, as in semantic mapping, discussed in Chapter 4. *Idea mapping* is a particular method of diagramming the structure of the text and bringing out important ideas and their relationships (Armbruster & Anderson, 1982), and may be suitable for use with advanced fifth and sixth graders. Idea mapping and other similar techniques can be effective because they focus students' attention on all of the ideas in the text. However, as with outlining, mapping must be carefully taught to students and can take a lot of time.

INSTRUCTIONAL GUIDELINES

Instruction in study skills is best embedded in content area instruction. That is, teach children to use a certain study technique as it fits with the criterion task in a content area unit. For example, suppose that your students have just completed a social studies unit on Japan. You plan to have them write a short essay comparing their own lives to the life of a student their age in Japan. Summarizing the text, bringing out the key information to be covered in the essay, might be appropriate here. To take another example, suppose that your students are working on a unit about the history of their region of the United States. You think it important for them to remember some of the causes of the events described later in the text. Outlining might be appropriate here.

Be careful in selecting a study skill to see that this kind of match exists. Do not have the children use a more complex strategy, such as summarizing or outlining, if no good purpose is served. For example, suppose that you are teaching a science unit about electricity. You want the students to learn certain concepts and terms, and you will be giving them a short-answer, fill-in-the-blank test. In this case, having the students underline and take a few notes may be sufficient.

The idea here is to give students a sense of the kinds of study skills they can use to meet different criterion tasks. Having them use an overly elaborate strategy for a simple criterion task will not give them this sense. Rather, try to give students the message that different study skills should be used to meet different goals.

Prediction guides

Nichols (1983) discusses the use of formal and informal prediction guides to increase students' understanding of content area material. Prediction guides are used to build students' interest before they begin reading. They can be used to motivate reading, to call students' attention to the information you think it important for them to retain, and to encourage skimming to find this information.

A formal prediction guide is one written in advance by the teacher. Construct such a guide by listing a number of statements relating to the topic to be studied, as shown in Figure 7.7. Include several incorrect statements in the set.

Have the students place a checkmark in Column A next to each statement they think their reading will show to be correct. When the students have finished reading, you could have them put a checkmark in Column B next to each statement actually supported by the text, a zero next to each statement shown to be incorrect, and a question mark next to each statement neither supported nor disproved. You could also have students rewrite incorrect statements to make them correct. Encourage them to refer to their textbooks to locate the information they need.

FIGURE 7.7 Prediction Guide

Directions: In Column A check those statements you think are true concerning the Twenties, the Depression, and the New Deal. Don't put anything in Column B yet.

A   B

1. Many Americans were characterized by their optimism, prosperity, and materialism at the beginning of the 20s.
2. Women voted for the first time in the 1920 election.
3. After a period of war and tension, people wanted to forget their problems and concentrate on enjoying themselves.
4. Richard Byrd conquered the South Pole.
5. Since booming business was certain to create a great future for Americans, government policies tended to leave it alone.
6. Auto makers were thrilled as cars rolled off the assembly lines, but some people felt this new invention only invited moral decay for America.
7. Movie theaters thrived on sex appeal, a new American ideal.
8. Television began to play an important role in politics.
9. The role of women changed drastically in the 1920s.
10. Prohibition laws were widely disobeyed.

From "Using Prediction to Increase Content Area Interest and Understanding" by James N. Nichols, December 1983 in the *Journal of Reading*. Reprinted with permission of James N. Nichols and the International Reading Association.

Two examples of informal prediction guides are given below (from Nichols, 1983, p. 228). When using the first prediction paragraph frame, have the students read just the title or first paragraph of the text. Then have them make predictions by completing the sentences below. Finally, have the students read to see if their predictions were correct.

From the title/paragraph, I predict that this chapter will be about ——.

The reason I believe this is ——————.

When using the second prediction paragraph frame, first have the students survey the chapter. Then have them complete sentences such as those shown below.

After surveying the chapter, I believe that the major figure(s) will be ——.

Some major events will be ——————.

Some important dates appear to be ——————.

Again, ask the students to read to verify their predictions.

Main idea comprehension

Being able to comprehend the main idea of a passage can be a skill useful across a whole range of criterion tasks. Often, understanding the main idea gives students a way of remembering and organizing information being studied. Baumann (1984) devised a program effective in teaching sixth graders to comprehend main ideas. The students received eight 30-minute lessons as described below. Distinctive features of this program included teaching students to identify supporting details along with main ideas, and not separately; giving them heuristics to foster concepts about main ideas (e.g., visualizing the main idea on an umbrella with supporting details beneath); and having them compose main idea statements instead of simply recognizing them.

In Lesson 1, students were taught to identify a main idea when it was explicitly stated in a paragraph (i.e., each paragraph had a clear topic sentence). They were also shown how to pick out details which supported the main idea.

In Lesson 2, students were introduced to the idea that the topic sentence can be implicit, as well as explicit. They were taught how to identify the "dominant relationship" described by the "subordinate topics" or details in a paragraph. Lesson 3 provided students with a review of the information presented in the first two lessons.

Lessons 4 and 5 moved students from working with paragraphs to working with passages. Students were taught in Lesson 4 to look for explicit statements of the passage theme, and in Lesson 5 for implicit themes. They were told when dealing with passages to think of a "detail" as the main idea of a particular paragraph. Thus, these two lessons built directly upon the foundation laid in the first lessons.

Lessons 6 and 7 focused on the generating of main idea outlines, first for passages with explicit main ideas and then for passages with implicit main ideas. Finally, in Lesson 8, the students reviewed and practiced all of the main idea skills previously introduced.

Instruction in each lesson followed a sequence of five steps. The instructor began by informing students of the purpose of the lesson and of the value of the particular main idea skill to be targeted. In the second step a sample text illustrating use of the skill was presented. The third step was direct instruction of the skill; the fourth, application activities; and the fifth, independent practice.

SQ3R

Robinson's (1961) studying technique, Survey-Question-Read-Recite-Review (SQ3R) is probably better known than any other. SQ3R gives students a systematic procedure for reading and learning text information. Included in SQ3R are the techniques of skimming and student questioning. Vaughan (1982) emphasizes the importance of working interactively with students when first introducing this technique. Give the students an overview of the technique. Discuss each step with the students, what it involves and why it is important. Guide them through each step.

As with any study technique, make sure to match SQ3R with appropriate criterion tasks in the study of content areas. Make sure students understand the purpose for reading (the topic to be targeted, for example) before they begin.

Here are the five steps in the technique:

Survey. Have the students preview the material in the manner described earlier, skimming for headings, introductory and summary statements, illustrations, etc. Get a sense of the content covered and the structure of the text.

Question. Have the students make up questions about information they expect the text to cover. Make sure these questions relate to the purposes set for reading (i.e., that they focus on the proper content and are at the proper level, either main idea or detail). The group may suggest questions, which you can then write on the chalkboard. Later, have the children write questions while working in small groups or in pairs, and then have them write questions individually.

Read. Have the students read the text, with the intent of locating answers to their questions. Encourage them to use note-taking as a memory aid.

Recite. Have the students close their books and try to answer the questions. At first, for group-generated questions written on the chalkboard, the answers can be given orally. Later, have the children try to write their answers.

Review. Have the students read the text to check their answers. Incorrect or incomplete answers should be rewritten.

Hierarchical summary procedure

Taylor (1982) designed this procedure to improve students' ability to deal with the structure and organization of expository text. It should enable fifth and sixth graders to learn and remember information and to write better expository compositions. Taylor reports that most students can master this procedure after eight one-hour lessons. The five steps in the hierarchical summary procedure (previewing, reading, summarizing in an outline, studying, and oral retelling) are described below. Taylor emphasizes the importance of having students write the idea *in their own words* rather than allowing them simply to copy from the text.

Previewing. To begin, students preview a three to five page segment from a content textbook that has headings and subheadings. With the aid of the teacher, students generate a skeleton outline for the segment by writing a Roman numeral for every major section in the reading selection, as designated by a heading. Then they write a capital letter for every subsection, as designated by a subheading. Finally, they leave five or six lines between capital letters where they will list important supporting details from each subsection. By the time students prepare their third hierarchical summary they should be able to generate skeleton outlines on their own.

Reading and outlining. After making skeleton outlines, students read the material subsection by subsection, writing a summary of each subsection as they go. With the teacher's guidance, they generate a main idea statement in their own words for an entire subsection, then they list two to four important supporting details for the main idea they just generated. As a class, they discuss the supporting details they wrote down. Then students repeat the process with the next subsection.

Before students go on to the new section of the text, they generate a topic sentence in their own words for the section they just finished reading. They write this topic sentence by the appropriate Roman numeral on their papers. In the left margin they write key phrases for any subsections which seem to go together. They draw lines between the key phrases and corresponding subsections. Finally, students discuss their topic sentences and key phrases with the teacher. An example of a hierarchical summary is presented in Figure 7.8.

After doing three hierarchical summaries, students should be able to complete them on their own after beginning them with the teacher. By their

---

FIGURE 7.8   *Hierarchical Summary for Social Studies Text Selection Containing One Heading and Six Subheadings*

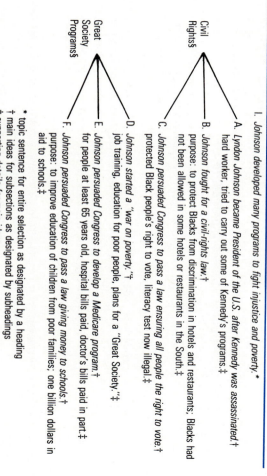

I. *Johnson developed many programs to fight injustice and poverty.* *

    A. *Lyndon Johnson became President of the U.S. after Kennedy was assassinated.*†

Civil
Rights§

    B. *Johnson fought for a civil-rights law.*†
        purpose: to protect Blacks from discrimination in hotels and restaurants; Blacks had not been allowed in some hotels or restaurants in the South.‡

    C. *Johnson persuaded Congress to pass a law ensuring all people the right to vote.*†
        purpose: to protect Black people's right to vote, literacy test now illegal.‡

    D. *Johnson started a "war on poverty."*†
        job training, education for poor people, plans for a "Great Society."‡

Great
Society
Programs§

    E. *Johnson persuaded Congress to develop a Medicare program.*†
        for people at least 65 years old, hospital bills paid, doctor's bills paid in part.‡

    F. *Johnson persuaded Congress to pass a law giving money to schools.*†
        purpose: to improve education of children from poor families; one billion dollars in aid to schools.‡

    * topic sentence for entire selection as designated by a heading
    † main ideas for subsections as designated by subheadings
    ‡ supporting details for main ideas
    § key phrases connecting subsections

From "A Summarizing Strategy to Improve Middle Grade Students' Reading and Writing Skills" by Barbara M. Taylor, November 1982 in *The Reading Teacher*. Reprinted with permission of Barbara Taylor and the International Reading Association.

sixth hierarchical summary, students should be able to write them independently and compare them to a model prepared by the teacher.

Studying and retelling orally.   After reading the textbook material and writing their hierarchical summaries, students study the material. They review the information in the summaries, distinguishing among topic sentences for sections, key phrases connecting subsections, main ideas of subsections, and important details in support of these main ideas.

Finally, students retell orally what they have learned. They tell a partner everything they can remember about the material, thinking of information they wrote on their hierarchical summaries. The partner looks at the summary as the student retells, reminding the student of unrecalled information (Taylor, 1982, pp. 202–204).

According to Taylor, the ideas described above can also be adapted to texts without headings. In this case, have the children first read part of the text. Then have them try to come up with their own main idea statements. Have them list details to support each main idea. Finally, help them compose a topic sentence for the text.

Idea mapping

The idea mapping technique developed by Armbruster and Anderson (1982) is a way of teaching students to locate important information by analyzing text structure. In other words, this technique may be used for the same purpose as the pattern guide. However, as modified by Mason and tried out by teachers, it differs from the pattern guide in that the relationships among important ideas are mapped. The goal is to have students understand the key concepts and their interrelationships. This procedure is best used with students in the upper elementary grades. Sample texts and their corresponding maps (from Armbruster & Anderson, 1982, p. 28ff) are shown in Figure 7.9.

The procedure requires the student to learn to use mapping symbols such as the following:

DEF =: After the equal sign, find and write in the *definition* of a key term or concept which appears in the text.

[[]]: Find *instances* or *examples* of a concept from the text and write them in the double brackets.

[]: Find *Properties* of a concept from the text and write them in the single brackets.

≡: Find information that is *identical* to the defined concept and write it after the symbol.

≈: Find information that is *similar* to a concept and write it after the symbol.

✗: Find information that is *not similar* to a concept and write it after the symbol.

FIGURE 7.9

Examples of Idea Maps

Description

Batholiths are the largest igneous rock bodies. They may form several kilometers below the surface of the earth. They are 50 to 80 kilometers across and extend for hundreds of kilometers in length. Batholiths are too thick for their lower surfaces to be seen. They are exposed at the earth's surface only when the overlying rock has been removed by erosion. Most batholiths are great masses of granite. They form the cores of the world's mountain systems.

(Bishop, M. S., Sutherland, B., & Lewis, P. G. *Focus on earth science.* Columbus, Ohio: Charles E. Merrill, 1981, p. 330)

Batholiths
Largest igneous rock bodies
May form several kilometers below the surface of the earth
50-80 kilometers across
Extend for hundreds of kilometers in length
Too thick for lower surfaces to be seen
Exposed at earth's surface only when overlying rock has been removed by erosion
Most are great masses of granite
Form the cores of world's mountain systems

Temporal Sequence

The iron ore in the ground is usually covered with a thick layer of dirt and rock. This layer must be removed before the actual mining can begin. After the dirt is taken away, huge power-driven shovels dig into the crumbly iron ore. The shovels carry load after load of ore from the pits to railroad cars that are standing nearby.

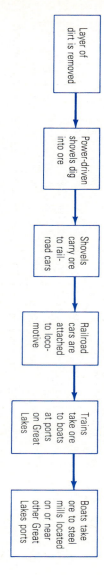

Layer of dirt is removed → Power-driven shovels dig into ore → Shovels carry ore to railroad cars → Railroad cars are attached to locomotive → Trains take ore to boats at ports on Great Lakes → Boats take ore to steel mills located on or near other Great Lakes ports

FIGURE 7.9   *(continued)*

When a long line of cars is filled, the cars are attached to a locomotive. These trains take the ore to boats that are waiting at nearby ports on the Great Lakes. The boats then take the ore to steel mills that are located on or near other Great Lakes ports.

(Gross, H. H., Follett, D. W., Gabler, R. E., Burton, W. L., & Ahlschwede, B. F. *Exploring Our World: The Americas.* Chicago: Follett, 1980. p. 224)

Explanation

In cold or mountainous regions, rocks are often subjected to the action of freezing water because of daily changes in the temperature. During the day, when the temperature is above the freezing point of water (0° C), rainwater or melted snow or ice trickles into cracks in the rocks. During the night, when the temperature falls near the freezing point of water, the trapped water expands as it changes into ice.

As freezing water expands, the expanding ice pushes against the sides of the cracks with tremendous force, splitting the rocks apart. In this way, large masses of rock, especially the exposed rocks on the topics of mountains, are broken into smaller pieces. . . .

(Lesser, M., Constant, C., & Wisler, J. J. *Contemporary Science Book 1.* New York: Amsco School Publications, Inc., 1977. pp. 282–283)

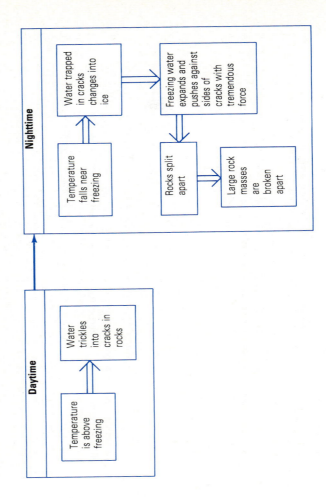

FIGURE 7.9 *(continued)*

Compare/Contrast

Body waves are of two kinds. The *P-wave*, or primary wave, travels forward in a horizontal direction. Rock particles vibrate back and forth. They are pushed close together, then move apart to their original positions. A slinky toy, held at one end, then given a slight jerk, shows the P-wave motion. The *S-wave* or secondary wave, vibrates at right angles to the P-wave. Particles move up and down, but the wave itself travels forward. The S-wave motion is like that of a rope fixed at one end and moved up and down at the free end.

(Bishop, M. S.; Sutherland, B., & Lewis, P. G. *Focus on earth science*. Columbus, Ohio: Charles E. Merrill, 1981, p. 292)

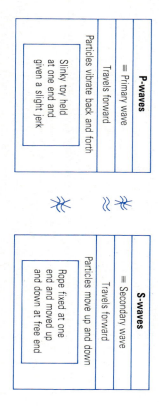

Definition—Example

In this forest biome, you would notice many deciduous trees. *Deciduous trees* grow leaves in the spring which fall from the trees in autumn. Oak, hickory, beech, and maple are deciduous trees.

(Sund, R. B., Adams, D. K., & Hackett, J. K. *Accent on science*. Columbus, Ohio: Charles E. Merrill, 1980, p. 142)

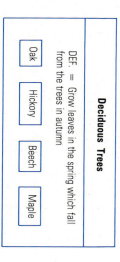

Excerpt from "Idea Mapping: The Technique and its Use in the Classroom" by Armbruster and Anderson from *Reading Education Report #36.* Reprinted with permission from the Center for the Study of Reading.

>: Find information that is *greater than* a concept and write it after the symbol.

<: Find information that is *less than* a concept and write it after the symbol.

->: Find information that *occurs after an event* and write it after the symbol.

=>: Find information that is *causally related* to a concept. Write the cause before the symbol and the result after the symbol.

≈>: Find information that *enables* a concept and write it before the symbol.

The following instructional procedure can be used:

1. To teach students how to recognize the symbols and read an idea map, begin with text they have recently studied. Choose a section organized according to only one structure. A list or an ordered list are good structures to use at first because they are likely to contain information easily found and mapped, such as definitions, examples, and properties of concepts. Read the text carefully and map it out yourself before discussing it with the children.

2. Show students the completely filled-in map. Help them understand how the map helps them learn and remember important information.

3. Work through several filled-in maps with students. As with the Niles procedure (described in Key Concept #2), have students use increasingly more complex and lengthy texts.

4. Make mimeographed handouts for students in which the symbols are mapped out but the text is missing. You can imagine the maps from Figure 7.9 with no text inserted. Hand these out for students to fill in as they read their assigned text. Upon completing the maps, students can discuss the information they found and how they figured out where in the map it belonged. Have them keep their maps as notes to study for tests. After a test has been given, ask students to talk about whether the maps helped them.

5. Older, more capable students who have learned to fill in maps may be taught to make maps of their own. Begin by having them work on well-organized texts and give them help in identifying the kind of structure. Later, they can be given less well-organized and longer texts and asked to identify the kind of structure as well as the relationships among ideas.

SUMMARY

We began by discussing the main reason for reading expository text, which is to learn and remember information. We suggested two means of increasing the opportunities students have to do this type of reading, in the context of either content area lessons or basal reading lessons. We recommended the *concurrent* approach, which calls for the teaching of content and strategies in the same lessons. Systematic procedures for planning and conducting these lessons were presented, along with three lesson frameworks: the concept-text-application approach, the SEARCH procedure, and the five phase instructional sequence.

The importance of making sure that the children understand the purposes for working with a particular expository selection was emphasized. Four activities (reciprocal teaching, informed strategies for learning, ReQuest, and the guided reading procedure) were recommended, because they all help students to learn content while at the same time making them more aware of strategies for comprehending expository text.

Expository texts often follow one of five common structures. These structures were described along with activities for helping students learn to recognize and then use them, to improve their understanding and recall of text information. Finally, we looked at study skills, bringing out the importance of helping students learn to achieve an appropriate match between study skills and the criterion task, or goal they have for studying.

Throughout this chapter, we emphasized the idea that teachers need to plan lessons carefully, both in terms of selecting the content they want students to learn, and of identifying the comprehension and study strategies they want students to use. As in previous chapters, we developed further the theme that students should be actively involved in constructing meaning from text and helped to become increasingly independent in the use of text comprehension strategies.

BIBLIOGRAPHY

REFERENCES

Alvermann, D. E., & Boothby, P. R. (1982). Text differences: Children's perceptions at the transition stage in reading. *Reading Teacher, 36* (3), 298–302.

Anderson, C., & Smith, E. (1984). Children's preconceptions and content area textbooks. In G. Duffy, L. Roehler, & J. Mason (Eds.), *Comprehension instruction: Perspectives and suggestions.* New York: Longman.

Anderson, T. H., & Armbruster, B. B. (1982). Reader and text—Studying strategies. In W. Otto & S. White (Eds.), *Reading expository material.* New York: Academic Press.

Ankney, P., & McClurg, P. (1981). Testing Manzo's guided reading procedure. *Reading Teacher* 1981, *34* (6), 681–685.

Armbruster, B. B. (1984). The problem of "inconsiderate" text. In G. Duffy, L. Roehler, and J. Mason (Eds.), *Comprehension instruction: Perspectives and suggestions.* New York: Longman.

Armbruster, B., and Anderson, T. (1982). *Idea-mapping: The technique and its use in the classroom or Simulating the "ups" and "downs" of reading comprehension.* (Reading Ed. Rep. No. 36.) Urbana, IL: University of Illinois, Center for the Study of Reading.

Baumann, J. F. (1984). The effectiveness of a direct instruction paradigm for teaching main idea comprehension. *Reading Research Quarterly, 20* (1), 93–115.

Baumann, J., & Serra, J. (1984). The frequency and placement of main ideas in children's social studies textbooks: A modified replication of Braddock's research on topic sentences. *Journal of Reading Behavior, 16*, 27–40.

Bridge, C., Belmore, S., Moskow, S., Cohen, S., & Matthews, P. (1984). Topicalization and memory for main ideas in prose. *Journal of Reading Behavior, 16*, 61–80.

Castagna, E. (1982). *Caught in the act.* Metuchen, NJ: The Scarecrow Press.

Charles, R. I. (1981). Get the most out of "word problems." *Arithmetic Teacher, 29*, 39–40.

Estes, T., & Vaughan, J. L. (1978). *Reading and learning in the content classroom.* Boston: Allyn & Bacon.

Gagne, R. M. (1970). *The conditions of learning.* New York: Holt, Rinehart & Winston.

Gaskins, I. W. (1981). Reading for learning: Going beyond basals in the elementary grades. *Reading Teacher, 35* (3), 323–328.

Guthrie, J. T. (1984). Literacy for science and technology. *Journal of Reading, 27* (5), 478–480.

Herber, H. L. (1978). *Teaching reading in content areas.* 2nd ed., Englewood Cliffs, NJ: Prentice-Hall.

Indrisano, R. (1983). *Independent application of SEARCH in reading and language arts.* Ginn Occasional Papers, No. 12. Columbus, Ohio: Ginn.

Kendall, J., Mason, J., & Hunter, W. (1980). Which comprehension? Artifacts in the measurement of reading comprehension. *Journal of Education Research, 73*, 233–236.

Langer, J. (1981). From theory to practice: A pre-reading plan. *Journal of Reading, 25*, 152–156.

Langer, J. (1984). Examining background knowledge and text comprehension. *Reading Research Quarterly, 19* (4), 468–481.

Le Blanc, J. F. (1982). Teaching textbook story problems. *Arithmetic Teacher, 29*, 52–54.

Manzo, A. (1969). The ReQuest procedure. *Journal of Reading, 13*, 123–126

Manzo, A. (1975). Guided reading procedure. *Journal of Reading, 18*, 287–291.

Meyer, B., Brandt, D., & Bluth, G. (1980). Use of top-level structure in text: Key for reading comprehension of ninth-grade students. *Reading Research Quarterly, 16*, 72–103.

Meyer, B. J. F., & Freedle, R. O. (1984). Effects of discourse type on recall. *American Educational Research Journal, 21* (1), 121–143.

Moore, D. W., & Readence, J. E. (1983). Approaches to content area reading instruction. *Journal of Reading, 26* (5), 397–402.

Nichols, J. N. (1983). Using prediction to increase content area interest and understanding. *Journal of Reading, 27* (3), 225–228.

Niles, O. (1965). Organization perceived. In H. Herber (Ed.), *Perspectives in reading: Developing study skills in secondary schools.* Newark, DE: International Reading Association.

Olson, M. W., & Longnion, B. (1982). Pattern guides: Workable alternative for content teachers. *Journal of Reading, 25* (8), 736–741.

Palincsar, A. (1984). The quest for meaning from expository text: A teacher-guided journey. In G. Duffy, L. Roehler, & J. Mason (Eds.), *Comprehension instruction: Perspectives and suggestions.* New York: Longman.

Paris, S. (in press). Teaching children to guide their reading and learning. In T. E. Raphael (Ed.), *The Contexts of school-based literacy.* New York: Random House.

Paris, S. G., Cross, D. R., & Lipson, M. Y. (1984). Informed strategies for learning: A program to improve children's reading awareness and comprehension. *Journal of Educational Psychology, 76*, 1239-1252.

Pearson, P. D., Hansen, J., & Gordon, C. (1979). The effect of background knowledge on young children's comprehension of explicit and implicit information. (Tech. Rep. No. 116.) Urbana, IL: University of Illinois, Center for the Study of Reading.

Robinson, F. P. (1961). *Effective study.* Rev. ed. New York: Harper & Row.

Roehler, L., & Duffy, G. (1984). Direct explanation of comprehension processes. In G. Duffy, L. Roehler, & J. Mason (Eds.), *Comprehension instruction: Perspectives and suggestions.* New York: Longman.

Roth, K. J., Smith, E. L., & Anderson, C. W. (1984). Verbal patterns of teachers: Comprehension instruction in the content areas. In G. Duffy, L. Roehler, & J. Mason (Eds.), *Comprehension instruction: Perspectives and suggestions.* New York: Longman.

Stevens, K. C. (1982). Can we improve reading by teaching background information? *Journal of Reading. 25*, 326-329.

Taylor, B. (1982). A summarizing strategy to improve middle grade students' reading and writing skills. *Reading Teacher, 36*, 202-205.

Taylor, B., & Samuels, S. J. (1983). Children's use of text structure in the recall of expository material. *American Educational Research Journal, 20* (4), 517-528.

Vaughan, J. L. (1982). Instructional strategies. In A. Berger, & H. A. Robinson (Eds.), *Secondary school reading: What research reveals for classroom practice.* Urbana, IL: ERIC Clearinghouse on Reading and Communication Skills and the National Conference on Research in English.

Wong, J., & Au, K. H. (1985). The concept-text-application approach: Helping elementary students comprehend expository text. *Reading Teacher, 38* (7), 612-618.

CHILDREN'S BOOKS CITED

Shogren, M. (1978). The Monster of Loch Ness. In R. B. Ruddell, M. Shogren, & A. L. Ryle, *Moon Magic.* Boston: Allyn & Bacon.

FURTHER READINGS

Barrow, L. H., Kristo, J. V., & Andrew, B. (1984). Building bridges between science and reading. *Reading Teacher, 38* (2), 188-192.

Berry, K. S. (1985). Talking to learn subject matter/learning subject matter talk. *Language Arts, 62* (1), 34-42.

Brown, A. L., Campione, J. C., Day, J. C. (1981). Learning to learn: On training students to learn from text. *Educational Researcher, 10* (2), 14-21.

Dishner, E. K., Bean, T. W., & Readence, J. E. (Eds.) (1981). *Reading in the content areas: Improving classroom instruction.* Dubuque, Iowa: Kendall Hunt.

Moore, D. W., Readence, J. E., & Rickelman, R. (1982). *Prereading activities for content area reading and learning.* Newark, DE: International Reading Association.

Poostag, E. J. (1984). Show me your underlines: A strategy to teach comprehension. *Reading Teacher, 37* (9), 828-830.

CHAPTER 8

Reading and Writing

Reading and writing are broadly defined in my grade one classroom. In October, Eric "wrote" a picture of a house. He paged through *My Puppy is Born* by Joanna Cole and "read" it by looking at the pictures and telling the story. Chrissy wrote her name and a book title. She read her invented spelling in her writing book. For Jessica, writing meant telling a story so she wrote about her house and yard. She read from a basal reader *Rhymes and Tales*.

These behaviors reveal a beginning awareness in the children of the complementary relationships between reading and writing. When asked to demonstrate reading abilities many children went directly to their own writing. And, when I asked children what they would do next to become better readers, they often responded, "Write another book." (Blackburn, 1984, p. 367)

OVERVIEW

In this chapter we emphasize the importance of the relationship between reading and writing. Writing has a great deal of value as an activity in and of itself, but because this is a textbook on the teaching of reading, we focus on how writing can be used to help students become better readers.

We begin by presenting a general perspective on the relationship between reading and writing—that both can be viewed as forms of constructing messages from text. We highlight the *writing process* approach as being particularly consistent with the idea of reading as the construction of meaning from text. We then discuss four key concepts. Each concerns a particular aspect of reading ability that can be strengthened through writing. A variety of instructional activities, some open-ended and some more structured, are described.

The key concepts in this chapter are:

PERSPECTIVE

READING AND WRITING AS CONSTRUCTIVE PROCESSES

Key Concept #1: Experience with the writing process can give students a better understanding of reading as the process of constructing meaning from text.

Key Concept #2: Writing can strengthen students' appreciation and comprehension of literature.

Key Concept #3: Writing can strengthen students' comprehension of expository text.

Key Concept #4: By sending and receiving written messages, students can learn more about literacy as a process of communication.

Writing can have a powerful positive effect on children's reading. To understand why, we need to see how the processes of reading and writing are related to one another. Recent research suggests many parallels between reading and writing. The general idea is that reading and writing both involve the use of language to communicate with others.

Another similarity is that both are *constructive* processes. To most of us, it is intuitively obvious that writing must involve construction, because the writer's efforts result in a physical product, a new text. It is almost as obvious that writing must involve a process, because we are familiar with the idea that writers often produce several drafts before arriving at a final text.

Readers construct messages from text already in existence. Writers, on the other hand, construct messages too but must bring the text into existence by putting together the words to form the messages. In this sense, readers and writers are both *composing* messages, as Tierney and Pearson (1983) point out:

We believe that at the heart of understanding reading and writing connections one must begin to view reading and writing as essentially similar processes of meaning construction. Both are acts of composing. From a reader's perspective, meaning is created as a reader uses his background of experience together with the author's cues to come to grips both with what the writer is getting him to do or think *and* what the reader decides and creates for himself. As a writer writes, she uses her own background of experience to generate ideas and, in order to produce a text which is considerate to her idealized reader, filters these drafts through her judgments about what her reader's background of experience will be, what she wants to say, and what she wants to get the reader to think or do. In a sense both reader and writer must *adapt* to their perceptions about their partner in negotiating what a text means.   (p. 568)

While the act of reading does not necessarily entail writing, the act of writing almost always involves reading. This is because writers usually go back and review what they have written before they go on writing. Thus, when they write, children produce texts which may be used to help them become better readers. Also, insights gained while producing these texts, because they encourage active involvement with print, may improve reading as well as writing ability.

Four subprocesses of writing

Before we spell out specific relationships between reading and writing, we present a more detailed explanation of the process of writing. As you read this section, try to guess at the parallels between reading and writing identified by researchers. According to Humes (1983), research on the process of writing shows it to involve four subprocesses: (1) planning, (2) translating, (3) reviewing, and (4) revising (the discussion below is based on Humes, 1983, pp. 205-212).

Planning. Writers are actively engaged in planning at all stages of producing a text, before, during, and after they have put down words. Writers think of the ideas they want to express, gathering material from external sources as well as their own minds. Then they organize the ideas, i.e., decide how the text will be structured, and set goals for themselves, i.e., decide what they will work on at that point. Good writers spend more time planning than poor writers. They use this time mainly to plan at a global level, while poor writers tend to focus planning at the level of words and sentences.

Translating. Humes defines translating as "the process of transforming meaning from one form of symbolization (thought) into another form of symbolization (graphic representation)." (p. 208) That is, in translating the writer puts thoughts down as written words. Other terms such as "writing," "recording," and "drafting" are also used for this same process. Translating is made extremely complex because of the many elements the writer must deal with at the same time, ranging from spelling and punctuation to clarity and audience. With good writers the "mechanics," many lower level writing skills such as proper spelling and grammar, become automatic. This enables them to concentrate on higher level writing skills such as clarity and elegance of phrasing.

Reviewing. This is the act of reading back over what has been written to determine whether the words convey the intended message. Writers review to see where they are in their overall plan for the text, whether more planning is needed, whether the text needs revision, whether the text is complete, whether words have been misspelled, and so on. Good writers tend to think over their text at the level of style and audience. On the other hand, poor writers generally review for errors, although they frequently fail to catch them. Good writers also seem to review their work more often than poor writers.

Revising. Revising is the process of making changes in the text and in one's thinking about it. According to Humes, revising occurs throughout the composing of a text, not only when a draft is completed. Revising may be at the level of correcting punctuation and spelling or at the level of substantially reorganizing or adding to the text. Humes points out that experienced writers "view revising as a process of structuring and shaping their discourse" (p. 211). They use their first draft to map out the territory to be explored, perhaps making changes in theme. Less experienced writers, however, tend to make changes at the word or phrase level.

Features common to both reading and writing

While reading the description of the writing process, you may already have guessed some of the important parallels between reading and writing. The first parallel, of course, is that reading and writing are both processes, with identifiable subprocesses, for constructing or composing meaning from text. In the act of constructing meaning when reading and writing, different sources of information, including one's knowledge of the world, come into play. Second, both reading and writing require people to control their thought processes. We pointed out in Chapters 5 and 6 the importance of control over one's reading activities, in the form of planning, monitoring, and evaluating. Similarly, planning, reviewing, and revising are of importance in writing. Third, we discussed in Chapter 3 how fluent reading depends on lower level word identification skills having become automatic. In a similar manner, proficiency at writing depends on the "mechanics" of writing becoming automatic.

Tierney and Pearson (1983) point out other similarities between reading and writing. Reading, like writing, requires the development of a "first draft" or some initial picture of what is going on with the text. Reading and writing both involve *alignment*, or the taking of a stance which allows one to collaborate, and hence communicate, with the author or audience. Revising is an activity commonly associated with writing and not reading, but Tierney and Pearson argue that readers can often benefit from the opportunity to pause and reflect on their "first draft" impressions of the text, and to develop alternate interpretations.

> . . . what drives reading and writing is this desire to make sense of what is happening—to make things cohere. A writer achieves that fit by deciding what information to include and what to withhold. The reader accomplishes that fit by filling in gaps (it must be early in the morning) or making uncued connections (he must have become angry because they lost the game). All readers, like all writers, ought to strive for this fit between the whole and the parts and among the parts. (p. 572)

Development of children's writing ability

Like reading, writing is an ability which develops gradually over time. Contrary to what we might expect, children do not move in a set manner from writing words, to writing sentences, to writing paragraphs. Rather, the process of learning to write appears to move forward in a much more exploratory and inventive way.

Consider, for example, the story *All About Ants* shown in Figure 8.1, written by a six-year-old boy named Kevin. The top half of the figure shows Kevin's work with *invented spelling,* or the arrangement of letters that he has chosen to represent words. The lower half of the figure shows the correct or conventional spelling of the words in Kevin's story. We can see that Kevin is simultaneously learning about words, sentences, and the features of an exciting story.

FIGURE 8.1 **Sample Stories**

"All About Ants," Showing Invented Spelling

Ains r mvn in a bld and ther wra insid and ot
A man kam to kal the adts and a lae was tik a baf
6 siks mnd kan to kal the adts ther r im tip fo the adts
Tje adts ther tid dkn the mi per siat bui
the r in the pis the man cot sime fo the adts
the adts cat a man
a man lqcd the adts
the adtst r tak the gid
the mans mrn kid sim fo the adts
2 mant kid 1 nis and a mid adts
the mant fir a lich ovf the adts daf
a man kid 10 adst
the mant r win the mant sisitt fir on the adts
the adst r at hie the adst r in the kins

Text as it appeared in the Student's Published Book

Ants are moving in a building. They are inside and outside.
A man came to kill the ants. A lady was taking a bath.
Six men came to kill the ants. They are on top of the ants.
The ants are tearing down the Empire State Building.
The ants are in the pipes. The men caught some of the ants.
The ants caught a man.
The man electrocuted the ants.
The ants are taking the gold
The man's machines killed some of the ants.
Two men killed one nest and a mother ant.
The ants are losing.
The man threw a latch over the ants' door.
A man killed ten ants.
The men are winning. The men shoot fire on the ants.
The ants are at Hawaii. The ants are in containers.

From "KDS CN RIT SUNR THN WE THINGK" by Susan Sowers. Reprinted with permission of the author.

In a study of her son, Bissex (1980) presents a detailed picture of one child's reading and writing development through most of the elementary school years, beginning at age 5. For the first two months she noticed that Paul was reading labels and signs and making labels on his pictures and for games. His word writing was at the stage where he could use the initial and other

EXERCISE

Reflect upon the processes that you would follow in writing a paper for one of your classes at school. Jot down answers to these questions:

Choice of topic

(1) How do you know what to write about? Does the instructor usually assign the topic or do you choose the topic yourself?

(2) Under which condition do you feel more motivated to write, when the instructor has chosen the topic or when you have?

Steps in writing

(1) What do you do when you first begin writing? For example, do you make an outline, draft a first paragraph, or draw a diagram of your ideas?

(2) How easy or difficult do you find it to begin writing?

(3) How many different drafts do you usually go through? Do you find it easy or difficult to revise what you have written?

(4) Do you find it helpful to talk to other people about your paper, or to have someone else read it and give you comments?

Attitude toward writing

(1) Do you enjoy writing? If so, what kinds of writing do you find enjoyable and why?

(2) If you don't enjoy writing, what do you dislike about it and why?

(3) Do you think it likely that an elementary student would share the attitude you have toward writing? Why or why not?

Many teachers, like most people, really don't like to write and are not very aware of the processes they use as writers. Perhaps your answers to the questions in this exercise also reflect this common pattern. Teachers need to be aware of their own attitudes, experiences and practices as writers, including the fears they have had to conquer, to be effective in teaching children to write. It's valuable in many writing lessons for teachers to share their own experiences as writers with students. In their behavior teachers model the role of adult writer, just as they model the role of adult reader. Thus, the most effective teachers of writing will often be those who have come to enjoy writing themselves and so transmit a positive attitude toward writing to their students.

As you read the rest of this chapter, and when you teach writing to children, reflect back on your answers to the questions above. See if insights into your own activities as a writer can make you more sensitive to the difficulties children might experience with different types of writing.

major consonants. During the next two months he began to analyze words into sound components and to read and write phonetically. When he was five and a half he began writing longer messages and tried to figure out how to separate words and syllables. When he was six he began to use more conventional spelling patterns and could represent most consonants and short vowels correctly. In the next year he read far more than he wrote. His writing consisted of his own spelling list (words that were harder than those given by the teacher) and a personal accounting of his activities and possessions. From age 7 to 9 he became interested in reading and writing about content area topics. Motivated by school assignments, he wrote stories and science reports, kept a personal diary, and worked on a newspaper and quiz booklets for friends. During his tenth year his writing centered around activities with friends, including a humor magazine, science fiction, and a movie script.

Studies also indicate that, while reading and writing are related processes, individual children are not necessarily at the same overall level of development in both reading and writing. Sulzby (in press), for example, found that children who were already reading in kindergarten varied in their writing development; some were able to use conventional spelling and some were only able to produce letter-strings. Teachers who follow a writing process approach (described below) often report that the students who are the best readers in the class are not the best writers. In short, while children's reading and writing ability develop together, they do not emerge as exact mirror images of one another.

KEY CONCEPT 1

Experience with the writing process can give students a better understanding of reading as the process of constructing meaning from text.

THE WRITING PROCESS APPROACH

In the *writing process* approach advocated by Graves (1983a), children take charge of their own development as writers. The children themselves choose what they want to write about. They have the opportunity to write every day, and so to gain experience with each of the four subprocesses outlined above. For example, children are encouraged to talk about or "rehearse" the ideas they would like to write about.

At the heart of this approach is the writing conference (discussed in more detail later), when children meet with the teacher or other students to discuss the information in their drafts. As a result of these conferences, children may decide to revise their drafts. Graves (1981) writes:

When children revise they demonstrate their changing visions of information, levels of thinking, what problems they are solving, and their level of control over the writing process. Revision is not only an important tool in the writer's repertoire, but is one of the best indices of how children change as writers. (p. 23)

In the writing process approach, children select certain pieces to be published. *Publishing* involves putting their writing in a form to be shared with others. In the classroom publishing may take many forms. For example, an individual child may publish a story by printing it neatly, and then adding drawings, in a booklet with a construction paper cover. Or the teacher may type the child's text. Publishing is important because it makes children aware of writing as an act of communication and heightens their sense of audience. Generally, children are encouraged to publish what they consider to be their best work or the work they would most like to share. They learn, as professional writers do, that not every piece should be published, only one's best work. This selectivity tends to lead children to the thoughtful revising and polishing of their writing.

Classroom connections between reading and writing

Teachers who use a writing process approach can develop children's understanding of the relationships between reading and writing and thus give them a deeper understanding of reading as the process of constructing meaning from text. Blackburn (1984), a first grade teacher experienced in the writing process approach, outlines five ways in which writing and reading can be connected to one another at the classroom level. In the discussion below, we emphasize how each connection strengthens children's concepts about reading, leading them to become more actively involved in directing their own learning to read.

According to Blackburn, the importance of *invention* is that it allows children to take charge of their own learning right from the start. In the reading of books, as in writing, children are permitted to approximate the performance of mature readers, as advocated in Chapter 2. For example, they can begin by paraphrasing the story lines in books and later start to attend more closely to the words and letters in the text itself. Allowing this type of approximation is consistent with the idea that reading is the process of constructing meaning from text, and the children can begin to construct meaning from text with whatever reading and language skills they have. They can write their own stories even though they are not yet able to spell many words or construct grammatically correct sentences.

Choice is valuable in helping children develop their own tastes in reading. Having a choice gives children the opportunity to reflect on what is important to them. Blackburn found her students often selected books on familiar topics. This made it easier for them to make predictions and to use context clues to identify words. Having a choice about what to write motivates children to put their thoughts down on paper and seek to express them in a coherent fashion.

Discussion occurs during writing conferences (described in more detail below) and around books. Children in classrooms with a writing process approach come to see themselves as authors and so tend to take a more critical and questioning attitude toward the writing of the adult authors whose works they read. They seem to feel that they are in a more direct *social interaction* with the author. They also seem more aware of the importance of the reader's purpose and reactions when reading a particular text. Reading, like writing, becomes an active process. Here, for example, are questions Blackburn's students asked of Chrissy, who had just read aloud to the group a story from a basal reader (*P*, *I*, and *E* are the students' initials).

P: Why did you want to read this story?
I: Do you think the author should have added more information?
E: Do you think this book is easy or hard?
P: How did you learn to read this?
P: Do you think you could write a better story than this?
I: I wonder who the author is.
P: What do you think you'll work on next?
E: Do you think it's going to be hard?
   (p. 372)

Notice that the children's last two questions highlight the idea that writing is an ongoing process.

Revision, according to Blackburn, requires lingering over a text and being able to see it from different perspectives. In writing, writers learn to rethink what they have written, while in reading they learn to look for different interpretations of the text. The principle of revision is reinforced for students through the discussion of text, books and one's own writing, with classmates and teacher.

Publication involves the public demonstration of the child's ability, whether in reading or writing. Blackburn (1984) writes:

The individual who writes a book or learns to read one sits in the author's chair and reads the book to the class. Each child is known for the books he or she has published and for the books he or she is able to read. The achievement gives the child status, but this status isn't conferred by the teacher through ranking and judging the child's performance and ability. It comes from the class as a whole in appreciation of what the author/reader has added to the community's resources. What is first an individual achievement, quickly becomes the accomplishment of all as they go on to master the new books they are introduced to.   (pp. 372-373)

INSTRUCTIONAL ACTIVITIES

Writing folders

The purpose of using writing folders (Newman, 1983, developed by Graves) is to show students that writing is an ongoing process of developing and expressing one's own ideas. This activity can be used with students of any age.

Give each student a file folder with his or her own name on it. Students keep all of the writing they are working on in their folders. Have students put the date on each piece of writing and keep pages for each piece clipped together. Often, they will have more than one piece in progress at the same time. Having all this material in one place gives students an awareness of the writing process and of their own development as writers.

When using this approach, *topic choice* is essential. That is, students should always be allowed to decide what they want to write about. In the inside front cover of their folders, students can keep a list of topics they might write about at some future time.

Teachers most often use folders simply as a means to keep a complete record of all of the writing an individual child has done. In Newman's approach, however, use of writing folders is meant to provide privacy, to encourage students to take risks when they write and to concentrate on the message of each piece, rather than the conventions of writing. For this reason, Newman recommends that the teacher ask students' permission before reading the material in their folders.

Writing conferences

Writing conferences give students the opportunity to gain insight into their own writing. The conference centers on a particular piece the student has written. It gives the writer the opportunity to learn about the effectiveness of his or her writing and to answer questions about the topic chosen or process used to write about it. The writer may meet with the teacher or with another student. In many classrooms the writer often meets in conferences with other students before meeting with the teacher.

Russell (1983), drawing upon the work of Calkins (1979, 1980), had sixth graders in her class refer to the following list of basic questions when conducting a writing conference with one of their classmates. The questions can be applied to any topic and give the child conducting the conference ideas to be discussed with the writer. A much shorter and less elaborate list may be used in a class with younger children.

1. What is your favorite part?
2. What problems are you having?
3. Which part are you having trouble with?
4. How do you feel?
5. Does your writing end abruptly? Does it need a closing?
6. Do you show feelings or events with specific examples or do you only tell about them?
7. Does your lead sentence "grab" your audience?
8. Do your paragraphs seem to be in the right order?
9. Is each paragraph on one topic?
10. Can you leave out parts that repeat or that fail to give details about your subject?
11. Can you combine some sentences?
12. Can you use precise verbs such as "sprinted" instead of "ran quickly" in places?
13. What do you plan to do next with this piece of writing?   (p. 335)

This girl is talking with the teacher about an idea she has for a story. The teacher uses these brief conferences to help her kindergarten students develop as writers.

Because students will be at different stages in their writing, Russell and others have found it impractical to have a set time when everyone in the class must take part in writing conferences. Instead, allow students to decide when they need a conference about a particular piece of writing, and with whom they would like to have the conference. You and your students may need to try a number of different arrangements before arriving at the best way to manage writing conferences. Russell and her students worked out the following set of procedures. Procedures will vary from class to class, but this is an example of a workable system and should give you an idea of the kinds of issues which may need to be resolved.

1. Three conference centers were designated. The students asked permission to conference. The rest of the students in the room were to be quiet and writing.
2. Students were to take their basic list of questions with them to a conference center so they could refer to them if necessary.
3. The writers were to read their drafts orally to their conferencing partners.
4. There was to be no proofreading or correction of mechanical errors at these sessions.
5. Students were to have a minimum of one conference session for each writing assignment.
6. Writers were to have the option of conferencing only with me.
   (p. 336)

Publishing children's writing

Graves (1983b) stresses that "[m]oving toward a more durable product that will be shared with other audiences leads children to fuss more over the exactness of their writing" (p. 845). Publishing children's writing in little books shows them that their work is valued and is good enough to be shared with others. Publishing emphasizes the idea that writing is a form of communication requiring a consideration of one's audience. Thus, it reinforces the concept of authorship, including the responsibilities authors have to their readers.

Children do not need to publish every piece they write, and they should be led to understand that authors often publish only a small number of the pieces they have written. Let the children select the pieces they want to publish. With younger children, these may be typed, one sentence to a page, using a primary typewriter. Include a title page with the author's name. Put the pages in a durable and attractive cover of some kind, using oaktag, wallpaper samples, etc., and staple or sew the book together. Allow the author to illustrate each page. Be sure the title is also printed on the front cover of the book.

Place the books the children have published in the library corner, to give them the same status as tradebooks. Treat the publishing of books as a special occasion by announcing the authors and titles of new books to the class.

The author's chair

The "author's chair" is a chair where individual children can sit and read aloud to the other students. The child sitting in the author's chair reads aloud to the class one of his or her own drafts or published books, a classmate's published book, or a tradebook. At times the teacher may also read a book to the class.

After the book has been read, the first response made by the audience is to receive or express acceptance of the piece. As Hansen (1983) describes it, the children will clap for the author and then make comments about the parts of the book they liked best. Then the audience addresses questions to the author.

If a tradebook has been read, and the author therefore is not present, the group speculates about the author's possible responses. When dealing with tradebooks, the children know that they, as readers, can agree or disagree with the decisions made by professional authors. A great deal of learning takes place in these sessions:

These children learn that sometimes authors leave out too much information and may have to explain their texts. But the questioners learn much more than just the answers to their queries. They have gathered to respond to another author's work, and they continue to learn it's their responsibility as readers to ask questions. (p. 973)

Besides setting up an author's chair, you can choose a child to be "author of the week" (Graves & Hansen, 1983). Put a photograph of the child on the bulletin board along with a list of the titles of the student's published books. Put the books in pockets and encourage the other children to post comments about them. From among these published books, have the author choose his or her favorite, and make copies for the other children to read. Give the author of the week several opportunities to sit in the author's chair and read aloud to the class, particularly his or her own published books.

Classmates respond with interest to the story being read by this boy, seated in the Author's Chair.

Having an author's chair in the classroom gives teachers the chance to observe the development of their students' concept of authorship. Using the author's chair as one of their focal points, Graves and Hansen (1983) studied first grade children's learning to read and write, especially development of their concept of authorship. They observed children going through three phases in understanding this concept. In the *replication phase*, the children began with a vague notion that authors somehow "write books." They had little or no understanding of what an author actually did when writing a book. In the *transition phase*, the children began to see themselves as authors. Once they had gone through the different parts of the writing process themselves, including publishing a book, the concept of authorship became real to them. In the *option-awareness phase*, the children recognized that authors made many decisions while writing. For example, they could decide in their own writing to describe what actually happened or to add a fictitious event to make a story better. Teachers could observe to see if their own students go through similar phases.

KEY CONCEPT 2

Writing can strengthen students' appreciation and comprehension of literature.

STRENGTHENING LITERARY APPRECIATION THROUGH THE CONCEPT OF AUTHORSHIP

When writing pieces on topics of their own choosing, children come to see themselves as authors and thus gain a deeper insight into the thinking of professional authors. They understand the many decisions the professional author has to make, for example, in choosing the words to convey an idea clearly and elegantly. They also have the opportunity to evaluate critically their own decisions as writers and the decisions of other writers in the class. This critical evaluation requires a thorough comprehension of the text, as it actually stands and as it might otherwise be. Thus, through their own experience as authors, children can learn to appreciate and comprehend literature.

Explicit instruction to strengthen literary appreciation and comprehension

Appreciation and comprehension of literature may be developed through teacher-directed activities. The activities to follow give children knowledge of specific genres and story structures. These activities place some restrictions on children's choice of topic and the form their writing will take for the purpose of having a group or the whole class share in a common experience or receive instruction in the same area. The goal of these activities is to involve students with different forms of literature in active and challenging ways. They may be used to broaden students' backgrounds as readers and writers in classrooms following either a process approach or another approach to writing.

INSTRUCTIONAL ACTIVITIES

The following activities present more structured ways to help children plan and write poems and stories.

Writing poetry

Freeman (1983) describes a program for encouraging children in the upper grades to write poetry. The first of the four steps in this program is described in detail below.

Meeting poetry. During the first session, read selected poems aloud to the children. Have them respond to the ideas in the poems, rather than to their language and form. Make books of poetry available to the children and encourage them to find poems they especially enjoy and would like to read aloud to the class. Harms and Lettow (1983) provide a listing of excellent collections of poetry for children published since 1970.

At the second session, let the children do most or all of the poetry reading. Encourage discussion of both ideas and form. Continue to hold readings like this so the children will have a variety of forms to choose from when they do their own writing.

In the third session, make language and word patterns the main topic of discussion. Freeman suggests using an alliteration word game developed by

Allen and Allen (1976) which results in a four line "poem." The first line consists of the name of something, the second of the name plus a descriptive term, the third adds an action word, and the fourth a word describing the action. Here is an example:

> Bees
> Buzzing bees
> Buzzing bees bumble
> Buzzing bees bumble boldly

Give the children the chance to make up a number of these poems on their own. Have them illustrate their favorites. Those who wish to do so may share their poems with the class.

Other steps. Later steps in Freeman's program involve introducing the children to two other forms of poetry, such as the *terquain*. The terquain is a three line form. A one word subject is given in the first line, two or three descriptive words are given in the second, and a word showing one's feelings in the third. Here is an example of a student's terquain (p. 240):

> Storms
> Horrifying, terrifying
> Destruction.

Written responses to literature

Atwell (1984) and Smith (1982) describe the enthusiasm for books generated by exchanging letters with comments on favorite books. The purpose of having students give written responses to literature is to encourage them to share their enthusiasm for reading with others, to feel that they are part of a *community of readers*. These activities have a different purpose and are structured somewhat differently from conventional book reports. Teachers often use book reports as a means of motivating students to read independently and of checking to see that they have actually done the reading. The audience for a book report, then, is usually the teacher, not the other students in the class.

Here are ideas for the sharing of books likely to be more interesting to students than writing book reports:

Create a space on the bulletin board where students can post "advertisements" for books recently read which they think their classmates would also enjoy. The advertisements could take the form of posters including the book's title and author, a short blurb meant to tantalize the prospective reader, and a recommendation (what the student who created the poster liked best about the book).

Have students write another story with the same main characters or in the same genre. For example, students who read a number of "Encyclopedia Brown" stories might write their own detective stories.

If you are using dialogue journals (described under Key Concept #4), suggest that the children write to you about the reading they are doing. In your responses you can share your own enthusiasm for reading and suggest other books they might find interesting.

Story patterns

This activity developed by Smith and Bean (1983) can help to improve children's comprehension of stories. It also gives them an opportunity to write stories of their own.

Select a short storybook with a simple plot (such as *The Wonderful Feast* by Slobodkina). Read the story aloud to the children, perhaps twice.

Ask if the children see a pattern in the story. Working from the children's responses, draw a chart presenting the events in the story in order, as shown in the left-hand column of Figure 8.2. In the story of the wonderful feast, the farmer feeds the horse. After the horse has eaten, there is enough food left over for the other creatures, each smaller than the one before, an ant being the last of them.

Reread all or parts of the story as necessary until the children give you the

FIGURE 8.2   *Story Pattern of "The Wonderful Feast" and a Classroom Story*

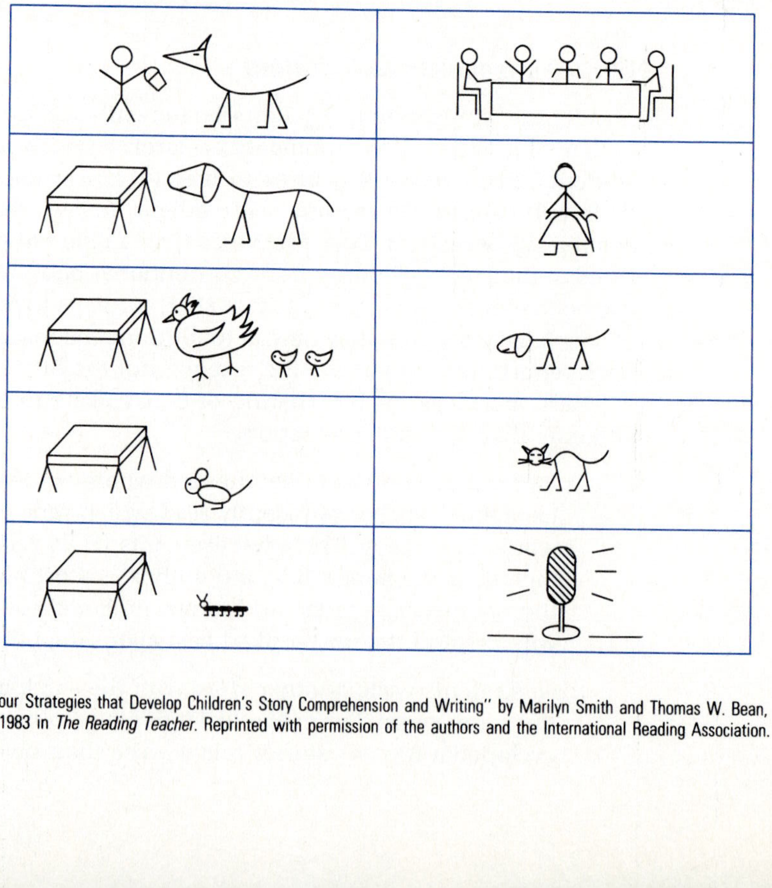

From "Four Strategies that Develop Children's Story Comprehension and Writing" by Marilyn Smith and Thomas W. Bean, December 1983 in *The Reading Teacher*. Reprinted with permission of the authors and the International Reading Association.

information needed to complete the chart. Have the children use the chart to retell the story.

Have the children make up a story of their own using the same pattern. In this case, the teacher might suggest starting with a family eating dinner. The children can then name other people and animals who might take some of the leftover food.

Have each of the children draw or write a story using the new version of the story pattern. The drawing a child might have done is shown in the right-hand column of Figure 8.2.

Probable passages

Teachers working with older children might wish to try Wood's (1984) probable passages activity, which is also based on familiarizing children with the structure of the story. This is a practical method for integrating writing with instruction centered on basal reader stories.

Preparation stage.   (1) Analyze the selection for the most significant concepts or for terms that may need extra emphasis. Present those words on the board or on an overhead projector. The words listed below and the sample lesson are from a basal reader story "The Doughnut Machine that Wouldn't Stop" (Sedgwick, 1978):

Tomas	machine
Mr. Tucker	delicious
doughnuts	customer
jelly-cinnamon-	bank loan
honey	Whirr!
huge	Buzz!
flour	invented
Clunk!	Mr. Redstone
start-button	

(2) Present the categories that correspond with the appropriate story frame (see Figure 8.3). You can change the categories and corresponding story frame depending upon the type of story to be read.

(3) On another section of the board or on another transparency, present the incomplete story frame that will be used both before and after reading. Note that the story frame corresponds with the categories listed in Step 2.

Incomplete probable passage

The story takes place _____ _____. _____ is a character in the story who _____ _____. A problem occurs when _____ _____. After that, _____ _____. Next, _____. The problem ends when _____ _____. The story ends _____ _____.

FIGURE 8.3 Incomplete Story Frame

Setting	Character(s)	Problem	Problem-solution	Ending

FIGURE 8.4 Completed Story Frame

Setting	Character(s)	Problem	Problem-solution	Ending
"doughnut shop" "bakery"	Tomas, "a little boy" Mr. Tucker, "the owner of the doughnut shop"	Whirr! Buzz! Clunk! machine flour start-button huge	bank loan invented customer "money"	delicious jelly-cinnamon-honey doughnut

From "Probable Passages: A Writing Strategy" by Karen D. Wood, February 1984 in *The Reading Teacher*. Reprinted with permission of Karen D. Wood and the International Reading Association.

Prereading stage. (4) Read the list of key terms to the students and have them repeat each word. (This practice is beneficial when words are in their hearing vocabularies but not in their reading vocabularies.)

(5) Tell the students to use the words to construct a story line mentally. Then have the students "slot" the words in the appropriate categories (see Figure 8.4). Point out that some words may fit in more than one category and that they can fill in with other words not listed that their background knowledge dictates are feasible predictions (see words in quotation marks in Figure 8.4). You can also require students to justify their responses. In this way they must verbalize their own version of the probable passage.

(6) Next, direct the students' attention to each line of the story frame and have them use these words to develop a logical probable passage. To help them reduce lengthy responses, you may need to ask questions such as, "How can we make that idea fit here?" or, "How can we reword that sentence to make it shorter and more meaningful?" The group thus reaches a consensus regarding the content and direction of the predicted passage.

Probable passage

The story takes place *in a doughnut shop. Mr. Tucker is a character in the story who owns the store. A problem occurs when Tomas, a little boy,* pushes the start-button. After that, the machine goes whirr, buzz, and clunk and a huge doughnut pops out. Next, a customer comes in. The problem is solved when they are given a bank loan and Mr. Tucker and Tomas invent a way to stop the machine. The story ends when Tomas eats a delicious, jelly-cinnamon-honey doughnut.

Reading stage. (7) The students either read or listen to the selection.

Postreading stage. (8) After reading, the class makes necessary changes in categorized words.

(9) Finally, they modify the story frame to reflect the actual story events.

Actual passage

The story takes place in *a doughnut shop. Tomas is the character who invented the jelly-cinnamon-honey doughnut. Mr. Tucker is the owner of the store. A problem occurs when Tomas pushes the start-button and can't figure out how to stop the machine. After that, he pushes all the buttons together, the machine goes whirr, buzz, and clunk and a huge jelly-cinnamon-honey doughnut pops out. Next, Mr. Redstone, a customer, comes in and buys all the doughnuts. The problem is solved when customers come from all around to buy the doughnuts and Mr. Tucker doesn't have to take out a bank loan. The story ends when Mr. Tucker lets Tomas have a free jelly-cinnamon-honey doughnut every day.*

The entire procedure may take two to three language arts/reading periods, depending upon the length of the story. After several experiences with this concept, students can work in small groups to construct their own probable passages. They can then share their predictions with the class to note the range of alternatives. Similarly, in the postreading stage students can reconstruct the actual selection in groups (Wood, 1984, pp. 497-499).

Story style

Acquiring an ear for differences in writers' styles may involve careful instruction, according to Church and Bereiter (1984). They developed the following approach for use with upper elementary and high school students. The texts used were those the students had already understood and studied.

Teachers first involved the students in "think alouds" (for a full description of think alouds, see Chapter 9). The students read aloud and talked about their reactions to the text. Then they were asked to describe everything they noticed about the way it was written. As a second task students compared two versions of a passage from the text, one written in a contemporary style, the other in a more ornate or archaic style. They were asked to choose the style they preferred and, given a different passage, to rewrite it in that style.

KEY CONCEPT 3

Writing can strengthen students' comprehension of expository text.

LEARNING ABOUT THE STRUCTURE OF EXPOSITORY TEXT

According to Hennings (1982), elementary school students may have few opportunities to work with headings and to learn about the structure of expository prose because the material in basal readers is primarily stories and poems. Especially in the primary grades, students are likely to receive much more exposure to texts written in narrative rather than expository forms. Yet much of the text students will have to deal with, in school as well as in the workplace and community, is expository in nature.

Writing can be a means of strengthening students' ability to deal with expository as well as narrative text. This can be accomplished by having students analyze expository text and then rewrite the ideas identified, and by having them express their own ideas in expository prose.

INSTRUCTIONAL ACTIVITIES

Teaching/learning strategies for developing understanding of expository text

Hennings (1982) proposes a series of eight teaching/learning strategies, centered on writing, to improve students' ability to comprehend expository text.

The starting point is to have the students read a text or gather information from other sources of information. Students then move through a process leading them to work with the information gathered, to produce their own report, and to use what they have learned to comprehend and evaluate other expository texts. The process consists of these strategies:

1. factstorming
2. categorizing the facts stormed
3. drafting paragraphs
4. sequencing paragraphs
5. drafting introductions and conclusions
6. organizing the report
7. interpreting texts with similar structures
8. summarizing, synthesizing, judging, and doing more writing

Brief descriptions of each activity follow (adapted from Hennings, 1982, pp. 9-15):

Factstorming. Begin by presenting the informational content to the students. Among other things, you could read a passage aloud to them or have them read a text themselves. Factstorming can then take place. In factstorming, students call out words and phrases on the topic. You or selected students write these items on chart paper or the chalkboard.

Categorizing the facts stormed. The next step is to organize the facts obtained. One method is to select an item and have the students identify others related to it. These items are circled and put into a list representing the first category. The students then sort the remaining items into a variety of lists representing the other categories. Be sure to have students give reasons for putting items together.

You can also help the students to develop a *data chart.* This is a matrix used to organize the facts. When working with first and second graders you might wish to give them the categories for organizing the data. With older children, you can guide them to infer the categories. Figure 8.5 shows a data chart on the topic of Thanksgiving developed after factstorming by a third grade class.

The next step is to have the students put the information in the text into a data chart. To accomplish this task, have them study the introductory and concluding paragraphs and the headings. This will help them to pick out labels for the rows and columns of the data chart (for an example, see Figure 8.6). Later, when discussing sections of the text, students can use the data chart to remind themselves of important points as well as details. Used in this way, a data chart can show them the value of having an organized set of notes.

Drafting paragraphs. Have the students use the category lists or data chart to draft short paragraphs. With younger children, you might guide the group through this activity. In this case, choose a list or section of the data chart and have the children try to come up with sentences using the information. Write the sentences on the board. Then guide the students to revise the draft. For example, have them suggest a topic sentence to begin the paragraph or

FIGURE 8.5   A Data Chart Used to Organize and Relate Facts

	Homes	Clothes	Food
1. Indians Squanto Samoset	longhouses	animal skins, feathers, furs, moccasins	fish, corn, deer, turkey, squash, cranberries
2. Pilgrims John, Hope, Sarah	cabins, loft	long dresses, pants, hat, knickers, shirts	salt pork, bread, turkey, squash, cranberries, corn, pie

Figure, "A Data Chart Used to Organize and Relate Facts" from "A Writing Approach to Reading Comprehension: Schema Theory in Action" by Dorothy Grant Hennings from *Language Arts*, Vol. 59, #1, January 1982. Reprinted with the permission of the National Council of Teachers of English.

FIGURE 8.6 A Chart for Summarizing Data

	The Monarchies of Europe in the 1600s and 1700s				
Country	The Sun King	The Habsburgs	Brandenburg-Prussia	The Romanovs	The Stuarts
Time period					
Key kings and queens of the period					
Good things done by this royal house					
Bad things done by this royal house					

Note: This chart was based on a section of the sixth grade text *The Human Adventure*, which is part of the Addison-Wesley social studies program. Figure, "A Chart for Summarizing Data" from "A Writing Approach to Reading Comprehension: Schema Theory in Action" by Dorothy Grant Hennings from *Language Arts*, Vol. 59, #1, January 1982. Reprinted with the permission of the National Council of Teachers of English.

perhaps a closing summary sentence. Help them put the sentences in a logical order and reword or combine sentences. Finally, ask the students to give the paragraph a title.

Older students, or those who have had more experience with this activity, can be asked to write paragraphs on their own. Those who composed paragraphs on the same category can later meet to share their writing and help each other with editing.

Sequencing paragraphs. Have students share their paragraphs by copying them onto chart paper or the chalkboard. Have them decide how the paragraphs should be ordered to form the group report. Encourage them to give reasons for thinking the paragraphs should be ordered in one way or another.

Drafting introductions and conclusions. Once the paragraphs have been ordered, help the students generate an introductory paragraph. Then have them draft a concluding paragraph, either one summarizing the information given or one stating generalizations derived from the information. Depending on the students' level of experience, the drafting of these paragraphs can be managed either as a teacher-directed group activity or an individual one.

Organizing the report. Select three students to put together the final class report, combining the introductory paragraph, the paragraphs on various categories of information, and the concluding paragraph. Have the students include headings based on the titles given to individual paragraphs.

Interpreting texts with similar structures.   Hennings suggests that the understanding students gain in creating the reports should give them a "mental map" for comprehending other expository texts. The next step, then, is to have students read informational texts to look for the same structures they used in creating their paragraphs. Choose texts with headings and well-organized introductory and concluding paragraphs. With these texts, Hennings recommends that you ask students questions such as the following (p. 13):

1. What are the big categories of information with which this writer is dealing? How do we know?
2. What system of heads and subheads is this writer using? What does the system of heads and subheads tell us about the way the topic will be developed in this section?
3. What is the main—or most important—topic of the section? How do we know?
4. What kind of information has the writer put into the introduction to the section? What clues have been given in the introduction as to the organization of the material to follow?
5. What kind of information has the writer put into the concluding section? Are there any clues given as to the most important points included in the section?

Through questioning you can guide students to identify the categories of information and organizing structures in the text. Point out how these might be similar to or different from those in the students' own reports.

Summarizing, synthesizing, judging, and doing more writing.   Data charts can also serve as the basis for developing additional writing assignments. These assignments strengthen understanding of the text and also give students other opportunities to practice their organizational and writing skills. For example, with the data chart in Figure 8.6, students could be asked to write a paragraph containing important information about the Sun King. Or they might write a paragraph synthesizing information, for example, one that tells how the monarchs were all similar. Finally, they might be asked to give their own judgments about the different periods, for example, writing a paragraph telling which period they would have preferred to live in and why. These paragraphs, too, can be organized in reports, using the same procedures that were followed earlier.

Writing a summary

When students write a summary of text information, they begin by analyzing the text and then restate the ideas in their own words. In this way, summarizing promotes their active involvement with both the structure and content of expository text. Summarizing is one of the abilities that differentiates good from poor readers, and learning to summarize can improve poor readers' comprehension (Brown & Day, 1983).

Summarizing is an activity which teachers may introduce as early as first grade, although systematic instruction (as described below) should probably occur in the fourth through sixth grades. Because even college students have difficulty with summarization, teachers should not expect elementary students to master this writing technique. Rather, the purposes of giving the children some direct instruction in writing a summary are to give them experience with the task, some knowledge of the procedures followed in producing an adequate summary, and a sense of the features which differentiate a good from a poor summary.

The following suggestions for helping elementary students learn to write summaries take them through the steps and rules recommended by Hare and Borchardt (1984), as shown in Figure 8.7. As you can see, the process is quite complex. For this reason, teachers may wish to introduce summarization to only some of the students in the class. Or they may find it easier to teach summarization to small groups of students, rather than the whole class at once.

Introduce the students to the four rules for writing a summary, as shown in Figure 8.7. Discuss each of the rules with them, so they have a general idea of the procedures involved. Using a familiar passage from a content area textbook, lead the group in constructing a rough draft of a summary, following the four rules. Write the summary on the board, using the children's suggestions for wording.

On the first day, discuss with the students why it can be useful to write a summary of text information. Help them to understand that, by analyzing the text and rewriting the important information, they will be better able to learn and remember it. If the children have prepared reports before, point out that summaries are often incorporated into reports.

On the second day, have the children work with you to improve the summary. Follow the suggestions for polishing presented at the bottom of Figure 8.7. When the summary is completed, allow the children to ask questions and make comments about the process of writing a summary. Help them to understand that writing a summary is a very demanding task.

Later group discussion lessons to practice preparing summaries may be timed to coincide with the children's completion of different sections in social studies or science textbooks. Teachers continue to lead the children in summarizing passages already read and understood, following the four rules.

FIGURE 8.7 *Four General Steps to Help With the Four+ Specific Rules for Writing a Summary*

1. *Make sure you understand the text.* Ask yourself, "What was this text about?" "What did the writer say?" Try to say the general theme to yourself.

2. *Look back.* Reread the text to make sure you got the theme right. Also read to make sure that you really understand what the important parts of the text are. Star important parts.

Now Use the Four Rules for Writing a Summary

3. *Rethink.* Reread a paragraph of the text. Try to say the theme of that paragraph to yourself. Is the theme a topic sentence? Have you underlined it? Or is the topic sentence missing: If it is missing, have you written one in the margin?

4. *Check and double-check.* Did you leave in any lists? Make sure you don't list things out in your summary. Did you repeat yourself? Make sure you didn't. Did you skip anything? Is all the important information in the summary?

Four Rules for Writing a Summary

1. *Collapse lists.* If you see a list of things, try to think of a word or phrase name for the whole list. For example, if you saw a list like eyes, ears, neck, arms, and legs, you could say "body parts." Or, if you saw a list like ice skating, skiing, or sledding, you could say "winter sports."

2. *Use topic sentences.* Often authors write a sentence that summarizes a whole paragraph. It is called a topic sentence. If the author gives you one, you can use it in your summary. Unfortunately, not all paragraphs contain topic sentences. That means you may have to make up one for yourself. If you don't see a topic sentence, make up one of your own.

3. *Get rid of unnecessary detail.* Some text information can be repeated in a passage. In other words, the same thing can be said in a number of different ways, all in one passage. Other text information can be unimportant, or trivial. Since summaries are meant to be short, get rid of repetitive or trivial information.

4. *Collapse paragraphs.* Paragraphs are often related to one another. Some paragraphs explain one or more other paragraphs. Some paragraphs just expand on the information presented in other paragraphs. Some paragraphs are more necessary than other paragraphs. Decide which paragraphs should be kept or gotten rid of, and which might be joined together.

A Final Suggestion

+. *Polish the summary.* When a lot of information is reduced from an original passage, the resulting concentrated information often sounds very unnatural. Fix this problem and create a more natural-sounding summary. Adjustments may include but are not limited to: paraphrasing, the insertion of connecting words like "and" or "because," and the insertion of introductory or closing statements. Paraphrasing is especially useful here, for two reasons: one, because it improves your ability to remember the material, and two, it avoids using the author's words, otherwise known as plagiarism.

From "Four General Steps to Help with the Four Specific Rules for Writing a Summary" by Victoria C. Hare and Kathleen M. Borchardt, *Reading Research Quarterly*, Vol. 20, No. 1. Reprinted with permission of the authors and the International Reading Association.

If the children show signs of understanding the overall process, teachers may wish to have them begin to work on summarizing a passage which has not already been studied. At this stage the children are introduced to the four steps at the top of Figure 8.7. The summary continues to be written through a process of group discussion.

After the children have had several teacher-led group experiences with unfamiliar passages, they may be ready to try writing summaries on their own, either individually or by working with partners. The children can discuss the strengths and weaknesses of their summaries and talk about parts of the process they are finding difficult. Again, the goal is to give students experience with summarization, not to have them produce perfect summaries, so the discussion should emphasize the process of writing a summary, and not only the qualities of the summaries they have prepared.

KEY CONCEPT 4

By sending and receiving written messages, students can learn more about literacy as a process of communication.

READING AND WRITING AS THE SENDING AND RECEIVING OF MESSAGES

As Taylor (1983) illustrates in her research, reading and writing are often embedded in the daily lives of children and their families. Writing to convey a message to a member of one's family is a common use of literacy, one described in Heath's (1980) work as its social interactional use. Writing notes and letters, to communicate to someone else a message they deem important, is a good way for children to develop an understanding of this particular use of literacy. This understanding can be strengthened further if children receive responses to messages they have written.

In a sense, all the writing activities described earlier in this chapter give children the chance to communicate through writing and to receive feedback about what they have written. Writing a piece and then participating in a writing conference, for example, provides this experience. The activities described below, however, are designed to bring out even more directly the idea that reading and writing are acts of communication, involving the sending and receiving of messages. They involve the exchange of letters or notes and encourage children to write in forms different from the narrative and expository ones targeted in other activities.

INSTRUCTIONAL ACTIVITIES

Just as acts of literacy are embedded in the lives of many families, the activities below should be embedded in the life of the classroom. They are another way of encouraging the development of a sense of community among the children, built around a sharing of reading and writing.

Message board and notices

The purpose of the message board (Newman, 1983, developed by Burke) is to show students that writing often involves a social interaction between two or more people. To help students grasp this idea, this activity focuses on the function or meaning of messages. The activity also highlights the fact that a single written exchange is often part of a chain leading to other exchanges.

Choose a place readily accessible to the children, where messages can easily be tacked up. Begin by leaving messages yourself for several or all of the students. Encourage the children to leave messages for one another. Point out that, in order to receive messages, one should begin sending them to others.

Notices (Newman, 1983) is a natural extension of the message board activity. Its purpose is to show students the use of writing to convey important news and to give them the responsibility for keeping informed through their own reading efforts. Instead of making routine announcements, for example of a change in the class schedule for that day, place a written notice with that news in a prominent location. Charge students with the responsibility of checking for important information on their own. Occasionally, students may have news of general importance to put on the Notice Board, too. You can help students to distinguish between news of general interest to the whole class, which should be shared through a notice, and information which would better be conveyed through a message to one or more children.

Classroom postal service

A classroom postal service can serve the same purpose as a message board. Create a mailbox out of a cardboard carton and have the children paint and label it. Start by writing short letters to several children or the whole class and deposit the letters in the box. Every few days a different child can be selected to distribute the letters. Children can receive mail at their desks or in their lockers or cubby holes. Encourage the children to write back to you and to send letters to one another. Letters might also be exchanged with another class, at the same or a different grade level.

Aulls (1982) suggests that the letters you write to the children be at a personal rather than academic level, and that you do no correcting of the letters you receive from the children. This will encourage the children to write back to you to share thoughts and news, so the exchange of letters mirrors their use in communication between friends and family members.

Dialogue journals

Staton (1980) describes the use of dialogue journals in a sixth grade classroom. With modifications, the procedures can be used with second graders and perhaps even with younger children. The purpose of the journals was to allow the teacher to give students individual attention, to motivate students to write about experiences important to them, and to help them improve their writing. Mrs. Reed, the teacher in this class, found dialogue journals to be an excellent way of getting to know her students and of building positive relationships with them. Staton writes:

From a language perspective, the openness of the journal as a forum for personal problems as well as academic ones captures the natural function of language as intentional communication about what matters most to the person. An attitude of trust and interest in everything the writer says characterizes Leslee Reed's attitude toward her students and what they write in their journals. "I learn something new every day about each one of them. They are fascinating to get to know." It is no

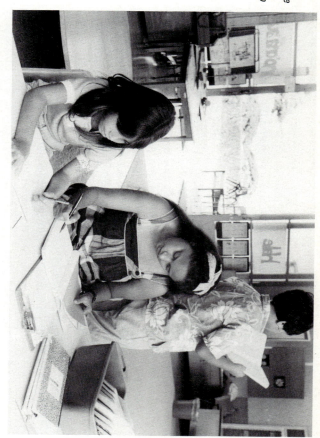

This teacher uses recess time to write responses to entries students have made in their dialogue journals. Children are often eager to read her replies and to write back.

wonder that their willingness to express their own ideas, feelings, and experiences in written language improves and creates in them a confidence about writing in general that too few people their age or any age enjoy. (p. 518)

Here are some guidelines for the use of dialogue journals based on the experiences of Reed and Staton:

1. Make sure each student has a notebook or binder to serve as a private journal. Let the students know that they will be writing to you, and that you will be writing back to them. Tell them that no one else will see the journals, except with their permission.

2. Let the students choose whatever they want to write about. Have them write on a regular schedule. In Reed's classroom the students wrote in their journals every day; once a week would seem to be the minimum. Have some minimum amount of writing the students must do each time. In Reed's classroom this was three sentences. Make some specific arrangements about when journal writing will take place. In Reed's classroom this was after the students had finished all their other assignments. Journal writing might also be done as homework.

3. Let the students know that the journals can be used to raise questions they might feel uncomfortable asking in class. For example, Reed encouraged students to ask her questions about lessons. These questions gave her valuable feedback about her own teaching. In their journals students also sought advice about personal problems, such as a conflict with a bully on the playground.

4. Make sure you have the time to write back to students, so they receive responses to their writing right away. Do not correct students' writing, but provide models for correct spelling and grammar in your responses. Respond to students' ideas and messages, rather than to the forms used in their writing.

Using computers as a writing and communication environment

Especially for children in the upper elementary grades, computers can serve as an aid to writing. There are a number of word processing or text editing programs, among them the Bank Street Writer and Story Writer, which appear to make writing and revision easier and more enjoyable for children. Newman (1984) suggests the following advantages of writing with a word processor:

It allows writers to become more willing to take risks, to be more tentative about meaning, to consider organization and word choices more freely than ever before. What this means is that children (and adults, too) can learn a great deal about language and the writing process each time they engage in writing.   (p. 495)

These advantages can be experienced even by primary grade children, as the work of Phenix and Hannan (1984) suggests. Over the course of a six-week pilot study, children in Phenix's first grade class learned to revise writing begun on previous days, instead of starting a new piece each day as they had been doing before. They enjoyed working on the computer and so spent more time writing. The pieces they produced were longer, so several conferences were usually held on the same piece. Having several conferences led the children to revise a piece more than once. As a result, Phenix and Hannan observed that the children learned to take a much more critical view of their own writing.

QUILL (Rubin & Bruce, 1984) is an example of a computer software package which shows students the connections between reading and writing and encourages the sending and receiving of messages. Among other things, a classroom newspaper can be readily composed and distributed with QUILL.

QUILL has four components. The Planner helps students generate and organize the ideas they will be writing about. The Writer's Assistant helps with text editing. The Library is essentially a data base management system that allows students to write and file information on a variety of topics, such as whales or Alaska. Other students may then call up the information.

Of particular interest is QUILL's fourth component, the Mailbag. It enables students and teachers to send and receive messages from one another. Messages can be sent to an individual, to a group, or to the whole class. A class may communicate with another class in the same school, or even with classes in schools far away.

The three reading and writing activities described earlier in this key concept can all be carried out in the computer communication environment provided when software packages such as QUILL are used. For example, the message board and notices can be presented via computer, with notices being accessible to a general audience and messages being sent only to particular students. A classroom mail system is readily set up. Letters can be printed out for distribution by a student mailman or the children can call up their own mail at the computer. Finally, dialogue journals may be handled on a computer. A file may be created to serve as each child's journal. The teacher may add a response to the same file whenever the child makes another entry.

SUMMARY

In this chapter we discussed relationships between reading and writing and some of the ways that writing can be used to strengthen reading ability. The perspective taken was that reading and writing are both forms of communication with language, requiring the construction of messages from text or a process of *composing*.

In our first key concept we discussed the *writing process* approach to improving children's reading and writing. This approach centers on concepts such as choice and publication and children's development of a concept of authorship. In the second key concept we looked at how writing can serve to develop children's appreciation and comprehension of literature. When following the writing process approach, this can be accomplished by beginning with the children's own experiences as authors. Direct, explicit instruction may be used to foster literary development.

In the third key concept we showed how children's comprehension of expository text might be improved through activities integrating reading and writing. Finally, in the fourth key concept we discussed ways of giving children an understanding of reading and writing as communication processes, involving the sending and receiving of messages. Computers can serve as communication environments to motivate and reinforce these understandings.

BIBLIOGRAPHY

REFERENCES

Allen R. V., & Allen, C. (1976). *Language experience activities.* Boston: Houghton Mifflin.

Atwell, N. (1984). Writing and reading literature from the inside out. *Language Arts, 61* (3), 240-252.

Aulls, M. W. (1982). *Developing readers in today's elementary school.* Boston: Allyn & Bacon.

Bissex, G. L. (1980). *GNYS AT WRK: A child learns to write and read.* Cambridge, MA: Harvard University Press.

Blackburn, E. (1984). Common ground: Developing relationships between reading and writing. *Language Arts, 61* (4), 367-375.

Brown, A. L., & Day, J. D. (1983). Macrorules for summarizing texts: The development of expertise. *Journal of Verbal Learning and Verbal Behavior, 22,* 1-14.

Calkins, L. M. (1979). Children learn the writer's craft. *Language Arts, 57,* 207-213.

Church, E., & Bereiter, C. (1984). Reading for style. In J. M. Jensen (Ed.), *Composing and comprehending*. Urbana, IL: National Conference on Research in English and ERIC Clearinghouse on Reading and Communication Skills.

Freeman, R. H. (1983). Poetry writing in the upper elementary grades. *Reading Teacher, 37* (3), 238-248.

Graves, D. H. (1981). Patterns of child control of the writing process. In R. D. Walshe, *Donald Graves in Australia—"Children want to write . . ."* Exeter, NH: Heinemann.

Graves, D. (1983a). *Writing: Teachers and children at work.* Exeter, NH: Heinemann.

Graves, D. (1983b). Teacher intervention in children's writing: A response to Myra Barrs. *Language Arts, 60* (7), 841-846.

Graves, D., & Hansen, J. (1983). The author's chair. *Language Arts, 60* (2), 176-183.

Hansen, J. (1983). Authors respond to authors. *Language Arts, 60* (8), 970-976.

Hare, V. C., & Borchardt, K. M. (1984). Direct instruction of summarization skills. *Reading Research Quarterly, 20* (1), 62-78.

Harms, J. M., & Lettow, L. J. (1983). Poetry for children has never been better. *Reading Teacher, 36* (4), 376-381.

Heath, S. B. (1980). The functions and uses of literacy. *Journal of Communication,* Winter, 123-133.

Hennings, D. G. (1982). A writing approach to reading comprehension—Schema theory in action. *Language Arts, 59* (1), 8-17.

Humes, A. (1983). Research on the composing process. *Review of Educational Research, 53* (2), 201-216.

Newman, J. M. (1983). *Whole language activities.* Monographs on learning and teaching, Publication #1. Halifax, Nova Scotia: Department of Education, Dalhousie University.

Newman, J. M. (1984). Language learning and computers. *Language Arts, 61* (5), 494-497.

Phenix, J., & Hannan, E. (1984). Word processing in the grade one classroom. *Language Arts, 61* (8), 804-812.

Rubin, A. D., & Bruce, B. C. (1984). QUILL: Reading and writing with a microcomputer. In B. A. Hutson (Ed.), *Advances in reading and language research.* Greenwich, CT: JAI Press.

Russell, C. (1983). Putting research in practice: Conferencing with young writers. *Language Arts, 60* (3), 333-340.

Smith, L. B. (1982). Sixth graders write about reading literature. *Language Arts, 59* (4), 357-363.

Smith, M., & Bean, T. W. (1983). Four strategies that develop children's story comprehension and writing. *Reading Teacher, 37* (3), 295-301.

Sowers, S. (1981). KDS CN RIT SUNR THN WE THINGK. In R. D. Walshe, *Donald Graves in Australia—"Children want to write . . ."* Exeter, NH: Heinemann.

Staton, J. (1980). Writing and counseling: Using a dialogue journal. *Language Arts, 57* (5), 514-518.

Sulzby, E. (in press). Writing and reading: Signs of oral and written language organization in the young child. In W. H. Teale & E. Sulzby (Eds.), *Emergent literacy: Writing and reading.* Norwood, NJ: Ablex.

Taylor, D. (1983). *Family literacy: Young children learning to read and write.* Portsmouth, NH: Heinemann.

Tierney, R. J., & Pearson, P. D. (1983). Toward a composing model of reading. *Language Arts, 60* (5). 568-580.

Wood, K. D. (1984). Probable passages: A writing strategy. *Reading Teacher, 37* (6), 496-499.

CHILDREN'S BOOKS CITED

Sedgwick, B. (1978). The doughnut machine that wouldn't stop. In I. E. Aaron, D. Jackson, C. Riggs, R. G. Smith, & R. Tierney, *Scott, Foresman Basics in Reading.* Glenview, IL: Scott, Foresman.

Slobodkina, E. (1967). *The wonderful feast.* Eau Claire, WI: E. M. Hale.

FURTHER READINGS

Britton, J. (1978). The composing processes and functions of writing. In C. R. Cooper & L. Odell (Eds.), *Research on composing: Points of departure.* Urbana, IL: National Council of Teachers of English.

Clay, M. M. (1975). *What did I write?* Exeter, NH: Heinemann.

Dyson, A. H. (1984). "N spell my Grandmama": Fostering early thinking about print. *Reading Teacher, 38* (3), 262-271.

Mehan, H., Miller-Souviney, B., & Riel, M. M. (1984). Research currents: Knowledge of text editing and control of literacy skills. *Language Arts, 6* (5), 510-515.

Rubin, A., & Hansen, J. (1985). Reading and writing: How are the first two "R's" related? In J. Orasanu (Ed.), *A decade of reading research: Implications for practice.* Hillsdale, NJ: Erlbaum.

Temple, C., Nathan, R., & Burris, N. (1982). *The beginnings of writing.* Boston: Allyn & Bacon.

CHAPTER 9

Teaching Reading to Students
with Special Needs

Intelligence is a mystery. We hear it said that people never develop more than a very small part of their latent intellectual capacity. Probably not; but *why* not? Most of us have our engines running at about ten percent of their power. Why no more? And how do some people manage to keep revved up to twenty percent or thirty percent of full power—or even more?

What turns the power off, or keeps it from ever being turned on?

During these past four years at the Colorado Rocky Mountain School my nose has been rubbed in the problem. When I started, I thought that some people were just born smarter than others and that not much could be done about it. This seems to be the official line of most of the psychologists. It isn't hard to believe, if all your contacts with students are in the classroom or the psychological testing room. But if you live at a small school, seeing students in class, in dorms, in their private lives, at their recreations, sports, and manual work, you can't escape the conclusion that some people are much smarter part of the time than they are at other times. Why? Why should a boy or girl, who under some circumstances is witty, observant, imaginative, analytical, in a word, *intelligent*, come into the classroom and, as if by magic, turn into a complete dolt?

(Holt, 1964, p. 5)

OVERVIEW

In this chapter we present background information critical to an understanding of teaching reading to children with special needs. We begin by emphasizing that the basic approaches to be used with these students grow logically from the foundation set in previous chapters. That is, reading instruction is still to be seen as developing children's ability to construct meaning from text, by building upon existing background knowledge and skills.

271

PERSPECTIVE

MEETING SPECIAL NEEDS

There are several major categories of students whose special needs require attention in teachers' planning and conducting of classroom reading instruction. While each student must, of course, be considered as an individual, teachers should also understand these major categories of special needs. Thus, we discuss how cultural differences and speaking another language or a dialect affect children's learning to read. We also consider the teaching of reading to children who are poor readers or gifted readers. To help teachers work more effectively with children with these types of special needs, we also present appropriate instructional activities.

The key concepts in this chapter are the following:

Key Concept #1: Teachers should know how to respond to cultural differences which can influence children's learning to read.

Key Concept #2: Teachers should know how to respond to differences in language which can influence children's learning to read.

Key Concept #3: Teachers should know how to provide sound classroom reading instruction to children who are poor readers.

Key Concept #4: Teachers should know how to provide sound classroom reading instruction to gifted readers.

In this textbook we have covered the basic aspects of sound reading instruction for all students. To review briefly, reading was defined as the process of constructing meaning from text. Thus, all classroom reading instruction, in one way or another, should help students learn to construct meaning from text, or foster their ability to comprehend text. Somewhat different skills seem to be required to comprehend narratives and stories, as compared to expository text. Therefore, most students will benefit from instruction in both areas. Instruction in vocabulary and word identification are also important aspects of the classroom reading program, because lessons in these areas give children other skills and knowledge needed to support text comprehension. We have emphasized the importance of helping students to become independent in directing their own reading activity. That is, students need to learn to set their own purposes for reading and to apply the skills they have been taught. Finally, we have discussed the idea that a well-balanced classroom reading program will give students the chance to develop an appreciation of literature and the incentive to read for their own enjoyment and information.

These are the areas of reading instruction we want to cover for all students, including *students with special needs*. We define students with special needs as those who may require an extra degree of teacher attention to become capable readers or to read at a level commensurate with their aptitude. In this chapter, we discuss the teaching of reading to several major categories of children with special needs, as evident in the list of key concepts: children who are culturally different, who speak another language or a dialect of English, who read poorly, or who read exceptionally well. Each type of special need is described in detail later. We will not be discussing every category of special need, but teachers should be able to gain a sense of how the major principles of reading instruction developed throughout this textbook should be applied to the teaching of reading to all students with special needs.

In short, while classroom teachers will make specific adjustments to meet their students' special needs, the overall approach to reading instruction will be very similar to that taken with other students, and consistent with the basic ideas set out in other chapters in this book. To make this perspective more concrete, we need to explain how the teaching of reading to students with special needs is often handled in school settings. We must also discuss why some common practices may even work *against* children's learning to read.

Coordinating instructional resources

In some schools, children with special needs remain in their homerooms all day. Sometimes the resource teacher, or an aide, enters the classroom to tutor the children or help them complete seatwork assignments. In many schools, however, the children are taken from the classroom and given reading or language instruction by a resource teacher. This type of pull-out procedure, in which children are removed from their regular classrooms, is often used in the federally funded Chapter 1 program for poor readers in low-income communities; bilingual or second language programs; and programs for the gifted and talented.

The danger in many of these situations is that the classroom teacher may no longer be responsible for providing reading instruction to children with special needs. The teacher loses touch with the children's needs in learning to read and fails to provide continued classroom support for reading.

For children who are experiencing difficulty with learning to read, the absence of classroom support may be quite damaging. Allington's (1983) findings, discussed in detail later in this chapter, point to the importance of setting aside adequate time to teach special students to read. For many children with reading difficulties, the time provided in resource room instruction is inadequate in and of itself. They continue to need the classroom teacher's help. For this reason, it seems best for the classroom teacher to view outside reading instruction as supporting or supplementing classroom reading instruction, rather than replacing it entirely. Also, outside instruction seems to be more effective if it is coordinated with classroom reading activities rather than being completely separate or different (e.g., Carter, 1984).

There are important reasons for classroom teachers to be actively involved in the reading instruction of special students. First, keeping in touch with all students' progress in learning to read helps in the planning of more effective whole-class lessons. Especially as students get older, most lessons involve some kind of reading. If teachers are familiar with the reading progress of special students, they will know how to structure such lessons to permit them to participate. This will be important if special students are to have valuable in-class reading opportunities, for example when reading instruction is being integrated with science and social studies lessons. Second, by taking the time to teach reading to all students, even those who receive outside instruction, teachers make it less likely that some students will feel neglected or inferior.

Curriculum scope

Often, whether children with reading problems are taken from the classroom or given reading instruction by their homeroom teacher, the tendency is to speeding it. The danger in programs which consist entirely of phonics ac-tivities, such as the learning of sound-symbol relationships, is that they give children with reading problems a misleading picture of what reading is all about. The children never have the opportunity to develop the concept that reading is the process of constructing meaning from text. The more they are deprived of experiences with constructing meaning from text, for example, as in the reading of storybooks, the less likely it is that they will ever become competent readers. A sound reading program for students with special needs will always include many comprehension activities in addition to those in word identification.

In fact, a sound reading program for students with special needs should go beyond just these basics. Research by Singer, McNeil, and Furse (1984) suggests that a broad curriculum, one which goes beyond the acquisition of basic reading skills, is likely to be beneficial for all students, including low achievers. A narrow curriculum is one that stresses only basic skills, while a broad curriculum covers the basics plus the content areas and fine arts. Thus, reading instruction for students with special needs should be broad

give them lessons which focus solely on word identification. Reading pro-grams which emphasize word identification or phonics to the exclusion of comprehension and vocabulary building are sometimes presented as a rem-edy for children's reading problems. Such programs are frequently repre-sented as being particularly effective with children from disadvantaged backgrounds or with children who learn more slowly. They cannot, however, be considered complete and balanced developmental reading programs.

As discussed in more detail in Key Concept #3, phonics-only instruction is not generally beneficial and may actually slow learning to read, instead of in scope, bringing out the many different functions of literacy, including its importance in learning information in the content areas, such as social studies and science. Such instruction should emphasize comprehension while also including opportunities for the development of writing, vocabulary, and word identification abilities. The idea is to provide special needs children with a complete and balanced program of reading instruction, one that touches upon the different functions of literacy and the different facets of reading ability.

Classroom climate

Often, students with special needs may develop feelings of inferiority and of not being valued as members of the class. This may occur because they are taken from the classroom for reading instruction and thus marked as being different. Or, if they remain in the classroom, they may not have many opportunities to succeed at reading and writing activities and to be recognized for their achievements. Teachers may need to work at helping students with special needs gain a feeling of belonging to the class and of being successful readers (refer to Chapter 12 for further discussion of this point).

This goal can be accomplished if teachers organize the classroom as a literate community, where readers and writers are constantly sharing their work, communicating with and learning from one another (e.g., Holdaway, 1979). We have highlighted the sharing of literature, information learned through reading expository text, and one's own writing as being particularly effective ways of developing the classroom as a literate community (refer to Chapters 6, 7, and 8). Students with special needs should be drawn into this community and encouraged to participate along with all of the other students. Teachers can play a key role in establishing the values of the classroom community which make it possible for special students to be accepted.

The sense of community in the classroom is best encouraged through reading and writing activities which promote cooperation, and not just competition. The students can also be led to discuss ways of helping one another and the value in applauding one another's efforts. All students, but especially those with special needs, benefit in such a classroom environment.

In summary, teachers need to be aware of several of the typical weaknesses in the reading instruction provided to students with special needs, especially those who are experiencing difficulties in learning to read. They should be sure to provide these students with adequate classroom time for learning to read, coordinating reading instruction with that provided by resource teachers. They should be sure that the reading instruction given to students with special needs is well balanced, with activities in comprehension as well as word identification, and in the content areas as well as basic skills. Finally, they should be sure to create a classroom climate which promotes a sense of community, so that all students have the chance to be recognized as successful readers.

KEY CONCEPT 1

Teachers should know how to respond to cultural differences which can influence children's learning to read.

CULTURAL DIFFERENCES

The ability to communicate with students is obviously critical to effective teaching. Differences in culture, we believe, often cause problems in learning to read because teachers find that they are unable to communicate well with culturally different students.

While we often think of the term *culture* as applying to physical objects, such as clothing and foods, it also applies to behaviors and values. According to Goodenough (1971), culture includes the standards we follow in our own behavior, as well as the standards we use to judge the behavior of others. Of particular significance in classrooms is the part of culture that involves rules for behavior in face-to-face communication. These are important in all kinds of teacher-led lessons, whether large group, small group, or individual.

Each culture has its own rules for what constitutes proper and respectful behavior. These rules reflect the deeply held values and beliefs of members of that culture. These rules and values make up what Philips (1983) terms *invisible culture*. They are invisible because neither the members of the culture nor the members of other cultures are usually aware of them. We can, however, learn about invisible culture if we make a conscious effort to do so.

The practical implication of this view of culture is that teachers should be aware of the rules for face-to-face communication likely to be followed by the culturally different students in their classes. They should also be aware of the cultural values reflected in those rules. Without this awareness, miscommunication and misunderstanding are likely to result, during reading lessons and at other times. Teachers may misunderstand and misjudge students, and in turn find themselves being misunderstood. Thus, if you are working with culturally different students, a primary goal will be to bridge the gap between the style of communication and values of the home and the school.

Examples of cultural differences in communication styles

To make this general idea more concrete, we discuss below three studies showing how differences in invisible culture may affect teachers' ability to communicate with culturally different children. In reading about these studies, keep in mind that there are often great differences among the students of any particular ethnic background, due to such factors as family income, parents' educational level, and family values and beliefs. The findings below, then, should be seen as *examples* of the types of cultural differences in communication style found to be important with particular groups of children in particular settings. They cannot automatically be applied to all children from those ethnic groups.

Questioning at home and at school.   Reading lessons often center on question-answer exchanges between teacher and students, as discussed in Chapter 5. Culturally different children, however, may not be familiar with classroom question answering routines (e.g., Boggs, 1972). This can make it difficult for them to learn during ordinary reading lessons.

Evidence for this idea comes from a study by Heath (1982). She compared the use of questions in three settings: Trackton, a working-class black community; the classrooms of the children from this community; and the homes of their teachers. In the classrooms and teachers' homes, Heath found that teachers often asked questions for the purpose of "training" children. The children were expected to give answers already known by the adult. When the child was looking at a book, such questions would include: "What's that?" "Where's the puppy?"

In Trackton, on the other hand, children were not generally asked questions for which the adult already knew the answer. Instead, they were asked open-ended questions with answers unknown to the adult. For example, in the passage below, the grandmother's first question has to do with what her grandson is planning to do next with the crayons. Another type of question often asked of Trackton children called for them to make comparisons, stating how one thing was like another. As shown in the passage, the grandmother's second question called the boy's attention to the fact that one of the crayons was the same color as his pants. Heath writes:

At early ages, Trackton children recognized situations, scenes, personalities, and items which were similar. However, they never volunteered, nor were they asked by adults, to name the attributes which were similar and added up to one thing's being like another. A grandmother playing with her grandson age 2;4 asked him as he fingered crayons in a box: "Whatcha gonna do with those, huh?" "Ain't dat [color] like your pants?" She then volunteered to me: "We don't talk to our chil'un like you folks do; we don't ask 'em 'bout colors, names, 'n things." (p. 117)

When they first entered school, then, Trackton children were unprepared to answer teachers' questions, which often had to do with such information as telling the colors or names of objects. With Heath's help, the teachers tried to adjust their teaching materials and questioning strategies, to incorporate familiar scenes and questions more like those asked of the children by Trackton adults. They started by using pictures of the community and countryside and, rather than asking known-answer questions, asked questions such as the following:

What's happening here?
Have you ever been here?
Tell me what you did when you were there.   (p. 124)

Questions like this drew many more responses from Trackton children.

The teachers also helped Trackton children develop the skills needed to answer typical classroom questions about situations or objects and their attributes. To do this, they taped certain lessons, and then added to them questions of the type unfamiliar to Trackton children. Children in the class who were able to answer this kind of question taped answers to them. All of the children were then able to listen to the tapes at the learning centers. By listening to the tapes, Trackton students were able to hear the kind of questions teachers typically asked and the kinds of answers teachers expected to hear. As time went on, the teachers invited Trackton students to assist them in preparing the questions and answers to be taped. In this way, the children were gradually able to learn classroom question-answer routines. The teachers also held discussions with the children about different types of questions and the kinds of answers called for.

If you think it appropriate to follow a plan like that described above, you might want to go one step further and make a direct connection to the kinds of questions asked in reading lessons and assignments. For this purpose, teach the children about question-answer relationships, following the program developed by Raphael (1982) and described in detail in Chapter 5. Have the taped questions and answers reflect all three types of question-answer relationships.

Other examples of cultural differences in communication style. As the work of Heath suggests, when teachers and children are unable to collaborate or "hook up" in a way that allows teaching to take place, students' learning to read is bound to suffer. Teachers who are able to work effectively with culturally different students seem to be those who use a communication style consistent with the values of the students' culture.

For example, research by Cazden, Carrasco, Maldonado-Guzman, and Erickson (1980) points to the importance of *cariño,* or a caring relationship, as seen in the interactions of a first-grade teacher with her Mexican-American students. Speaking in Spanish, the teacher communicated a sense of caring by using terms of endearment in addressing the children, reinforcing norms of politeness and respect, and in showing her knowledge regarding their families.

Another example is provided by the work of Erickson and Mohatt (1982). Building on earlier work by Philips (1972), these researchers found that it was important for teachers of Odawa Indian students to avoid exercising direct social control. According to their findings, teachers were likely to have more difficulty providing effective lessons if they ordered students around, singled them out before the class, and waited for all the students to do the same thing at the same time. In contrast, teachers were likely to have less difficulty if they gave orders in a less direct way (saying, for example, "It's time for people to stop running around" instead of "Sam, stop running around"), questioned children individually or in small groups, and allowed the students to shift from one activity to another in a gradual fashion. According to Erickson and Mohatt, this second style of interaction is effective because it is consistent with the high value the Odawa attach to respecting individual autonomy. In this view, one person should not openly order another person around or otherwise openly try to contol his or her behavior.

Differences in background knowledge

Teachers should also be aware that differences in background or cultural knowledge may lead to different interpretations of the same text. For example, Reynolds, Taylor, Steffenson, Shirey, and Anderson (1982) had a group of black and a group of white eighth graders read the same letter. The letter could be interpreted either as describing "sounding," a ritual form of verbal insult likely to be familiar to black students, or as describing a physical fight. Black students applied their knowledge of sounding in interpreting the text, while white students, who did not have this same kind of cultural knowledge, thought the text was about a fight. Differences in culture thus led to differences in students' understanding of the text.

With texts used to teach reading, as with any other texts, readers are expected to "fill in the gaps" in text from their own background knowledge. If the background knowledge of culturally different students differs from that of their teachers, the students may use sound logic, yet arrive at interpretations teachers think incorrect. For example, with the text described above, teachers might not recognize that students are applying knowledge of sounding. Thus, teachers should be careful not to reject answers which, on the surface, seem to be wrong. Rather, they should try to find out how the child arrived at the answer. By focusing on the process of thinking, rather than simply on whether the answer was right or wrong, teachers will be able either to offer the child other useful background knowledge or a sounder line of reasoning.

Guidelines for dealing with cultural differences

Teachers can and should be optimistic about their ability to work with culturally different students. This is because we know that teachers are able to adjust their interactional styles in order to communicate more effectively with their students (e.g., Erickson & Mohatt, 1982). Furthermore, students often can learn to communicate more effectively with their teachers. Following the guidelines below will get you and your students off to a good start.

1. Be aware of cultural differences as a source of children's problems in learning to read. Read to find out more about the differences which may be affecting your ability to work effectively with some children (see, for example, Cazden, John, & Hymes, 1972; Trueba, Guthrie, & Au, 1981; and Chu-Chang, 1983). Consult with other teachers and school staff or with parents and members of the community about possible sources of difficulty.

2. Try to adjust your own style to help bridge the communication gap. This is often difficult to accomplish on your own. If possible, have someone observe or videotape you so you can become more aware of exactly how you are interacting with your students.

3. Help the children understand conventional school styles of speaking and

INSTRUCTIONAL ACTIVITIES

Listed below are several instructional activities likely to prove especially effective with culturally different students.

answering questions. You might wish to try the procedure developed by Heath or other means to make the children aware of typical school expectations for speaking and turntaking. Even if you can teach effectively by bridging the communication gap, you will still need to prepare your students to deal with the ways of the school. Their future academic success usually depends on their making this adjustment. This does not mean asking the children to give up the communication style and values of their own culture. Rather, it is a matter of helping them understand that a different communication style may be appropriate in certain kinds of situations.

4. Build upon the children's strengths, by looking for areas of knowledge and interest they already possess. All children have background knowledge and interests which can and should serve as the starting points for reading instruction. If you are working with students whose background is different from your own, the students' knowledge and interests may not be immediately obvious to you. During lessons or when children are working on assignments, watch for signs of interest. Try a range of topics and activities to spark enthusiasm, and repeat those that seem successful. For some children, times other than formal classroom lessons, for example, informal chats at recess or lunch, may offer you a better opportunity for learning about their interests.

Experience-text-relationship method

While it can be used with all children, the experience-text-relationship (ETR) method, described in Chapter 5, can be an especially effective way of organizing text comprehension lessons given to culturally different children. This is because the opening experience phase of discussion gives the teacher a chance to see what the children already know about the topic of the text. Starting from the children's background knowledge, the teacher can then make meaningful connections to text ideas. This method thus offers a good way of building upon the children's strengths.

Shared book experience

While the shared book experience (Holdaway, 1979; refer also to Chapter 2) is an excellent approach for any group of beginning readers, it was originally

These children have heard the story once and, with the teacher's encouragement, are now trying to reread the big book on their own.

developed in classrooms with students who were from several different cultural backgrounds, and is an especially sound approach for culturally different children. At the heart of the shared book experience is the reading together of stories, some in "big books." The "big books" are versions of storybooks enlarged so that the text can be seen clearly when lessons are given to the whole class. When reading, the teacher tries to capture the children's interest and attention, just as a parent would when reading a child a bedtime story. The children are encouraged to "chime in" and then to discuss the story. The books are placed where the children may easily get hold of them, and they are encouraged to try to read them on their own. Favorite books are reread for the whole class, sometimes by the children themselves. Later, the teacher may introduce word identification activities with these same books. For a complete description, refer to Holdaway (1979, especially Chapter 4; see also Slaughter, 1983). Figure 9.1 outlines the objectives and activities in the three stages of work with each new storybook or other literary experience, such as a poem or song.

FIGURE 9.1   Three Stages in the Course of a New Literary Experience

A. Discovery

Introduction of the new experience in the listening situation with maximum participation in predictable, repetitive structures, and in the problem solving strategies of decoding.

Objectives

To provide an enjoyable story experience to all of the children. *(This objective should not be sacrificed to any other purpose.)*
To induce a desire to return to the book on subsequent days.
To encourage participation by inducing children to chime in
   on repetitive sections,
   suggest an obvious word,
   predict possible outcomes,
   engage in suitable expressive activities.
To provide a clear and spoken model for the book language.
To induce sound strategies of word solving by encouraging and discussing suggestions, at an appropriate skills level and without unduly interrupting the story. Remember that the thrill of problem-solving is a natural and proper part of the enjoyment of a story.

B. Exploration

Rereadings—usually on request—for familiarization and teaching where applicable. Increasing unison participation is natural to this re-experience.

Objectives

To establish firm oral models for the language of the book.
To deepen understanding and response.
To provide opportunities for all children to gain oral practice of the language of the story by unison, group and individual participation.
To help children become aware of the special structures of the story so that these may be used in reconstructing and decoding in later independent readings, or be used as patterns for personal expression.
To teach relevant reading skills in relation to the text, especially sight vocabulary, structural analysis and the use of letter-sound relationships in strategies of decoding.
To provide further expressive activities based on the language of the book both to personalize response and to provide purposeful practice of the language models.
To provide additional, enjoyable listening experience for slower children who require more repetition than others to develop strong memory models. Listening post activity is most useful for this purpose.

Using literature to develop children's understanding of different cultures

The guided reading of literature to develop positive attitudes about oneself and others can contribute to a sense of community in classrooms with students from different cultural backgrounds. Through books, perhaps read aloud by the teacher or recommended as independent reading, students can gain an appreciation of other cultures and of individual differences. They may also come to a better understanding of their own problems and the problems of others (Bohning, 1981). Among the books you read to your students, be sure to include some to help your students feel pride in their own cultures as well as respect for the cultures of others. For listings of suitable books see Rollock (1974), Aoki (1981), and Gilliland (1982), or check the book selection aids listed in Sutherland and Arbuthnot (1986).

FIGURE 9.1 (continued)

C. Independent Experience and Expression

Independent retrieval of the experience in reading or reading-like ways by individuals or small groups. Creative exploration and expression of meanings from the experience, involving all the expressive arts.

Objectives

To provide opportunities for independent reading by individuals or very small-groups (Sometimes one child will act as teacher in guiding others through the book).

To give a sense of individual achievement and competence.

To encourage the development of self-monitoring and self-correction, using the familiar language models.

To encourage expressive activities using the interests and the language arising from the book so that children will identify more fully with the story and internalize the language as a permanent part of their competence.

However, the total programme is concerned with a great wealth of literary experience happening together, and within this richness different children seek out their own preoccupations, determining for themselves where their own 'working face' in language learning will be from day to day. To give some order and security to this diversity of experience, the daily input session tends to have a predictable structure something like the following:

1. **Tune-in**   Verse, song, and chant—favourite and new. Enlarged print and charts are always central.

2. **Favourite stories**   Rereading of stories, usually by request but sometimes planned. Unison participation. Learning reading-skills in context. Dramatic and other relaxing counterparts. Exploring syntax—substitution, simplification, extension, transformation, innovating on verse and story structure.

3. **Language activities**   Alphabet study and games. Learning other cultural sequences. Exploring language—riddles, puzzles, vocabulary games; exploring writing—approximations towards spelling.

4. **New story**   Introducing new story for the day either in normal or enlarged form. Word-solving strategies induced within the unfolding context of a new language experience. Modelling how print is unlocked.

5. **Independent reading**   Enjoying old favourites—individual or group. Pointing encouraged—pointers available. Much playing at being teacher—children teach each other.

6. **Expression**   Related arts activity either individual or group. Painting, group murals, construction, mask-making for drama. Group drama, puppetry, mime. Writing—innovating on literary structure (teacher as scribe).

(Note: 5. and 6. interchangeable in order.)

From *The Foundations of Literacy* by Don Holdaway. Copyright © 1979 by Don Holdaway. Reprinted with the permission of Ashton Scholastic.

KEY CONCEPT 2

Teachers should know how to respond to differences in language which can influence children's learning to read.

DIFFERENCES IN LANGUAGE

In this section, we first discuss the teaching of reading to students who speak English as a second language, and second, the teaching of reading to students who speak a dialect. In both cases, we focus on teaching the students to read texts written in Standard English. Biliteracy, or the ability to read and write in two languages, is a highly desirable educational outcome (for a discussion, see Goodman, Goodman, & Flores, 1979; Cummins, 1979) but a topic beyond the scope of this textbook.

It is important to remember that cultural and language differences are usually operating together. That is, children who speak a language other than English or a dialect of English often come from nonmainstream cultural backgrounds, as well. Thus, in classroom settings, teachers will generally need to be thinking simultaneously of the information covered under Key Concepts #1 and #2 in this chapter.

STUDENTS WHO SPEAK ENGLISH AS A SECOND LANGUAGE

Students who speak English as a second language (referred to as ESL students) have in common the fact that the first language they learned to speak was not English. Other than that, they are a tremendously diverse group. When teaching reading to ESL students, then, you will want to have some knowledge about the children's family background, cultural background, and native language, as well as their proficiency in English.

The arrangements for providing English reading instruction to ESL students differ from school to school. In some schools students are taken from their regular classrooms to receive instruction in a class designed for ESL students. In others they remain in their homerooms but may receive tutoring or small group lessons from a bilingual aide. In still others no special services may be available for them.

The approaches used to teach reading to ESL students vary greatly. In some cases the children may be taught in a manner which emphasizes the learning of English exclusively. In others one of a number of approaches to *bilingual education* may be followed. Bilingual education involves programs specially designed for ESL students or students who can use two languages. However, bilingual education approaches reflect differences in the value attached to the students' first language. In transitional bilingual education, use of the native language is encouraged primarily as a means of helping the children make the transition to English language instruction. In maintenance approaches students are given the opportunity to develop skill in both English and the native language. English may be emphasized, the two languages may be given equal instructional time, or the children's first language may be emphasized.

Teachers working with ESL students should realize that bilingual education is often a controversial topic. Thus, it is important to be aware of the views the community and school system have about bilingual education. Different views naturally lead to different educational goals and practices. For example, in some communities, parents may have the goal of biliteracy. In others, parents may be most concerned that the schools assist their children to speak and read only in English.

Obviously, one major difference between a classroom reading program for children who speak English as a second language, and one for children whose first or only language is English, must be in the attention given to language development in English. In other words, the teacher will want to help ESL students develop the knowledge of English needed to support the understanding of texts written in English.

In terms of their knowledge of English, ESL students include (1) those who speak some English but are more proficient in a language other than English, and (2) those who are monolingual speakers of another language. These students are also referred to as LEP (limited English proficiency) students.

All of these children, even monolingual speakers of another language, should be encouraged to work with print and books during the time that they are acquiring further knowledge of English. With ESL students, as with others, the reading of books can itself be an effective means of learning about language, as demonstrated in research by Elley and Mangubhai (1983). Elley (1981) argues that an early exposure to books and reading is likely to be beneficial to ESL students. He recommends that high interest books be used to encourage students to read to satisfy their own curiosity, rather than satisfying the teacher.

Remember also that ESL students come to school with a knowledge of their own language and its uses in communicating with others. They also bring with them a vast amount of knowledge of the world. The effective teacher recognizes that the students have these strengths. In teaching ESL students to read in English, then, the teacher should help them make use of this prior knowledge to learn to speak and read English.

There continues to be considerable debate about whether ESL students will progress best if first taught to read in the native language (for a detailed discussion of these issues, see Hudelson & Barrera, 1985; Barrera, 1983, 1984). Current research suggests that it is *not* necessary to delay teaching children to read in the second language until after they have learned to read in the first. Barrera (1983) points out that children can and do learn to read successfully in two languages, the native and non-native, and that some bilingual children may even move themselves into reading through the non-native language first. She has observed these to be common occurrences in classrooms where the reading program is oriented to comprehension rather than to phonics. This is the case because young ESL students in comprehension-emphasis programs approach reading as a meaning-making process in both languages. That is, they do not see reading in Spanish (or other native language) as one thing and reading in English as another. Rather, in trying to construct meaning from text, they pay less attention to the particular language code, Spanish or English, than to the overall message of the text.

Barrera suggests that the problems supposedly presented by the child's having to deal with two languages at once may lie primarily in the way the teaching of reading to ESL students has typically been conceptualized in the past, largely as phonics training. This limited view of the issues probably does not lead to the most effective reading instruction for young ESL students, either in the native language or in English. However, if the reading program focuses mainly on comprehension, the children can be taught to read simultaneously in both the native and non-native languages, or in the non-native language first.

Knowledge of this point may be a comfort to teachers who find their options limited by practical realities. Often, teachers may have little choice: ESL students may have to be taught to read first in English, and reading instruction will probably have to begin well before the students have a great deal of knowledge of English. These situations may come about because there is a shortage of qualified teachers and suitable instructional materials. Matters are further complicated, particularly in urban classrooms, if the ESL students come from many different language backgrounds.

In any event, even when students receive reading and language instruction from well-qualified ESL teachers, classroom teachers still should monitor students' progress in learning to read and make sure that they receive adequate classroom opportunities to develop English reading and writing skills. Moll and Diaz (in press) emphasize the importance of giving Spanish-dominant students the opportunity to apply Spanish speaking and reading skills in learning to read texts written in English. For example, although reading an English text, the children could be allowed to discuss the ideas in Spanish. They recommend that English reading lessons focus on comprehension, whether ideas are discussed in English or in Spanish. If the children speak in English, they suggest that the teacher concentrate on the ideas the children are expressing and not spend much time correcting their grammar and pronunciation.

In general, then, we suggest that the reading instruction provided for ESL students be much like that for students who speak English as a first language, in the sense that it should be oriented largely to the teaching of comprehension, or the constructing of meaning from text. If comprehension-oriented

Displaying words written in both Spanish and English is one way of showing students that their Spanish-language skills are valued in the classroom.

reading instruction can be provided, ESL students can learn to read simultaneously in both the native language and in English. If the children are being taught to read first in the native language, the teacher should try to allow them to use native language reading and speaking skills to promote learning to read in English. To further students' knowledge of English and appreciation for literature, the teacher's reading aloud of good books should be an integral part of the reading and language program.

Guidelines for improving students' English proficiency

The most important general guideline teachers should follow is to focus on children's *ideas* rather than the exact form used to express them. The teacher's goal is to try to understand the messages the children are seeking to communicate, however limited their proficiency in English, and to respond positively to these messages. Correcting children's grammar or drilling them on proper pronunciation does little to develop language (for discussion of this point, see Gonzales, 1980) and might discourage them from continuing to speak up. Refer to Chapter 2 for guidelines on encouraging language development in all children. The guidelines below are those recommended by Gonzales (1981) specifically for use with ESL students (adapted from Gonzales, 1981, pp. 178-180).

1. *Create a comfortable atmosphere for ESL students to try speaking English, and encourage them to begin speaking when they feel ready to do so.* According to Gonzales, ESL students may go through a "silent period" when they are in fact learning English but not yet ready to speak it. Remind yourself to be patient and supportive while the children are starting to learn English, and do not expect instant proficiency.

2. *Accept the children's accents.* Do not drill them on standard pronunciations or isolated sounds. Making sure that ESL students have many opportunities to speak and listen to native speakers of English will lead naturally to improvement in this area.

3. *Make your meaning as clear as you can and check for understanding.* Gonzales recommends using gestures and other nonverbal means to show children what you want them to do. Model the steps in completing assignments. Use alternate wordings. Perhaps have other children explain directions to the class in their own words. Then ask the children if they have understood, and be prepared to offer more help if necessary. Ask questions requiring answers with several words. This will ensure that you do not just get back rote answers and so have a better chance of uncovering the misunderstandings an ESL student may have.

4. *Speak warmly in a normal and natural tone of voice to ESL students. It is not necessary to speak more slowly or loudly.*

5. *If you can, explain the purpose of the lesson in the students' native language.* Giving ESL students a preview of what to expect will make it easier for them to follow directions and explanations given in English.

INSTRUCTIONAL ACTIVITIES

Listed below are a number of instructional activities to be used in the classroom with ESL students.

Reading aloud to ESL students

ESL students, like all other students, need to become familiar with English in its written form, which of course differs from spoken English. Thus, the reading aloud of picture books and other forms of children's literature is extremely important. Regardless of their proficiency in English, ESL students can benefit from this activity. Refer to Chapters 2 and 6 for guidelines for reading aloud to children and drawing responses from them. The shared book experience, an activity described earlier in this chapter, is also highly recommended.

Make the books you read aloud available to ESL students. Encourage them to look at the pictures and words and "tell the story" in English even if they cannot yet read most of it word-for-word.

Language experience

Using the language experience approach helps young ESL students, who cannot yet read in any language, to get started in reading. Refer to Chapters 2 and 11 for a discussion of LEA. With ESL students as with all other children, the reading aloud of books should always be used along with LEA. This ensures that the students will be exposed to a wide variety of written, and not only oral, language patterns.

Hudelson and Barrera (1985) recommend using a variation of the language experience approach with ESL students who are just beginning to speak English, for the purposes of involving them in lessons. In this procedure, the teacher writes cloze sentences on the board for the children to complete. For example, suppose that the teacher has brought a grocery sack containing different kinds of vegetables. The children could be asked to complete sentences such as:

_____ said, "I like to eat _____."

_____ said, "I don't like to eat _____."

_____ said, "The biggest vegetable is _____."

_____ said, "The smallest vegetable is _____."

After the blanks have been filled in, the children could reread all the sentences.

Predictable books

Along with lessons following the language experience approach, young ESL students can be given reading instruction with predictable books, books where the same patterns of language, descriptions, and events occur again and again (Feeley, 1983). For a list of suitable books, refer to Rhodes (1981) and Tompkins and Webeler (1983). Bill Martin's *Sounds of Language* series and the *Little Owl* books are other examples. When just beginning work with predictable books, you might first read the book or selection aloud to the children, and then have them read it aloud with you as a group. Ask the children questions and encourage them to use words and phrases from the book in answering you. Write words, phrases, and sentences from the book on the chalkboard, in such a way that the children can easily see their similarities and differences.

Feeley (1983) suggests that you tape readings of predictable books so the children can later listen and follow along. Or you can purchase book and tape sets. The children can reread the books silently and retell the stories during a small group lesson. Feeley also recommends having the children complete cloze exercises based on sentences from the text.

Book floods

Elley and Mangubhai (1983) found that "book floods" improved ESL students' reading achievement. Approximately 50 new books were introduced to each class of ESL students (ages 9 to 11) at four or five week intervals. Children benefited from the book floods whether they learned through the shared book experience or silent reading method. In the silent reading method, the books were displayed and the teachers regularly read some of them aloud, with 20 to 30 minutes per day allotted for sustained silent reading.

Elley and Mangubhai offer the following conclusions and practical suggestions. First, allow the children to have access to a variety of books. Elley and Mangubhai feel that books should be selected for interesting content rather than for controlled vocabulary or sentence length. Second, they recommend having a large number of books, perhaps 150, available to the children. Included among these should be a number of popular western children's stories, such as versions of the Three Pigs, Cinderella, and Red Riding Hood, which they found many children to enjoy. Books from the Ladybird series were also popular.

Writing

Feeley (1983) and others recommend giving ESL students many opportunities to write. In addition to the writing activities recommended in Chapter 8, you might also encourage ESL students to make their own dictionaries. Older children should be allowed to use native language skills to support their learning of English words. For example, Feeley writes:

I saw a 10-year-old Korean girl's dictionary of her "own" English terms, loosely alphabetized, and defined by a mixture of English words and Korean ideographs. She was very proud of her collection. (p. 654)

STUDENTS WHO SPEAK A DIALECT OF ENGLISH

In the view of linguists, *all* speakers of English are speakers of a dialect (Barnitz, 1980). What we commonly refer to as Standard English or as "good" or "proper" English is itself a dialect or version of the English language. The difference between this particular dialect and all others is that it has the greatest prestige, being widely used by television broadcasters, business leaders, government officials, and others in influential positions.

While there are differences between written and oral versions of English, spoken Standard English is generally considered to be closer to the commonly published forms of English, in terms of grammar and vocabulary. Thus, children who speak a nonstandard dialect of English have often been thought to be at a disadvantage in learning to read. There is, however, little evidence to support the view that speaking a dialect actively interferes with learning to read (e.g., Hart, Guthrie, & Winfield, 1980; Au, Tharp, Crowell, Jordan, Speidel, & Calkins, 1984). In particular, its effect on comprehension (spoken or written) is minimal (Alexander, 1979). Nor is there evidence to support the view that drilling children on Standard English grammar and pronunciation improves learning to read.

In teaching reading to dialect-speaking students, current research suggests that the source of the problem is probably in cultural differences in communication styles and teachers' attitudes toward children's language, rather than just the children's speaking of a nonstandard dialect (e.g., Au et al., 1984). Thus, teachers working with children who enter school as speakers of a nonstandard dialect should be aware of cultural differences, as discussed earlier, and seek to develop a positive attitude about the children's language and abilities. They should have some understanding of nonstandard dialects in general as well as of their students' particular dialects.

Alexander (1979) makes the following points in discussing black dialect (also referred to as Black English or Black Vernacular English), and these points apply as well to other dialects. First, most dialect speakers are actually bidialectal. That is, they speak the dialect in informal situations or when addressing other speakers of the same dialect, but can easily switch to Standard English in formal situations or when addressing those who do not speak the dialect. Second, there are many different versions of Black English or black dialect. Dialects vary by region as well as by social class, younger speakers may use different vocabulary from older speakers, and so on. All dialects, like Standard English or any other version of a language, follow definite rules and are complete, effective language systems.

Teachers should be aware that dialect speakers' use of speech features different from those of Standard English is *not* a sign of inferior language or thinking ability. Rather, it is simply a sign that the children are expressing themselves in an alternate, more familiar language code. For example, Barnitz (1980) gives the following examples of frequently cited syntactic differences between black dialect and Standard English:

"Be" verb: To show ongoing action or states of being, VBE speakers may say "I be pretty [everyday]." However, to show a particular instance instead of habitual aspect, the speaker may delete the *be* verb: "My friend pretty [today, wearing make-up]."

Past tense: The past tense marker is often deleted. "The man walk yesterday." This process often results from the consonant cluster simplification rule.

Existential it: The speaker may say "It ['s] a man in our yard" instead of "There [is] a man in the yard." (p. 781)

But while teachers must show respect and appreciation for the children's own language, they should still be aware of making sure that the children are becoming more and more familiar with Standard English. Having knowledge of Standard English will make it easier for the students to learn to read texts written in Standard English, which will make up the vast majority of the material they encounter.

Guidelines for developing dialect speakers' knowledge of Standard English

The most important general guideline is the same as that stated for working with ESL students: focus on the child's ideas rather than the exact form used to express them. Other recommendations are as follows:

1. Create an accepting atmosphere for the use of language, one where students will feel comfortable using the dialect but also have the opportunity to learn Standard English. This is accomplished by allowing students to express their ideas in the dialect. You will, however, respond in Standard English, modeling the use of Standard English pronunciation, vocabulary, and syntax for the students. You will not need to correct the students. Rather, the way to encourage learning is to continue to engage them in discussion of the topic, so they will have the opportunity to use the Standard English forms you modeled.

2. Accept the children's accents. As with ESL students, correcting pronunciation or providing drill on isolated sounds is ineffective. Variations in pronunciation generally do not affect dialect speakers' ability to make themselves understood. Allow students to use dialect pronunciations or substitutions when reading orally. Do not correct their reading unless it is apparent that the meaning of the text has been changed.

3. With older students, discuss in a sensitive manner how Standard English may be appropriate in some situations, and the dialect in others. Help them to understand the advantages of being able to use Standard English at certain times. Encourage them to practice using Standard English forms during reading lessons, for example, but do not correct them when they use the dialect instead.

Recommended sequence of instruction for beginning readers

The following variation of the language experience approach may be beneficial in increasing children's knowledge of Standard English (adapted from Gillet & Gentry, 1983, pp. 361-363).

The recommended sequence of beginning reading instruction for young dialect speakers is like that recommended in Chapter 2 for most other kindergarten and first grade students, and in this chapter for young ESL students. In other words, begin by reading aloud to the children and by using the language experience approach. Move on to predictable books and, if possible, give the students the opportunity to write every day, preferably on topics of their own choosing. When working with young dialect speakers, the teaching of reading using a basal reader should always be supplemented with these other activities.

INSTRUCTIONAL ACTIVITIES

Extending the language experience approach

Step 1. Begin the lesson following the usual method for having the children dictate a story. In other words, introduce a stimulus for discussion, and take down the children's story without changing the language used. See Figure 9.2 for a story dictated by first grade children in Jamaica and then transformed following the procedures outlined by Gillet and Gentry.

Step 2. Introduce a Standard English version. Gillet and Gentry recommend that the teacher rewrite the children's original story in Standard English. This story is then printed on chart paper in the same manner. Alternately, if the children are already somewhat familiar with Standard English, the teacher could work with the group to arrive at a Standard English version. Introduce this version as "another story" about the same topic and have the children read it aloud, in the usual way.

Step 3. Have the children revise their sentences. Reintroduce the original story and have the children review it. Then have each child revise and expand upon his original statements. Encourage the children to make each sentence longer and more detailed and interesting, using phrases such as, "Can you think of another way to say that?" and "What would you like to add?" Do not use wordings (such as "How can you make this sentence correct?") which

FIGURE 9.2   Sentence Transformations from "Funny Fruits"

They	were	in	a	bag.
(Cookies)	were	in	a	box.
Cookies	were	in	a	jar.
(Words) and (pictures)	were	in	the	books.
Shoes and *socks*	were	(under)	the	big bed.
A *dog* and a *cat*	were	inside	the	red barn.
The fruit	felt	squishy	and	round.
The (apple)	felt	hard	and	bumpy.
The (puppy)	felt	soft, warm	and	wiggly.
The (new) baseball	felt	(very) hard.		
The *ripe mango*	(tasted)	sweet	and	delicious.
The *old shoes*	(looked)	dirty	and	worn out.

Teacher's suggestions in parentheses, children's in italic type.
Figure: "Sentence Transformations from 'Funny Fruits'" from "Bridges between Nonstandard and Standard English with Extensions of Dictated Stories" by Jean W. Gillet and J. R. Gentry, January 1983 in *The Reading Teacher*. Reprinted with permission of the authors and the International Reading Association.

suggest that the earlier sentence was inferior. While you may wish to make a few corrections at this point, do so sensitively and do not expect the children's new story to be entirely in Standard English. Have the children practice reading the new story.

Step 4. Have the children practice sentence transformations. Use sentences from any of the three versions of the story to show the children how sentences can be produced by substituting different words. Write the original sentences on the chalkboard or on chart paper. Put a copy of the sentence below, leaving a blank to indicate where the new words can be substituted. Have the children suggest words to fill the blank.

Sample story obtained in Step 1

Funny Fruits

Mandy said, "They was in a bag—a lunch bag."
Kareem said, "They was some kind of fruits."
Tonya said, "Teacher say feel it."
Jerome said, "They was real squishy."

Version developed for Step 2

The Mystery Bag

Mandy, Kareem, Tonya, and Jerome learned about some funny fruit. First, we looked at a lunch bag. Second, we each put one hand into the bag. We each felt the funny fruit. Then, we talked about the fruit. We tried to guess what the fruit was. Last, we wrote a story about the funny, squishy fruit.

Version developed during Step 3

Funny Fruits

Mandy said, "First, we looked at the lunch bag."
Kareem said, "There were some fruits in the bag."
Tonya said, "Our teacher said to put in your hand and feel around but don't tell what it is.
Jerome said, "The fruit felt squishy and sort of round."

Sentence transformations from Step 4. See Figure 9.2

Activities for older students

Among others, Alexander (1979) recommends the following classroom activities which are in keeping with guidelines presented earlier. All may, of course, be adapted for use with children who speak any nonstandard dialect.

Have your students read some of the poems of black literature which offer opportunities for performance-response, perhaps the poetry of Gwendolyn Brooks and Langston Hughes.

Discuss the major dialect areas in the United States.

Discuss reasons for the different dialects and why we should respect dialectal differences.

Read passages in other English dialects to your students to help them appreciate the variability of English and the legitimacy of their own dialect.

Discuss and role-play different situations in which vernacular Black English dialect and Standard English dialect would be used.

Teach the grammatical constructions of Standard English dialect. Provide time for practice of grammatical constructions. (pp. 575-576)

KEY CONCEPT 3

Teachers should know how to provide sound classroom reading instruction to children who are poor readers.

WHY DO SOME CHILDREN BECOME POOR READERS?

In teaching reading, many classroom teachers experience the greatest difficulty in working effectively with children in the "low group," those in the bottom third or quarter of the class. We will refer to these students as *poor readers*. These students appear to be making very slow or, in some cases, inconsistent progress in learning to read. Some may also appear to be more inattentive or restless than the good readers in the class.

Children will, of course, enter school differing in many ways, including aptitude for learning to read and previous experiences with literacy. The

EXERCISE

(1) Arrange to observe the same teacher providing instruction to two different groups of students, one a group of high achievers and the other a group of low achievers.

(2) While observing, write down as much as you can about what the teacher and children say and do during the lesson. Try to record information enabling you to answer the following questions:

What were the children supposed to learn during this lesson (i.e., what was the teacher's purpose for teaching the lesson)?

What questions or tasks did the teacher pose for the children?

How interested and involved were the children?

What materials were used?

(3) Analyze your observation notes for similarities and differences in the answers you obtained to the four questions above. In what ways were the lessons similar? In what ways did they differ? What do you think accounts for the differences? In your opinion, was instruction equally beneficial for both groups?

Keep your observations in mind while reading about the research findings described below. Compare these findings to the patterns you discovered. This research highlights the fact that teachers are often unaware of how differences in the lessons given to good and poor readers may be handicapping poor readers even more. Even with the best of intentions, we may make serious errors in our approach to improving the reading ability of some children.

---

research suggests, however, that *many students' slowness in learning to read is highly related to the quality of the instruction they receive.* In general, it seems that poor readers never have the opportunity to learn to read well because they consistently receive lessons of poor quality. Thus, our point of view is that teachers should work to provide high quality instruction to poor readers.

Allington (1983) summarizes evidence to support the view that *"good and poor readers differ in their reading ability as much because of differences in instruction as variations in individual learning styles or aptitudes"* (p. 548; italics in the original). His review indicates five areas in which the instruction given to poor readers differs from that given to good readers.

1. Allocation of instructional time. Teachers seem to allocate about the same amount of time for teaching reading to good and poor readers. However, Allington argues that this treatment is in fact unequal, because poor readers need *more* instructional time to overcome their reading deficits.

2. Engaged instructional time. During reading lessons, poor readers show more off-task behavior or less engagement with the reading task than good readers. According to Allington, the problem is *not* that poor readers are naturally inattentive or hyperactive. Rather, he suggests that much off-task behavior results because the type of instruction given to poor readers allows them to be distracted by signals from a number of different sources. This is related to the fact that poor readers engage in oral reading more often than good readers.

3. *General instructional emphases.* While the lessons given to good readers tend to focus on meaningful discussions of the text, those for poor readers are generally organized around oral reading. Poor readers appear to receive more instruction on word identification and less on comprehension. Thus, poor readers seem to have less chance than good readers to gain an understanding of reading as the process of constructing meaning from text.

4. *Quality and mode of assigned reading.* In first grade classes, Allington found that good readers did more reading every day than poor readers (about three times as many words). Furthermore, good readers do about 70 percent of their reading silently, while poor readers do most of their reading orally. This is a dangerous trend because, in general, the amount of time spent in silent reading seems to be positively related to reading achievement. Also, good readers tend to be questioned and evaluated on their understanding of the text, while poor readers are assessed on the word-for-word accuracy of their oral reading.

5. *Teacher interruption behavior.* Teachers tend to correct and interrupt poor readers much more frequently than good readers. These practices are damaging to poor readers, Allington suggests, because they prevent them from engaging in self-monitoring and self-correction when reading. As discussed at many points in earlier chapters, both self-monitoring and self-correction are important components of reading comprehension, but poor readers apparently have little opportunity to practice them.

INSTRUCTIONAL GUIDELINES

On the basis of this review, Allington arrives at the following recommendations for working with poor readers (adapted from Allington, 1983, pp. 554–556):

1. *Assess the teaching behaviors you use when giving lessons to poor readers.* Before changing anything, become aware of what you are already doing. Tape record a number of the lessons you give to your slowest learners, review the tapes, count such features as the number of interruptions, and identify behaviors to be changed. Try to make the needed changes and then tape record lessons to make comparisons. Over time, see if you can detect any changes in the students' behavior. A good way to measure your success is by the number of low-group students you are able to move into other, regular-ability reading groups.

2. *Give poor readers a second daily reading lesson.* Try to give slow learners the extra instructional time they need to overcome their disadvantage. Remember, however, that these lessons must be of high quality. Not just time, but what happens during reading lessons, is the critical factor.

3. *Be sure poor readers spend a substantial amount of time in silent*

reading. If you add a second reading lesson, Allington suggests that you allow only silent reading during this time. In any event, anticipate the students' having difficulty with silent reading at first, since few of them will have had much previous experience with it. Be sure to set purposes for silent reading and remind the children to use strategies such as skipping over unknown words and then coming back to them later. Try not to offer too much help. In the beginning, use a highly structured lesson framework, such as the DRTA, and break the story into relatively short segments for silent reading. Begin with texts the students should find quite easy.

4. *Every day, give students the opportunity to read easy material for the purpose of increasing their reading fluency.* Poor readers often have developed the habit of labored, word-by-word reading. Thus, you want to give them the feeling of moving smoothly through the text often experienced by good readers. This is a matter both of selecting easier-to-read texts and of giving poor readers the chance to develop reading habits more like those of good readers. To develop a sense of fluency, a suitable procedure is the method of repeated readings, described below.

5. *Teach students to monitor their own reading performances.* Emphasize to poor readers the importance of "making sense" when reading, and be sure to give them the chance to correct their interpretations of the text. Through tape recordings or other means, check to be certain that you are not encouraging them to become dependent on *your* monitoring. Do not jump in immediately and correct a student's error during discussion or oral reading, but give students the chance to correct themselves. For example, ask for an explanation of the answer or have the student reread. Set purposes for reading and have students check to see if their reading has met these purposes.

6. *Have poor readers spend more time in recreational reading, or in reading for information, and less time with worksheet and workbook assignments.* The reading required by worksheet and workbook assignments is unlike the reading of text and tradebooks (e.g., Osborn, 1984). Especially for poor readers, valuable time is wasted if students are doing these peripheral assignments rather than actually reading for meaning. Use easy texts for independent reading and hold students responsible for discussing their reading or for writing a brief report. If a teacher's aide is available, he or she can be asked to listen to students' retellings or summaries and to discuss their reading with them.

HANDICAPPED STUDENTS

Among the poor readers in the classroom may be a number of handicapped students. Included in this broad term are students who are learning disabled, mentally retarded, visually or hearing impaired, speech impaired, physically handicapped, or emotionally disturbed. Some may be multiply handicapped. Under the provisions of Public Law 94-142, referred to as the Education of the

Handicapped Act, handicapped students are to be given individualized instruction and *mainstreamed*, or educated as much as possible in regular classroom environments.

As it concerns the classroom reading program, the first implication of this law is that teachers should participate in developing the individualized education plan (IEP) drawn up for each handicapped student in the classroom. The IEP should present in writing the educational program, including provisions for reading instruction, the school is providing to meet the student's special needs. The IEP is usually developed by the special education teacher and/or other school personnel with expertise in special education, and the classroom teacher, with the cooperation of the child's parents.

The second implication of the law, because it emphasizes mainstreaming, is that teachers need to know how they can help the handicapped student learn to read in the regular classroom. Handicapped children who are poor readers should probably be provided with instruction consistent with the guidelines above and including activities such as those listed below. This means that their overall program of reading instruction will emphasize comprehension, with special provisions for developing their awareness of thinking and reasoning processes, for increasing their reading fluency, and for encouraging independent silent reading.

INSTRUCTIONAL ACTIVITIES

Be sure to give poor readers a full range of instruction, just as you do good readers. Include comprehension activities described in Chapters 5 through 7, writing activities in Chapter 8, and vocabulary activities in Chapter 4. Comprehension activities mentioned earlier, found to be particularly effective with poor readers, are the inferential comprehension strategy (see Chapter 6) and reciprocal teaching (see Chapter 7). The activities described below can be used to *supplement* the basic developmental reading program for poor readers.

Confirmation strategy

The purpose of the confirmation strategy developed by Holmes (1983) is to improve poor readers' ability to draw inferences from text by giving them a systematic approach for checking their hypotheses. The method developed by Holmes is consistent with a theme developed in Chapters 5 through 7—that of teaching students specific comprehension strategies and encouraging them to become aware of their own thinking while reading.

The confirmation strategy helps students identify and then make use of important text information. Holmes emphasizes the importance of beginning with easy materials and then moving on to more difficult ones. This enables the students to be successful and then motivates them to continue. The procedure was tested with poor readers in the fourth and fifth grades. The description below is adapted from Holmes (1983, pp. 145–146).

Step 1: Reading the passage. Have the students read the passage, along with an inferential question about it. As an example, Holmes gives the following passage and question:

The more Roy walked, the darker it grew. He had to crouch to keep from bumping the damp rocks overhead. To his left ran a small underground brook. It was the only sound he heard besides his footsteps crunching over stones and earth. When he turned around, Roy saw the place where he had come in. It was a small, bright spot of light.

Question: Where is Roy?

Step 2: Hypothesizing an answer. Ask the children to draw upon their background knowledge to come up with possible answers to the question. In this instance, the children might think of responses such as "at the beach" or "in a cave."

Step 3: Identifying key words. Have the students go through the passage from the beginning and identify key words and phrases. Be sure to tell them to start with the first sentence, so that they will be able to begin the task without hesitation. In the sample passage, the key words and phrases are *walked, darker it grew, crouch,* and *damp rocks overhead.*

Step 4: Formulating and answering yes/no questions. At this point you are modeling for the children the kinds of questions you would eventually like them to be able to ask themselves. Ask the students yes/no questions about one of the answers proposed earlier, to see whether it can be supported by the key words. Continue until you receive a "no" response. For example, for the answer "at the beach," the teacher might ask the following questions:

If Roy is at the beach could he walk? [yes] Could it be getting darker? [yes, if it's evening] Could he be bumping damp rocks overhead? [no]

Step 5: Making a final confirmation. If the first answer proposed is eliminated, go through the same procedure of using yes/no questions with another of the proposed answers. Continue on through the list of answers until one of them is finally confirmed.

After the children have had some experience with the confirmation strategy, encourage them to conduct the yes/no questioning themselves. Have them take turns being the teacher and asking yes/no questions of the other students.

Think-alouds

Davey (1983) suggests that teachers model for poor readers the techniques good readers use to overcome comprehension problems. The purpose of this procedure is to make poor readers aware of the different strategies they can use when they experience difficulty with a particular text. The teacher thinks aloud, verbalizing thoughts while reading orally. Like the confirmation strategy, this activity is also consistent with the theme of helping children to acquire particular comprehension strategies and to become aware of the thought processes used while reading.

First, select a passage to read aloud that contains points of difficulty, contradictions, ambiguities, or unknown words. (You may want to develop your own materials for this step—short, with obvious problems.) As you read the passage aloud, students follow along silently, listening to how you think through these trouble spots. Here are some examples of points to make during think-alouds:

1. *Make predictions.* (Show how to develop hypotheses.)

    From the title, I predict that this section will tell how fishermen used to catch whales.

    In this next part, I think we'll find out why the men flew into the hurricane.

    I think this is a description of a computer game.

2. *Describe the picture you're forming in your head from the informa-tion.* (Show how to develop images during reading.)

    I have a picture of this scene in my mind. The car is on a dark, probably narrow, road; there are no other cars around.

3. *Share an analogy.* (Show how to link prior knowledge with new infor-mation in the text.) We call this the "like a" step.

    This is like a time we drove to Boston and had a flat tire. We were worried and we had to walk three miles for help.

4. *Verbalize a confusing point.* (Show how you monitor your ongoing comprehension.)

    This just doesn't make sense.
    This is different from what I had expected.

5. *Demonstrate fix-up strategies.* (Show how you correct your lagging comprehension.)

    I'd better reread.
    Maybe I'll read ahead to see if it gets clearer.
    This is a new word to me—I'd better check context to figure it out.

When you have completed your oral reading, encourage students to add their thoughts to yours.

After several modeling experiences, students can work with partners to practice think-alouds, taking turns in reading orally and sharing thoughts. The listening partner may add thoughts after the oral sharing has been completed. Again, carefully developed materials should be used initially (short, with ob-vious problems). Move then to school materials of various types and lengths. Finally, encourage readers to practice thinking through materials silently. This is the final step toward using the strategies independently. We used checklists of various types (see an example in Figure 9.3) to stimulate student involvement and verify that readers were using this procedure.   (Davey, 1983, pp. 45–46)

FIGURE 9.3   Self-Evaluation of Think-Alouds

While I was reading how did I do?   (Put an X in the appropriate column.)

	Not very much	A little bit	Much of the time	All of the time
Made predictions				
Formed pictures				
Used "like-a"				
Found problems				
Used fix-ups				

From "Think Aloud: Modeling the Cognitive Processes of Reading Comprehension" by Beth Davey, October 1983 in the *Journal of Reading.* Reprinted with permission of Beth Davey and the International Reading Association.

Repeated readings

The purpose of the method of repeated readings described by Samuels (1979) is to improve the reading fluency of poor readers. In this method students read a short, meaningful passage several times until they can read it fluently. They then move on to a new passage. This procedure allows poor readers to experience ease in reading and improves their word identification ability. The method can be used with students at all grade levels.

According to Samuels, fluency has two components: speed and accuracy. He advises teachers to have students read with greater speed rather than with complete accuracy. This prevents poor readers from being overly hesitant or fearful when reading. Each time students' reread the text, they find it easier and easier to recognize the words. Because little attention is then required for word identification, more attention can be paid to comprehension. Thus, Samuels argues, repeated readings should also lead to improved comprehension of the passage.

Here are some suggestions Samuels makes for using the method of repeated readings:

1. Match the amount of material to be read to the students' reading skill. With very poor readers, begin with passages as short as just 50 words, and increase the length of passages gradually. (In our experience, we find it important for students beginning to work with the method of repeated readings to be motivated to participate in the activity and not to become discouraged. Therefore, teachers should look for short passages on topics of interest to the students.)

2. If working with very poor readers, first read the passage with or to them, and then have them practice it. You could also make a tape recording of the passage and have them read along with the recording until they are able to read the passage on their own.

3. Have somewhat more capable students select the books or other materials they wish to read. Break longer texts into segments of about 200 words for the students to work with. This enables the students to experience much more success.

4. Time the students' reading, or have them time themselves. Have each student keep a graph showing improvement in reading times.

5. To build comprehension, ask students a different comprehension question after each rereading of the text. We think another possibility would be to have students report on anything new or interesting noticed during the rereading.

6. Enlist the help of other students, aides, or parents. Have them listen to the students read and time their readings. They can also keep records of word recognition errors. You can then work with other students, knowing the poor readers have others to help with their practice.

Lauritzen (1982) suggests two modifications to the method of repeated readings to make it easier for classroom teachers to use. These modifications may be especially useful if you are working with younger children.

1. *Choose selections with rhyme, rhythm, and sequence, following oral literature patterns.* Lauritzen recommends folktales such as *Henry Penny, Old Mother Hubbard, The Gingerbread Boy, The Three Little Pigs, The Turnip,* and *The Old Woman and Her Pig.* Poetry and song lyrics are also good choices.

2. *Have the students read in a group rather than individually.* First, read the selection aloud. Then have students follow along by looking at the words. Have them work from copies of the book or from a chart, or print the words on the chalkboard. Then have the children echo your reading, saying each line, sentence, or paragraph (choose the length of the segment according to the structure of the text). Finally, have the group read the entire selection in unison.

Let the children read the text as many times as they wish, working individually, in pairs, or in small groups. Have them listen to a tape if you have made one. Let them continue to read in unison for two days or more. When the children can read the text fluently, let them read it to other students, parents, or the principal.

To develop word identification skills, break the text into segments by putting verses, sentences, or words on cards or strips of oaktag. Have the students put the cards or strips together in the proper order in a pocketchart or on a table top.

Oral reading for meaning

The purpose of this procedure, developed by Taylor and Nosbush (1983), is to improve poor readers' ability to identify words in context. Specifically, the student is encouraged to correct his or her own errors and to consider whether miscues make sense in the context of the passage. The four steps in the procedure involve having the student read orally, praising the student for self-correcting, instructing the student to make sure words make sense in the context, and providing direct instruction in word identification skills. Word identification instruction is based on the kind of errors just made.

The procedure requires the classroom teacher or a tutor to spend a brief time working with individual students. It proved effective with poor readers in the third grade, and can probably be used with students from the second grade on up.

Step One: To conduct oral reading for meaning, work with a student on a one-to-one basis for 10 to 15 minutes. The student reads 100–300 words aloud from material on his/her instructional level. Record any miscues the student makes, but, to avoid interruption, provide as little feedback as possible while the student is reading. Encourage the student to do the best she/he can without teacher assistance.

Step Two: After the student has finished reading aloud, praise the student for something she/he has done well during the oral reading. If possible, focus this praise on any self-corrections the student made, particularly on miscues which interfered with meaning. Encourage the student to engage in more self-correcting in the future when she/he comes across miscues that don't make sense.

Step Three: Discuss one or two miscues that the student didn't self-correct. They should be ones that didn't make sense but that occurred in sentences with good context clues. For example, if a student read, "The shepherd came and stood before the *thorn* where the king sat" (for "The

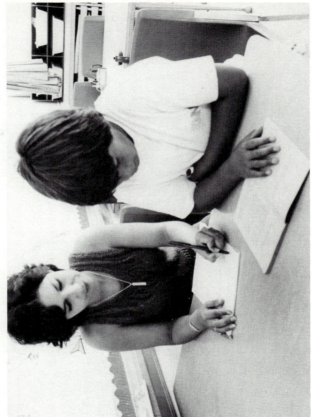

This student is reading aloud a passage from a favorite book while his teacher records words read incorrectly. She will use these words in later instruction on word identification skills.

shepherd came and stood before the throne where the king sat"), "thorn" would be a good miscue to discuss because it doesn't make sense for a king to sit on a thorn. On the other hand, if a student read, "He had *barely* read the words" (for "He had scarcely read the words"), "barely" would not be a good miscue to discuss because the error hasn't interfered with meaning.

To discuss an uncorrected, semantically inappropriate miscue, read the sentence in which the miscue occurred just as the student read it. Then ask the student if there seems to be a word in the sentence which doesn't make sense, giving guidance if necessary. Then help the student decode the troublesome word, stressing the use of context and phonics. For example, you might say, "What word beginning with *thr* would make sense here? Where would a king sit?" Also, continually remind the student that, in the future, after decoding a word like "thorn" that doesn't seem to make sense, she/he should stop and correct the error. It is through repetitive reminders to self-correct that eventual improvements in the student's self-correcting behavior will be seen.

Step Four: Finally, provide the student with on-the-spot instruction in a word identification skill that the student has had difficulty with during oral reading. You may decide to skip this step if you do not have an additional five minutes or so to spend with an individual student on a particular day.

On days when you are able to carry out this last step, however, select just one area which seems particularly troublesome. Perhaps you noticed the student had a problem with a word identification skill that had also caused problems for that student on a previous occasion. If a student has read "know" for "now," you may choose to provide five minutes of instruction on words with two different sounds for *ow*. Or, if the student has read "though" for "thought," you might provide instruction on this frequently confused pair of basic sight words. Perhaps the student has made several errors involving the endings of words, for example, endings have been frequently omitted or inserted. You might work for a few minutes on these words, stressing the need to pay more attention to word endings when decoding.

As an alternative to focusing on a problem, you might choose to reinforce a word identification skill that was recently taught. For example, if the students recently studied common sounds for *ea*, you and the student might locate and discuss words containing *ea* in the material just read aloud. (Taylor and Nosbush, pp. 235–236)

To be effective, the oral reading for meaning procedure should be used with individual students on a regular basis, probably two or more times per week. You may wish to work with two or three poor readers at first, and concentrate on their instruction for a four to six week period. Then, select a second set of poor readers to receive the procedure for a second four to six week period. Monitor the progress of the students in the first group and provide maintenance lessons as needed.

KEY CONCEPT 4

Teachers should know how to provide sound classroom reading instruction to gifted readers.

GIFTED READERS

The term *gifted* is generally applied to students with above-average intellectual ability. Usually, this means the students have IQs above 120 or 130. Having a high IQ, however, does not mean that a child is equally gifted in all fields of endeavor. For example, one child may have exceptional musical talent while another may excel in science. These two students are both gifted, but not in the same way.

It makes sense, then, not to treat all gifted students identically, but to address their needs according to areas of special talent and interest. Thus, because this textbook is about reading instruction, we will be concerned here with ways teachers can meet the needs of children who have exceptional ability in reading and working with text information. We will refer to these students as *gifted readers*.

In identifying gifted readers, teachers cannot rely on IQ score alone. They should look at how well the children are able to handle classroom reading and writing assignments. They should also examine the children's reading achievement test scores and criterion referenced reading test results. As you will learn in Chapter 10, a score at stanine 9 (or perhaps 8) on standarized tests is likely to indicate a gifted reader.

The following profile of a gifted reader is intended to give teachers a sense of the pattern of behavior often shown by such a child, although some gifted readers may not show exactly this same pattern. First, gifted readers are often able to comprehend both the details and larger ideas in text much more readily than other students in the class. Second, they appear to have a much broader base of knowledge, across many different topics, than do most children at the same grade level. In a related vein, they have larger vocabularies, in the sense that they know the meaning of many more words than most students. Third, they generally experience no problems at all with word identification.

In terms of standardized achievement test scores, teachers will generally find gifted readers to be at least a year above grade level by the time they are in the second and third grades, and two or more years above grade level by the time they are in the fourth grade and above. The results of criterion-referenced testing will show the same high levels of performance, reflecting the students' ability to master reading skills at a much faster than average rate.

But while gifted readers may show a similar pattern of reading ability and achievement, they may be very different in terms of such factors as study

INSTRUCTIONAL GUIDELINES

1. *Provide gifted readers with systematic and challenging instruction in comprehension.* Such lessons should encourage gifted readers to think deeply and not superficially about text ideas, so that they learn to make good use of their special talents. For lesson ideas, refer to the Instructional Activities section under this key concept.

2. *Have gifted readers spend more time in recreational reading, or in reading for information, and less time with worksheet and workbook assignments.* Often, gifted readers do not need the type of practice provided by worksheets and workbooks. During time that other students might be spending with these activities, gifted readers can be allowed to read independently, following their own interests or a plan worked out with the teacher. You may wish to use an individualized reading approach as described in Chapter 11.

3. *Be sure to give gifted readers a balance between opportunities for independent discovery and participation in reading activities involving other students.* Gifted readers, even when able to work independently for relatively long periods of time, should also be given ample time to interact with other children. They can be valuable contributors to the classroom community and so should be given the chance to discuss their ideas with others. Gifted readers may be placed in reading groups in some cases, or given other, somewhat less structured ways of sharing their ideas with other students. For example, a gifted reader who especially enjoys reading independently might be encouraged to discuss favorite books with other children.

4. *Be sure to give gifted readers the opportunity to work actively and creatively with the ideas gained through reading.* Gifted readers, along with other children in the class, can benefit from being given time to write every day. Part of their writing may be reflections on what they have read, stories in the style of a favorite author, or a report to be shared with the class. Other expressive activities might include dramatizations and art projects. Gifted readers might also conduct science experiments or interview experts to develop more fully ideas gained through reading. In short, reading can be used as a springboard to further the students' own literary or content area interests.

INSTRUCTIONAL ACTIVITIES

The following instructional activities are designed to challenge gifted readers by encouraging independence and the use of higher level thinking. All allow teachers to work in a systematic, but not restrictive, way with these students.

Inquiry reading

In the inquiry reading approach recommended by Cassidy (1981), the gifted reader conducts independent research on topics of interest. The student selects the topic, carries out the research, and then presents the findings to others. This cycle takes about four weeks and occupies time otherwise spent in basal reader instruction. The approach can be used by classroom teachers working with gifted readers in the third through sixth grades. Here are the steps in the instructional sequence:

First week

1. *Defining the term "inquiry."* Have the students discuss the meaning of inquiry, looking the word up in a dictionary if necessary.

2. *Presenting the requirements.* State the requirements for conducting the inquiry: that the students will each choose a question to investigate, that the inquiry will take up about four weeks, and that the end product will involve communicating the results.

3. *Discussing areas of interest.* Hold a brainstorming session and help each student to arrive at a list of interesting topics.

4. *Formulating questions.* Tell the students to develop three questions for possible investigation. Help each student to settle on one of these questions, neither too narrow nor too broad, to be the subject of the inquiry.

5. *Discussing references and resources.* Hold another brainstorming session to help the children come up with a list of references, such as the encyclopedia, books, or magazines. Also have them identify someone they can consult about the topic. This may be a parent or a professional in the field.

6. *Reviewing interview procedures.* Help the students draw up plans to conduct an interview of their chosen expert. Have the students write or phone the person for an appointment and then make up a list of interview questions.

7. *Identifying a sharing activity.* Early on, have the children decide how they will be sharing their findings. This procedure helps add direction and focus to their inquiry efforts.

8. *Developing a contract.* Help the students to set deadlines for completing each step in the inquiry.

Second and third weeks

1. *Reviewing methods for taking notes.*

2. *Locating references in the school or public library or at home.* If the students are unfamiliar with the process, assist them (or enlist the help of the librarian) in finding useful sources of information. The students then proceed to gather facts and ideas, writing the information on file cards or sheets of paper.

3. *Keeping a folder.* Have the students collect their notes in a folder. Staple a card with the student's question to the outside of the folder. Remind students to check back to be sure that their notes are all addressed to this question.

4. *Sharing problems and successes.* Conduct one or two sessions for the purpose of having the children share with one another the progress being made in their inquiries. Allow the students to offer suggestions to one another.

5. *Holding individual conferences.* Meet with each student individually to review his or her contract and make any adjustments needed.

6. *Constructing projects.* By the third week, students are usually spending most of their time putting their projects together.

Fourth week

1. *Completing projects.* Help students finish up, perhaps also suggesting adjustments to their original plans.

2. *Holding a dress rehearsal.* Have members of the group act as the audience for one another. Let the children suggest ways that other students' projects might be improved. Help the children adjust their presentations so the entire session, encompassing the sharing of all of the children in the group, will last no longer than 90 minutes. The presentations may take different forms. For example, a child may give a talk, speaking from an outline and notes, or read just part of a written report aloud and let the other members of the class know that the full report will be placed in the class library.

3. *Presenting to an outside audience.* The outside audience may consist of other students in the class, parents, or another homeroom.

4. *Evaluating the inquiry.* Meet with each student to go over the contract and finished project. Discuss what went well as well as areas that might have been handled differently.

Inquiry reading might be followed with experiences with the SEARCH procedure, described in Chapter 7. In this way, gifted readers can have the chance to work on projects with other students in the class, as well as with one another.

Instruction to improve purpose-setting and question-asking

Gifted readers often benefit from activities giving them the opportunity to learn to set their own purposes and to raise their own questions for reading. In keeping with this idea, Bates (1984) recommends that gifted readers be given instruction with the DRTA (see Chapter 5) and the ReQuest procedure (see Chapter 7). They may also make up their own study guides (see the pattern guides activity in Chapter 7), instead of working from a study guide prepared by the teacher.

In these activities the teacher will generally wish to guide, rather than totally direct, the students' reading efforts. At the same time, the teacher has the chance during these lessons to monitor the development of the children's reading comprehension abilities. It is important to do so to ensure, for example, that gifted readers learn to read carefully as well as quickly, and that they learn to base conclusions on text information and not just background knowledge.

Great books approach

Trevise (1984) recommends that teachers have gifted readers from the second grade on up work with the Junior Great Books Reading and Discussion Program developed by the Great Books Foundation. While reading the recommended "classics" students could meet for group discussions. Students in the discussion groups need not all be in the same grade. Discussion should focus on the universal themes in the books, as well as on the author, particular content, and style of writing. If teachers ask many open-ended questions and make the discussions challenging and interesting, the approach can have many advantages. These include encouraging gifted readers to read more widely, by reading books besides basal readers and textbooks; to read more critically, by having to analyze the texts read; and to read more creatively, by being asked to share individual responses to what they have read.

Curriculum compacting

The classroom program for gifted readers should, of course, be based on the children's needs and interests in learning to read. Occasionally, however, other school personnel or parents may be concerned that gifted readers "cover" all of the objectives in the standard reading curriculum used in the school. In this event, although the classroom teacher realizes that the curriculum may not be entirely appropriate for gifted readers, he or she may wish to use parts of the strategy of *curriculum compacting* (Renzulli, Smith, & Reis, 1982). This is a method for checking to make sure that the students have, indeed, mastered basic reading skills, and so can have the time to pursue more advanced and independent reading activities.

SUMMARY

Throughout this chapter we emphasized the importance of providing high quality, comprehension-oriented classroom reading instruction to students with special needs. In the first key concept, we discussed how differences in culture and communication styles can influence children's learning to read. We recommend that teachers see their goal as bridging the gap between the culture of the home and that of the school.

In the second key concept we addressed the issue of differences in language. We looked at the teaching of reading to students who speak a language other than English, then at teaching students who speak a dialect. In both cases we emphasized the importance of attending to students' ideas rather than only to their pronunciation and grammar.

In the third key concept we looked at means for providing effective instruction to poor readers. The main reason poor readers continue to progress slowly in learning to read seems to be that they often receive faulty instruction. We stressed the importance of the classroom teacher's role in helping poor readers, including those who might be handicapped. Guidelines and activities for overcoming this problem were presented. Finally, in the fourth key concept, we covered methods teachers can use to provide instruction to gifted readers, providing opportunities for inquiry as well as comprehension lessons when students set their own purposes for reading.

BIBLIOGRAPHY

REFERENCES

Alexander, C. F. (1979). Black English dialect and the classroom teacher. *Reading Teacher, 33* (5), 571–577.

Allington, R. L. (1983). The reading instruction provided readers of differing abilities. *Elementary School Journal, 83* (5), 548–559.

Aoki, E. M. (1981). "Are you Chinese? Are you just a mixed-up kid?" Using Asian American children's literature. *Reading Teacher, 34* (4), 382–385.

Au, K. H., Tharp, R. G., Crowell, D. C., Jordan, C., Speidel, G. E., & Calkins, R. (1984). KEEP: The role of research in the development of a successful reading program. In J. Osborn, P. T. Wilson, & R. C. Anderson (Eds.), *Reading education: Foundations for a literate America.* Boston: D. C. Heath.

Barnitz, J. G. (1980). Black English and other dialects: Sociolinguistic implications for reading instruction. *Reading Teacher, 33* (7), 779–786.

Barrera, R. B. (1983). Bilingual reading in the primary grades: Some questions about questionable views and practices. In T. H. Escobedo (Ed.), *Early childhood bilingual education: A Hispanic perspective.* New York: Teachers College Press.

Barrera, R. B. (1984). The teaching of reading to language-minority students: Some basic guidelines. In F. W. Parkay, S. O'Bryan, & M. Hennessy (Eds.), *Quest for quality: Improving basic skills instruction in the 1980s.* Lanham, MD: University Press of America.

Bates, G. W. (1984). Developing reading strategies for the gifted: A research-based approach. *Journal of Reading, 27* (7), 590-593.

Boggs, S. T. (1972). The meaning of questions and narratives to Hawaiian children. In C. Cazden, V. John, & D. Hymes (Eds.), *Functions of language in the classroom.* New York: Teachers College Press.

Bohning, G. (1981). Bibliotherapy: Fitting the resources together. *Elementary School Journal, 82* (2), 166-170.

Carter, L. F. (1984). The sustaining effects study of compensatory and elementary education. *Educational Researcher, 13* (7), 4-13.

Cassidy, J. (1981). Inquiry reading for the gifted. *Reading Teacher, 35* (1), 17-21.

Cazden, C. B., Carrasco, R., Maldonado-Guzman, A. A., & Erickson, F. (1980). The contribution of ethnographic research to bicultural bilingual education. In J. Alatis (Ed.), *Current issues in bilingual education.* Georgetown University Round Table on Language and Linguistics. Washington, DC: Georgetown University Press.

Cazden, C. B., John, V., & Hymes, D. (Eds.) (1972). *Functions of language in the classroom.* New York: Teachers College Press.

Chu-Chang, M. (Ed.) (1983). *Comparative research in bilingual education: Asian-Pacific-American perspectives.* New York: Teachers College Press.

Cummins, J. (1979). Linguistic interdependence and the educational development of bilingual children. *Review of Educational Research, 49,* 22-51.

Davey, B. (1983). Think aloud—Modeling the cognitive processes of reading comprehension. *Journal of Reading, 27* (1), 44-47.

Elley, W. B. (1981). The role of reading in bilingual contexts. In J. T. Guthrie (Ed.), *Comprehension and teaching: Research reviews.* Newark, DE: International Reading Association.

Elley, W. B., & Mangubhai, F. (1983). The impact of reading on second language learning. *Reading Research Quarterly, 19* (1), 53-67.

Erickson, F., & Mohatt, G. (1982). Cultural organization of participation structures in two classrooms of Indian students. In G. B. Spindler (Ed.), *Doing the ethnography of schooling: Educational anthropology in action.* New York: Holt, Rinehart & Winston.

Feeley, J. T. (1983). Help for the reading teacher: Dealing with the Limited English Proficient (LEP) child in the elementary classroom. *Reading Teacher, 36* (7), 650-655.

Gillet, J. W., & Gentry, J. R. (1983). Bridges between nonstandard and standard English with extensions of dictated stories. *Reading Teacher, 36* (4), 360-364.

Gilliland, H. (1982). The new view of Native Americans in children's books. *Reading Teacher, 35* (8), 912-916.

Gonzales, P. C. (1980). What's wrong with the basal reader approach to language development? *Reading Teacher, 33* (6), 668-673.

Gonzales, P. C. (1981). How to begin language instruction for non-English speaking students. *Language Arts, 58* (2), 175-180.

Goodenough, W. (1971). *Culture, language and society.* Addison-Wesley module. Reading, MA: Addison-Wesley.

Goodman, K., Goodman, Y., & Flores, B. (1979). *Reading in the bilingual classroom: Literacy and biliteracy.* Rosslyn, VA: National Clearinghouse for Bilingual Education.

Hart, J. T., Guthrie, J. T., & Winfield, L. (1980). Black English phonology and learning to read. *Journal of Educational Psychology, 72,* 636-646.

Heath, S. B. (1982). Questioning at home and at school: A comparative study. In G. B. Spindler (Ed.), *Doing the ethnography of schooling: Educational anthropology in action.* New York: Holt, Rinehart & Winston.

Holdaway, D. (1979). *The foundations of literacy.* Sydney: Ashton-Scholastic.

Holmes, B. C. (1983). A confirmation strategy for improving poor readers' ability to answer inferential questions. *Reading Teacher, 37* (2), 144–148.

Holt, J. (1964). *Why children fail.* New York: Dell.

Hudelson, S., & Barrera, R. (1985). Bilingual/second language learners and reading. In L. Searfoss & J. Readence (Eds.), *Helping children learn to read.* Englewood Cliffs, NJ: Prentice-Hall.

Lauritzen, C. (1982). A modification of repeated readings for group instruction. *Reading Teacher, 35* (4), 456–458.

Moll, L. C., & Diaz, S. (in press). Bilingual communication and reading: The importance of Spanish in learning to read in English. *Elementary School Journal.*

Osborn, J. (1984). The purposes, uses, and contents of workbooks and some guidelines for publishers. In R. C. Anderson, J. Osborn, & R. L. Tierney (Eds.), *Learning to read in American schools: Basal readers and content texts.* Hillsdale, NJ: Erlbaum.

Philips, S. (1972). Participant structures and communicative competence: Warm Springs children in community and classroom. In C. Cazden, V. John, & D. Hymes (Eds.), *Functions of language in the classroom.* New York: Teachers College Press.

Philips, S. U. (1983). *The invisible culture: Communication in classroom and community on the Warm Springs Indian Reservation.* New York: Longman.

Raphael, T. E. (1982). Question-answering strategies for children. *Reading Teacher, 36* (2), 186–190.

Renzulli, J. S., Smith, L. H., & Reis, S. M. (1982). Curriculum compacting: An essential strategy for working with gifted students. *Elementary School Journal, 82* (3), 185–194.

Reynolds, R. E., Taylor, M. A., Steffenson, M. S., Shirey, L. L., & Anderson, R. C. (1982). Cultural schemata and reading comprehension. *Reading Research Quarterly, 17,* 353–366.

Rhodes, L. K. (1981). I can read! Predictable books as resources for reading and writing instruction. *Reading Teacher, 34* (5), 511–518.

Rollock, B. (1974). *The black experience in children's books.* Rev. ed. New York: New York Public Library.

Samuels, S. J. (1979). The method of repeated readings. *Reading Teacher, 32,* 403–408.

Singer, H., McNeil, J. D., & Furse, L. L. (1984). Relationship between curriculum scope and reading achievement in elementary schools. *Reading Teacher, 37* (7), 608–612.

Slaughter, J. P. (1983). Big books for little kids: Another fad or a new approach for teaching beginning reading? *Reading Teacher, 36* (8), 758–762.

Sutherland, Z., & Arbuthnot, M. H. (1986). *Children and books.* Seventh ed. Glenview, IL: Scott, Foresman.

Taylor, B. M., & Nosbush, L. Oral reading for meaning: A technique for improving word identification skills. *Reading Teacher, 37* (3), 234–237.

Tompkins, G. E., & Webeler, M. (1983). What will happen next? Using predictable books with young children. *Reading Teacher, 36* (6), 498–502.

Trevise, R. (1984). Teaching reading to the gifted. In A. Harris & E. Sipay (Eds.), *Readings on reading instruction.* New York: Longman.

Trueba, H. T., Guthrie, G. P., & Au, K. H. (Eds.) (1981). *Culture and the bilingual classroom.* Rowley, MA: Newbury House.

CHILDREN'S BOOKS AND PROGRAMS CITED

Junior Great Books Reading and Discussion Program for Students from Second Grade through Senior High School. Great Books Foundation, 307 N. Michigan Ave., Chicago, IL 60601.

Ladybird series
Ladybird "Easy Reading" Books (1973). Loughborough, England: Ladybird Books, Ltd.

Little Owl books
Bill Martin, Jr. (General Editor). *Little Owl Books*, Grades K–2. New York: Holt, Rinehart & Winston.

Sounds of Language series
Bill Martin, Jr. in collaboration with Peggy Brogan (1974). *Sounds of Language Readers*. New York: Holt, Rinehart & Winston.

FURTHER READINGS

Andersson, B. V., & Barnitz, J. G. (1984). Cross-cultural schemata and reading comprehension instruction. *Journal of Reading, 28* (2), 102–108.

Au, K. H., & Kawakami, A. J. (1985). Research currents: Talk story and learning to read. *Language Arts, 62* (4), 406–411.

Gilmore, P. (1984). Research currents: Assessing sub-rosa skills in children's language. *Language Arts, 61* (4), 384–391.

Lass, B., & Bromfield, M. (1981). Books about children with special needs: An annotated bibliography. *Reading Teacher, 34* (5), 530–533.

Sinatra, R. C., Stahl-Gemake, J., & Berg, D. N. (1984). Improving reading comprehension of disabled readers through semantic mapping. *Reading Teacher, 38* (1), 22–29.

Ward, M., & McCormick, S. (1981). Reading instruction for blind and low vision children in the regular classroom. *Reading Teacher, 34* (4), 434–444.

CHAPTER 10

Testing and Assessment

To be unable to evaluate what teachers are doing and what children are doing is to be lost in the forest with no compass. Evaluation, then, is an essential topic for the person working in the field of reading. One must not only understand some of the technicalities about how to give tests and how to score them and look up norms, but also try to discover the inner purposes of the tests—what are the tests for, and at what times evaluative procedures other than tests are needed.

(Harris, 1984, p. 146)

OVERVIEW

Testing is an integral part of classroom instruction. This chapter will explain how you can use testing instruments effectively. Similarities and differences among tests must be understood. You must be able to distinguish among the different purposes for using a test, whether to screen a child, keep records, or assess your own teaching. You should know the limits of commercial tests and how your own informal assessments can be used in their place. Finally, you should understand how tests and other assessment instruments are constructed and interpreted, as well as their benefits and disadvantages.

There are three generally recognized methods of assessment. We begin the chapter by describing the development of their use in schools. Three key concepts in the chapter follow, each focused on one method of assessment. The first assessment approach, referred to as norm-referenced tests, is achieved by comparing students' scores with a large group of students who were tested by the test developers. The second, criterion-referenced tests, focuses on the amount of information students know about a topic or to what extent they have mastered a skill. The third section, concerning informal tests, describes a variety of ways that you can measure your students' progress and evaluate your own teaching. The chapter concludes with a fourth key concept in which we show how testing must be an integral part of instruction, using the concept of the teaching-learning cycle.

The chapter is organized around the following key concepts:

Key Concept #1: The teacher should understand the purposes served by norm-referenced tests, how to administer them, and how to interpret the results.

Key Concept #2: The teacher should understand the purposes served by criterion-referenced tests, how to administer them, and how to interpret the results.

Key Concept #3: The teacher should understand the purposes served by informal tests, how to construct them, and how to interpret the results.

Key Concept #4: The teacher should understand how to integrate tests into the curriculum and make effective use of testing programs.

PERSPECTIVE

PURPOSES OF TESTING

Reading tests given to schoolchildren have many different purposes. Teachers use reading tests for instructional purposes, such as to determine how well a child can read, what reading group a child should be in, and whether a lesson was successful. Principals use tests to measure whether teachers have been effective in teaching reading over an academic year. They determine whether overall gains by students are equivalent to a year's growth in achievement. School system administrators use tests to evaluate the effectiveness of curricular programs and materials and to determine whether a special program is worthwhile or whether monies have been appropriately spent. Since most of you will be giving and interpreting tests to evaluate students' progress and organize and improve your lessons, we focus in this chapter on teachers' purposes.

Pictures of children's reading ability

To introduce the concept of interpreting test information for your teaching, we have taken an account of successful and less successful readers presented by Clay (1979, pp. 176–178).

The first example is a child from the top 25 percent of the children that Clay studied. Helen entered school at age five and made a good adjustment. Her IQ score of 118 was at the lower limit of the superior group. After five weeks she was given a caption reader, and after nine weeks the first supplementary reader, which she read easily, using several cues to figure out unknown words. At eleven weeks she was placed in the basic reader. After six months at school, Helen had read a supplementary reader every two weeks. She read at the rate of 120 words per minute and her accuracy was about 95 percent. It was estimated that she read about 20,000 words during that first year. Her comprehension responses were fast and accurate.

When reading easy material, Helen sometimes read so fast that she made errors that she did not notice. When she did notice an error, she usually returned to the beginning of a line or sentence and relied on text meaning and knowledge of syntax to guide her guesses. She usually did not sound out unknown words but asked to be told the word. After one prompt, she was able to read the word when it appeared later.

Jerry made average progress in the school year. He was given a caption reader after seven weeks at school and a supplementary reader after 19 weeks. After 26 weeks he was given the first basic reader. After one year of school, he was where the high progress child had been after six months. He read more slowly, 90 words per minute, with about 90 percent accuracy. It was estimated that he read between 10,000 and 15,000 words in the first year.

This child made moderately good progress and seemed to have the right approach to reading but had not developed reliable methods for sampling text cues and figuring out how to correct his errors. He needed to learn to use sentence structures to anticipate what might follow and to learn better ways to check his guesses about words.

Terry, who made poor progress in reading, was also given a caption reader at seven weeks. He did not receive the first supplementary reader until the 28th week, and the basic reader until the 36th week. By the end of the year, he had moved through the three basic readers, but had been generally unsuccessful. He made one error in every three words (accuracy rate of 67%) and was able to correct only one word in 20. He was trying to read at the same rate as the average reader, about 90 words per minute, though he read far fewer words than other children (an estimate of 5,000 words in the year). Over the vacation period he forgot more of the skills he had begun to use than did the other children.

These brief sketches give you an idea of how information from both formal and informal tests can be put together to give a picture of a child's knowledge and progress in reading.

EXERCISE

Pick a child who is in a grade that you would like to teach. If possible, make arrangements to look at the child's cumulative folder in order to analyze the formal tests given over the last three years. Observe the child at school during the reading period and take notes about what the child reads, what errors are made, how corrections are attempted, how well independent work time is used, and how attentive the child is during the teacher-directed lesson.

Next, arrange to have the child read for you. Use a 100-200 word passage (comparable in difficulty to those in the child's reading book. Give the child the following directions: "Look over the beginning of this story and then read it out loud for me. Read it as well as you can and try to remember what it said. I'll tell you any words that you can't figure out." After the reading close the book and ask the child to give a summary of what was read. Keep track of the length of time it took to read, what errors were made, and what information was remembered. Try to make an estimate of how many words per minute the child read, how accurately, and how much was remembered.

Finally, use all the information obtained to write a few paragraphs giving a picture of the child's current reading abilities. Even though you will not have made observations over time, as in the examples of the children taken from Clay's work, try to provide a picture with a similar degree of clarity and objectivity.

KEY CONCEPT 1

The teacher should understand the purposes served by norm-referenced tests, how to administer them, and how to interpret the results.

PURPOSES OF NORM-REFERENCED TESTS

Norm-referenced, standardized tests are intended to show whether students have learned what others in the same grade typically have learned. That is, they assess students' performance in relation to the performance of a large, representative group of students. The scores represent overall achievement rather than a particular ability. These tests are used in nearly every school system in America. In some schools the tests are given every year, while in others they are used for gatekeeping or sorting purposes, typically in the first, fourth, and seventh grades. Scores are likely to be in every child's cumulative folder to mark progress through school.

Typically, norm-referenced reading tests contain subtests of decoding, comprehension, and vocabulary to measure the *relative success* of the student in these areas. You can examine and compare reading achievement of your students with students the test makers have determined are typical. You can use them at the beginning of the school year to learn which students are below the norms for that grade and are likely to need a more concentrated reading program, and which are above and will benefit from an accelerated program. You may also use the test scores to group students for reading. However, you cannot use them for diagnosis of individual students.

How norm-referenced tests are constructed and used

Items on norm-referenced reading tests are intended to sample the reading skills typically developed at the kindergarten, primary, and intermediate levels. Because most schools rely on basal reading programs, the items at each level are quite closely related to the content of these programs. Items on the kindergarten and primary tests are limited as well by children's lack of reading competence. These tests have a more restricted vocabulary and range of comprehension skills than do the intermediate level tests.

An ideal norm-referenced test is developed as follows: First, many different test items are created. The acceptable items are tried out with a larger number of students in order to eliminate very easy and very hard items, as well as items that do not discriminate good from poor readers or students in higher grades from students in lower grades. After a large enough pool of satisfactory items is created, the test must be tried out with thousands of students who are representative of all schoolchildren in the country. The results of the field test yield information about the "normal distribution" of the test scores. These norms provide the information needed to compare students to one another. You can read the test maker's description of how a particular test was developed to see whether the test you plan to use has been carefully prepared in this way.

When you give a standardized test, you must follow the same procedures as were used by the test maker. Otherwise your students' scores cannot be compared against the norms. This means you must read the directions and give the example as stated, follow the time limits, and avoid helping any children. For example, if a child doesn't understand how to do the test, you can repeat the directions or the example but you can't provide other information. Appropriate responses are, "Do the best you can" or "Figure out as many of the items as you can. I can help you with your other work later but not now."

How norm-referenced tests are scored and reported

All items on the test are scored as either right or wrong. The total number that a student gets right is called a raw score. By itself, the raw score means little. Instead, interpretation is based on one of several kinds of "derived scores." The derived score indicates how a child's performance compares with the performance of the norm group. Typically, comparisons are made in terms of percentile ranks, stanines, and grade equivalents. Baumann and Stevenson (1982a) present a complete description of each. Here is a brief explanation:

A percentile rank describes the likely rank of a student's score in terms of the percent of the total. A rank of 1 percent is given to students who score the lowest, while a rank of 50 percent is given to students in the middle. To calculate a child's percentile rank within your class:

1. Determine the number of children who got lower scores;
2. Divide by the total number of children in the group;
3. Multiply by 100.

To determine children's percentile ranks in comparison to national norms, refer to the tables provided by the test maker. Merely read across the table from the raw score to the normed percentile equivalent.

Another derived score on a norm-referenced test is the *stanine*. A stanine is a number from one through nine, where one represents the poorest performance, five is average, and nine is the best. Stanines are derived from a normal, bell-shaped curve of scores that clusters many scores in the middle region and very few at the extreme. While each stanine includes a range of percentile ranks, more ranks are represented by the middle stanines than by the extreme stanines. Stanines and percentiles are related as follows:

Stanine	Percentile
9	96–99
8	89–95
7	77–88
6	60–76
5	40–59
4	23–39
3	11–22
2	4–10
1	0– 3

Stanines are useful because they show each child's score in terms of deviations from the normed average, or the population mean. Read from the test maker's table the conversion of a raw score to a stanine. You can interpret a stanine of 4, 5, or 6 as representing a fairly typical score, a stanine of 3 as borderline, and a stanine of 2 as a low score. A stanine of 7 represents an above average score and 8 is a high score. A score in stanine 1 is exceptionally low, while a score in stanine 9 is exceptionally high.

A *grade equivalent score* compares the performance of a child to the average performance of groups of children in the different grades. The number expresses level of reading achievement in grades and tenths of grades. For example, a score of 3.9 is supposed to mean the score that would be earned by the average third grader at the end of the school year.

We do not recommend relying on grade equivalent scores because they do not have adequate statistical properties either for making comparisons among children or decisions about instruction. For example, a third grader who obtains a grade equivalent score of 6.5 on a reading test is not necessarily reading at the sixth grade level. Likewise, a third grader who tests at grade 1.5 may not need a first grade book. A small change in the raw score of either of these children can mean an alarming advance or decline in the supposed grade level.

Instead of using grade equivalent scores to evaluate children and your instruction, learn to use stanines or percentiles. To do this, study the raw and derived scores of your average students. Get a sense of whether the middle-of-the-roaders are indeed performing at the 40–60th percentile, at a stanine of 4 to 6. Having established a sense of the middle group, look at the groups at either end. If a child seems misplaced, go back to the cumulative record and study earlier test information to see if there has been a change in relative performance. That is, do not assume that one test score yields a complete picture or a final judgment of a child's performance.

While a particular test score is not useful instructionally, the stanines or percentiles from several tests or subtests from one test can be placed together to study a child's performance in various dimensions of reading. If a child does very well on a particular test relative to his or her own average on the other tests, this may indicate a special strength. Similarly, a score much lower than the child's average may suggest an area of weakness. However, remember that all tests contain a margin of error. Don't make too much of small fluctuations from one test to another. Test makers always list the margin of error. (This is called the standard error.) Or you could use the rule of thumb that a difference of two stanines might be important while one less than that might just show a temporary fluctuation.

Strengths of norm-referenced tests

Norm-referenced tests which are properly constructed are useful for ranking and comparing children. Most test makers have gone to great lengths to prepare reliable instruments. This means that if the test were given to the same child again or to another child of similar ability, the score obtained would vary little from the first one. It is extremely unlikely that you could construct as reliable a test. As a result, and because of the use of the sampling techniques to make the test scores representative, your students' scores can be compared with students across the nation.

Norm-referenced tests can be the most efficient way to obtain performance information. Data can be gathered on large numbers of students in a short time. Standardized procedures exist for administration and for accurate scoring. Because of the multiple-choice format, the data can be marked and analyzed quickly by machine. The whole procedure takes little of a teacher's or student's time. The field test information allows the construction of tables that list derived scores and comparison information.

Weaknesses of norm-referenced tests

Norm-referenced tests are thought to be overused in our schools. They categorize, group, or track students, and their scores become a key part of student records. In high school they can dictate which courses students may select and stand as a prime factor in awarding scholarships. Such pervasive use puts students at risk for being educationally mislabled and therefore misdirected.

A weakness of standardized reading tests is that they represent a limited sample of reading concepts. Their focus is too much on some measures of reading at the expense of others. Armbruster, Stevens, and Rosenshine (1977) found that reading comprehension subtests were poorly related to comprehension lessons, calling on identification of factual information at the expense of higher level thinking and reasoning. Passages may be too short for adequate evaluation of comprehension, and some questions can be answered without reading the text. Moreover, according to Petrosky (1982), an overuse of these tests may keep children from learning effective reading comprehension habits. He based his conclusions on the reading performance of about 2,500 seventeen-year-olds who were asked not only to answer multiple-choice questions but also to write out explanations of their answers. While they did very well in selecting the correct answers, showing good literal and inferential skills, they did not explain or justify their responses well.

Tests given to younger children are less reliable than those given to older children; that is, the standard error is higher for younger children than for older children. Moreover, according to Arter and Jenkins (1978), standardized diagnostic reading tests may not be valid indicators of important ability differences. As a result, you must be careful that decisions made about children's potential in the early grades do not keep them from receiving appropriate instruction.

Reading achievement tests are also thought to be biased in favor of white, middle-class students. While test makers attempt to build tests around information available to everyone, all children are not necessarily exposed to the information needed to answer a test question. Unequal opportunity to learn at school and at home means that a test score does not reflect only an ability to learn. As a result, children may misinterpret questions or answers not because they can't read but because they lack sufficient background knowledge about that topic.

INSTRUCTIONAL ACTIVITIES

Children do not necessarily know how to take tests. That is, test scores may be depressed because students lack test-taking skills, and their scores will not be accurate indicators of their reading ability. It may be helpful, then, to teach students how to take a test and give them opportunities to practice the test format.

Approaching test-taking

Stewart and Green (1983) describe several ways to prepare children for test-taking:

1. Teach children how to take tests well before the formal testing date. Explain to them why tests are given, why there are special rules for test-taking, and how tests are made and scored.

2. Find practice materials that match the format of the test. Explain to children how to answer the type of question in order to make the best use of their time. Younger children need practice in how to mark correct items. If they use a separate answer sheet, they need advice about how to keep track of the items on the score sheet. Older children taking a reading comprehension cloze test should know to scan a whole paragraph before trying to fill in most of the items. On a multiple-choice comprehension test, they should read the questions before reading the text and look for the answers in the text. If they can't find the answer they should read the alternatives and use a process of elimination to make a best-guess response.

3. During test-practice sessions, set up a test-taking atmosphere. Separate children's desks, establish quiet, have them all turn the test over at the same time, and make them aware of the time limitations.

4. At first, give additional time to children who cannot complete the task within the specified limit. Gradually decrease the allotted time.

5. Children need to develop a serious attitude toward test-taking. You may need to give advice to individuals about their performance. For example, discuss with slow test-takers how they can move through items in the test more efficiently. Convince children who go too fast and miss many items that they need to work more carefully. Help anxious children realize that they really do know much of the information and will do better when they relax. Impress upon all the children that they should try to be accurate and to complete as many items as possible.

Teaching children strategies for interpreting test questions

The nature of questions on a comprehension test can influence how well children appear to know the information from a passage. For example, choosing the correct answer, such as finding the main idea of a passage, is usually much easier than writing out an answer. Explicit or literal questions are usually easier than inferential questions. Furthermore, the situation in which the questions are asked can influence performance. Children often do less well in answering questions in a formal testing situation than during an informal reading lesson discussion because they are worried about the test, the teacher or other students can't provide hints, and the context for thinking about and remembering the information is less evident.

Raphael (1982) developed one approach to this problem as discussed in Chapter 5. This is to teach children how to recognize three different kinds of comprehension questions: questions in which the answer is from one sentence in the text, called RIGHT THERE items; questions in which the informa-

FIGURE 10.1 Example of a Test Chart for an Individual Child

Name		Age	Grade
Standard tests	Dates	Scores	Comments
Aptitude tests	Dates	Scores	Comments
Classroom behaviors			
Teacher evaluations			
Other comments			

tion is in the passage but has to be integrated from more than one place, called THINK AND SEARCH items; and questions that are generally related to the text but with answers that must come from the reader's prior knowledge, called ON YOUR OWN items. Encourage children to analyze test questions in this way. Point out that RIGHT THERE question-answer relationships are by far the most common in norm-referenced tests.

Using norm-referenced tests for instructional decision-making

The test scores, as we emphasized earlier, do not tell you what children know. However, if the test is well-constructed, and the scores are used in conjunction with other information, they can help you decide how to rank your students for reading instruction. Baumann and Stevenson (1982b) offer advice about how to interpret the scores. You will need to construct a chart for each child (see Figure 10.1 for example). Make multiple copies of a grid that provides space for a child's name and grade at the top, the four types of measures listed below on the left, and room for scores and your written comments. Be sure you include the name of the test and the date it was given. Complete the sheet with the following information:

1. A standardized reading score, converted to a stanine or percentile.
2. A general aptitude score, such as an IQ test score, converted to a stanine or percentile.
3. The child's test-taking behavior, which you can note while children are taking the reading test. Look for signs of concentration or distraction, relaxation or anxiety, speed or slowness, and understanding or puzzlement about the task procedures.

4. Your own evaluation of the child's reading ability based on informal and criterion-referenced tests you have given, placement for reading lessons, and your summary of reading progress in the previous two grades.

Now, to make an instructional decision, compare achievement with aptitude, past performance, current classroom performance, and test-taking skills. Similarity among all the measures for average and high performers would suggest that appropriate instruction is being provided, but for low performers it would indicate that more instructional support ought to be considered. Discrepancies among the measures could signal a need for a different type of reading instruction. For example, a child with high achievement and aptitude scores and low classroom performance could be bored and might work more effectively if moved to a higher instructional group. A child, with low achievement scores but high classroom performance might need coaching on test-taking. In general, the chart provides a good summary of test performance that you can refer to when discussing instructional or testing problems with children, parents, or other professionals.

CHARACTERISTICS OF CRITERION-REFERENCED TESTS

Criterion-referenced tests are widely used in schools. Unlike norm-referenced tests which tap a general assortment of subjects, criterion-referenced tests are narrowly focused on particular skills or topics. They are intended to measure the extent to which students have mastered that information. This is done by comparing the number of items answered correctly with some absolute standard. Increasingly, criterion-referenced tests are used in school systems. Students' progress through their curriculum is often tested several times each year.

An example will clarify the difference between a criterion- and a norm-referenced test. If you say, "Jane is ranked in the 90th percentile in comprehension achievement," you are making a norm-referenced statement. If you say, "Jane understands summarization because she gave good summaries for over 80 percent of the paragraphs on that test," you are then making a criterion-referenced statement.

Criterion-referenced tests typically measure what children are taught from particular programs and curriculum packages. They appear, for example, as end-of-level tests in basal reading programs. They are intended to check children's competence on the particular skills taught and to estimate whether students are ready to proceed to the next level. There are also criterion-referenced reading testing programs that can be purchased for more general use. An example of a page from a more general comprehension test appears in Figure 10.2. However, tests such as this do not necessarily measure what the students were taught.

Criterion-referenced tests are developed by defining first a set of concepts or skills that form the backbone of the subject being taught. Reading is organized into skills that are listed in the *scope and sequence* chart of published reading programs (this is discussed in Chapter 11). The general construct for the approach is found in Bloom's taxonomy (1956). It is assumed that children should understand and master certain skills and that the skills are

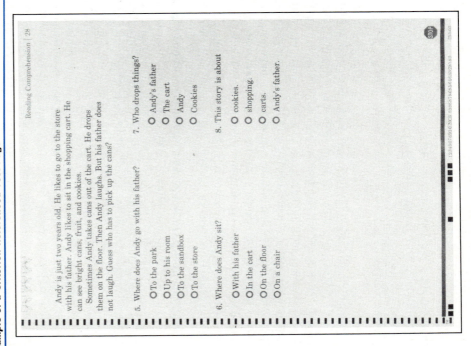

FIGURE 10.2   Example of a Criterion-Referenced Test Page

ordered from easy to difficult. For example, Bloom's taxonomy describes *recognition* of information as an easier skill than *analysis* or *synthesis* of information. It is also assumed that once the skills are mastered, children can use them both with the materials they used for learning and with new materials. For example, if children learned to recognize the sequence of events in the *Three Billy-Goats Gruff* story, they would also recognize the sequence of events in other stories. Based on these assumptions, a set of test questions is developed to measure children's mastery of the skills.

Administering commercial criterion-referenced tests

If you want to use a criterion-referenced test you should administer it directly after teaching the instructional unit. You may give it individually or to groups. In either case, seat children so they can work independently, and give them enough time to complete all items. If children get tired, testing may be stopped at the end of a subtest and continued another day.

If test directions are in the children's test booklet, you can give them a copy of the test and, after they have read the directions, let them proceed at their own pace until the test is completed. If children ask for clarification about a test item, you may help them understand the questions, but do not give the answer, and then note that aid was given to the child. With teacher-administered tests, the directions are read to the children by the teacher. If children do not understand the directions, you may reinterpret them. Again, children are allowed to work at their own pace because these tests usually measure knowledge of the topic or skill rather than speed of response.

How criterion-referenced tests are scored and reported

Scoring is done by marking answers as right or wrong, though if an unclear answer is given, you may question the child and give partial credit. Interpretation depends on the approach used by the test maker. Typically, tests in basal readers use a score of 80 percent or above as a passing score. A score of 80 percent or higher indicates that a child has mastered most of the information and is ready for the next unit in the textbook. A low score could mean that the children did not understand the lesson, that they needed more practice examples, or that they understood the lesson but not the test-taking procedure. Discussing the task with the children should help you determine whether to give instruction or practice on the skills or another opportunity to take the test.

Finding out that children did not learn the material means that you need to study the instructional situation. Was the failure the result of poor classroom instruction? Perhaps children needed a more complete explanation or more guided practice. Were the children not ready for the instruction in the first place? Perhaps you needed to present background information or a clearer introduction to the unit.

One advantage of a criterion-referenced testing system is that the teacher can show children the progress they are making. The teacher explains to this student how his test results have been charted on an individual profile sheet.

Keeping individual records of students' progress can be an effective and objective way to monitor children's growth. You could make a record sheet that lists all students' names alphabetically at the left. Put the test name and when it was given at the top. Fill in the sheet with students' scores, comments about their reactions to the test or your observations of them as they worked, or merely that they completed and obtained an acceptable grade on the test.

Strengths of criterion-referenced tests

The principal advantage of a criterion-referenced test is its close tie with actual instruction. If it measures what you taught, it can help you to evaluate whether your instruction was effective and whether children are ready to move to the next level. You can look for scores of 80 percent or higher to help you judge whether you can move to the next instructional unit.

Another advantage is that when children do poorly on a test, it offers the opportunity to study patterns of error. Consistent patterns of error show areas that should be targeted in future instruction.

Weaknesses of criterion-referenced tests

Criterion-referenced tests of reading, particularly of reading comprehension, have serious limitations. The skills that are to be measured, which must be identified and arranged into an instructional sequence, have not been validated by research. In fact, there is still a disagreement about whether there is a true sequence to reading subskills (Mason, Osborn, & Rosenshine, (1977). This

INSTRUCTIONAL ACTIVITIES

The first activity below helps teachers involve students in charting their own progress on criterion-referenced tests. The other two show teachers how to construct suitable tests.

Test recording

A cumulative record of particular skills can be kept by the students themselves as an incentive to studying. Smith (1926) suggested a good approach for testing and keeping track of reading comprehension accuracy and reading rate:

> In giving the tests (at regular, two-week intervals), the teacher selects some portion of a story in a reader and explains to the children why they are to read it. She should take care to have the selections for all the tests of as nearly the same degree of difficulty as is possible. At a given signal the pupils open their books and read silently for a specified time, at the end of which they are given a signal to stop. They close their books, number their papers from one to ten, and write "yes" or "no" in response to the questions which the teacher asks on the content of their reading. . . . In taking a speed test, the pupil finds the designated place, puts his finger in his reader at this place, and then closes the book. At a given signal each one opens his book and reads for one minute silently, when the teacher gives the signal to stop by saying "Mark." He then places a dot after the last word read and counts the total number of words covered during the entire minute.   (pp. 95–96)

Smith suggests that graphs be constructed for comprehension accuracy and for reading speed. For comprehension accuracy, list the scores from 0 to 10 on the left margin, placing 0 at the bottom of the graph, as shown in Figure 10.3. The child's name would be on the top and the testing dates along the top or bottom margin. After the test is scored, children fill in the square marking

means you cannot rely solely on commercial reading tests to evaluate the progress of your children or the effectiveness of your reading instruction.

Test items do not necessarily measure what was taught or what was emphasized in lessons. Even when using a commercial reading program, it is not only difficult but unwise to follow lessons exactly. When you adjust the commercial lesson to the needs of the children, you must also adjust the end-of-level tests. You should make sure that the test items you have children answer match the actual instruction that children received.

A third problem is a variation of test items' closeness to the skill. Some items are so similar to the original task that children could answer them by remembering the lesson rather than by understanding the underlying construct. At the other extreme are items couched in such different language that they actually test skills in addition to the one taught. You should evaluate children's performance in light of the variation in item difficulty.

FIGURE 10.3 Cumulative Record of Comprehension Accuracy

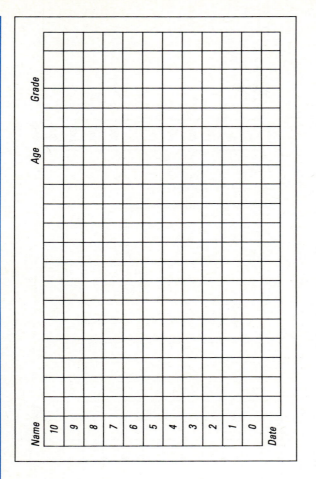

the score they received or make a bar graph by filling in the squares from 0 to the score they received. A reading speed graph lists words per minute on the left margin, beginning at the bottom with 40 and, counting by 20's, going to 240. The top and bottom margins would be identical to the reading accuracy graph. Graphing could be done in the same way or as a series of dots connecting one score to the next (see Figure 10.4).

While there are other ways of testing comprehension than a yes-no test, as suggested by Smith, we think the general approach for keeping track of children's progress is sound. You would be testing children on what they are learning, frequent records would be kept, even young children would be able to do the record-keeping, and you would have an easy way for children to monitor their own progress.

Constructing a criterion-referenced comprehension test

Johnston and Pearson (1982) recommend that you construct criterion-referenced tests to measure reading comprehension instruction because you will have tests that fit the text sections that children are studying.

Decide how to measure comprehension. The first step is to decide what you want to measure. Here are four possibilities:

1. Measure children's *prior knowledge of the subject* before you teach it. For example, before having children read an expository selection, you

FIGURE 10.4 Cumulative Record of Reading Speed

Name													Age				Grade	
240																		
220																		
200																		
180																		
160																		
140																		
120																		
100																		
80																		
60																		
40																		
Date																		

can have them try writing out answers to a set of questions about the text. After they have read the selection, have them write the answers again and compare their two sets of answers.

2. Measure children's *ability to comprehend different text structures.* Find two texts about the same topic that are written in quite different ways. For example, you could find differently organized selections about the desert in two social studies textbooks. One might be written as a narrative and the other as a descriptive passage. Construct questions that focus on the information found in both texts. Have students read one, discuss answers to the questions, then read the other and discuss the answers again as a way to measure their ability to find information in different kinds of texts.

3. Measure children's *reasoning and critical thinking* as they read. You might have children explain information from the text, have them evaluate text information, or ask them to justify their answers. For example, you could have children explain or justify how they determined the most important idea in a paragraph. You would learn whether they can go beyond selecting answers, such as explaining how they chose important information.

4. Measure children's *ability to read text information quickly and remember it accurately.* For example, you could have children read a text and answer questions in a fixed period of time. You would evaluate separately their reading speed and accuracy in order to help

them realize that both are important and may be practiced by using different reading strategies.

Decide how to set up test items. The second step to constructing a comprehension test is to decide how to ask your questions. Johnston (1981) suggests five alternatives:

1. Free recall questions. Ask children to write down what they remember after reading a text selection and with their books closed. What they have written gives information about their organization of stored information; it indicates what they thought was important and it suggests how they interpreted it. This kind of question is useful for evaluating their understanding of the whole text, such as to determine whether children are paying attention to the sequence of information or are able to pick out initiating events and resolutions in stories or the important ideas in an expository text.

2. Short answer or fill-in-the-blank questions. Ask children to complete sentences where important information must be filled in. You might use this approach to test their memory of the critical parts of a text, to measure their ability to reconstruct part of the text or to explain, justify, relate, or interpret information.

3. Sentence verification. List a set of sentences—some taken directly from the text, some changed a little, and some unrelated to the text—and ask children to circle those they think appeared in the passage. This helps you determine whether they can recognize information that appeared in the text.

4. True-false questions. Ask children to differentiate sentences containing information found in the text from sentences that present inaccurate information about the text topic. However, while this approach can tell whether information appearing in the text is recognized, it can lead to interpretation and scoring problems, since a score of 50 percent correct can be obtained by chance.

5. Multiple-choice questions. Ask children to choose from among about four choices, only one of which is correct. An alternative approach for use with older children is to have them order the answers from best (most plausible) to worst. The multiple-choice approach can be given to groups of children and easily scored. However, it is difficult to construct items that contain four equally plausible alternative answers. Furthermore, text facts are often easier to set up as questions than more complicated and important text ideas.

Trying out the test. The third step is to choose materials and try out the test. Suppose you want to measure children's ability to reason and think as they read. One appropriate testing approach is to use a short answer question. You might ask children to complete the statement, "This paragraph is mainly about ——," followed by a request for a justification of their answer. Materials for this test may be drawn from familiar content area textbook material that children are using or have completed. Easier test materials would consist of paragraphs that present the main point at the beginning. Harder tests could include paragraphs in which the main point is at other locations or has to be inferred.

Constructing a vocabulary test

You can apply these three test construction steps to other reading skills. For example, to construct a vocabulary test, your *first step* is to decide what to measure. Let us assume you want to measure children's knowledge of words from the last unit of their content area textbook.

Your *second step* is decide how to ask the vocabulary questions. Here are four possibilities listed in the approximate order of difficulty, with the last, definition-construction, being much harder than the others:

1. Find sentences from the textbook that contain the new words. Delete one new word from each sentence and have children select the correct words from a list and write them in the blank spaces.
2. List the new words and ask children to construct an appropriate sentence for each word.
3. List under each new word four possible meanings and have children select the correct definition or synonym from the choices.
4. List the new words and ask children to explain the meaning of each by definition or by example.

The *third step* is to select materials and try out the test. If you use the first approach listed above, you might take ten to twenty sentences from last week's science lesson. Delete the new words, putting them in a list along with some that will not fit. Give students the sentences and test whether they can fill in the deleted words. Alternatively, you might list some of the new words and ask students to construct a plausible sentence for each word or list the words and ask for definitions of each.

USING INFORMAL TESTS AND INTERVIEWS

KEY CONCEPT 3

The teacher should understand the purposes served by informal tests, how to construct them, and how to interpret the results.

In this section of the chapter we describe alternatives to the use of norm-referenced or criterion-referenced tests. Informal tests or interviews with children can be given without advance preparation while you are teaching or monitoring children as they work independently. They can be directly related to the lesson you are teaching or to an on-the-spot problem that you notice individuals or a group of children having.

Because informal measures can be adapted for particular situations and problem children, you are likely to obtain more accurate information from them than from a norm- or criterion-referenced test. We describe several representative examples, focusing on concepts of print, word recognition, vocabulary, informal reading inventories, comprehension, and observation.

Concepts of print tests

A number of informal tests and tasks have been developed to measure young children's knowledge of reading even before they can read from books. For example, Clay (1979) and Sulzby (in press) have suggested ways to ask children about how they might read a book. Mason (1980) and Mason, Stewart, and Dunning (in press) have evaluated letter, letter-sound, and word knowledge. Morris (1981) and Ferreiro and Teberosky (1982) have developed word-concept tests.

Informal tests and interview questions can help you learn what concepts children have acquired about reading and writing at home. If you are a kindergarten or a first grade teacher, you might measure how children think people read, how they try to read or spell words, or what they know about reading conventions. One intent of these informal measures is to determine what children know about reading. Another is to determine whether they are using appropriate reading strategies.

The informal concepts of print tests that follow are based on tasks developed in early reading and literacy research. You could use some as individual or group tests and others could be adapted and merged with your instruction. They are particularly fitting for measuring young children's knowledge about how to read.

Orientation to a book. Hand children a book upside down. See if they can turn the book right side up, open it to the first page, point to where to start reading, show you where to continue reading after the first page, and show where the story ends. This task can reveal their familiarity with books and their readiness to be able to follow directions when they are asked to use books in school.

Knowledge about reading terms. Look through your teaching notes and teacher's guide for the special words used to talk about reading. Ask children to explain terms such as "letter," "word," "sentence," and "page." Check their knowledge of procedural terms such as "underline," "circle," and "cross out" and directional terms such as "left," "right," "top," "bottom," "beginning," and "end." You will learn to what extent they are familiar with terms that are used to talk about reading assignments, workbook exercises, or writing tasks.

Knowledge about how to learn to read. After children have had several months of reading instruction, ask them to describe what next year's class should do to learn to read. After they discuss their ideas as a group, have them draw or write three ideas. As they are working, have children explain their ideas. Write out what they tell you next to their picture or writing attempts. Studying their responses helps you understand how they perceive what you have taught and what they think is important to learn.

Relating written and oral language. Read children a short story that repeats the same words over and over or a poem or nursery rhyme that they have heard many times. Ask children one by one to point to the text as you read. Observe whether they are able to find the words as you say them. Then have them read part of the text back to you. When they finish, repeat their last word and ask where in the text it says that word and how they know. This task lets you know whether they can find the actual print, and whether they are following the print or just memorizing the text.

Separating phrases into words. Say a phrase or short sentence and ask children to clap as you say each word. Do they clap for every word? Or do they clap for syllables, suggesting they may be confused about where words end? Or do they clap only for important nouns and verbs, suggesting a tracking of ideas but not individual words? The purpose of this task is to assess children's concept of words and whether they can distinguish words from phrases and syllables.

Spelling words. If children can name and print letters, you can ask them to spell a few three-letter words such as *top, cat, sit, pat.* Observe these developmental changes: (1) they simply make a random array of letters; (2) they use the correct initial letter; (3) they use the first and last consonant; or (4) they attempt the vowel. When you give this test, do not correct children's attempts at spelling. Then they will be more likely to show you what they understand about letter sounds rather than what they think you want to see. If you have a writing program that allows children to use their own spelling system, you can also observe changes in letter-sound understanding in their everyday writing. You can then determine whether children are beginning to separate words into phonemes and which letters they assign to the phonemes they hear.

Conventions of reading. Give children a pencil or felt-tipped pen and ask them to write something for you. Ask what they have written and notice whether they use real letters, English-like words, real words, words separated by spaces, etc. Show them a page from a book and have them point out spaces between words, periods, and question marks. Ask them to explain why the punctuation marks are there and see if they use the correct terms as part of their explanation. This task measures children's concepts about how words and sentences are formed in print.

Informal word recognition tests

Word recognition tests have been the most common means used to evaluate beginning reading achievement. On standardized tests, word recognition is typically measured by asking children to circle the words that were read aloud. However, you obtain more useful information about their word reading if you ask them to read a list of words. You might test whether children recognize new words you taught by presenting these words in the sentences in which they were learned. Then place the same words in new sentence contexts (an approach evaluated by Francis, 1977). You can evaluate whether they make "good" or meaning-preserving word-reading errors when reading part of a story aloud (Goodman & Goodman, 1977). You also can evaluate whether they can make appropriate generalizations of phonetic patterns that you taught (Mason, 1976, 1977).

Reading words out of context. If you are teaching phonics your goal is for children to apply their knowledge of letter-to-sound patterns to words they have never seen before. An ability to do this means they are learning to make general use of the regular letter-to-sound correspondences that exist in English (Mason, 1976; Juel, 1983). You can test this general ability by following these steps with a phonics rule you have taught:

1. Choose two phonics rules or patterns that you have recently taught and list the words children have learned that follow the pattern. Take, for example, the long vowel, silent *e* pattern. Children might have learned *cake, made, poke, hole.*

2. Think of new words that fit the pattern and are about the same length as the words children learned, such as *lake, take, home, role.* Construct a list of about ten to twenty words.

3. List the words on the blackboard, mixing the examples from each pattern. In this way the children will have to think about which pattern applies instead of automatically applying the same one to every word.

4. Ask children to say each word, reading quickly but accurately. Mark down their errors.

5. Study the kind of errors made (Mason, 1976). You can categorize them as (1) wild guesses, (2) using the first letter and then guessing, (3) using most consonant information and then guessing, or (4) substituting or inserting a word that uses most of the letter information including the expected regular vowel pattern.

Recognizing words in their learned context. After children have studied the new words that appeared in a story they read, have them read sentences containing the new words taken directly from the story. This could be done during the reading group lesson by having children read directly from the book or from sentences written on the blackboard or paper. The purpose of this activity is to determine whether children recognize the new words in their story context.

Recognizing words in new contexts. A more difficult task for some children, but important for your assessment of what they have learned, is to determine whether they can recognize the new words in a different context. Using familiar words, make up sentences that use each new word. For example, if they learned the new word *park* in the sentence, "Pam went to the park to play ball," you might give a new sentence such as, "The snow is all over the park." You could also give a more difficult sentence that uses a different meaning of the word such as, "The woman said to park the car near the house." Put sentences such as these on the blackboard for children to study and read aloud.

Reading in context. While teaching a small group lesson or during an individual conference, have children read aloud sentences and paragraphs from stories. If possible, make a photocopy of the material to be read so that you can note word-reading errors directly and accurately. Your analysis of the miscues (Goodman & Goodman, 1977) helps you sort out the extent to which a child is paying attention to letter cues (graphic information), the arrangement or expected order of words in a sentence (syntactic cues), and the expected meaning (semantic cues). When a child substitutes one word for another or adds or omits words, notice whether most of the letters, particularly the consonants, are in the substituted word, whether the word is the same part of speech, and whether the changed wording fits the meaning up to that point in the sentence.

For example, a child who substituted the word *pick* for *park* in, "He went to the park," relied on graphic cues. A child who said, "He threw the ball was gone" for "He thought" probably relied on both graphic information (word beginning) and syntactic information (the first four words of the sentence). A child who said, "Put the pencil down" for "Put the pen down," was relying on all three sources, graphic, syntactic, and semantic. The important analysis here is to notice which cue sources the child is using. Miscues that show use of only one cue source are much more serious than those that show use of all three sources.

Informal reading inventories

Using an informal reading inventory (IRI) is a popular approach for measuring children's reading ability (Betts, 1960). It may provide information about children's word reading, their reading fluency, how they try to correct their errors, and what they comprehend. This means that an IRI can give you a more holistic or integrated account of reading problems and help you judge reading progress. You can use IRI results to decide on the appropriate reading group placement of children who join the class part way into the school year. Some teachers also use IRI's to help select appropriate independent reading materials for children.

Setting up an IRI.   Choose sections of texts of at least 100 words long that begin a chapter, story, or text section. Choose sections from materials that are below, at, and above the average reading level for the grade you teach. Photocopy the sections and place each on a separate page. Make multiple copies of each page. Next, construct five to ten post-reading comprehension questions for each selection. Be sure the questions assess a range of information. Betts (1960) recommends questions on:

Recall of facts
Association of an appropriate meaning with a term
Identifying a sequence of events
Drawing conclusions
Applying information

Another approach for measuring comprehension in conjunction with an IRI is to ask the child, "What do you remember about this selection? . . . What else do you remember? . . . Anything else?"

Arrange a 20 to 30 minute time limit for administering the inventory to each child, perhaps using an aide to give it or to monitor the class while you give it. Hand the child the text, beginning with the easiest selection, and allow the child to scan or read it silently before reading aloud. When the child reads aloud, use your copy of the selection to mark reading miscues. Here are some types of errors and the way you can mark them:

Omission—circle words that are left out.
Substitution—add substituted words above the misread words.
Insertion—mark a caret for the extra words.
Repetition—place a wavy line beneath repeated words.
Unknown word—place a circled *p* ⓟ over words that the examiner
   must pronounce for the child.

Figure 10.5 (page 338) shows a sample passage with the child's oral reading errors marked and scored.

Scoring and interpretation of an IRI.   To score word reading errors, count the number of mistakes that the child made, ignoring repetitions. Then count the number of words in the text. To score comprehension from questions that were asked, count the number of questions answered correctly. To score free recalls, make up a 0–10 point scale to indicate how complete the retelling was. You could, for example, give two points each for description of story beginning, story characters, problem, attempted solution, and ending.

The next step is to transform each score into a percentage of the total. The accuracy percentile is the number of words read correctly divided by the total number in the text. The comprehension percentile is the number of correct responses divided by the total possible score (usually 10). Then you may interpret the scores. You can use the percentage of words read accurately and the percentage of information remembered to determine whether a text is at the appropriate level of difficulty for reading.

A text is thought to be at the right level for instruction if a child reads 85 to 95 percent of the words correctly and answers at least 80 percent of the questions. It is thought to be appropriate for independent reading if the child can read 95 percent or more of the words correctly. Scores below 80–85 percent are thought to be at the frustration level, indicating that the passage is far too difficult for the child.

Judging the pattern of word recognition errors is another way to use IRI results. You could look at the pattern of omissions, substitutions, and insertions and the amount of words needed to judge how a child is trying to read, refer to Silvaroli (1973) for more detailed suggestions, or study the errors using the miscue analysis discussed earlier.

Criticism of IRI's. Estes and Vaughan (1972) recommend that IRI results be used only as indications of how the child approaches reading, and not as measures of reading performance. Jongsma and Jongsma (1981) and McKenna (1983) also point out substantial difficulties with these instruments. Fuchs, Fuchs, and Deno (1982) recommend their use for measuring performance, but only if you give a child many texts to read. They found that you may need as many as ten IRI's in order to obtain a stable result.

IRI's that are commercially produced may be less useful than the ones that teachers construct. Schell and Hanna (1981) found that published IRI's do not describe true strengths or weaknesses of children's comprehension ability. Many questions are not reliably labeled and can be answered without reading.

FIGURE 10.5   Example of Oral Reading Miscues and Scoring

Text	Error	Score
A cat sat in his boat. ℗	(unknown word)	1/6
The wind blew ʌit the boat.	(insertion)	1/5
The boat ~~tipped~~ over.	(repetition)	0/4
The cat fell (in the water.)	(omission)	1/6
The cat was mad. wet.	(substitution)	1/4
Total words 25	Total errors	4/25
	Total correct	21/25
	Percent correct	84%

Despite these criticisms, we think IRI's can be useful informal measures of children's reading. After all, they involve reading in context, they provide a way to measure both word recognition and comprehension, and they let you view how a child reads both more and less difficult texts. We recommend them particularly when you are not sure about what text materials to use with a child or when you are puzzled about a child's reading performance and suspect that a change in instruction is needed.

Informal comprehension testing

Comprehension is at the heart of reading and obviously must be evaluated. And, in fact, most teachers do evaluate comprehension frequently, using informal approaches. They ask questions after children read text selections, they ask children to locate information, and they listen as children read aloud for their ability to express the ideas with feeling and appropriate meaning. When you use these and other informal comprehension tests, consider *what* questions to ask, *when* to ask questions, and *how* to measure children's answers. We give examples of each in this section.

What questions might be asked?   As was apparent in the comprehension instruction chapters, your questions should go beyond text facts and details. Here are three suggestions that require children to think about other concepts:

1. Awareness of words that signal a connection between two ideas or events (e.g., *and, or, then, until*). After children have read the passage have them find the cue words that connect phrases and sentences. Ask them why they think those words were there, what they thought when they saw them, and then how the words helped them to understand the text.

2. Awareness of the author's plans, intentions, and purposes. Have children think about why the author wrote the text. For example, was there a moral to the story or information to be remembered? Lead a discussion after the text is read about why the author wrote it, what the author seemed to want the reader to learn or appreciate, and how the children gained new insights from the author.

3. Critical evaluation of the author's writing or plan. Ask children if there was something in the text they did not understand or disagreed with. Discuss problems the author might have had in writing clearly, organizing the ideas effectively, or in explaining or giving sufficient evidence for his or her position.

When comprehension should be measured.   You can ask questions before you teach or have children read, while the lesson is proceeding, and after the lesson. Each gives somewhat different information.

Ask questions before teaching to learn about children's prior knowledge of the topic. If children are more familiar with the topic of a passage, for instance, they are better able to answer inferential questions and will know more of the answers without looking at the text. Asking children questions about the topic before you teach lets you know whether you are measuring information gained from reading or simply from children's previously existing knowledge of a topic.

Ask questions while you are teaching if children need help with their reading comprehension, such as what to focus on or how to interpret certain information. Have them read short segments of text and ask questions about what they have read so far, what it means, or how to summarize it. In this way you can assess whether they are ready to read longer sections and if not, what kind of interpretation problems they are having.

Ask questions after the text has been read or the lesson is completed to see if children have an adequate mental model of the text. You can evaluate whether they can summarize and interpret the important ideas. You can also ask questions that have them relate the text information to their own experiences, to other lessons on the topic, and to other authors or texts.

How might comprehension be assessed? We describe several informal ways to evaluate comprehension, focusing on explanation and interpretation. A problem with comprehension evaluation is that it frequently does not require children to interpret or explain. Even teachers' informal questions are more often directed at facts and details than at an understanding of the larger concepts. Petrosky (1982) recommends the following ways to evaluate comprehension:

1. Test children with exercises that encourage the use of critical thinking.
2. Give assignments that ask children to write about their reading.
3. Create tests that ask them to make text interpretations and then give evidence from the texts or from their knowledge to support them.
4. Have children give text interpretations during science and social studies periods as well as language arts and reading periods. This extends their opportunity to practice forming interpretations and justifying their evaluations.
5. After children have read a text that puts forward an argument and provides evidence for it, set up discussions or debates to give children practice in evaluating arguments, in critical reasoning, and in explaining and justifying an argument.

Another problem with comprehension evaluation is the difficulty of assessing understanding of poetry and imaginative literature. Even though you might want to determine whether students have wrestled with deeper meanings of a text, it is not possible to measure objectively their "experiences," "happenings," or "personal realizations" from reading literature. There cannot be one "correct" reading of a piece of literature, and assessment questions cannot be graded as right or wrong but must be individually interpreted. Galda (1982) suggests that literature assessment be the "consideration and analysis of individual responses rather than comparison with an arbitrary standard" (p. 112). In that way, assessment becomes closely tied to the written expression of the reader's ideas and is interpreted by the teacher in terms of individual children's ability to express, explain, and interpret what they had read.

Children's responses to literature could be evaluated according to their ability to relate literature to themselves, to retell the text, and to evaluate the quality of the text. We suggest tasks drawn from Odell and Cooper (1976):

1. Evaluate students' ability to relate the work to self with an auto-biographical account or with an expression of their personal engagement with it.

2. Evaluate whether students can retell part of the text or describe language, character, setting, etc.

3. Evaluate whether students can interpret parts of the text or the whole text.

4. Evaluate students' ability to make evaluative statements about the evocativeness of the text, about the structure of the text, and about its meaningfulness or applicability to life.

Observing children

Observing individual and group responses to activities and materials may be one of the best ways to assess children's reading. It is a way, as Clay (1979) explains, to know why children are learning or failing to learn. A teacher can make good decisions about how to teach a child:

With children all working on the same assignment, this teacher is able to make notes about how well individuals handle a particular type of academic task.

if she knows the child well;

if she has some records which catch current behavior in such a way that it can be referred to some weeks later;

if she sets aside time for observation periods when she pays close attention to precisely what individual children are doing. (p. 180)

Knowing what to observe and making arrangements to do it should be part of your general teaching plan. Although what you should observe will vary with the age and reading difficulties and successes of the children, your approach will usually include observing how children approach reading and writing, the kinds of errors they make, and their reading and writing interests.

Observing writing. Children's early writing attempts provide an excellent way to observe their progress. You can measure their ability to sequence letters in words, use capital letters and periods, use the correct form of letters and order them from left to right, and construct sentences. Older children's writing gives you insights into their letter-sound knowledge, grammar, sense of the structure of stories and reports, and ability to use different styles of written language. Their errors let you know how they visualize words and sentences. If they are asked to write out all they remember about a story they read, what they leave out tells you what they found unimportant or did not understand or remember. The topics they write about give you insights into their interests and experiences.

Observing reading. Once children begin to read stories, you can observe their attempts to read. According to Clay (1979), you can observe the child's (1) paying attention to the print rather than the picture, (2) remembering rules about the direction for reading words and sentences, (3) changing the voice when reading aloud to "talk like a book," and (4) hearing the sound sequences of words and phrases. Reading errors can show the information (letters, sentence structure, text meaning, or picture) they are using. Unusual pauses or searching and checking for words are signs that the child is making progress with a problem-solving approach to word identification and comprehension.

Older children's reading can be observed by noting their capacity for independent, resourceful reading, their decisions to read or not at spare moments, and their choice of reading material when they do read. Resourceful reading is the ability to monitor reading, to self-correct, and to know what to do when something is not understood. Errors in comprehending, figuring out why something doesn't make sense, predicting, or summarizing information help you know which children do not have effective reading strategies or are not doing enough self-monitoring of their reading. It is also important to observe, for example, whether children read on their own, set up their own purposes for reading, use odd bits of time to read, show interest in books you have read aloud, develop a sustained interest in topics and authors, and borrow books to read at home.

Recording observations. There are many ways to record your observations of children's reading and writing behaviors. Here are four suggestions: (1) You might make notes in a lesson diary of group or individual children's responses to your teaching procedures, topics, or materials. (2) At the end of the day you might write a brief description of your attempts to teach difficult children and their reactions to the attempts. (3) You could focus on a different set of three to four children each week, observing them more intently for that time and writing out your observations of their attitude toward reading, work habits, interactions with classmates, and effective use of time. When you have observed every child once, repeat the cycle, so that over the school year you have two or three close observations of each child. (4) Finally, you could set aside occasional five-minute periods to observe all the children as they work independently or in small groups. Watch how well they concentrate, whether they give help or work with others, and whether they maintain a cheerful and interested attitude in reading and learning.

KEY CONCEPT 4

The teacher should understand how to integrate tests into the curriculum and make effective use of testing programs.

INTEGRATING THE TESTING PROGRAM WITH INSTRUCTION

The *teaching-learning cycle* is a sequence of steps that allows you to use tests to improve reading instruction. It is not the only set of procedures you could use to integrate a testing program with instruction, but it is a straightforward and practical one. It synthesizes ideas from the detailed instructional approaches we have recommended in the earlier chapters of this book with the suggestions made in this chapter for using norm-referenced, criterion-referenced, and informal tests and observations.

Step 1: Assessing students' needs before teaching

With respect to overall goals, effective teachers want to have some idea of what their students already know and can do. You can identify these goals from the strands (sets of related skills) listed in the scope and sequence chart of the commercial reading program or in your district's curriculum. The purpose of assessment is to find out which goals or objectives individual students already seem to have met, and which they appear ready to learn next.

Knowing what children are expected to learn is the halfway mark. Now you need to measure their knowledge. While you won't have the time and resources to conduct extensive testing, there are some straightforward and reasonable possibilities. For example, if you are using a basal series, there may be criterion-referenced tests matched to the strands in its scope and sequence chart, and these tests may be administered to the whole class at once or to smaller groups of children. This pretest assessment gives an idea about how much children know about the topic and helps you decide whether it needs to be taught, and if so, how much work it will be to teach it.

Your skill as an *observer*, rather than as an interpreter of test scores, is most valuable in establishing a system of useful, ongoing assessment within the classroom. Listen carefully to students' responses during the instruction of a reading lesson to determine their level of understanding. For further information about their capabilities, carefully examine their first completed assignments. At times you may want to interact with students while they are completing seatwork assignments, to get an idea of the problem-solving strategies they're using or need to learn. In other words, every contact with the students, in person or through their work, can provide you with information about their needs in learning to read.

You won't want to omit this initial step, even if you are just doing some kind of informal checking. Obviously, an effective classroom reading program cannot be developed on the basis of sheer guesswork. This step allows you to gather information about your students in order to make informed rather than haphazard instructional decisions.

To illustrate the idea of assessing needs before teaching, let's suppose that you were working with a fifth grade class. You were particularly concerned about the long-term development of their reading comprehension abilities, and your major goals were mostly in that area. You suspected that your middle and low ability reading groups needed to work on learning to summarize what they had read. You checked this by noticing their reluctance to respond and tendency to give vague or poorly worded story summaries during small group, teacher-led discussions. When looking at their first completed seatwork on that topic, you also noted that they were unable to locate or write down the main idea on their own.

Step 2: Setting immediate goals for instruction

Next, set immediate goals for instruction, or specific objectives for student learning. On the basis of your assessment, formal or informal, which of course includes information obtained from observations of the students, you determine where the students are along the strands you have decided to emphasize. Once students are "placed" on the strands, you have some idea of the immediate goals to help them reach. The reason for being as accurate as possible in setting realistic immediate goals for students' learning is to use your time and theirs to the best advantage.

Seek to meet these goals through a combination of activities. Instruction may be through teacher-led activities (see Step 3 below), through assignments pursued by small groups of students working with indirect teacher supervision, through independent seatwork assignments (these last two are part of Step 4), or other arrangements.

In our example, suppose you had set as an immediate goal for your middle group to develop an understanding of how to summarize paragraphs from expository prose passages, using already covered chapters from the social studies textbook. Because the concept of summarizing is such a difficult one, you would not use unfamiliar materials. Also, you would not ask them to summarize whole passages because you wanted them to understand the approach first with short pieces of text. You intended to teach them how to summarize by modeling the approach yourself and then giving them opportunities to "be the teacher" and try out the approach, getting corrective feedback from you and then from other students in the group. For independent practice seatwork, you decided to have them write summaries from paragraphs in easy, second grade expository texts.

Step 3: Providing instruction to meet goals

In Step 3 focus is primarily on giving teacher-directed lessons which are "on target" or at the students' *instructional* level. This is the level of difficulty at which students are challenged but at the same time, with the teacher's assistance, able to acquire new skills and knowledge. Because students within a class of 25 or more will generally have very different needs in learning to read, you may regroup them for particular reading topics. These groups should be more similar in instructional level, and so Step 3 lessons are often given to eight to ten students, rather than to the class as a whole.

In our example, you began by having a general discussion of what a summary is, why it might be important to construct one, and how you are going to help them do it, following the ideas in Chapter 8 of this textbook. You gave them the first paragraph in the social studies text, asked them to read it to themselves, and then modeled how you would summarize the paragraph. You invited students to comment on your summary. Next, you called on a student to "be the teacher," having everyone read the next paragraph and then seeing if the student teacher could come up with a summary. You carried this basic plan on in several lessons or until the students were able to use the same kind of thinking without corrective feedback from you.

Step 4: Providing opportunities for student practice and discovery

In Step 4 focus is on lessons and assignments which are easier or "below target." Having introduced the new process or information in Step 3, students are to practice and apply the concept or skill in a slightly different way. Opportunities for discovery would involve assignments requiring them to use their skills and background knowledge to gain new understandings on their own. These lessons and assignments are said to be at the students' *independent* rather than instructional level. More often than not, Step 4 involves seatwork or other assignments the children are to complete largely on their own, with little or no assistance from the teacher.

Neither in Step 3 nor Step 4 does the teacher give lessons or assignments at the students' *frustration level*, or so far "above target" as to be of practically no benefit at all. In preparation for meeting future goals, it's sometimes wise in Step 3 to introduce students to skills and knowledge they aren't yet able to master or grasp completely. But a lot of time can be wasted if students are faced with teacher-directed lessons on material much too difficult for them or left to struggle on their own with frustration level seatwork assignments.

In our example, you followed your plan of having the children work with short, easy text materials. When they could summarize them, you had them try to summarize more difficult and longer materials. You expected that they should eventually be able to write down the main ideas of text from current lessons. In addition to summarizing, you had them read and answer multiple-choice questions on reading comprehension passages, taking passages from old tests. You did this in order to measure their reading performance more generally.

Step 5: Checking on student progress

Check often to see if the children are progressing in a satisfactory way toward meeting both the narrowly defined goals and the broader goals of learning to read. Observe them when working on seatwork assignments or participating in group lessons, look at writing samples, and, if available, administer criterion-referenced tests. This process, much like that described in Step 1, now determines if the students are ready to move ahead to face new goals. Again, in practice, your observations and judgment are generally the deciding factors. But test results can provide converging evidence about what the children have learned.

In our example, you found on the first day that the children had to struggle quite a bit. Their responses during the lessons improved, but several members of the group did not seem to be able to construct a summary without considerable help from others. The seatwork assignments were similarly of an uneven quality and the criterion-referenced comprehension test showed only small gains.

Going ahead: Setting new goals

If your check shows that students have met the immediate learning goal, new goals are set for their instruction. The students are now ready to enter a new teaching-learning cycle, focused on another goal or set of goals. Thus, having completed Step 1, the assessment step, you can pick up with Step 2 and move on through the rest of the cycle.

In our example, you might have decided after five days that you would spend more time on this immediate goal. This was because of its importance and because most of the children seemed almost, but not quite, able to apply the concept at this basic level. If all went well, you would then have moved on to another goal, perhaps targeting vocabulary development related to science lessons. The children had begun the study of growing plants, so it looked like a good time to relate the important concepts to the new terms. The concept of summarizing texts could now be introduced with a different factual selection, thus allowing for some review as well as new learning.

Continuing to target the same goals: Providing further instruction and opportunities for practice and discovery

What you teach isn't the same as what students learn. If the goal hasn't yet been met, as shown by the evidence gathered in Step 5, provide more instruction. This means going back through Steps 3 and 4 within the same teaching-learning cycle. Several different methods are often available for teaching particular types of reading skills so that a variety of means can be employed to reach the same end. Simple repetition may also be used selectively.

In our example, you decided to work for three more days on summarizing social studies paragraphs and to continue with seatwork assignments along similar lines. In addition, you decided to have the children include in their book reports a summary of the central theme of the books they had chosen for independent reading. Children in the group were invited to share their book reports at the end of several lessons, and you pointed out how the concept of summarization could be applied to these books, as well. At the end of the three days, you repeated the criterion-referenced test using new examples, and gave a set of norm-referenced comprehension paragraphs with multiple-choice questions. You found that the children did very well on the criterion test (85% or better) and made a moderate improvement on the other test. You and the children were now ready to move on to another comprehension topic.

SUMMARY

In this chapter we provided you with a perspective about testing and assessing instruction and children's performance. In the first section we described how test information could be used to extend knowledge about individual children. The first and second key concepts provided an explanation of norm-referenced and criterion-referenced tests. We described how they are constructed, administered, and scored. We then advised you of their strengths and weaknesses so that you would have a better idea of when and how to use them appropriately. The third key concept provided descriptions of informal tests that you could use or adapt. Ways to assess reading concepts, word recognition, and comprehension and to use informal reading and observational techniques were described. The point here was to extend your knowledge about testing and assessment to those approaches that could be used during classroom lessons. In the last key concept we explained how you might integrate information from observations and tests into classroom instruction, by following the teaching-learning cycle and applying an understanding of various forms of formal and informal assessment.

BIBLIOGRAPHY

REFERENCES

Armbruster, B., Stevens, R., & Rosenshine, B. (1977). *Analyzing content coverage and emphasis* (Tech. Rep. No. 26). Urbana: University of Illinois, Center for the Study of Reading.

Arter, J., & Jenkins, J. (1978). *Differential diagnosis-prescriptive teaching: A critical appraisal* (Tech. Rep. No. 80). Urbana: University of Illinois, Center for the Study of Reading.

Baumann, J. F., & Stevenson, J. A. (1982a). Understanding standardized reading achievement test scores. *Reading Teacher, 35*(6), 648–654.

Baumann, J. F., & Stevenson, J. A. (1982b). Using scores from standardized reading achievement tests. *Reading Teacher, 35*(5), 528–532.

Betts, E. (1960). *Handbook on corrective reading for the American Adventure Series.* New York: Row, Peterson & Company.

Bloom, B. (1956). *Taxonomy of educational objectives.* New York: David McKay Company.

Clay, M. (1979). *Reading: The patterning of complex behavior.* Portsmouth, NH: Heinemann.

Estes, T., & Vaughan, J. (1972). Reading interest and comprehension implications. *Reading Teacher, 27,* 149–153.

Ferreiro, E., & Teberosky, A. (1982). *Literacy before schooling.* Portsmouth, NH: Heinemann.

Francis, H. (1977). Symposium: Reading abilities and disabilities: Children's strategies in learning to read. *British Journal of Educational Psychology, 47,* 117–125.

Fuchs, L., Fuchs, D., & Deno, S. (1982). Reliability and validity of curriculum-based informal reading inventories. *Reading Research Quarterly, 18,* 6–26.

Galda, S. L. (1982). Assessment: Responses to literature. In A. Berger & H. A. Robinson (Eds.), *Secondary school reading: What research reveals for classroom practice.* Urbana, IL: ERIC Clearinghouse on Reading and Communication Skills and the National Conference on Research in English.

Goodman, K., & Goodman, Y. (1977). Learning about psycholinguistic processes by analyzing oral reading. *Harvard Educational Review, 47,* 317–333.

Harris, A. (1984/1966). Areas of concern in evaluation. In A. Harris & E. Sipay (Eds.), *Readings on reading instruction,* 3rd ed. New York: Longman.

Johnston, P. H. (1981). *Implications of basic research for the assessment of reading comprehension* (Tech. Rep. No. 206). Urbana: University of Illinois, Center for the Study of Reading.

Johnston, P., & Pearson, P. D. (1982). Assessment: Responses to exposition. In A. Berger & H. A. Robinson (Eds.), *Secondary school reading: What research reveals for classroom practice.* Urbana, IL: ERIC Clearinghouse on Reading and Communication Skills and the National Conference on Research in English.

Jongsma, K. S., & Jongsma, E. A. (1981). Test review: Commercial informal reading inventories. *Reading Teacher, 34,* 697–705.

Juel, C. (1983). The development of mediated word identification. *Reading Research Quarterly, 18,* 306-327.

Mason, J. (1976). Overgeneralization in learning to read. *Journal of Reading Behavior, 8,* 173-182.

Mason, J. (1977). Questioning the notion of independent processing stages in reading. *Journal of Educational Psychology, 69,* 288-297.

Mason, J. (1980). When *do* children begin to read? *Reading Research Quarterly, 15,* 203-227.

Mason, J., Osborn, J., & Rosenshine, B. (1977). *A consideration of skill hierarchy approaches to the teaching of reading* (Tech. Rep. No. 42). Urbana: University of Illinois, Center for the Study of Reading.

Mason, J., Stewart, J., & Dunning, D. (1986). Measuring early reading: A window into kindergarten children's understanding. In T. Raphael (Ed.), *Contexts of school-based literacy.* New York: Random House.

McKenna, M. (1983). Informal reading inventories: A review of the issues. *Reading Teacher, 36,* 670-679.

Morris, D. (1981). Concept of a word: A developmental phenomenon. In J. Jensen (Ed.), *Composing and comprehending.* Urbana, IL: ERIC Clearinghouse on Reading and Communication Skills and the National Conference on Research in English.

Odell, L., & Cooper, C. (1976). Describing responses to works of fiction. *Research in the Teaching of English, 10,* 203-225.

Petrosky, A. (1982). Reading achievement. In A. Berger & H. A. Robinson (Eds.), *Secondary school reading: What research reveals for classroom practice.* Urbana, IL: ERIC Clearinghouse on Reading and Communication Skills and the National Conference on Research in English.

Raphael, T. E. (1982). Question-answering strategies for children. *Reading Teacher, 36,* 186-190.

Schell, L., & Hanna, G. (1981). Can informal reading inventories reveal strengths and weaknesses in comprehension subskills? *Reading Teacher, 35,* 263-268.

Silvaroli, N. (1973). *Classroom reading inventory,* 2nd ed. Dubuque, IA: Wm. C. Brown.

Smith, N. (1926). *One hundred ways of teaching silent reading for all grades.* Chicago: World Book.

Stewart O., & Green, D. (1983). Test-taking skills for standardized tests of reading. *Reading Teacher, 36,* 634-639.

Sulzby, E. (1986). Writing and reading as signs of oral and written language organization in the young child. In W. Teale & E. Sulzby (Eds.), *Emergent literacy: Writing and reading.* Norwood, NJ: Ablex.

FURTHER READINGS

Allington, R. L., & McGill-Franzen, A. (1980). Word identification errors in isolation and in context: Apples vs. oranges. *Reading Teacher, 33,* 795-800.

Bruton, B. (1977). *An ounce of prevention plus a pound of cure: Tests and techniques for aiding individual readers.* Santa Monica, CA: Goodyear.

Burns, P. C., & Roe, B. D. (1980). *Informal reading assessment: Preprimer to twelfth grade.* Chicago: Rand McNally.

Crowell, D. C., Au, K. H., & Blake, K. M. (1983). Comprehension questions: Differences among standardized tests. *Journal of Reading, 26(4),* 314-319.

Goodman, K. S. (1969). Analysis of oral reading miscues: Applied psycholinguistics. *Reading Research Quarterly, 5,* 9-30.

Hood, J. (1978). Is miscue analysis practical for teachers? *Reading Teacher, 32,* 260-266.

Kubiszyn, T., & Borich, G. (1983). *Educational testing and measurement: Classroom application and practice.* Glenview, IL: Scott, Foresman.

Pikulski, J. (1974). A critical review: Informal reading inventories. *Reading Teacher, 28,* 141-151.

Readence, J. E., & Moore, D. W. (1983). Why questions? A historical perspective on standardized reading achievement tests. *Journal of Reading, 26*(4), 306-313.

Shuy, R. W. (1981). What the teacher knows is more important than text or test. *Language Arts, 58,* 919-929.

Wixson, K. L. (1979). Miscue analysis: A critical review. *Journal of Reading Behavior, 11,* 163-175.

Yarborough, B. H., & Johnson, R. A. (1980). How meaningful are marks in promoting growth in reading? *Reading Teacher, 33*(6), 644-651.

CHAPTER 11

Instructional Approaches

and Materials

An observer senses definite changes in moving from a classroom where one method is taught to one where another is taught, and yet many of these changes cannot be measured; they can only be described. Take pupil interest, for example. Interest is a subtle thing to measure—indeed, even to observe. Every method ever proposed has claimed pupil interest as one of its strengths. Ironically, it is the one effect that experimental classroom tryouts have not measured in any objective way. . . . .

How interested pupils are in learning to read, I concluded, is not determined by what method or set of materials they are using. I saw excitement, enthusiasm, and general interest exhibited in classes using every reading program. I also saw children respond to each with listlessness, apathy, boredom, and restlessness.

Generally, it was *what the teacher did* with the method, the materials, and the children rather than the method itself that seemed to make the difference. More specifically, I would say that interest is highly related to pacing—how instruction is geared to that tenuous balance between ease and difficulty for the child. In classes where pupils seemed to enjoy the reading period, the children knew what was expected of them, and the pace was neither too slow nor too fast. Instead, where classwork belabored the obvious or when only one or two pupils were working while others watched, interest seemed to wane.
(Chall, 1970, pp. 269-270)

OVERVIEW

Commercial reading materials are intended to help children learn to read. Yet, when they are too closely followed, negative consequences have been reported (Durkin, 1981; Shannon, 1983). An over-reliance on commercial reading materials seems to limit instruction or keeps teachers from developing a flexible attitude toward reading instruction.

PERSPECTIVE

CHANGES IN TEACHING READING

In this chapter we explain *why* there are different instructional methods and materials and *how* they differ. Contrasting methods are described, with suggestions for ways to adapt and evaluate them to strengthen comprehension instruction. In the perspective we describe the many changes in reading methods and materials which have taken place since the beginning of the century. We explain how the changes are related to changes in society and ideas about the reading process.

The first three key concepts describe different approaches to the teaching of reading, while the fourth is on the uses of computers in reading instruction. These are followed by two key concepts on the effective use, modification, and evaluation of reading materials.

The six key concepts are:

Key Concept #1: Basal reading programs are intended to provide a complete, skill-organized approach for teaching all levels of reading.

Key Concept #2: Teaching children to read with a language experience approach can foster the integration of reading with writing and speaking.

Key Concept #3: An individualized reading approach can foster reading with a diverse assortment of books and other materials that suit children's interests.

Key Concept #4: Computers can offer opportunities for children to think about and practice reading and writing.

Key Concept #5: Establishing goals for reading instruction can help teachers make more effective use of reading materials.

Key Concept #6: Teachers should evaluate the appropriateness and quality of reading instructional materials and procedures.

You will have a better understanding of reading instruction in the United States if you see the connection between contrasting approaches to reading instruction and the changing needs and attitudes of the society. Smith (1926) pointed out the earlier historical connections, as summarized below.

ABC texts. In colonial times reading education was bound to religious concepts. Young children were taught letters and words with religious verses and moral messages. Older children read or memorized selections from the Bible. For most adults reading meant the exact recollection of information and so instruction was directed to this purpose. Smith reported, for example, that the

New England Primer used complex statements to teach the letters of the alphabet. They could be used even for beginning readers, because children were required only to memorize the texts. Here are three examples:

F Foolishness is bound up in the heart of a child, but the rod of correction shall drive it far from him.

  G Grieve not the Holy Spirit.

  H Holiness becomes God's House forever.

Oral reading. As our country was being settled and wars for independence were fought, other reading purposes arose. Children's reading began to focus on patriotism and political freedom as well as moral values. Since there was little printed material available for children or adults, oratory was emphasized for transmitting news and ideas. Children were trained to become eloquent and expressive oral readers. The text was to provide a useful message, but was simplified for beginning readers. Here is an example of a selection from the popular reader, the *McGuffey's Eclectic Primer* (1881). The two-page text also listed nine new story words, gave a pronunciation key for four letters and included a picture of a cat and children at the seashore. It is reproduced in Figure 11.1.

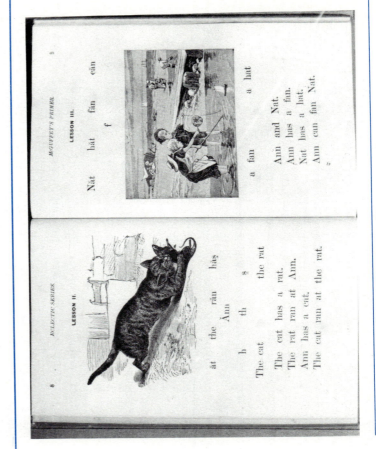

From *McGuffey's Eclectic Primer,* American Book Company, 1909.

FIGURE 11.1

Basic readers. At the beginning of the twentieth century the social conditions for reading changed in many ways. Abundant reading materials such as newspapers, periodicals, and books were published. Rapid transportation facilities brought them to rural as well as urban areas of the country. Compulsory education laws made it necessary for all children to attend school and learn to read. Philosophers were beginning to propose that instruction be centered on interpretation of text meaning rather than on its exact recall. Moreover, with the decrease in the length of the working day and increase in mechanical devices for household care, reading was becoming a leisure time activity. Smith (1926) described these accompanying social changes:

> The goal of reading instruction is no longer solely that of teaching the child to read the Bible, nor is it that of training him to read orally with such expression and eloquence that he will sway his audience. There is now no particular need for oratory. The chief emphasis is placed upon training the child to get the *complete thought* from the page and to get it as *quickly and accurately as possible*. (emphasis by Smith, p. 9)

After the turn of the century, then, ABC and syllable recitation methods were gradually replaced by whole word instruction, and silent reading and text comprehension became the new emphasis. Children were to be taught fluent silent reading, and to learn to comprehend and interpret printed information. More care was taken that first-read texts be understandable to young children. These changes were reflected in a heavily used primer developed by Bryce and Spaulding in 1916. The first lesson, for example, had children memorize a set of phrases that rhymed. The teacher was to introduce it by telling children a story that made the little text meaningful. The text is reproduced in Figure 11.2.

Individualized reading. During the first quarter of the century with the advent of standardized testing, an alternative instructional approach was developed that emphasized wide reading according to children's interests. Smith (1965) suggested that it came about when educators realized there were large individual differences among children in reading. Called *individualized reading* or a *book-centered approach*, it favored the replacement of reading textbooks and group instruction techniques with children's independent reading of books that fit their interests and reading ability, and with individual conferences with the teacher.

One late nineteenth-century proponent of individualized reading was Charles Eliot, then the president of Harvard University. According to Smith (1965), Eliot collected all the elementary school reading materials being used to teach reading at that time and had two adults read them. Although 37 percent of all school time was devoted to the study of reading and the English language, he found that two adults could read in only 46 hours everything that elementary school children were supposed to spend six years reading. Eliot (1898) argued that children should be reading far more books.

FIGURE 11.2

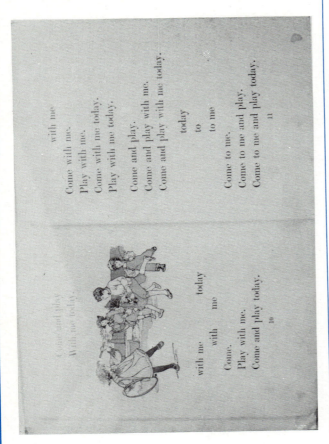

From *Aldine Readers: Primer* by Catherine T. Bryce and Frank E. Spaulding. Newson & Company, 1916.

Individualized reading has never won wide acceptance. Even though it can be effective, it is cumbersome to use because teachers must provide a set of books for every child and develop lessons and practice materials on their own.

Linguistic programs. Another method of teaching reading arose from analyses of the letter-to-sound patterns of English. According to Fries (1963), linguistic research between 1850 and 1925 encouraged Bloomfield, a linguist, to formulate letter pattern rules to teach beginning reading. Relying on his understanding of the letter-sound regularities of English, Bloomfield argued that high frequency words were often not regular and should not be used in beginning reading materials because they would mislead children. If words exhibiting regular letter-sound patterns were taught first, children would be able to understand how English words are structured and how to identify countless new words.

In the 1960s, then, a movement began to construct beginning reading materials made up of regularly patterned words. This approach appeared first in materials by Bloomfield and Barnhart (1961) who demonstrated that texts could feature words with regular letter-sound patterns (such as the phonograms presented in Chapter 3). These words could be taught in sets and presented in stories. The following example is from the first reading lesson (p. 60) by Bloomfield and Barnhart. It is designed to teach the *an* pattern which is then practiced with nine new words. There are no pictures to go with this 42-word text.

Dan ran. Nan ran.
Van ran. A man ran.
Nan can fan Dan.
Can Dan fan Nan?
Dan can fan Nan.
Nan, fan Dan.
Dan, fan Nan.
Dan ran a van.
Dan ran a tan van.
A man ran a tan van.

Basal reading programs. Today, reading is taught with materials that are published by about 150 independent publishers, about five of whom serve most of the school market. The materials are called *basals*, or *basal readers*, a term derived from that used at the turn of the century, basic books. Basal reading companies produce materials used by about 90 to 95 percent of all American school children several times a week, if not daily (Mason & Osborn, 1982; Shannon, 1983).

Basal programs are intended to provide a complete set of materials for teaching, practicing, and testing reading. Texts in children's reading books or readers are graded by difficulty according to *readability formulas*. The formulas are based on sentence length and either the number of syllables in words or the number of uncommon words. Texts with short sentences and one syllable or common words are considered to be easier to read than texts with a larger proportion of long sentences and many multisyllable words. Using these texts, children are to read under the teacher's supervision, learn reading skills in lessons taught by the teacher, and practice the skills by completing workbook exercises.

Forecasting change in reading practices

At the present time reading instructional principles are on the edge of another change, this coming about with the use in the workplace of scientific reading materials, including those related to the use of computers, and a predicted reduction in the need for low-skill jobs. The present requirement for literacy goes beyond fluent silent reading or an ability to decipher or interpret printed information. There is now a need for critical and analytic thinking, as discussed further in Chapter 13.

The new demands for tougher educational standards and higher levels of literacy include the ability to express one's ideas effectively, the ability to identify propaganda and use reasoning and disciplined thought, and the ability to evaluate, not merely remember, information read. This means that teachers will be asked to go beyond teaching children to read fluently and comprehend text information. They are to teach them to be reflective thinkers, capable of analyzing and judging information, and able to express themselves in written as well as oral form.

We interpret this shift in literacy to indicate the importance of teaching children extensive comprehension skills and of looking upon reading as an active, problem-solving activity. Reading instruction will need to involve widespread reading and writing, advanced reading comprehension skills, and an understanding of how to use the computer for reading, writing, and information storage. These expected changes have been taken into consideration in the descriptions of reading methods and suggestions for modifications and alternative approaches presented in the body of this chapter.

KEY CONCEPT 1

Basal reading programs are intended to provide a complete, skill-organized approach for teaching all levels of reading.

CHARACTERISTICS OF BASAL READING PROGRAMS

A basal reading program is a sequentially arranged series of reading textbooks, workbooks, teacher's guides, scope and sequence charts, tests, and supplementary practice materials. When using these materials, a teacher should not forget that reading instruction is meant to focus on the children's reader, the textbook containing stories and other selections. The texts are selected for their high interest to children and for their usefulness in teaching skills. Materials for one grade level are all at about the same level of difficulty, at least in terms of word and sentence length. Children are assumed to achieve reading fluency and to develop effective comprehension strategies from the readings. Evaluation is typically carried out by asking children comprehension questions, listening to them read, and giving end-of-unit tests.

Reading skills

The skill lessons, presented in the teacher's guide, explain how to teach a skill and provide follow-up practice. The skills covered in these lessons are applied to increasingly difficult texts as children move up the grades. The teacher is expected to select from the lessons only those skills that children need to study, to integrate the text reading with instruction in those skills, and to provide guided and independent practice using the skills. The skills are listed at the beginning of the lessons and also in the scope and sequence chart in the teacher's guide. The skills are grouped under headings such as:

Decoding and word recognition
Vocabulary
Comprehension
Resource and study skills
Language and literature skills

Decoding is taught from word analysis lessons located in the teacher's guide and with practice materials found in the workbook. However, because basal programs use both high frequency and words of regular letter-patterns in stories, children must learn to recognize many of their story words by sight rather than by decoding.

Vocabulary is usually taught by definition, by reading words in context, and by morphemic analysis. New vocabulary words are repeated several times in the stories, giving children practice reading them, but they usually appear infrequently in workbook exercises.

Comprehension is taught through story questioning and skill lessons in the guide. Among the strategies taught are understanding the main idea, drawing conclusions, predicting outcomes, recognizing cause-effect relationships, and understanding an author's purpose. Workbook exercises are available to reinforce the lessons.

Reference and study skills are taught through lessons appearing in the guide and in short texts in the children's reader. These skills include locating information, using references, organizing information, and evaluating information. Practice exercises appear occasionally in the workbook.

Literary and language skills are taught in lessons from the guide, often in postreading story activities. The skills include analysis of types of literature, elements of stories, writing devices, grammatical relations, and word forms.

Basal program examples

To give you an idea about lessons in basal readers, we have chosen examples for a readiness text, two contrasting first grade texts, a third grade text, and a fifth grade text.

A reading readiness lesson. Basal reading materials for kindergarten children are in workbooks instead of hardcover readers. Most of the workbook pages contain pictures or pictures and letters and relatively few words and sentences.

Letters and their sounds are typically taught by presenting children with pictures of objects beginning with the same letter. Only a few new words are introduced at a time, and children are then given frequent practice in reading them. Either CVC clusters or high frequency words are introduced. As we discussed earlier, linguistic programs emphasize words in certain clusters so as to provide practice with regular patterns. Conventional basal programs emphasize high frequency words to enable children to read short stories. In both types of programs, linguistic and conventional, children are taught to recognize, copy, and match words and short phrases. Many of the words are put into sentences. In some programs, pictures of objects are substituted for words not yet introduced to the children. This mixing of words and pictures, called a *rebus* approach, allows the presentation of more meaningful and interesting sentences.

Here is an example from one conventional basal program (Ginn, 1982). We chose the first lesson in which children are to read more than one sentence. The text is representative of those appearing in other basal programs.

The readiness book reviews letters and letter sounds with twenty basic words (names of five children and the high frequency words *and, ball, can, cat, dig, here, hop, is, it, play, run, she, the, to, with*). Sentences and brief stories also appear. As shown in Figure 11.3, the first story (pp. 46-47) is written with just

EXERCISE

Becoming familiar with a teacher's guide

Choose a recently published basal reader, if possible one that you have used or will use for teaching, and go through as many of the steps below as possible.

Overview. Locate the scope and sequence chart for that grade, looking over the skills to be taught. Determine whether the program features mostly regularly patterned words or high frequency words to teach beginning reading. Choose one skill listed on the chart and find a lesson where it is taught. Read the accompanying story and figure out a way to teach the skill in conjunction with the story.

Using the guide. Locate in the introduction of the teacher's guide the publisher's explanation of how lessons are organized. Choose one lesson and complete these activities:

(1) Describe how you might teach the lesson, relate it to the story, and provide examples of guided and independent practice.

(2) Determine whether the lesson you chose was intended to teach new information, review information, or provide practice.

(3) Explain the meaning of the colored headings and different type fonts.

(4) Determine whether the lesson was intended for all children or for high or low achieving readers.

(5) Determine whether the end-of-unit test covered information from the lesson you chose.

(6) Describe how new words in the story are identified. Find out how to distinguish words that the publisher suggests you teach, words that children are to figure out on their own, and words that are pointed out but not practiced.

(7) Study the questions provided for teachers to ask children before, during, and after storyreading. Explain the distinctions among question types.

FIGURE 11.3

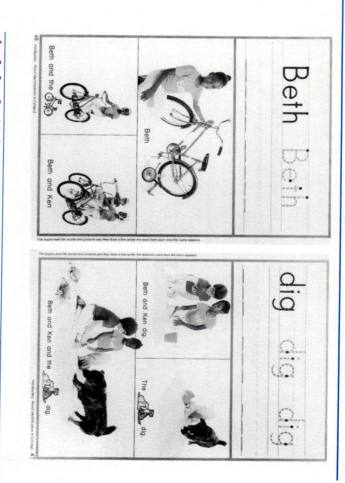

From *One Potato Two* of the *Ginn Reading Program* by Theodore Clymer and others, © Copyright 1985, 1982 by Ginn and Company. Used with permission.

five different words, and a picture accompanies each line of print. The words *Beth* and *dig* appear at the top for the child to trace and copy. Pictures are substituted for some words.

Notice the repetition of words in the context of sentences. The lessons rely on repetition to teach children to recognize a small set of words. If you use one of these programs, remember that one of your instructional goals is for children to recognize those words anywhere, not just in those sentences. So, be sure not to limit the children to reading and copying only these materials. Try to get them to use the words in their oral responses, in language experience stories, and in labeling their pictures. Help them make phrase cards that include the words, and include the words in some of your bulletin board labels. You could also expand the lessons, for example by substituting children's names for the names in the basal text.

First grade linguistic reader. The Lippincott basal reader (1975) exemplifies a linguistic approach for beginning readers. The first story is on pages 13–14. It contains six different words in a running count of twenty words, and two pictures describe the events in the text. One new word, *the*, is taught as a sight word. The children are to figure out all the rest of the words by using the letter sounds they have been taught (*a, n, r, d, u, m, p*).

FIGURE 11.4

Three Nights of Magic

by Michele Spirn

Once there was a pretty house.
Mr. and Mrs. Green and Pat and Sue
lived in the house.
But the Greens were not happy.

"Things are always the same around
here," said Mrs. Green.

"All the days are the same in this
house," said Pat.

"We need something new around here,"
they all said.

Skills Unit 6

84

"Three Nights of Magic" by Michele Spirn from *SF Reading: Kick Up Your Heels* by Ira E. Aaron et al., Scott, Foresman and Company, 1981, 1983, p. 84.

Pam and the Pup

Pam ran up the ramp.
Up the ramp ran the pup.
The pup and Pam nap.

Notice that this text features the phonograms *-an, -am, -ap, -up*. The advantage to materials of this sort is that phonics instruction is deeply embedded in the text. Children are not likely to be confused about how to pronounce words and can learn about the regularity of letter-sound correspondences. The disadvantage is that the first texts are quite stilted, relatively meaningless, and likely to contain unfamiliar words.

If you use one of these programs, you can also give the children other CVC words in the same pattern and see if they can figure them out. Your aim is to have children recognize words quickly and accurately by applying knowledge of letter-sound regularities.

First grade conventional basal reader. An example of a first grade text, which is typical of stories from most basal programs, is taken from a Scott, Foresman (1983) reader. The first page of this story is shown in Figure 11.4. In the teacher's guide eight words are listed as mastery words (words to be learned) along with four other new words. The mastery words are *once, night, elves, large, might, became, while, such*. Of these, *night* and *elves* have easily pictured meanings. The others are important, high-frequency words with hard-to-describe meanings. Three of the fourteen (*while, became, such*) are listed as decodable. This means that you are to have children figure out these three words using letter-sound rules taught earlier. The rest are to be learned when you introduce them and as the children read the story, where the words are repeated several times. For example, *once* appears four times and *might* appears nine times.

When introducing the story you are to go over the new words. Then you are to have children look at the first page, name the four story characters, and ask how they think the characters feel. After reading each page of the story, you ask several questions. The questions help children focus on the story information, and their answers help you determine whether they are following the story. Because you know from children's answers whether they can read the story, you do not need to have children read aloud, except for brief sections that are fun to read or particularly important to read carefully.

We recommend modifying this kind of lesson in order to strengthen your comprehension instruction. First, as we described in Chapter 5, you can use the ETR approach with basal stories. With this approach, focus the prereading segment of the lesson on children's understanding of the topic. This story, which is about having wishes come true, could be introduced with a discussion of children's experiences with having a wish come true. Modify the guided reading segment of the lesson to ask children to predict what might happen next and to sum up what they have read so far. Devote the postreading segment of the lesson to interpretations and the drawing of relationships of the story information to the children's own lives. Or teach children to analyze the story's structure. In these ways the story can be used to give children practice with new words in an interesting context, as well as to help them analyze and interpret text information.

Third grade basal reader. Our example is Lesson 6 from a grade three Scott, Foresman (1983) reader. It contains a one-page expository selection about how to make a hand puppet, a skill lesson on ordering text information, and a story, "Somebody Stole Second." Children are asked to pronounce and then define the seven new words. The teacher is then to tell children what the story will be about and to remember the order of story events as they read. Several questions are provided for checking comprehension. Shown in Figure 11.5 is the first page of the eight-page story.

To use a lesson like this effectively, be sure to read over the guide lessons and the story carefully, making notes about their purpose and approach. Be sure you know how to relate the skill lessons to the text so that you can bring out the connections when you teach. You must also decide whether the skill lesson, the vocabulary words, and the text content and structure all should be

FIGURE 11.5

Somebody Stole Second

by Louise Munro Foley

"It's GONE!" Pete yelled. He stopped running. Scooter stopped throwing and Jenny ran in from left field.

Pete was right. It was gone. Second base had disappeared.

"Fine thing," said Pete. Pete was captain of the Jets. "First time this year that I hit a double and when I get here, second base is gone."

"Somebody stole second!" yelled Scooter as he jumped up and down. "Somebody stole second!" He poked Pete in the ribs. "Just like the Giants," yelled Scooter. "Somebody stole second!"

93

Skills Unit 6

taught. They should challenge and not bore or discourage children. Here are the factors you would consider in making these decisions:

1. Since the comprehension skill lesson is about ordering information, ask yourself whether your students have any idea about how to order a set of events as they read. Will this activity be totally new or is it something that could be done with guided practice? If new, you may need to add exercises and plan on taking most of the group's reading period for the skill lesson. On the other hand, if it is familiar, the children may just apply the skill, under your guidance, while reading the story.

2. If the new story words are difficult for children to pronounce, list them on the board for children to practice pronouncing. If the meanings of the words are not known, you can have them read the story sentences in which they appear and try to figure out the meanings from context or by relating them to words they know. This might be done after the children read the story. Refer to Chapter 4 for further suggestions.

3. Consider what your instructional purpose for the story will be. If it is to be read purely for fun, you can introduce the topic and let children read it independently. If it is to be read for reading fluency

practice, you might have them read aloud as a group, read after you read, or read with partners. If the story is going to be studied for the purpose of improving comprehension ability, you need to consider how to set up a lesson. You could follow the suggestion in the guide on ordering information, or you could highlight the problem in the story. Have the children read the first page, discuss the problem, and then predict what the characters might do. On subsequent pages ask the children for predictions and have them focus on the setting and characters. After reading, have them describe events in the correct order or fill out a diagram on the blackboard of the ordered informa- tion. Refer to Chapter 6 for other suggestions.

Fifth grade basal reader. In this example (Scott, Foresman, 1983) we look at expository reading instruction for fifth graders. Here the skill lesson is on using an index. There is a one-page index for an imaginary book about South America, followed by a five-page article about the Theodore Roosevelt family and an index page related to the article. The first pages of the article are shown in Figure 11.6. The article contains 18 new words. The teacher's guide provides prereading questions to be used with children who can read the article independently and additional questions to be used with those who need a guided reading approach.

As previously suggested, in this case also you should study the guide lessons and text beforehand, decide on the purpose for reading, and develop a plan to teach the text content. Again, the same three factors need to be considered.

1. Since the suggested skill lesson is on indexing, think about whether your students need the lesson and if so, how it can be related to the story or their work with social studies or science textbooks. For ex- ample, you might ask them questions similar to those in the teacher's guide but have them use an actual index from one of their textbooks. Consult Chapter 7 for other ideas.

2. With regard to vocabulary instruction, think about what words stu- dents need help in pronouncing and what words are likely to have unknown meanings. If instruction is needed, try to use words the students have recently studied, with related pronunciations or mean- ings that can be used to help them learn and remember the new words.

3. Decide whether the text should be read independently or with your guidance. If students need guidance, decide whether to emphasize the topic (such as by relating events in the article to historical events already familiar to the children), the skill of indexing suggested for the lesson (such as by having children construct an index for impor-

tant topics in the article), or the text structure (such as by having children analyze how the author blended interesting and plausible events with documented facts). For other possibilities, refer to Chapter 7.

CHARACTERISTICS OF A LANGUAGE EXPERIENCE APPROACH

The language experience approach (LEA) to reading instruction, originally developed in the 1950s, is intended to make beginning reading easier by using children's own language and experiences in the stories they read. It fosters active participation in reading and writing because children dictate and later compose and write their own stories. LEA can be particularly effective in kindergarten and first grade and may be used before or while children are

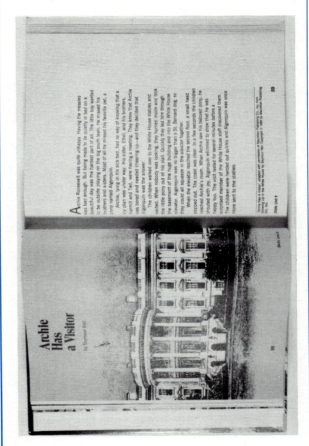

FIGURE 11.6

Adapted with permission of Macmillan Publishing Company from *Growing Up in the White House* by Seymour Reit. Copyright © 1968 by Macmillan Publishing Company.

INSTRUCTIONAL ACTIVITIES

A systematic instructional program is important to the success of LEA. Mallon and Berglund (1984) recommend the following five-day sequence.

Five-day sequence

Day one: Introduce an object or topic that will stimulate discussion. It might be an animal, toy, special event, or picture. Follow this with a discussion in which numerous ideas are expressed. End the discussion with a review of the ideas and list the suggestions on the chalkboard.

Day two: Briefly review the first day's discussion, refreshing children's memories of the listed ideas. Have children draw pictures of their ideas and then individually dictate the ideas. You write the words on their pictures or on a separate piece of paper for them to copy. More advanced writers can write their own ideas directly on their pictures. Help the children reread their sentences to see if everything is in order.

Day three: Have children read their stories independently or to you. Have them underline words they know and help them with unknown words, if any.

Day four: Have children reread their stories to you. Again underline words they know and help them with difficult words.

Day five: Use this day for skill development, adding words the children know to their word boxes. A rule of thumb is to allow a word to be in the box if they have recognized it on at least two different days.

Language experience activities for beginning readers

The application of the language experience approach described here can be used to prepare either kindergarten or first grade children for textbook or tradebook reading. Allen and Laminack (1982) developed this application, documented with a day-to-day journal account. While this particular application is more rigidly structured than most other LEA applications, it does offer clear procedures for introducing children to reading and writing. Here are samples of the instructional ideas used by Allen and Laminack to begin language experience reading and writing:

The text continues on the right side of the page

reading basal stories. Some teachers use LEA when high-quality written materials are unavailable or materials are uninteresting to children.

LEA can also be effective with older children in the study of social studies, science, and other content areas as part of an experience-based approach to new concepts. By allowing children to read texts based on their own oral language, teachers can help them talk about and grasp concepts that might otherwise have been difficult to understand.

1. Have children draw pictures of themselves and then write their own names on the picture. As children finish, ask them to complete the sentence, "I feel . . ." Print in manuscript letters what each child says, saying each word as you write it. Read it aloud and then ask the child to read it back to you.

2. List each child's name on chart paper. As you write the name, ask the child to stand and tell something he or she likes to do. Say the words as you write them on the paper, "_____ likes to . . ." Then have the whole class read the sentence.

3. Hand out to each child a sheet of paper with the following written on the bottom: "On my way to school I saw . . ." Ask each child to draw something seen, write the complete sentence with the child's idea, and have the child read it aloud.

4. Hand out a sheet of paper with, "At school I like to . . ." Have the class draw the idea that completes the sentence and then write the word(s) for them. Print the most popular responses on chart paper and have children read them in their sentence contexts. Have children locate particular words on the chart, including the same words appearing in different locations.

5. After they have learned a color word, have children draw something of that color. Write out for each child a sentence that includes the color word, such as "_____ is red."

Advantages of this approach, according to the authors, are that the children learn a large number of new words rapidly and willingly. Comprehension is not abandoned because texts begin with children's real experiences. Words are learned in their story context first and then apart and in reconstituted sentences to give children a more flexible approach to word identification.

Language experience activities for older children

McClure (1982) recommends using a thematic unit approach for integrating fiction, poetry, and exposition. Begin with a topic interesting to children and related to a topic to be covered in a content area. For example, McClure describes how you might foster reading and writing while studying the life cycle of frogs. She also includes examples of informational books about frogs students might read.

1. Bring in nature photography books so children can look at, read, and hear about frogs.

2. Have children generate questions about frogs' growth, eating habits, where they live, etc.

3. Have children make observations of frog eggs and pond water using a magnifying glass and microscope.

4. Have them record their observations daily and share their observations with partners or larger groups.

5. Have them read informational articles on frogs' life cycles and life in ponds. Lead discussions about what they learned and have them write reports or stories about frogs.

KEY CONCEPT 3

An individualized reading approach can foster reading with a diverse assortment of books and other reading materials that suit children's interests.

CHARACTERISTICS OF INDIVIDUALIZED READING

In an individualized reading approach, children choose their own reading materials so their reading is directly related to their interests and knowledge. Since reading choices are made individually, teachers have conferences with children to discuss each text and give help with word recognition, word meanings, and comprehension. Teachers evaluate children's reading by giving them questions to answer and by listening to them read aloud. They also keep track of the number of books that children read, topics they are interested in, and their progress toward reading more complex materials.

According to West (1964), the individualized method of reading allows for:

> . . . individual differences while at the same time recognizing interest and purpose as prime factors in the learning process. It is designed to allow the child to develop his own unique direction and pace rather than to fit him into a prescribed mode of development supposed typical or normal for his age group. It makes provision for reading activities which develop the needed reading skills in functional settings, capitalizes upon opportunities for the development of skills in other areas of the curriculum and throughout the school day, and recognizes the interrelationship of all the language arts—speaking, listening, reading, and writing—which are based on a wide variety of interesting experiences closely related to the real activities and interests in the child's life that provide entries into learning situations. (p. 37)

Individualized reading can be recommended because it helps children enjoy reading and fosters more reading. Another advantage cited by Stott (1982) and Yamada (1983) is that children have the opportunity to read long selections. Stott had children read novels while Yamada had them read historical fiction. Individualized reading can be criticized because it does not provide step-by-step skill instruction and evaluation. However, research in the 1950s and 1960s summarized by West (1964) suggests that well-planned individualized reading programs do not hamper children's progress in learning to read.

General guidelines for organizing an individualized reading program

Because research supports the value of an instructional emphasis on comprehension, silent reading, and the reading of good literature, we believe individualized reading should have a definite place in classroom reading programs. However, use of an individualized reading approach, or even the supplementing of a basal program with tradebooks, does require the teacher to do more advance preparation. The individualized approach cannot be carried out merely by providing children with an assortment of books to read. Thus, West (1964) recommends attention to these basic elements:

1. Choosing book materials.
2. Organizing the classroom.
3. Monitoring reading activity.
4. Evaluating reading growth.
5. Providing reading strategy instruction.

Choosing book materials.   You need to know where or how to find appropriate books for children to read and you must decide what guidelines to follow for helping children to choose topics and books.

Arbuthnot (1957) offered the following good advice for identifying well-written stories and informational materials. Of stories, she said, "In general children like stories with an *adequate theme*, strong enough to generate and support a *lively plot*. They appreciate *memorable characters* and *distinctive style*" (p. 16). Of informational texts, she wrote:

The best we can do here is to set up criteria for judging these books on the basis of *scrupulous accuracy* (unless our text is accurate our reading is worse than useless; accuracy is the most important criterion for judging any informational book), *convenient presentation* (we want the material presented in such a way that we can find what we are looking for quickly and comfortably; this is equally true of children), *clarity* (information for any age level should be written directly and sensibly, with obvious respect for the reader's intelligence), *adequate treatment* (it is essential that enough significant facts be given for a realistic and balanced picture), and *style* (a lively, well-written text is an invaluable bait to learning). [p. 545, emphasis added].

In your classroom library, you should plan to have at least fifty different books at a time. Bring in new books regularly from the library. Some multiple copies are necessary for books that you will want several children to read and discuss together, or that you know are going to be very popular. To build up a diverse collection of books, magazines, and children's reference materials at the lowest possible cost, check possible resources in your community (for example, children's books may be purchased from library, church, and garage sales). There are probably books in the back cupboards of your school building, and extra or older books in your school district's resource materials center. Have your children join school book clubs and purchase and exchange paperback books. Then encourage children to lend their books to one another and your classroom library.

One way to locate good books is to look at journals, including *Language Arts*, *The Horn Book*, and *The Reading Teacher*, which regularly publish topically organized lists of children's books. Some examples of anthologies of

Creative dramatics: While classmates watch, these children pretend to be sea turtles dragging themselves along the sand.

special purpose tradebooks published in *The Reading Teacher* are included in the list of further readings at the end of this chapter. These lists appear regularly, so be sure to consult new issues of journals yourself.

Once a year *The Reading Teacher* also publishes a list of the new books children reported they liked the best. Free copies of the most recent list can be obtained by sending a stamped self-addressed envelope to:

Children's Choices
International Reading Association
P.O. Box 8139
Newark, DE 19714

Another way to identify good books is from the list published yearly by the American Booksellers Association, Children's Book Council. The year's best-selling tradebooks are organized under the headings *Very First Books, Picture Books, Fairy Tales, Beginning-to-Read Books, Fiction for Readers 8–12, Informational Books for Readers under 8,* and *Informational Books for Readers 8 and Older.* Copies of the list can be obtained through your local librarian or bookseller. There are also lists of interesting children's books in language arts textbooks.

Finally, high quality stories, poems, and informational texts can be found in anthologies of children's literature. An anthology by Sutherland and Livingston (1984) provides examples of poetry, folktales and myths, realistic and historical fiction, biography, and informational articles. It also contains articles on how to present and explain good literature to children.

Organizing the classroom. Most classrooms, because they use basal reading programs, are organized into three ability groups. Individualized reading requires a different approach. For example, Burrows (1952) developed this weekly pattern:

At the beginning of each reading period the class discusses who needs new materials, who needs to go to the library, and who needs the teacher's help. It takes five to ten minutes to get everyone reading.

Monday: The teacher invites children reading books difficult for them to sit near her for help. This procedure encourages children of different reading abilities to sit and read together.

The teacher has individual conferences with two or three children while the others in the class read silently by themselves. Conferences are set up at the teacher's request or by the children's signing up on a list.

Tuesday: The Monday program is continued with more individual conferencing.

Wednesday: The period is devoted to group discussion about favorite books, dramatization, reading aloud, or sharing of illustrations. Individual conferences may be needed to help some children plan or prepare their presentations.

Thursday: Conferences are held with six or seven children while the rest read independently or work on written assignments.

Friday: Children bring their reading records up to date. The teacher checks their records and holds conferences with several individuals. Most of the children do some independent reading and some get books ready for weekend reading at home.

Monitoring reading activity. Regularly scheduled conferences are an integral part of individualized reading. The teacher begins with questions that lead the child to describe what was learned from the text. Questions could lead the child to describe characters, their problems, and attempted resolutions. Questions could also focus on the sequence of events central to the plot and their relationship to the characters' goals and problems. The children might be asked to summarize the main ideas or discuss important factual information. Any problems the child has had in interpreting the text or reading particular words ought to be discussed. Finally, oral reading fluency can be checked by asking the child to read a favorite section as well as a section that the teacher chooses.

Evaluating growth. The teacher uses checklists and brief notes to describe the quality and accuracy of children's comprehension and their oral reading fluency. These help the teacher keep track of children's reading problems and over time show where improvements have been made. The children keep chronological records of the books they have read. For each completed reading, a child should list the date the book was completed, book title, author, publisher, and number of pages. Children could also list each book they have read on a separate card and give a 2–3 sentence commentary such as what interested them the most or what they learned from their reading. Commentaries can be kept with the book to help other children decide whether they want to read it.

Providing skill instruction. One problem with individualized reading is that no provision is made for systematic skill instruction. Most children will need to be taught more effective ways to read and learn from their reading. To get an idea of the areas of instruction you might need to teach, refer to a basal scope and sequence chart for your grade (its use is discussed in the fifth key concept) or rely on suggestions from Chapters 5, 6, and 7. You probably will want to set aside one or two hours a week for group comprehension instruction lessons.

INSTRUCTIONAL ACTIVITIES

Picture books and storybooks available in libraries and bookstores generally are not written for the purpose of teaching children to read. While they certainly can be used for instruction, teachers may wish to be aware of both the strengths and weaknesses which may be found in tradebooks for beginning readers.

Using tradebooks with beginning readers

In comparison to basal reader selections, tradebooks usually have longer texts and harder words. Yet Gourley (1984) found that children do not necessarily make more errors as they try to read tradebooks. She also found that tradebooks often contain devices to support young children's reading. These devices include rhyming and the repetition of phrases.

Another possible problem with tradebooks is that their plots are often more complicated than those of basal selections. Thus, children may miss the main point of a story. One solution, recommended by Galda (1982), is to have children act out the stories. Since dramatic play does not come easily to some children, you may need to help them learn how to participate. Galda had children imagine themselves as the character and asked questions such as, "What are you going to do now, Wolf?" Sometimes she modeled participation by acting out one of the characters herself. She relied on six criteria for the dramatic play (from Smilansky, 1971). These were applied following the reading of favorite, familiar stories such as "The Three Bears" or "The Three Billy-Goats Gruff." You can use these guidelines when you want children to have a better understanding of a story.

1. Imitate or role-play the actions and words from the story;
2. Substitute make-believe objects for real objects;
3. Use make-believe actions and situations;
4. Have the play last about ten minutes;
5. Be sure the children interact within the framework of the storyline as they act out their parts;
6. Encourage verbal communication in expressing the ideas from the story.

Using tradebooks to foster report writing

Moss (1982), a language arts teacher, suggests ways to lead children from reading stories to writing their own texts. She demonstrates the approach with a reading instructional unit for fourth graders around the contrast between traditional folk tales and contemporary tales. To begin, the class reads and listens to a variety of traditional folk and fairy tales from different countries. Then a series of discussions get children to identify the common patterns and themes. Moss suggests that children work independently or with a partner and then as a group to discuss the distinctive features of folktales. This phase of the unit is likely to go on for several days before an adequate list is compiled.

In the next phase, children read and listen to several modern fairy tales. She recommends stories by J. Williams (for example, *The Practical Princess and Other Liberating Fairy Tales*, 1978) because they are amusing spoofs on folktales. Children answer questions such as the following:

How is this story similar to traditional fairy tales?
How is this story different from the traditional fairy tale?
What techniques did the author use to create humor or surprise?
How are the characters similar to or different from those in traditional fairy tales?
What message is today's author trying to convey, different from that of the traditional fairy tale?

When the children are adept at reading, interpreting, and comparing folktales, you can have them create their own modern fairy tales. First, they need to review the characteristics of the classic and modern tales. Then they should review ways that make modern tales different. Children are then ready to draw from their experiences with traditional as well as modern stories, in terms of structure and purpose to create their own imaginative versions of a contemporary folktale.

Using tradebooks for bibliotherapy

Jalongo (1983) recommends that teachers provide children with sensitive guidance to select the "right" book at the right time. Children who are under stress, who lack sufficient sensitivity toward their classmates, or who need to hear about how children like themselves resolved their problems, will probably profit from a bibliotherapeutic technique.

Jalongo points out that to to be successful you must plan carefully. First, consider what you expect to accomplish and how you might carry through after finding an appropriate book. The second step is to decide who will be involved. A book might be presented to one child, several children, or the entire class. The third step has to do with timing. Be sure the books you present are directed to classroom problems and are understandable to the children. The fourth step regards evaluation of your success in using this technique. For example, you might ask children whether the books influenced their thinking, feelings, and attitudes. Or you might have them rank order the value of a set of books.

Bibliotherapy is useful because children can profit from reading books about other people who shared their sentiments or experienced similar problems. From this type of book reading, children can be reassured that people make mistakes but can learn to change and be loved and accepted.

COMPUTERS IN THE CLASSROOM

According to De Sola Pool (1982), four revolutionary changes in the history of human communication have profoundly affected education. The first, occurring some 5000 years ago, was the invention of writing. It freed people from face-to-face communication, and information could be collected and saved without laborious acts of memory. The second change was the invention about 500 years ago of printing. Printed materials could be spread to scattered audiences and later generations. Paper was cheap and, with mass production of written materials, ordinary individuals could, if they learned to read, make use of the information. As a result, literacy became more widespread and education became dependent upon book learning. The third change occurred 150 years ago with the invention of devices that allowed the symbolization of messages by electronic communication. First it was the telegraph. Then came the telephone, phonograph, camera, motion picture, radio, and television. The audiovisual revolution, leading to enormous changes in work and recreation habits, continues to affect education.

The fourth revolutionary event was the advent of the computer. More than

7 million people are doing their work with the aid of a computer (Compaine, 1983). The computer is being used for information storage, analysis, writing, and retrieval of documents. It allows communication with others; selection, display, and summarizing of information; organization and analysis of information in ways impossible for a human; and storage of one's written ideas for efficient editing, revision, and retrieval.

Because it is a new educational device, the computer should be critically evaluated by teachers (Baker, 1984). Baker suggests:

Computer-based learning programs carry a mystique, an illusion of progression, a sense of being in the 21st century. . . . Once the mystique of the new technology is removed then many of the programs appear to be a step backwards in learning and teaching . . . the majority of maths, reading skills, modern language programs presently circulating follow a rote learning, drill and practice pattern which is exalted in computer jargon to the title of computer aided instruction. Limitations include atomistic concept of knowledge, artificiality of reinforcement, loss of a dynamic interaction with the teacher, and the desirability of reducing all curriculum areas to a sequential structure. (pp. 112–114)

The computer has yet to be utilized to any significant extent for individual tutoring, monitoring student progress, or even recording tests and assessments. Still, according to Starr (1983), who calls the computer the "electronic reader," programs are being developed for self-instruction as a substitute for

These boys discuss possible revisions to their writing which is done on the computer.

some textbooks, training manuals, and how-to guides. Some of the best programs are set up as a dialogue between the machine and the learner, with responses marked and commented on, with graphics to describe a concept or event, or with a product that the computer outlines or initiates and guides the learner to complete.

With networks being constructed among libraries, schools, and industries, there is rapid access to dictionaries, bibliographies, financial data, judicial decisions, medical information, and ideas for teaching and learning. This means that teachers and their students are able to store and retrieve large amounts of information at their convenience.

Not only is information being transmitted instantaneously, it is also easily updated or revised. Teachers who use computer-stored texts may revise or expand these reading materials to suit students' needs, improve the quality of the writing, or add important new information. Students can do the same, developing their writing as well as analytic skills by reading, modifying, and expanding upon written texts. Computer-stored reading texts can be revised, not merely read.

Preparing for the use of computers in the classroom

If you have the opportunity to purchase programs, begin by studying literature describing the programs available for the types of computers in your school. Look particularly for programs that provide feedback to children or that establish a dialogue. Do not limit your choices to "skill and drill" programs. Refer to the *Reading Teacher*, *Journal of Reading*, *Language Arts*, and other educational journals for new ideas about using computers for reading and writing. Whether you are purchasing new programs or limited to using those already in your school, learn to run them yourself before introducing them to the children.

When introducing computers to students who have had no experience with them, Obrist (1983) recommends following these guidelines:

1. Teach the children to load the programs. Not only will it free you from that supervisory task, it will help children understand an important aspect of computer use.

2. Have regular small group instructional sessions to teach the use of new programs.

3. Begin with simple programs such as letter and word recognition or word meaning programs, so that children understand how to operate the equipment before they try complicated games or learn to use the computer for writing texts or their own programs.

4. Help children realize that they usually cannot damage the equipment merely by striking keys. Experimentation with the various operations of a program need not be discouraged.

INSTRUCTIONAL ACTIVITIES

Two types of programs are described briefly: those for letter and word recognition (which tend to be skill and drill programs) and those for word processing and writing.

Letter and word recognition programs

Some dub this kind of program the electronic workbook because it usually offers little more than the kind of practice available in workbooks. Better programs of this type include computer-generated responses to children's answers and provide for the storage and analysis of students' responses.

Examples of skill and drill programs include the following. To help young children learn letters, CBS Software has a program to be used with large plastic pieces which fit over the keyboard. A program by Henson Associates, creators of the Muppets, uses large keys placed in alphabetical order and a "help" key picturing Miss Piggy. To help children learn words in context, Chrosniak and McConkie (1985) developed an approach where the child touches an unknown word with a light pen, leading the computer to "speak" that word.

Word processing and writing programs

Computer programs can be used to help children draft, edit, sort or rearrange text, and then print a hard copy. An example of such a program is the Bank Street Writer (see Chapter 8).

Marcus (1984) discusses ways the computer can be used to improve children's writing. Marcus points out that professional writers spend about 85 percent of their time in planning and prewriting, only 1 percent drafting, and 14 percent rewriting. It may be important, then, to increase the time children spend on ideas rather than the mechanics of writing. For example, children can be asked to do "freewriting" on the computer, getting ideas out rather than attending to grammar, spelling, or punctuation. Another method is to have children adjust the brightness control to eliminate the visual display. With the writing made invisible, children may attend for longer times to the ideas and development of their line of thought. Another approach is to work on two unrelated sentences, move the cursor to the end of the first sentence and develop a story which connects them. Another approach is to have pairs of students, each with a computer, see only the other's screen as they begin drafting text on a topic. If they lose their train of thought they type *???* to ask the other person for information about what they were typing. If they run out of ideas, they type *XXX* to ask for a new idea or an additional perspective on the current thought.

Marcus recommends the use of revision and editing programs, for example IBM's "Epistle," Westinghouse's "Writing Aids" system, Bell Lab's "Writer's

Workbench," or Marcus' "Sherlock" program. These help users realize how little time they need spend on editing and lead to new ways to learn as well as to new uses for computer-stored texts.

THE IMPORTANCE OF GOAL-SETTING

In the first part of this chapter we looked at how reading methods have changed. Then we described how reading can be taught and what kinds of materials can be used. It should be apparent now that because you have many methods and materials to choose from, you need to plan carefully before you begin teaching. Our purpose here is to give you a framework for thinking systematically about reading instruction. Ask yourself what you want to accomplish and then ask what kinds of materials will help your students do that kind of learning.

Setting up instructional goals

The first thing to think about in setting up the classroom reading program is, what is it the students should be learning? Set clear goals for instruction, based on what you think your students need to learn. This is not easy to do. Many teachers begin, not with learning goals, but by thinking about their students and activities (Clark & Yinger, 1979). However, without setting goals, you may waste a lot of time on lessons and activities which do not advance students' reading achievement or enjoyment of reading in any particular way.

Many teachers rely primarily or even exclusively on commercial basal reading programs. Even if you do also, you should make a conscious decision to set overall goals for reading instruction. You need not slavishly follow the goals of any commercial program. Keep in mind that commercial programs are designed to attract as large a share of the market as possible. Thus, it is extremely unlikely that any commercial program will be tailored perfectly to the needs of your particular group of students.

You may also find that your school or district has "mandated" certain goals. Sometimes highly specific goals in reading are set and students tested to see how well they are progressing toward those goals. Often, though, goals for reading instruction stated in these mandates are sufficiently broad or generally worded to give the teacher considerable latitude in setting goals.

While it isn't necessary for you to invent your own goals, it is necessary to use your judgment in selecting appropriate goals from among the different sources of goals available. Two of the sources commonly used by teachers are

(1) commercial programs, and (2) state or district curriculum guides. Throughout this book we have suggested a third source, your own knowledge derived from this book, other reading courses, and your understanding of students' needs. We explain next how ideas from these three sources can be coordinated to guide your organization of lessons and materials.

Scope and sequence charts: How goals for instruction are explained in commercial programs

Figure 11.7 shows two pages of a *scope and sequence chart* from the curriculum guide for a basal reading program (Scott, Foresman, 1983). Its overall structure is typical of how goals for student learning in reading are organized for presentation to the teacher. Scope and sequence charts undoubtedly have a great deal of practical value. They are readily understood and therefore can be extremely useful to the classroom teacher, in essence providing a "road map" for guiding students' learning.

First, let's address the notion of *scope*. This term covers the categories of skills the students should be learning. Scope thus refers to all the different aspects of reading ability the curriculum covers. The six broad areas in this program are readiness skills, word identification, comprehension, study and research, literary understanding and appreciation, and language skills. These

FIGURE 11.7

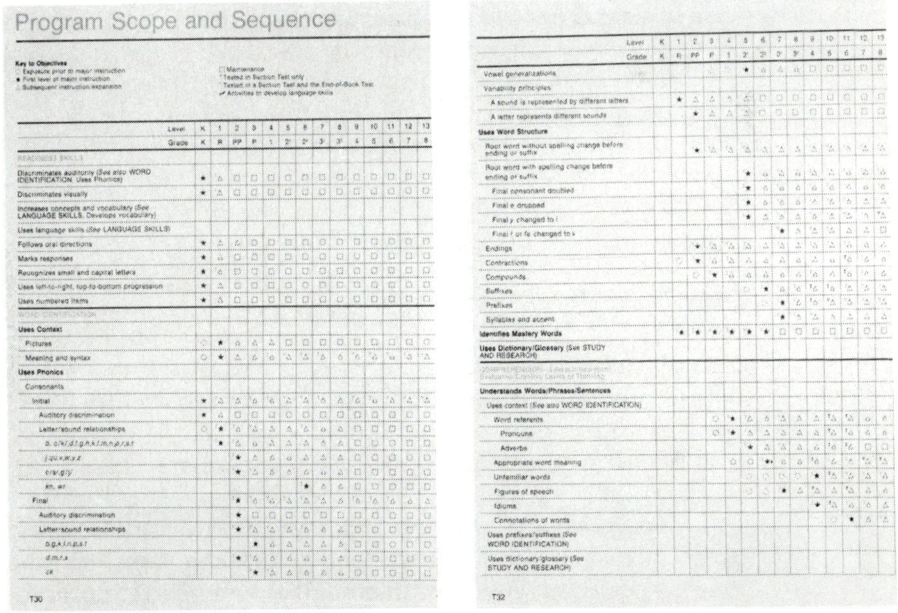

From *SF Reading: Hang On to Your Hats* by Ira E. Aaron et al., Scott, Foresman and Company, 1981, 1983, pp. T-30; T-32.

are the major *strands* in the curriculum. There are also *substrands* within each of these strands. For example, within the Scott, Foresman comprehension strand are five substrands (beginning with *Understands words/phrases/sentences*) and under those, a number of specific skills.

These specific skills are listed in the chart as *exposed, taught, expanded or retaught,* and *maintained.* It is assumed that you will focus on instruction of the skill for the "teaching" lesson and at later times make sure that all the children understand and practice the skill with the story and workbook materials. The intent is for students to receive skill instruction and practice with a variety of texts and practice pages.

Now, consider the notion of *sequence.* This term has to do with the steps students should go through in mastering the skills in any given strand or substrand. Generally, these steps or individual objectives are comprised of skills or knowledge which it seems logical to have students learn in an order moving from easier to more difficult.

When we consider word identification skills, we see a logical order. For example, the chart (Figure 11.7) shows that most initial consonants are taught before final consonants, and final consonants before vowels. It is probably wise to follow this ordering if you use the basal because there is an instructional hierarchy in the lesson and practice materials.

An ordering of skills is not so evident for comprehension. Many skills are exposed before being taught. Most of the skills represented by the substrand *Understands paragraphs/selections,* for example, are exposed in the preprimer or primer, although some are not taught until second or third grade. Moreover, some instructional distinctions are not clear. For example, is it really possible to teach children to recognize main ideas before teaching them about supporting details or drawing conclusions? Probably not, and certainly there is no research to support such an ordering. This may be why commercial publishers introduce most of the comprehension skills fairly early and then apply them to increasingly more difficult texts (Rosenshine, 1977). This means that you do not need to follow the exact order in the chart when providing comprehension instruction. Instead, you can use the text materials flexibly to foster whatever comprehension skills you find the children need.

Modifying a basal reading program

Teachers in most schools rely upon a basal reader series when organizing their classroom reading program. You are likely to do the same, particularly when you begin teaching, but you will want to understand how to take advantage of good ideas while avoiding common problems in the way basals are typically used.

Many schools or districts "adopt" a particular basal reader series. This means that all classroom teachers at all grade levels are expected to use that series. However, you want to avoid the thoughtless approach of simply taking as many students as possible through the basal materials from the first to last page. Consult the teacher's guide for the program and read the sections giving an overview of the goals for student learning. Study the scope and sequence chart to determine how the major strands as well as substrands are represented at different reading levels. Then study the sequence for particular skills and how they are taught.

Modifying the lessons in a basal program could be done by using the text materials but critically evaluating the skill lessons of the basal program against the suggestions we have made in the earlier chapters and your own analysis of what the students need. Often you may find a good match between the skills suggested for instruction and those you think ought to be taught at that time. At other times you will place more emphasis on some skills, rearrange lessons to match a particular story, or add lessons not present in the program. Examples of this approach appeared in the first key concept of this chapter.

Another way to modify a basal reading program is to use the goals listed in the scope and sequence chart but vary the text and worksheet practice materials from those recommended in the teacher's guide. This approach (suggested in the previous three key concepts) gives you a support system for teaching but allows you to modify what the children read and how they practice the skills. You could substitute language experience charts, tradebooks, or computer-presented text for the reader selections, and substitute independent reading or writing activities for some of the workbook pages. This way you can gradually adjust and enrich the menu provided by the basal program to better meet the needs of your students.

With either modified approach you can move systematically toward making sure that your major goals for classroom reading instruction are met. You are using the basal program as a foundation but not limiting students' learning to the opportunities that "by the book" use of the basal would provide. You avoid the main danger of using basals in the all-too-common practice of using them in an unthinking and inflexible way, without regard for students' needs. There are many more effective strategies for teaching reading than could be incorporated in any one commercial program. You will have knowledge of these strategies and know when they should be used.

KEY CONCEPT 6

Teachers should evaluate the appropriateness and quality of reading instructional materials and procedures.

EVALUATION OF READING MATERIALS AND METHODS

To become an effective teacher you need to learn how to choose the best materials from basal programs or other sources and how to adapt them to fit your children's interests and instructional needs. In so doing, you can accumulate a set of high quality materials and a repertoire of effective methods.

Evaluation of textbooks

In the 1940s and 1950s text writing began to be tailored to readability formulas. Lowered readability levels, it was argued, helped students more readily assimilate their lessons and increased motivation in the classroom. By the 1960s school officials had become aware of the concept of readability and began to ask publishers about the readability levels of textbooks. Readability is now a criterion for textbook adoption used by many states and school districts.

As readability formulas became more widely used as screening devices, publishers and authors came to produce materials to meet readability ranges for particular grade levels. Critics suggest, however, that texts produced in adherence to the formulas are not a solution to learning problems but a contributor to them. This is in part because the quality of writing, level of interest and challenge, and conceptual difficulty cannot be taken into account with readability formulas. Materials low in challenge may have low appeal. Materials consisting of short sentences and one-syllable words are not necessarily easy to understand, while some materials with long sentences are.

Texts for children should be evaluated on more dimensions than just readability. They could be analyzed in terms of their literary quality, their interest and appeal to children, or their content. We provide examples here of each of these other factors in evaluating text materials.

Evaluation of literary quality.   One approach to evaluation is to compare the adapted text with the original. Many folktales, for example, are rewritten to be quite different from the original. Egan (1983) argues that current versions of classic folktales "usually contain poor versions of the old stories, giving prominence to incidental points, entirely missing others of far greater importance, and often finishing up with a new story that has only a superficial resemblance to the 'original'" (p. 228).

He suggests it is worth the effort to locate texts that are closer to the original language. These will represent more clearly the depth and richness of possible or intended meanings. Instead of projecting only innocence and lightheartedness, original fairy tales bring out evil as well as good, or tragedy as well as happiness. As Egan explains:

> In mythology and folktales, we are taken into a strange world which glitters with gold and precious stones, but which is also menacing. . . . Goodness wins out in the end, but it always remains interwoven with its darker side, and we cannot remove one without destroying the other as well. (p. 230)

Evaluation of text interest.   Abrahamson and Shannon (1983) analyzed the 61 most popular picturebooks from 1982, based on the Children's Choices in *The Reading Teacher* for that year. Nearly three quarters of the children liked materials which had a conflict, opposing views, or several episodes. Less appealing were travel stories, nonfiction, and other types of writing. Their evaluation categories are listed here for you to use:

Stories in which characters must confront and resolve a problem;
Stories in which characters have opposing viewpoints, come from contrasting settings, or are involved in contrasting situations;
Stories featuring several episodes played out by the main characters;
Travel stories in which characters embark on a real or imaginary adventure away from home;
Nonfiction or biography or explanation of an observed phenomenon;
Poetry or verse;
Quest or aspiration stories;
Other: Jokes, riddles, story collections, ABC books, counting books.

Evaluation of text content. Schmidt, Caul, Byers, and Buchmann (1984) recommend that children's reading selections contain more *subject matter* content, *functional* content, or *ethos* content. They advise that texts without at least one of these contents ought to be considered deficient.

Subject matter is categorized as follows:

language skills	music
fine arts and crafts	science
physical education	philosophy
mathematics	social science

The functional dimension has the following categories:

reasoning/problem-solving	initiative/persistence
moral reasoning	absurdity/paradox
contemplation	humor in use of language
creativity	cunning/mother wit
feeling/catharsis	

The ethos dimension contains these categories:

humility	kindness/generosity
patience/forbearance	honesty
courage	hope

Expository text evaluation. Expository texts need a different sort of evaluation. Writing a perfect text for children to read and learn from is not easy. For example, after criticizing the quality of content area texts, Armbruster and Anderson (1984) attempted to write a good text. They discuss just how difficult this was to do. Be sure to evaluate the quality of the expository texts you plan to use. Because high quality texts are few and may be difficult to find, you may still end up using some inconsiderate (poorly written) texts. However, if you have carefully evaluated these texts, you will know where the problems lie and be able to compensate for weaknesses by providing students with extra instruction.

The following guidelines for evaluating the quality of a text are adapted from those formulated by Anderson and Armbruster (1984). The guidelines cover both the structure of the text and its topic:

1. The outline of the text should be apparent from reading the headings. The headings should be an accurate reflection of the most important ideas in each section.

2. The author's principal message should be coordinated with the structure of the text. For example, an author should not list facts when trying to express a cause and effect relationship.

3. The same text structure should be repeated, so the information on each subtopic can be presented in a parallel manner. For example, if the author is describing several countries, the same information (such as location, climate, history, and natural resources) should be presented for each, in about the same order.

4. The key relationships among ideas should be explicitly stated. Such relationships should not have to be inferred. For example, historical events are often most clearly understood by children as problems that the people of that time met and resolved. In this case, the problem and its solution should be directly stated and related.

5. Events should be presented in their natural order, especially in texts written for younger children. This guideline applies both to descriptions of historical events and of processes or procedures.

6. A close reading should show that each idea in the text contributes to the author's stated purpose. Watch out for loosely written passages which simply list unrelated information.

7. Adequate information should be presented about each major concept. The information should be complete enough for a child to be able to grasp the underlying ideas.

8. Technical terms should be introduced only if they are important to an understanding of the topic. Clear and complete definitions should be included.

9. Figurative language, such as similes and metaphors, should be used only if their referents are likely to be known to most children.

Evaluation of workbooks

Osborn (1984) notes that developers of workbooks do not always use research knowledge about instructional design, the giving of directions, or the sequencing and concentration of activities. Workbook practice pages seldom build upon students' reading of the basal selections, stories, or expository texts. Furthermore, the materials are seldom field-tested before being marketed.

As a result, workbook materials vary substantially in their quality. Whether you plan to use commercial practice materials or develop your own, you should be aware of how to evaluate their quality. We have grouped Osborn's suggestions for evaluation into three categories: tasks, format and language, and procedures.

Tasks. Workbook tasks should be related to other aspects of a reading lesson. A task should:

be related to lesson and text
provide review
have importance in the greater scope of a topic
provide practice for hard-to-teach children
have an obvious payoff for students

Format and language. A workbook practice page can be arranged in many different ways and use a variety of words, phrases, and illustrations to communicate what the task is and how it is to be done. A page should:

repeat language and concepts used in the lesson
use a small number of different response modes and task types
have a layout that helps, not interferes, with the task
highlight the text, not illustrations

Procedures. Workbook exercises are meant to provide guided and independent practice of skills taught in the lesson. They must be critically evaluated for quality of presentation, accuracy, and appropriateness. A procedure should:

provide clear, unambiguous, easy-to-follow instructions
use accurate information in both questions and answers
use a response mode that yields complete and meaningful information
use a response mode for reading and writing practice
make the purpose of the task clear
be part of a pattern of responses and a sequence of concepts

Evaluation of teacher's guide materials

Teacher's guides may not give adequate advice about comprehension instruction, according to an analysis of materials by Durkin (1981). The guides often offer precise help with easy comprehension instructional issues but can be obscure or silent on difficult issues or when specific help is needed. Difficult-to-teach topics may often be mentioned rather than explained, and definitions of terms are substituted for instruction about the topic. Often, instruction in a concept is replaced by practice in doing a task. Thus, inadequate attention is generally paid to the instruction itself. To make matters worse, guided practice may not be directly related to the concept being taught or the text being read.

If a teacher is relying on the guide, and the guide does not give adequate advice about how to organize lessons or teach comprehension, then the teacher must improvise. Some teachers will be successful, but others will not be. In the latter situation, story and expository text reading may be sacrificed or poorly taught while the more completely described workbook and skill instruction activities become overemphasized (Mason, 1983). To keep that from happening, you will need to develop a critical eye to distinguish good from not-so-good activities and the confidence to insert, replace, and modify lessons and practice materials.

Evaluate the teacher's guide to see if it has the weaknesses identified by Durkin and may therefore lead you to the questionable practices observed by Mason. If you find serious weaknesses in the guide, use it selectively. That is, implement exactly only the activities you judge to be sound, and adapt or skip over others.

Here are some questions to ask when deciding whether it will be necessary to adapt guide activities or skip them and develop lessons of your own:

1. Does the activity place story or expository text materials at the center of instruction?

2. Is comprehension instruction adequately designed, according to the concepts discussed in Chapters 5, 6, and 7 of this textbook?

3. Is there a good match between the activity and the text to be used?

4. Do the students have the opportunity to practice the skills taught?

5. Will giving directions for the workbook or other practice exercise take more time than students will spend completing it?

6. Will use of the workbook or other practice exercises take up more time than the actual reading and writing of connected text?

SUMMARY

This chapter focused on the instructional approaches and materials used in the teaching of reading. In the perspective section we explained how reading instruction has changed over time in response to social needs. This background was provided to help you see how different instructional approaches, meant to achieve different goals, came about.

The first three key concepts covered the major reading approaches and materials. Basal reading programs were described in considerable detail, and suggestions were given for using them in a flexible manner. The language experience and individualized reading approaches were then described. Both of these approaches have much to offer, especially if attention is paid to the careful organization of sequences of instruction. Possible use of these approaches in an eclectic manner, perhaps in conjunction with a basal reading program, was discussed.

In the fourth key concept we considered two ways of using computers to strengthen classroom reading instruction. In the fifth key concept we emphasized the need for goal-directed instruction. Finally, we covered various ways of evaluating reading materials.

From the classification and analysis of materials and methods in this chapter, we hope you have gained an understanding of the strengths and weaknesses of various reading methods and materials. Our aim was to help you learn to select appropriate methods and materials according to the needs of your students. In short, we believe the preferred approach will usually be an eclectic one, over a period of time incorporating quite a variety of methods and materials.

BIBLIOGRAPHY

REFERENCES

Abrahamson, R., & Shannon, P. (1983). A plot structure analysis of favorite picture books. *Reading Teacher, 37,* 44-50.

Allen, E., & Laminack, L. (1982). Language experience reading—it's a natural. *Reading Teacher, 35,* 708-714.

Anderson, T., & Armbruster, B. (1984). Content area textbooks. In R. Anderson, J. Osborn, & R. Tierney (Eds.), *Learning to read in American schools.* Hillsdale, NJ: Erlbaum.

Arbuthnot, M. (1957). *Children and books.* 2nd ed. Glenview, IL: Scott, Foresman.

Armbruster, B., & Anderson, T. (1984). Producing "considerate" expository text: or Easy reading is damned hard writing (Reading Education Report No. 46). Urbana, IL: University of Illinois, Center for the Study of Reading.

Baker, C. (1984). A critical examination of the effect of the microcomputer on the curriculum. In C. Terry (Ed.), *Using microcomputers in schools.* New York: Nichols.

Burrows, A. (1952). *Teaching children in the middle grades.* Boston: Heath.

Chall, J. (1967/1970). *Learning to read: The Great Debate.* New York: McGraw-Hill.

Children's choices for 1984 (1984). *Reading Teacher, 38,* 58-75.

Chrosniak, P., & McConkie, G. (1985). *Computer-aided reading with reading-discouraged students.* Paper presented at the annual meeting of the American Educational Research Association, Chicago.

Clark, C., & Yinger, R. (1979). Teachers' thinking. In P. Peterson, & H. Walberg (Eds.), *Research on teaching.* Berkeley, CA: McCutchan.

Compaine, B. (1983). The new literacy. *Daedalus, 112,* 129-142.

De Sola Pool, I. (1982). The culture of electronic print. *Daedalus, 111,* 17-32.

Durkin, D. (1981). Reading comprehension instruction in five basal reader series. *Reading Research Quarterly, 16,* 515-544.

Egan, O. (1983). In defense of traditional language: Folktales and reading texts. *Reading Teacher, 37,* 228-233.

Eliot, C. (1898). *Educational reform.* New York: Century.

Fries, C. (1963). *Linguistics and reading.* New York: Holt, Rinehart & Winston.

Galda, L. (1982). Playing about a story: Its impact on comprehension. *Reading Teacher, 36,* 52-55.

Gourley, J. (1984). Discourse structure: Expectations of beginning readers and readability of text. *Journal of Reading Behavior, 16,* 169-188.

Jalongo, M. (1983). Bibliotherapy: Literature to promote socioemotional growth. *Reading Teacher, 36,* 796-803.

Mallon, B., & Berglund, R. (1984). The language experience approach to reading: Recurring questions and their answers. *Reading Teacher, 37,* 867-871.

Marcus, S. (1984). Computers and the teaching of writing: Prose and poetry. In C. Terry (Ed.), *Using microcomputers in schools.* New York: Nichols.

Mason, J. (1983). An examination of reading in third and fourth grades. *Reading Teacher, 36,* 906-913.

Mason, J., & Osborn, J. (1982). *When do children begin "Reading to learn"?: A survey of classroom reading instruction practices in grades two through five.* (Technical Report No. 261.) Urbana, IL: University of Illinois, Center for the Study of Reading.

McClure, A. (1982). Integrating children's fiction and informational literature in a primary reading curriculum. *Reading Teacher, 35,* 784-789.

Moss, J. (1982). Reading and discussing fairy tales—old and new. *Reading Teacher, 35,* 656-659.

Obrist, A. (1983). *The microcomputer and the primary school.* London: Hodder & Stoughton.

Osborn, J. (1984). The purposes, uses, and contents of workbooks and some guidelines for publishers. In R. C. Anderson, J. Osborn, & R. Tierney (Eds.), *Learning to read in American schools: Basal readers and content texts.* Hillsdale, NJ: Erlbaum.

Rosenshine, B. (1977). Skill hierarchies in reading comprehension. In J. Mason, J. Osborn, and B. Rosenshine, *A consideration of skill hierarchy approaches to the teaching of reading* (Technical Report No. 42). Urbana, IL: University of Illinois, Center for the Study of Reading.

Schmidt, W., Caul, J., Byers, J., & Buchmann, M. (1984). Content of basal text selections: Implications for comprehension instruction. In G. Duffy, L. Roehler, & J. Mason (Eds.), *Comprehension instruction: Perspectives and suggestions.* New York: Longman.

Shannon, P. (1983). The use of commercial reading materials in American elementary schools. *Reading Research Quarterly, 19,* 68-85.

Smilansky, S. (1971). Can adults facilitate play in children? Theoretical and practical considerations. In *Play.* Washington, DC: National Association for the Education of Young Children.

Smith, N. (1926). *One hundred ways of teaching silent reading for all grades.* New York: World Book Company.

Smith, N. (1965). *American reading instruction.* Newark, DE: International Reading Association.

Starr, P. (1983). The electronic reader. *Daedalus, 112,* 143-156.

Stott, J. (1982). A structuralist approach to teaching novels in elementary grades. *Reading Teacher, 36,* 136-143.

Sutherland, Z., & Livingston, M. (1984). *The Scott, Foresman anthology of children's literature.* Glenview, IL: Scott, Foresman.

West, R. (1964). *Individualized reading instruction.* Port Washington, NY: Kennikat Press.

Yamada, Y. (1983). How much can children learn from a single book? *Reading Teacher, 36,* 880-883.

CHILDREN'S BOOKS CITED

Bloomfield, L., & Barnhart, C. (1961). *Let's read: A linguistic approach.* Detroit: Wayne State Press.

Bryce, C., & Spaulding, F. (1907, 1916). *The Aldine Readers: A primer.* New York: Newson.

Clymer, T., & Venezky, R. (1982). *One Potato Two.* Lexington, MA: Ginn & Company.

Foley, M. (1983). Somebody stole second. In I. E. Aaron & R. Koke (Eds.), *Hidden wonders.* Glenview, IL: Scott, Foresman.

McCracken, G., & Walcutt, C. (1975). *Book A: Basic reading.* Philadelphia: Lippincott.

McGuffey's Eclectic primer. Rev. ed. (1881). New York: American Book Company.

Program scope and sequence chart. In L. G. Botko, J. K. Heryla, V. K. Klassen, & J. Manning (Eds.), *Hang on to your hats.* Teacher's edition. Glenview, IL: Scott, Foresman.

Reit, S. (1983). Archie has a visitor. In R. G. Smith & R. J. Tierney (Eds.), *Sky climbers.* Glenview, IL: Scott, Foresman.

Spirn, M. (1983). Three nights of magic. In R. E. Jennings & D. E. Prince (Eds.), *Kick up your heels.* Glenview, IL: Scott, Foresman.

Williams, J. (1978). *The practical princess and other liberating fairy tales.* New York: Parents Magazine Press.

FURTHER READINGS

Abrahamson, R. J. (1981). An update on wordless picture books with an annotated bibliography. *Reading Teacher, 34,* 417-421.

Balajthy, E. (1984). Reinforcement and drill by microcomputer. *Reading Teacher, 37,* 490-494.

Baumann, J. F. (1984). How to expand a basal reader program. *Reading Teacher, 37,* 604-607.

Bork, A. (1984). The fourth revolution—computers and learning. In C. Terry (Ed.), *Using microcomputers in school.* New York: Nichols.

Burris, N., & Lentz, K. (1983). Caption books in the classroom. *Reading Teacher, 36,* 872-875.

Chall, J. & Conrad, S. Resources and their use for reading instruction. Chapter VIII. In A. C. Purves & O. Niles (Eds.), *Becoming readers in a complex society.* Part I, 83rd Yearbook of the National Society for the Study of Education. Chicago, IL: University of Chicago Press.

Cox, J., & Wallis, B. (1982). Books for the Cajun child—Lagniappe or a little something extra for multicultural teaching. *Reading Teacher, 36,* 263-266.

Dole, J., & Johnson, V. (1981). Beyond the textbook: Science literature for young people. *Journal of Reading, 24,* 579-582.

Gamby, G. (1983). Talking books and taped books: Materials for instruction. *Reading Teacher, 36,* 366-369.

Greenlinger-Harless, C. S. (1984). Updated cross-referenced index to U.S. reading materials, grades K-8. *Reading Teacher, 37,* 871.

Hennings, D. (1982). Reading picture storybooks in the social studies. *Reading Teacher, 36,* 284-289.

Jalongo, M., & Bromley, K. (1984). Developing linguistic competence through song picture books. *Reading Teacher, 37,* 840-845.

Judd, D. (1984). *Mastering the micro: Using the microcomputer in the elementary classroom.* Glenview, IL: Scott, Foresman.

Kerr, S. T. (1981). How teachers design their materials: Implications for instructional design. *Instructional Science, 10,* 363-378.

Koenke, K. (1981). The careful use of comic books. *Reading Teacher, 34,* 529-595.

Mason, G., & Blanchard, J. (1979). *Computer applications in reading.* Newark, DE: International Reading Association.

Miccinati, J., Sanford, J., & Hepner, G. (1983). Teaching reading through the arts: An annotated bibliography. *Reading Teacher, 36,* 412-417.

Pozsic, F. (1982). The Ukraine—children's stories in English. *Reading Teacher, 35,* 716-722.

Reimer, B. L. (1983). Recipes for language experience stories. *Reading Teacher, 36,* 396-401.

Sharp, P. (1984). Teaching with picture books throughout the curriculum. *Reading Teacher, 38,* 132-137.

Smardo, F. (1982). Using children's literature to clarify science concepts in early childhood programs. *Reading Teacher, 36,* 267-273.

Stauffer, R. (1970). *The language-experience approach to the teaching of reading.* New York: Harper & Row.

Storey, D. C. (1982). Reading in the content areas: Fictionalized biographies and diaries for social studies. *Reading Teacher, 35,* 796-798.

Swaby, B. (1982). Varying the ways you teach reading with basal stories. *Reading Teacher, 35,* 676-681.

Truett, C. (1984). *Choosing educational software: a buyer's guide.* Littleton, CO: Libraries Unlimited.

Wagoner, S. (1982). Mexican-Americans in children's literature since 1970. *Reading Teacher, 36,* 274-279.

Wood, K. (1983). A variation on an old theme: 4-way oral reading. *Reading Teacher, 37,* 38-43.

CHAPTER 12

Organizing and Managing

the Classroom Reading Program

Because I had no sense of myself as a teacher, I took my cues from the people above and below me. I mimicked older teachers, when I wasn't arrogantly telling them how much I knew. I followed all the rules of the administrators and worried about my supervisor. If a student said, "But this is not the way we did it last year," I would change the procedure. Much of what I did was determined by fear that I would look like a fool in front of my students.

At the same time that I was filling everyone else's expectations, I was exhilarated by teaching. I loved interacting with so many students; I loved to think and write and talk about teaching; and I loved being in control. . . . I thought that I could control everyone's learning. If I prepared the perfect lesson, or devised the perfect exercise, every student would learn. I controlled discussions, tests, assignments, everything.

I enjoyed being the center of attention, and I worked hard at giving a good performance. Even when students worked in groups, I prided myself on my ability to "keep an eye on everyone" and squelch any "irrelevant" talk. . . .

Five years later, I began to feel competent, not just flashy, in a classroom. Because I was building a stronger sense of myself as a teacher (and as an adult outside of school), I could shed the external definitions of myself. I did not need student or administrative approval for what I did, and I could act and judge independently. As my competence grew, the loneliness and isolation of the classroom began to feel like an opportunity for freedom. . . .

As I returned to teaching [after having a baby], I carried with me a new understanding of what it meant to nurture others. Although I had less time to be obsessed about teaching, the time I spent thinking about classrooms was focused differently from before. I no longer thought so much about myself—what I would say, how I would appear, how I would judge and correct. Instead I thought about the students and what I could do to allow them to take more responsibility for their own learning. I wanted to accompany them through learning. (Lightfoot, 1983, pp. 253-254)

OVERVIEW

The purpose of this chapter is to provide information about how effective teachers organize and manage their classrooms for reading instruction. To prepare you for considering these ideas, the perspective section introduces a set of overriding principles of teaching and instructional decision-making. The key concepts that follow describe both classroom organization and management issues. Some relate specifically to the teaching of reading and others are an important component also for teaching other subjects.

The first key concept describes how the location of furniture and materials in your classroom can help provide an appropriate learning environment. The second key concept sets out the more general classroom management issues and suggests how you might prepare for them. The third key concept provides advice about scheduling and organizing reading lessons in the school day. The fourth explains how the success of your reading program is complexly related to decisions you make about grouping children for instruction and to the climate for learning. Each key concept describes what you need to consider and organize in order to create an effective instructional atmosphere.

The key concepts in this chapter are:

Key Concept #1: Teachers should pay attention to arranging the physical environment to support reading and learning to read.

Key Concept #2: Teachers should have an understanding of classroom management principles, an essential background for effective reading instruction.

Key Concept #3: Reading should be scheduled at the most opportune time and in the most effective way possible.

Key Concept #4: Teachers need to understand the complex instructional and motivational issues involved in grouping children for instruction.

PERSPECTIVE

ESTABLISHING AN EFFECTIVE SETTING FOR READING INSTRUCTION

We know from the research on teacher effectiveness that there are many "ifs," "ands," and "buts" when it comes to organizing a classroom for effective teaching. There are no simple formulas or lists of procedures which you can follow. Rather, your effectiveness will depend on understanding some of the complexities of instruction. Three overriding principles, presented next, will help you establish an effective classroom environment. One is to pay attention to how class time is spent, a second is to learn to make instructional decisions while you are teaching, and a third is to understand how to construct simplified models of teaching.

Instructional time and its efficient use

An effective reading program obviously depends on there being adequate time for instruction. Students are not likely to progress well in learning to read unless there is enough time allocated to teaching and practicing reading. A beginning step is for you to arrange your schedule to allow enough time for reading on a daily and weekly basis.

The average amounts of time that elementary school teachers reported allocating to various subject areas were presented by Goodlad (1983). The times shown below are for hours per week. We consider this average time for reading, which in the early grades works out to about one hour and 45 minutes per day, to be the minimum amount of time you should set aside for reading and language arts. You might keep these average times in mind when you set up your schedule.

Early elementary

Reading-language arts	8.46
Mathematics	4.65
Social studies	2.09
Science	1.65
Art, music, drama, dance	2.97
Physical education, recess	1.49

Upper elementary

Reading-language arts	7.41
Mathematics	5.12
Social studies	3.83
Science	2.93
Art, music, drama, dance	2.88
Physical education, recess	2.26

There is an average of 180 days in the school year, with approximately eight hours per week of reading and language arts instruction or about 288 hours per year. However, instructional time in school will be affected by child and teacher absences, snow days, and teacher strikes. Time for reading should also be considered beyond the classroom. For example, actual reading time is affected by outside-of-school reading opportunities. Some parents foster library book reading, enforce homework-reading, and send their children to academic after-school and summer camp lessons.

Of course, just setting aside *time* for reading is not sufficient. Rosenshine

(1979) pointed out that teachers need to distinguish between *allocated time* and *academic engaged time*. While allocated time is the amount of time scheduled, academic engaged time is the amount of time students spend working on academically relevant tasks. During the time allocated, students must be doing constructive work, work designed to encourage learning to read and reading to learn.

Finally, allocated and academic engaged time are usually affected by another factor, the reading group in which children are placed. Instruction given to low ability groups is typically of lower quality than that for high ability groups. There is less engaged time, a larger proportion of time is taken by management, the pace of instruction is slower, and there is an overemphasis on decoding and oral reading (Hiebert, 1983). This means that time and quality of instruction are often reduced for children assigned to low ability groups.

You can now see that thinking about time for instruction requires us to consider at least these three dimensions: the number of hours available for instruction, children's attentiveness to the lesson, and the quality of the lesson for the group. Each dimension contributes to the amount that children learn. It is up to you to keep track of each so that you can provide maximum opportunities for reading, keep children engaged with worthwhile reading tasks, and develop higher quality instruction for children in low ability groups.

Making good decisions while teaching

Effective reading instruction is an extremely complex process, and a teacher has to consider many factors at once. One solution is to sharpen your *decision-making* skills as you teach. This involves learning to make better on-the-spot instructional decisions and to adjust your plans in view of the immediate situation.

Taking appropriate action in an instructional situation requires you to understand *interactive decision-making*, or how to make decisions while giving instruction (Good, 1983; Clark & Yinger, 1979). In interactive decision-making, you begin by following a plan but, as the lesson moves forward, you see that the planned activities or topics may not be working. You adjust to the changes or new demands by modifying your lesson.

For example, we observed a reading lesson given to second graders who seemed unable to see cause-and-effect relationships in the basal story. Judging from the children's responses, the teacher identified the source of their confusion to be story events that had been presented in a flashback, a literary device unfamiliar to them. Although she hadn't planned to do so, the teacher decided to explain about flashbacks. She took the children through a review of story events, an exercise ending when they were able to tell her how to list the events on the chalkboard in sequential order. Only then did she resume the discussion of cause-and-effect relationships. Now the children were easily able to answer her questions.

As we see in this example, if you want your lesson to be a successful one, beneficial to the students' learning, you can't always stay with your original plan. Instead, you must make decisions about how to reorganize the lesson. In this example, if the teacher hadn't digressed from the discussion originally planned, her students probably would have learned very little. But because the teacher made a sound decision to modify the lesson, the students learned something about how to analyze stories with flashbacks, a comprehension ability likely to be useful in the future.

Situations similar to this will frequently arise; you will find you are not able to follow your original plan. Do not feel that you have failed. While it is true that more experienced teachers know better what to expect from their students and are less likely to have to depart radically from their plans, they also know that almost all lessons have moments when the unexpected happens. Among such unexpected occurrences may be the discovery that children know more about a certain topic than the teacher expected, or find uninteresting an activity that had been expected to capture their interest.

At times, these unexpected occurrences provide *teachable moments* for engaging children in learning and helping them recognize new ideas or make new connections among ideas. Teachable moments are those occasions when a child asks a question or makes a comment indicating a special readiness to learn something. More often than not, the teachable moment comes as a surprise to the teacher. For example, a teacher told us about giving a reading lesson during which a second grade student had a remarkable insight. One of the opening episodes in the basal story was about sighted children who wouldn't allow a blind boy to join in their game. The student commented that those children were actually "blind" in their own way. The teacher was then able to build upon this idea to develop the group's understanding of how the blind must sometimes cope with the mental blindness or ignorance of others, in addition to their physical handicap.

As you can see, given the many complexities in teaching effective reading lessons, it is not necessarily a good idea to map out in advance every detail of a lesson, and then stick rigidly to that plan. This kind of inflexibility could prevent you from taking advantage of the prime opportunities for learning provided by unexpected occurrences. While good planning is essential, it is equally important to learn how to make informed decisions in the course of teaching lessons. This line of reasoning led Brophy (1984) to suggest:

". . . lessons that go entirely according to plan may be less successful, at least in some respects, than lessons that go generally according to plan but that require some interactive decision making involving shifts to alternative strategies to respond to unforeseen developments. (p. 73)

As a decision-maker you will learn to take advantage of prime but unanticipated opportunities for learning as they arise, and to respond to cues from the children that they are understanding, or not understanding, the points you are trying to get across. You will try to provide instruction in a responsive manner, always keeping in touch with the students' thinking. A study by Peterson and Clark (1978) suggests that such responsive instruction may help students learn to think more reflectively.

Of course, making the proper "in-flight" adjustments to lessons is easier said than done. Brophy (1984) suggests that teachers go through three stages in developing their skills as decision-makers. Beginning teachers' earliest concerns are with "survival." They first address issues of classroom management and scheduling. Once these areas are under control, they turn to issues of instruction. In this second stage teachers are concerned with "procedure" or the mechanics of instruction. They generally rely on detailed written plans or the teacher's guide, referring to these materials frequently during the course of the lesson. This may cause them to behave somewhat too rigidly and not responsively enough. However, Brophy believes it wise for most beginning teachers to follow such scripts, because this practice allows them to deal with what they might otherwise find to be an overwhelmingly complex task.

In Brophy's view, teachers do not become good decision-makers, in the sense described above, until they reach the third stage. At this point they have gained enough experience and knowledge to feel comfortable and confident during lessons. Only then is it possible to adjust to unexpected occurrences, such as unplanned teachable moments.

We recommend that you set as a long-term, but not immediate, goal development of the ability to make sound in-flight decisions. As Brophy suggests, most beginning teachers will find themselves with immediate concerns for survival and procedure, and if so, these problems should be tackled first. Some of these techniques are described next and in the first two key concepts of this chapter. The use of scripts and routines, as well as simplified models, are possible and acceptable solutions. As you become a more effective manager, you will be more flexible and responsive to students' needs in learning to read, as shown in moment-to-moment interactions with them during lessons.

Using simplified models of teaching

Although teaching is very complex and has far too many aspects for a beginning teacher to consider all at once, there are ways to simplify it. In fact, effective teachers do not try to attend to all aspects of instruction at one time. Instead, they construct simplified models of the classroom (Shulman, 1983). To simplify your own teaching, do not try at first to manage the children, create perfect lessons, set up smooth and meaningful interactions with students and understand what and how children are learning. No one can achieve instant and complete success on all aspects of teaching. According to Hawkins (1973): "It may be possible to learn in two or three years the kind of practice which then leads to another twenty years of learning" (p. 7).

In keeping with Brophy's notion of stages of teaching, at first simplify your instruction so that you can pay particular attention to classroom management. After all, children will not learn if they are inattentive to the lesson. Rely at first on clearly structured or even scripted lessons until the children are listening to you and to each other, working in groups and by themselves, and helping you maintain an orderly, smooth-running working environment. Then you can begin to experiment with your own instructional ideas.

Here are some examples of ways you can simplify the teaching situation in order to reduce its complexity:

1. For the first one or two weeks of the school year, imagine that all the children are "average-ability" students in reading. Use whole class instruction and have all the children read from the same textbook (perhaps a textbook meant for the grade you are teaching but no longer being used in your school), participate in the same skill lessons, and do the same writing activities and practice exercises. Listen to children as they read aloud together, in partners, or to you individually. Watch as they complete workbook exercises and look at their creative writing assignments. Notice which children answer your questions, talk to them about what they like to read, and ask what they find difficult about learning to read. Using this simplified, whole class model of instruction at the beginning of the year allows you the time to understand better how your students read, write, and learn. You will be able to make informal diagnoses of children's reading and gain information about how to group them for instruction.

2. Classroom discipline is the major problem faced by first year teachers, according to Veeman (1984). Since it takes time to establish appropriate lessons and effective management techniques, begin teaching reading by laying out a clear routine for reading lessons and setting up classroom rules for lessons, independent reading, and seatwork activity. Resolve discipline problems as quickly and quietly as possible. Eventually, you will learn to spot problem situations before they arise and will know how to keep children focused on their lessons or independent work.

3. As you teach a reading skill or concept, don't try to figure out whether all the children understand it. Instead pick out those children who are slightly below average as readers. Watch them as you teach and ask them questions to see if they understand. If they do, you are probably moving through the lesson at about the right pace, not so slow that most become bored and not so fast that too many become "lost" and stop trying to understand.

4. An idea for simplifying discipline problems, and which can lead to other ways to view grouped instruction, was suggested by an Indiana teacher of the year, Susan Talbot. When a group is about to begin a new story she announces the story name to the class and allows anyone else to join the group to read and discuss the story. Children from higher groups often join because they want to read a story again, and children from lower groups often take part in reading a more difficult story. The approach allows children more story reading opportunities and gives the teacher a way of keeping hard-to-manage children working.

Using reasonable means such as these to reduce the number of different things you have to think about while teaching reading will help you to be more effective. When you are more experienced, you will know how to expand on these ideas and fit instruction more closely to your particular situation and the children you teach.

In summary, then, fulfilling the intent of these instructional principles means going beyond setting aside one hour a day to teach reading following preplanned lessons. It means making more efficient use of your students' lesson time, working toward proficiency in interactive decision-making, and using simplified teaching procedures.

KEY CONCEPT 1

Teachers should pay attention to arranging the physical environment to support reading and learning to read.

ORGANIZATION OF THE CLASSROOM

Before you meet your students on the first day of class, many important decisions should already be made. We describe those decisions that have to do with organizing classroom spaces and setting up learning centers.

A well-organized classroom is usually one with a regular place for everything. Children know where to go for supplies and have a designated place for their own belongings. A well-organized classroom then can become a literacy-rich environment, filled with useful and interesting printed information. Children's work and art samples can decorate the walls. There can be displays including pictures and other materials related to topics being studied, notices about work activities and listings of child helpers, the classroom schedule, and new books.

Placement of desks, chairs, tables, learning centers, and materials should be determined before children arrive. Consider each in terms of the way you expect to work and how you want children grouped to work with you and to work independently.

Place your desk so that it serves a useful purpose. That is, decide how you will use it, whether as a place from which to watch children work, a place where children come for help, a center for correcting papers, or a storage place. If it is principally a place where individuals are helped, the desk ought to be at the back or side of the room. Then your interactions with children will be more private and less distracting to other children. If it is a place from which you monitor the class, place the desk at the front of the room. If you do not plan to use it except to store papers, put it in an out-of-the-way corner.

Your classroom is likely either to have separate desks for each child or tables where four to six children sit. If there are desks, you might place children in rows or in tablelike groups. The advantages to rows are twofold: Everyone can be facing you and see the blackboard as you conduct whole-class lessons. Children can see and hear you more easily and are less likely to talk to one another (especially if you place talkative and easily distracted children near the front of the room). One advantage to grouped desks is that you can foster cooperative learning by having children work together. The instruction we have recommended in this book slightly favors the grouped desk arrangement, although either could be used. You should make your decision based on whether you are going to emphasize teacher-directed or peer-supported activities.

Materials ought to be placed on shelves and labeled so that children can use them without help. Places need to be set up for children to hand in their completed work and to pick it up after it is corrected. Supplementary writing materials, learning games, and books need convenient and well-labeled places so that children can find and replace them without help. Tables for learning centers are often placed at the back or side of the classroom, away from your small group teaching area.

Organization of learning centers

We strongly recommend that you put learning centers in your classroom. Learning centers are areas of the classroom set aside for specific kinds of activities. For example, a teacher might create a reference center consisting of a table and chairs, and a shelf with several dictionaries, an almanac, atlas, and a set of encyclopedias. Groups of children might work in this area when working on reports, and individuals might go there for a few minutes at a time to look up specific pieces of information.

Learning centers allow you to establish a wide range of independent work activities and provide opportunities for children to follow their own interests and work with classmates. Children can choose useful and interesting inde-

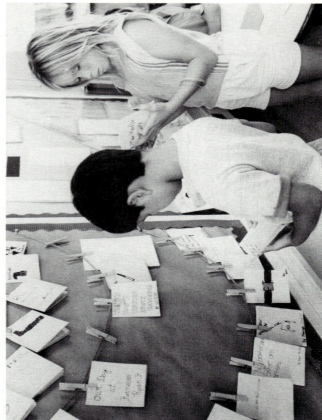

A bookline, with children's published books attached with clothespins, is prominently displayed in this classroom.

pendent activities when they finish their work or when waiting for school to begin. Moreover, you can set up alternative and longer term activities to replace workbook exercises. You might set up a library corner, a writing table, a listening area, and math, science, computer, or natural science tables.

Library center. Begin by establishing a library center. It has demonstrated benefits to children and much is known about how it can be set up. You probably want it to be a place where four or five children sit and read to themselves or read quietly to one another. You can set up guidelines for activities such as recreational reading, locating or studying important information, and choosing books to take home or to read in school. You might assign small groups of children each day to read there in place of doing workbook activities, making sure that everyone in the class has this opportunity at least once a week. Finally, you might allow children to read to each other or to tell stories to others through the use of flannel boards, roll movies, or puppets.

After determining your purposes for the center and how it will be used, decide where it should be placed, what materials it should include, how to introduce it, and what rules it needs. You will want children to appreciate the opportunity to work there, know the standards of conduct, and be able to work on their own. You will also want it to be a place that children can keep in order without your help. Independent and responsible behavior must be fostered at all learning centers, including the library center. This is important if children are to benefit from the center, and if you want to be free to work with other groups or individuals without frequent interruptions.

To decide where and how to set up a library center, we rely on work by Arbuthnot & Sutherland (1977), Huck (1976), and Morrow (1982). A relatively quiet space in the room (which means away from the door, coat rack, and your small group discussion center) is recommended. It should be physically accessible and well lighted. If possible, it should be carpeted and contain chairs or pillows for seating, have shelves for storing books, an open-faced shelf for displaying new or recently discussed books, a bulletin board for promoting certain books, a list of rules for its use and for borrowing books, and (for younger children) a flannel board. Two or three books per child ought to be in the library and new books should be introduced at regular intervals by bringing in books from the school library. Books should be arranged either by topic or alphabetically, by the author's last name. We favor an alphabetical listing because children can more easily locate books by a favorite author and keep the books in order.

The children should be carefully introduced to the library center. First, explain when children may go to the center and what they may do while they are there. They need to know how to sign up to borrow books for desk or home reading and how to keep the center orderly. Anyone should be able to borrow any book in the library, although books might be coded in some way to indicate which are harder to read. The second step is to assign two children each week as monitors to keep the books in order and to keep track of borrowed books. The third step is to promote book reading. You might talk about interesting new books, read the first part of a good book to the class, relate some lessons or content area topics to particular books, or have children talk about their favorite books and authors. You could set up regular times when everyone is required to choose a book and read to themselves (*sustained silent reading*; see Chapter 6). Sustained silent reading, in conjunction with a library center, helps children realize that reading is a regular part of the academic schedule, not merely a supplementary activity.

Research by Morrow (1982) with nursery school through second grade classrooms showed that a good location and set-up led to more frequent use of a classroom library. Morrow and Weinstein (1984) found that teacher-promoted library reading greatly influenced in-school reading. Even poor readers demonstrated a high interest in book reading when independent reading and use of the library center were promoted. The teachers were enthusiastic about the library center because it fostered excitement about reading and provided a favorable social context for learning. Children can tell stories together, read to each other, and read separate books while sitting near one another. The center also encourages children from different ability levels to mingle with one another.

Writing center.   A writing center offers a way to introduce writing and to integrate writing with reading and language arts. It gives children a way to work together and help one another write out their ideas. It provides a place for children to read and discuss with others what they have written. Thus, a writing center can promote the sharing of information with classmates.

A writing center requires a table, writing implements, lined and unlined paper or notebooks, scissors and tape, a stapler and materials for making book covers, and a space for a few children to work. Other useful accessories include a computer with word processing or writing programs and a bulletin board to display work, notify children about writing assignments, or give them ideas.

Listening post.   Young children and those who cannot yet read benefit from a listening post. This is a place that has one or more tape recorders attached to earphones, a number of taped stories, and accompanying books for children to follow as they listen. As with a library center, the place should be comfortable and well-lighted with cushions or chairs for children to sit on. Picture-word directions for use and identification of the tapes should be available so that children can use the materials unassisted.

Computer center.   Materials needed in a computer center begin with the computer, video display device, and printer. These should be on a rolling cart if you have to share the equipment with other classrooms, otherwise on a table. Since several children are likely to use the computer together, be sure there is enough room for about three or four children. Programs should be kept at the table, each with prominently labeled directions for use. If there is a bulletin board nearby, children can post their latest computer ideas or written stories, activities they want to share or set up with others, and suggestions or requests for help.

On graph paper, draw the floor plan of the way you would like to set up your classroom. Use a scale of one inch to represent four or five feet. Mark the likely location of chalkboards, bulletin boards, doors, windows, and coat and storage areas. Then show where you would place desks and learning centers. Indicate the areas you would use for large and small group activities. Draw arrows for the children's likely traffic patterns. Based on the way you expect to teach reading, write a brief explanation or justification for your plan.

KEY CONCEPT 2

Teachers should have an understanding of classroom management principles, an essential background for effective reading instruction.

CLASSROOM MANAGEMENT PRINCIPLES

Large-scale studies of schools and classrooms have led to the identification of a set of management characteristics that make a difference in learning. They show what teachers should do to improve their reading instruction. Rutter (1983) describes the following characteristics:

Appropriate classroom management [characteristics] include a high proportion of lesson time spent on the subject matter of the lesson (as distinct from setting up equipment, handing out papers, dealing with disciplinary problems, etc.); a high proportion of teacher time spent interacting with the class as a whole, rather than with individuals; a minimum of disciplinary interventions; lessons beginning and ending on time; clear and unambiguous feedback to pupils on both their performance and what was expected of them; and ample use of praise for good performance. (p. 29)

Effective management involves gaining students' attention and providing an orderly environment for learning. Little time is wasted by distributing papers, making transitions from one activity to the next, or dealing with discipline problems. With group-based discipline standards, children know what is expected, and individuals are not singled out for criticism. Rule enforcement is carried out on the spot, with a minimum of lesson interference. Finally, criticism and physical punishment are avoided. As Rutter explained: "In the long run good discipline is achieved by the majority of pupils wanting to participate in the educational process rather than doing so merely through fear of retribution" (p. 31).

Setting up routines

Children need to know what they are supposed to do and when. Most want to learn and be cooperative. If you give them a chance to follow your rules, provided the rules are reasonable, most will be agreeable and will even help you monitor those who do not appreciate a regular, predictable structure. Prepare clear, simple rules for the whole class, small groups, and individual readers. Let children know how to conduct themselves in each learning setting and how to deal with problems without bothering you or others.

Children need to carry out routine activities without supervision. For example, they should know the rules for sharpening a pencil (some teachers have everyone check that they have two sharp pencils each day before school begins), leaving the room, lining up for recess, and waiting for class to begin or for groups to change. Orderly classrooms have children who are responsive to the teacher's signaling, such as for reading groups to change places. Children in orderly classrooms bring the correct materials with them to small group reading lessons, they have a serious attitude about reading, and they adapt to the established and predictable schedule.

Teaching children ways to get help on independent work, when the teacher is working with other children, can be a knotty problem for a beginning teacher. You should let children know how to signal their need for your help (e.g., raise their hands, come to your desk, write their names on the board), and how they might secure help from classmates. It is particularly important to establish these rules early in the school year because otherwise great confusion will occur while you are trying to teach lessons to small groups or work with individuals.

What children should do when finished with assignments is often another problem for beginning teachers. Solving it depends partly on the extra resources you have made available to children and also on children's ability to work without disturbing others. Ideally, children should look upon the time as an opportunity to do independent reading or writing, complete or correct back work, work on a long-term project, help other children, or work on supplementary science, math, or computer activities. As children become adept in working on their own, you can make more options available to them. At first, however, too many options will probably create confusion for the children and distract them from regular classroom tasks.

Setting up effective instruction for small groups

Instructional research by Anderson, Evertson, and Brophy (1982) has led to a list of six general principles for teaching reading to small groups (p. 2). These are listed and explained below:

1. *Reading groups should be organized for efficient, sustained focus on the content to be learned.* Anderson et al. recommend that teacher time with each

reading group average 25 to 30 minutes per day. Teach students to move into the reading group with their materials as soon as you give the signal. If appropriate for children from this cultural background, use an ordered turn arrangement to avoid wasting time waiting for volunteers and to allow all students to be prepared to respond. To maintain a focus on the academic task without having to deal with managerial problems, avoid letting children outside the reading group interrupt you. This can be accomplished in part by positioning yourself so that you can monitor the rest of the class as you teach a reading group.

2. *All students should be not merely attentive, but actively involved in the lesson.* One way to do this is to begin lessons with an overview describing what students will learn and why it is important. Another way is to use questions, particularly those that require students to predict the content of the next segment of the story. Concentrate the discussion on the academic content and keep students focused on the topic, concept, or skill to be learned.

3. *Questions and tasks should be easy enough to enable the teacher to move the lesson along at a brisk pace.* They recommend about an 80 percent success rate for answers to your questions about new material and about a 95 percent success rate for review material.

4. *Students should receive frequent opportunities to read and respond to questions, and should get clear feedback about the correctness of their performance.* Choral responses and ordered turns give everyone the opportunity to answer. When they do answer, begin the lesson by acknowledging correctness briefly (nod, repeat what was said, or say "right"). Later in the lesson when children understand whether responses are correct or not, you can omit acknowledgments. Use praise sparingly unless you are trying to change the behavior of a problem student; for the most part, reserve it for particularly well phrased answers or answers to difficult questions. Avoid criticism; instead, help students correct their wrong answers. Use follow-up questions occasionally to help students integrate or better understand an important idea.

5. *Skills should be mastered to overlearning, with new ones gradually phased in while old ones are being mastered.* When presenting new information (such as new words), do not merely give the information and move on. Explain it, relate it to other work, or have students relate it to their knowledge or experience. Be sure that students know what to do and how to do it before they begin to work independently. One way to check is to have one of the slowest students in the group demonstrate how to accomplish the task. If necessary, give guided practice by doing the first two or three problems with the students.

6. *Although instruction takes place in the group setting for efficiency reasons, the teacher monitors the progress of each individual student and provides whatever specific instruction, feedback, or opportunities to practice each student requires.* Be sure everyone has opportunities to respond to your questions. You may need to keep children from calling out answers so that shy and slower children have an opportunity to answer. When using a choral reading approach, watch carefully that everyone responds together. If some children delay responding give them individual chances to answer or coach them until

they can answer. When asking individuals to respond, wait for answers (though not so long that others become impatient or the child being asked to respond becomes embarrassed). If a child cannot respond without help, give clues or simplify the question. If that does not work, give the answer or call on another to answer. If part of the answer is given, rephrase it so that children hear the correct part. If you are not sure they understand, amplify on the answer or have someone explain why it is correct.

Responding to different types of learners

Kedar-Voivodas (1983) reviewed research on teachers attitudes toward their students. Teachers appear to distinguish three kinds of students:

1. *Pupils*—children who are "patient, docile, passive, orderly, conforming, obedient, and acquiescent to rules and regulations, receptive to and respectful of authority, easily controllable and socially adept" (p. 417).

2. *Receptive learners*—children who are able to "perform adequately in established curriculum areas, on prescribed measures, at set times, and by set criteria . . . [also] the ability to work independently and efficiently despite distractions. . . Furthermore, related educational activities, such as homework and class assignments, have to be punctually and adequately performed" (p. 417).

3. *Active learners*—children who go beyond "the established academic curriculum both in terms of the content to be mastered and in the processes for gaining such mastery. . . . Scholarly traits include curiosity, active probing and exploring, challenging authority, an independent and questioning mind, an insistence on explanations, and a self-imposed discipline that serves the demands of scholarship rather than the wishes and desires of other people" (p. 418).

Children who fit the "active learner" description tend to be rejected more often by teachers than "pupils" or "receptive learners." This is because active learners are harder to discipline and work with. Furthermore, since more boys than girls seem to be active learners, a bias against those children can lead to a preference for instructing girls over boys.

We caution you to observe your own responses to active learners and avoid a bias in favor of pupils or receptive learners. While active learners are undoubtedly more difficult to teach and will challenge and be more critical of your instruction, they have an attitude and approach toward learning that other children in the classroom would do well to emulate.

Fostering a sense of responsibility for learning

An important long-term instructional goal is for children to take on the responsibility for their own learning. Children should read, study, and learn because they want to know about something or master a skill. They should strive to be more like *active learners*. Marshall and Weinstein (1984) reviewed

EXERCISE

Observe, or watch a videotape of, an experienced teacher during the first ten minutes of the school day. When did children make the shift from talking to friends to getting ready to work? How long did it take? Did the teacher do anything to foster that shift, or was the routine so well established that the teacher did not need to signal the change? How did the teacher prepare for the first lesson (e.g., put work on the board, have children get out books, hand back papers, work with individuals)? Describe differences you saw in individuals' willingness to begin to work, and if the teacher had to encourage some individuals to begin working, how that was done.

the approaches that teachers can take to foster this attitude. From their work, we suggest the following guidelines:

Figure out ways to share the responsibility for learning with your students. To encourage students to be more involved in their reading lessons, offer them work choices, give them several things to do but let them choose what to do first, or let them choose whom to work with to get the task done.

Have students help you create the reading tasks and the goals. Discuss both short-term and long-term learning goals with them. Foster the concept of individually-determined goals.

Encourage students to check their own answers and evaluate their own performance. Give students opportunities to monitor their progress. Help them to understand how their performance on each assignment can foster a gradual improvement in their reading as well as mastery of different learning goals (such as reading fluency, word knowledge, problem solving, outlining, etc.).

KEY CONCEPT 3

Reading should be scheduled at the most opportune time and in the most effective way possible.

SCHEDULING READING

Because elementary school reading is generally held to be highly important but difficult to teach, most teachers schedule reading for the first period in the day, every day of the week. Children are more likely at that time to be alert and willing to concentrate. Set aside as much as two hours for reading if the children you teach are from homes that do not provide much support for literacy development or if you are going to merge reading with the other language arts.

Setting up instructional groups

When you teach reading, you will need to decide whether to group students, and if so, the basis on which groups will be formed (e.g., by ability or by interest), the size of the groups, and when and for how long each will be taught.

Although many variations are possible, we present these options for you to consider: (1) whole class instruction, (2) small group instruction, and (3) individualized instruction and peer work groups. You will probably use one of these approaches most of the time and rely on the others less often. Each requires a different type of schedule.

Whole class lesson schedule.   Whole class lessons are appropriate when you want to teach skills that all the children can learn together and need to practice. Depending on the class, these skills might include phonics, word analysis, comprehension and reading-to-learn strategies, and study skills. The sample schedule presented in Figure 12.1 is adapted from Good, Grouws, and Ebmeier (1983), who conducted instructional research on the teaching of mathematics.

FIGURE 12.1   Sample Schedule for Whole Class Instruction

Daily Review (first eight minutes except Monday)

1. Review the concepts and skills associated with the homework
2. Collect and deal with homework assignments

Development (about twenty minutes)

1. Briefly focus on prerequisite skills and concepts
2. Focus on meaning and promoting student understanding by using lively explanations, demonstrations, process explanations, illustrations, etc.
3. Assess student comprehension

Seatwork (about fifteen minutes)

1. Provide uninterrupted successful practice
2. Momentum—keep the ball rolling—get everyone involved, then sustain involvement
3. Alerting—let students know their work will be checked at end of period
4. Accountability—check the students' work

Homework assignment

1. Given on a regular basis at the end of each class except Fridays
2. Should involve about fifteen minutes of work to be done at home
3. Should include some review

Special Reviews

1. Weekly review/maintenance
   a. Conduct during the first twenty minutes each Wednesday
   b. Focus on skills and concepts covered during the previous week
2. Monthly review/maintenance
   a. Conduct every fourth Monday
   b. Focus on skills and concepts covered since the last monthly review

From *Active Mathematics Teaching* by T. L. Good, D. A. Grouws, and H. Ebmeier. Copyright © 1983 by Longman Inc. Reprinted by permission.

FIGURE 12.2   *Sample Daily Schedule for Small Group Instruction*

Introduction to day's activities (first five minutes)

Teacher explains to the whole class any new activities and reminds children about ongoing activities and projects. Children ask questions about the work.

Small group lessons (one hour and forty minutes)

Teacher signals that children should begin work. Teacher meets for twenty minutes with each of the five reading groups. Teacher gives lessons with an ETR or other systematic method of comprehension instruction and also teaches particular word identification or vocabulary skills.

Wrap-up (last five to ten minutes each day)

Completed assignments are handed in. Teacher discusses with the whole class their progress at learning centers. Teacher also asks for reactions to the work and for suggestions for future work. Occasionally, children present their completed work to the class.

This is a fast-paced whole class schedule. It might be appropriate if used perhaps two days a week during part of a reading period.

Small group lesson schedule. Small group lessons are appropriate when you want to teach certain skills or topics to some children but not others. In other words, you have found considerable diversity in the reading instructional needs and in the interests of the children in your class. Thus, whole class lessons may not be an effective way of furthering the learning to read of the majority of your students.

The following is an example of a small group plan, one used successfully in primary grade classrooms (Au & Kawakami, 1984; Tharp, 1982). The class is first divided into four or five instruction groups, with grouping being based on criterion-referenced test results. The assumption is that children in each group will benefit from receiving the same lessons and independent practice activities, because they are at about the same reading level. Each group is usually composed of three to seven children. We recommend, however, that you try to place fewer children in the lowest ability group, because these children typically need the most teacher attention.

In this plan teachers meet with each group for 20 to 25 minutes every day. Usually they meet with one of the lowest ability groups first. While each group is receiving direct instruction from the teacher, the remaining children are working independently at one of several learning centers set up around the room. At the signal for a change from the teacher, everyone moves, either to another learning center or to the center for teacher-directed instruction. By the end of the reading period every child has received instruction from the teacher and has worked at several different learning centers. A sample schedule is shown in Figure 12.2.

Schedule for individualized instruction or peer work groups. Individualized instruction can be conducted by having children work on individual readings and other assignments, for example, as in the individualized reading approach discussed in Chapter 10. Recent investigations suggest, however, that student-led small group activities may lead to greater learning than individual activities where children work alone. The small group in this case is often called a "peer work group." There are three to four children in each group, one each of high and low reading ability and one or two of average ability. There is one task for every group to carry out with each member of the group contributing to the end product. For example, groups might be asked to read and write a brief summary of an expository text. To accomplish this task would require children first to read the text, perhaps aloud if one child in the group is a very poor reader or perhaps silently but with the children helping one another with unknown words. Then the children discuss the text and compose a summary. The teacher circulates among the peer work groups, helping them negotiate who will do which tasks and advising them about the assignment. The completed assignment is evaluated by the teacher or by the groups themselves.

An alternative, less structured approach is called a "multitask" organization. Here there are a number of possible tasks such as independent reading, writing, and research projects for children to carry out. These are chosen by the children to be carried out at their own pace in small groups at learning centers. Children are encouraged to help one another as they work on the same assignments, but they complete and hand in their own work. Again, the teacher works with the small groups for large portions of the reading period.

These two approaches have in common the reliance on students' taking the initiative, assuming responsibility for learning, and cooperating to accomplish tasks. In both, the teacher manages behavior problems on an individual basis, talking with children privately while the others work. Lessons still need to be formulated by the teacher and taught either to small groups or to the whole class. What is unique is the use of groups in which students help one another and work together on projects.

A schedule for this type of classroom organization would be more flexible than the others we described. It is likely, however, to have a structure such as that shown in Figure 12.3.

EXERCISE

Observe, or watch a videotape of, the first five to ten minutes of time a class is organized for whole class instruction, small group instruction, and in peer work groups. Notice how each is set up, how the teacher organizes the work activities, and the nature of the work. Estimate how long it takes for everyone to begin working in each setting, how children who are confused get help, and how the teacher monitors the whole class while still working with groups or individuals.

Set up (five to ten minutes)

The teacher explains what children are to do for the day or week and gives deadlines for completion. Children ask questions about the work and materials are handed out. Children might work with those who select the same task or might be put into working groups by the teacher.

Worktime (sixty to seventy minutes)

The children work in small clusters at their desks or at learning centers. They might be discussing the tasks and figuring out how they should be done and who will work on each part. They might be reading or writing by themselves and giving help to one another as it is requested. The teacher circulates around the room instructing and providing information to individuals or groups.

Wrap-up (five to ten minutes)

The teacher might discuss with the children what they accomplished and learned, how or why it was important, and how it fits with their other work. Assignments might be collected or corrected, and children might share completed projects with the rest of the class.

Advantages of various arrangements for reading instruction

Decisions about how to organize your class into instructional groups are among the most difficult for beginning teachers to make. While grouping children into small, ability-defined groups (homogeneous grouping) is the most common approach, it may not be the best for your students, certainly not on all occasions. You should consider the advantages and disadvantages of each alternative. A listing of some of the advantages is presented in Figure 12.4.

GROUPING CHILDREN

Children in most American elementary school classrooms are placed into groups for reading instruction. Three or four groups are common and placement in one or another group is almost always determined by reading ability. Instruction centers on the group, not on individuals. Moreover, grouping decisions are usually permanent arrangements, as few children are moved from one instructional group to another over the course of the school year.

These practices, while long-standing and based on reasonable ideas, can be detrimental to some students. Grouping sometimes has the effect of limiting opportunities for learning. Less effective instruction is often given to low-ability groups. Grouping can also reduce low-ability groups' interest in or motivation to work and learn and can lead to a low academic self-concept.

A study by Eder and Felmlee (1984) compared lessons given to the low and high ability groups in a first grade class. They found that the teacher set lower standards for conduct in the low groups and taught more structured lessons. The children in the low groups were less able to help the teacher maintain attention to the lesson. As a result, children in the low groups lost lesson time because the teacher had to spend more time on management.

A study by Allington (1984; related to research discussed also in Chapter 9) indicates in another way how ability grouping can affect reading lessons. High and low ability groups in grades one, three, and five read about the same amount orally but not silently. Low ability groups read much less silently, as much as a twenty-to-one difference. Most teachers have good readers read one story per session while poor readers often read only a few pages from a story. Good readers are paced at a faster rate and given more comprehension lessons; poor readers read fewer stories and are given more lesson drills and worksheets. While high ability learners can move at a faster pace, we believe the differences in instruction are often greater than necessary and tend to hold low ability children back.

FIGURE 12.4 *Advantages of Different Instructional Arrangements*

Advantages of the whole class arrangement:

1. You can use one lesson and set of practice materials.
2. You can often give longer lessons.
3. You can supervise all children during practice activities.
4. You can give private help as children are working.
5. You can lessen problems of labeling, low expectations, elitism, and poor self-concepts because children of lower ability are less obviously identified.

Advantages of the small, homogeneous group arrangement:

1. Because children are more similar in ability, you can match instruction to ability.
2. You can provide individualized feedback for comprehension responses and oral reading.
3. You can monitor and hold the attention of all children in the group.
4. You can maintain an orderly instructional environment without having to depend on the children to do so on their own.
5. By varying the size of the groups, you can put fewer children in the low group and give lower achieving children somewhat more attention.

Advantages of the peer work group arrangement:

1. You can use mixed ability groups which allow grouping by interest, a reduction of elitism, and an opportunity for children to work cooperatively and learn from one another.
2. You can circulate among and work with all of the groups.
3. You can give children more choices of tasks and options in learning and perhaps improve motivation.
4. You can place responsibility for learning more directly on the children and perhaps improve their sense of control over their own learning.
5. Since children are helping one another, you can assign more difficult practice materials.

Alternative approaches

Considering the problems that can arise when children are taught in groups based on ability, an obvious question is whether it is necessary to use ability grouping for reading instruction, especially on all or most occasions. Here are four options you can consider:

1. Keep an ability grouping arrangement but foster a multidimensional concept of ability for your students, the view that children have different special abilities and that no one is best in every way.

2. Take special steps to give low ability students the chance to achieve higher status.

3. Encourage cooperative learning by using different kinds of peer work groups.

4. Use various types of heterogeneous (mixed ability) grouping. Each of these options is discussed in turn.

Fostering a multidimensional concept of ability. Teachers should try to evaluate children on more than one dimension. In that way they find out that different children are "smart" in different areas. According to a review by Marshall and Weinstein (1984), when teachers foster a multiple- rather than single-ability concept of academic ability, children will begin to look for and talk about each other's different strengths. This means that no child will need to feel incompetent at everything, and everyone can be praised for some special ability. It could also help children see hard work and skill learning as undertakings that will increase their competence.

In your teaching you need not view children's ability only in terms of their overall reading scores. Instead, look for special reading talents such as an ability to act out the part of a story character, give good definitions of words, make interesting predictions about stories, remember information that was read, find important ideas in a text, or read with expression. Although children who are not fluent readers are less likely to be good in other aspects of reading, you can find or help children develop a special skill. Pointing out and making use of their special abilities will help children not only to differentiate aspects of their own reading but will encourage them to work on their deficiencies.

Improving the classroom status of low ability children. A serious problem of separating children by ability is the lowered sense of self-esteem and social status that children who are not in the "fast track" feel. Ability grouping can be detrimental to average- and lower-ability groups, particularly depressing achievement for students in low groups (Hallinan, 1984). Since, however, there are instructional advantages to ability grouping, a possible solution is for the teacher to enhance the status and self-esteem of lower-achieving children.

One approach for enhancing status was studied by Morine-Dershimer (1983). The basic idea is that children's academic status is influenced by their participation in classroom discussions. Teachers usually call on children who volunteer, and children volunteer if they know the answer. Because children who are called on become visible to their classmates as *children-who-know*, they achieve a high status and become children that others turn to and learn from.

Morine-Dershimer studied how three teachers created or supported children-who-know. One teacher, who emphasized text content, factual information, and short answers, more often called on, and so supported, the best readers in the class. The other two teachers, who emphasized children's lesson-related experiences and problem-solving ideas, called on high, middle, and low-achieving readers about equally. The effect for these two teachers was the creation of high status children among low ability (and, originally, low status) children.

This means that high status can be given, even to low-achieving readers, if teachers encourage discussions that allow them to describe relevant experiences and ideas rather than only to remember and describe what they read. Possible additional advantages found by Morine-Dershimer are better attention among children to each other's answers and higher end-of-year gains in reading.

Cooperative learning and flexible grouping.   Effective teachers encourage students to collaborate or learn from one another, rather than to compete or refuse to help one another. The advantages of a cooperative classroom atmosphere are several. It enables students to teach one another, lessening the instructional burden for the teacher. It can increase time on task for seatwork activities, while the teacher is working with a small group. It can enhance students' ability to explain, allow them to see another child's perspective, and improve low achievers' academic self-concept. Finally, it allows alternative and more flexible grouping arrangements.

Stodolsky (1984) distinguished five types of peer work groups sometimes used by teachers who use alternative grouping arrangements:

1. Completely cooperative—Children have one common goal or product to complete. It might be a group discussion or preparation for a debate or a demonstration. They work together and share in all aspects of the process, with everyone expected to contribute to the activity. Evaluation is directed to the group-accomplished result, and everyone in the group is similarly evaluated.

2. Cooperative—While there is a common end or goal, there is a division of labor. All members of the group are expected to contribute, although not in the same way, and the result or product is evaluated as a group. The approach might be used with a research report, a written story or play, or a reading/art project. For example, with a research report each child might write a section.

3. Helping obligatory—Each child works on a task, often the same task for everyone, but the work is done together at a convenient table. Children are to assist one another but each child's product is sepa-

These girls are part of a helping-permitted peer work group. Children spend much of the time working on their own assignments but occasionally seek one another's advice.

rately evaluated. This kind of cooperative work could be carried out with workbook exercises or teacher-constructed seatwork. It could also be used when children are reading independently and need help understanding or identifying some words, or writing a story.

4. Helping permitted—While children work and are evaluated on their own completed product, they are allowed to help one another. Children can ask whom they please but others are not obligated to help. This approach can be used with most reading and writing tasks.

5. Peer tutoring—Children do not share a common goal. Rather one child acts as an expert and help is expected to flow in one direction only. The accomplished work is evaluated only for the child who was being tutored. This approach can be used for oral reading, workbook tasks, and drill on new words.

Wilkinson and Calculator (1982) set up an arrangement for helping-permitted work groups. The groups were comprised of four to six children of similar reading ability. They met briefly with the teacher, who explained their work. The same tasks were given to all the children in a group, who then worked together at a small table. The children were encouraged but not required to cooperate with others in the completion of the tasks. The results of working together varied with the ability of the group. Better readers were more likely than poor readers to make clear and explicit requests for help and to receive the help they asked for. Similarly, Cohen (1984), who studied mixed ability groupings, found that low ability children were less likely to ask for and receive help than were other children. She suggested that these children need more support from the teacher to work in a helping-permitted structure.

Heterogeneous grouping. Instead of setting up ability-determined groups that remain stable over time, Marshall and Weinstein suggest using small groups, putting together children of differing abilities, and having children work together for many different purposes. With this procedure children have the chance to work with a larger number of their classmates. This has the advantage of giving children more opportunity to observe their own and other's strengths in a variety of tasks and situations. It may also give lower achieving children more opportunities to receive recognition for their work and effort.

Heterogeneous groups can be set up in reading even when a basal or other commercial reading program is being used and children are working with different readers. For example, while keeping ability groups for story reading, you could form other groups for writing, spelling, vocabulary development, and discussion of books read for recreation. You could group children interested in the same topic, such as rock collecting, and have them read tradebooks, magazines, and other materials. You could also group high, middle, and low readers together to work on reading-related projects, such as the presentation of a scene from a play.

Webb and Cullian (1983) studied the use of cooperative groups on children's social interactions and achievement. They successfully mixed children of high, middle, and low ability together in small groups of three and four. The teachers assigned tasks to be completed by the groups and emphasized cooperation, helpfulness, and coordination of effort. The teacher circulated among the groups, giving help as requested.

In another study (Webb & Kenderski, 1984), cooperative peer work groups were composed either of a mixture of high and middle or of middle and low ability children. The important result here was that the groups were more effective if children explained things to one another. This suggests that in order to promote helpfulness, a teacher should encourage children to explain their ideas and answers to one another.

SUMMARY

In this chapter we presented information to help you understand how principles of classroom organization and management can be applied to enhance children's progress in learning to read. In the perspective we discussed three important areas of research contributing to our understanding of effective organization and management. These had to do with time and the efficiency of teaching, interactive decision-making, and simplified models of instruction.

We suggested in the first key concept that you prepare for the school year by arranging your classroom in a way expressly designed to foster learning to read. We recommended that you consider the use of learning centers, particularly one for a classroom library. In the second key concept we focused on principles of effective classroom management. Among the procedures presented were those for establishing routines, setting up effective small group instruction, and giving attention to individual students.

We considered in the third key concept how reading instruction might be scheduled. A detailed discussion was provided for three alternative types of scheduling: for whole class instruction, for the instruction of small groups formed on the basis of ability, and for peer work groups. In the fourth key concept we explored the complex issues raised by grouping children for reading instruction on the basis of ability. The chief problem with this practice seems to be its detrimental effects on low ability children. We recommended that you consider remedying this problem by improving other children's opinions of low ability children, encouraging cooperative learning, and forming groups heterogeneous in ability.

We covered many different ideas and procedures, more than you will be able to use right away. However, we hope you will eventually try many of the less widely used, but possibly more effective, alternative approaches presented in this chapter. As you try a variety of approaches to organizing and managing your reading program and become comfortable working with your class, you will gradually understand how to provide effective instruction for all your students.

BIBLIOGRAPHY

REFERENCES

Allington, R. (1984). Content coverage and contextual reading in reading groups. *Journal of Reading Behavior, 16,* 85-96.

Anderson, L., Evertson, C., & Brophy, J. (1982). *Principles of small-group instruction in elementary reading.* (Occasional Paper #58). East Lansing, MI: Institute for Research on Teaching, Michigan State University.

Arbuthnot, M., & Sutherland, Z. (1977). *Children and books.* 5th ed. Glenview, IL: Scott, Foresman.

Au, K., & Kawakami, A. (1984). Vygotskian perspectives on discussion processes in small-group reading-lessons. In P. Peterson, L. Wilkinson, & M. Hallinan (Eds.), *The social context of instruction: Group organization and group processes.* New York: Academic Press.

Brophy, J. (1979). *Teacher behavior and its effects* (Occasional Paper #25). East Lansing, MI: Institute for Research on Teaching, Michigan State University.

Brophy, J. (1984). The teacher as thinker: Implementing instruction. In G. Duffy, L. Roehler, & J. Mason (Eds.), *Comprehension instruction: Perspectives and suggestions.* New York: Longman.

Clark, C., & Yinger, R. (1979). Teachers' thinking. In P. Peterson & H. Walberg (Eds.), *Research on teaching.* Berkeley, CA: McCutchan.

Cohen, E. (1984). Talking and working together: Status, interaction, and learning. In P. Peterson, L. Wilkinson, & M. Hallinan (Eds.), *The social context of instruction: Group organization and group processes.* New York: Academic Press.

Eder, D., & Felmlee, D. (1984). The development of attention norms in ability groups. In P. Peterson, L. Wilkinson, & M. Hallinan, (Eds.), *The social context of instruction: Group organization and group processes.* New York: Academic Press.

Good, T. (1983). Research on classroom teaching. In L. Shulman & G. Sykes (Eds.), *Handbook of teaching and policy.* New York: Longman.

Good, T., Grouws, D., & Ebmeier, H. (1983). *Active mathematics teaching.* New York: Longman.

Goodlad, J. (1983). *A place called school.* New York: Harper.

Hallinan, M. (1984). Summary and conclusions. In P. Peterson, L. Wilkinson, & M. Hallinan (Eds.), *The social context of instruction: Group organization and group processes.* New York: Academic Press.

Hawkins, D. (1973). What it means to teach. *Teachers College Record, 75,* 7-16.

Hiebert, E. (1983). An examination of ability grouping for reading instruction. *Reading Research Quarterly, 18,* 231-255.

Huck, C. (1976). *Children's literature in the elementary school.* New York: Holt, Rinehart & Winston.

Kedar-Voivodas, G. (1983). Impact of elementary children's school roles and sex roles on teacher attitudes: An interactional analysis. *Review of Educational Research, 53,* 415-437.

Lightfoot, S. (1983). The lives of teachers. In L. Shulman & G. Sykes (Eds.), *Handbook of teaching and policy.* New York: Longman.

Marshall, H., & Weinstein, R. (1984). Classroom factors affecting students' self-evaluations: An interactional model. *Review of Educational Research, 54,* 301-326.

Morine-Dershimer, G. (1983). Instructional strategy and the "creation" of classroom status. *American Educational Research Journal, 20,* 645-662.

Morrow, L. (1982). Relationships between literature programs, library corner design, and children's use of literature. *Journal of Educational Research, 75,* 339-344.

Morrow, L., & Weinstein, C. (1984). *The impacts of a recreational reading program on children's voluntary use of literature.* Paper presented at the annual meeting of the National Reading Conference, St. Petersburg, FL.

Peterson, P., & Clark, C. (1978). Teachers' reports of their cognitive processes during teaching. *American Educational Research Journal, 15,* 555-565.

Rosenshine, B. (1979). Content, time, and direct instruction. In P. Peterson & H. Walberg (Eds.), *Research on teaching: Concepts, findings, and implications.* Berkeley, CA: McCutchan.

Rutter, M. (1983). Complexities of schools and classrooms. In L. Shulman & G. Sykes (Eds.), *Handbook of teaching and policy.* New York: Longman.

Shulman, L. (1983). Autonomy and obligation: The remote control of teaching. In L. Shulman & G. Sykes (Eds.), *Handbook of teaching and policy.* New York: Longman.

Stodolsky, S. (1984). Frameworks for studying instructional processes in peer work-groups. In P. Peterson, L. Wilkinson, & M. Hallinan (Eds.), *The social context of instruction: Group organization and group processes.* New York: Academic Press.

Tharp, R. (1982). The effective instruction of comprehension: Results and description of the Kamehameha Early Education Program. *Reading Research Quarterly, 17,* 503-527.

Veeman, S. (1984). Perceived problems of beginning teachers. *Review of Educational Research, 54,* 143-178.

Webb, N., & Cullian, L. (1983). Group interaction and achievement in small groups: Stability over time. *American Educational Research Journal, 20,* 411-423.

Webb, N., & Kenderski, C. (1984). Student interaction and learning in small-group and whole-class settings. In P. Peterson, L. Wilkinson & M. Hallinan (Eds.), *The social context of instruction: Group organization and group processes.* New York: Academic Press.

Wilkinson, L., & Calculator, S. (1982). Requests and responses in peer-directed reading groups. *American Educational Research Journal, 19,* 107-120.

FURTHER READINGS

Anderson, L. M., Evertson, C. M., & Brophy, J. E. (1979). An experimental study of effective teaching in first-grade reading groups. *Elementary School Journal, 79,* 193-223.

Brophy, J. E. (1982). Fostering student learning and motivation in the elementary school classroom (Occasional Paper #51). East Lansing, MI: Institute for Research on Teaching, Michigan State University.

Cazden, C. B. (1981). Social context of learning to read. In J. T. Guthrie (Ed.), *Comprehension and teaching: Research reviews.* Newark, DE: International Reading Association.

Duffy, G. (1982). Fighting off the alligators: What research in real classrooms has to say about reading instruction. *Journal of Reading Behavior, 14,* 357-374.

Ellis, D. W., & Preston, F. W. (1984). Enhancing beginning reading using wordless picture books in a cross-age tutoring program. *Reading Teacher, 37,* 692-698.

Guthrie, J. T. (1982). Effective teaching practices. *Reading Teacher, 35,* 766-768.

Levine, D. U. (1982). Successful approaches for improving academic achievement in inner-city elementary schools. *Phi Delta Kappan, 63,* 523-526.

Mason, J. (1984). A question about reading comprehension instruction. In G. Duffy, L. Roehler, & J. Mason (Eds.), *Comprehension instruction: Perspectives and suggestions.* New York: Longman.

Walker, J. (1984). *Behavior management: A practical approach for educators.* Third edition. New York: Mosby.

Webb, N. (1982). Student interaction and learning in small groups. *Review of Educational Research, 52,* 421-445.

CHAPTER 13

Reading in the School, Home, and Community

When Ernie was fourteen his father died and the children were left to cope as best they could. Ernie talked of attending school until he was in the fifth grade, but he explained that he was never there long enough to understand what was going on. Similarly, Ernie's wife had never learned to read. She described how the school had been twelve miles from her home and therefore she had never managed to attend on a regular basis.

Among the difficulties Ernie spoke of were the problems he experienced when traveling. He spoke of coping with street names. He would have the word written on a piece of paper, and he would try to match it with the street name. With unmistakable sincerity, he added that it was no good if the first letter matched, that did not mean it was the right word. The whole word had to match. Another difficulty was being able to prove that the items he owned really belonged to him. He pointed to the ring I was wearing, and he repeated several times how important it was for me to be able to prove the ring was mine. Ernie went on to talk of the house he was buying; he had to rely on friends to tell him that the house was legally his.

Although Ernie faced these immense problems on a daily basis, they did not compare with the formidable task of finding employment. Ernie spoke of the application forms for his present job. He explained:

> I sat in school and the teacher helped me fill in the application. Well, it wasn't bad. Getting it was bad. But she showed me and it wasn't too bad. I filled it out at school and she showed me. So when I went to the job I filled it out again on my own and so I passed and so I got the job.
> (Taylor, 1983, pp. 85–86)

OVERVIEW

We begin this chapter by taking a look at reading in the community. With this perspective of how reading fits into the lives of many adults, teachers should have a better idea of the wide variety of reading activities they will want to help their students learn to carry out. Because reading is such an important activity for adults in the workplace, we discuss workplace demands for literacy in the

419

PERSPECTIVE

PROFILE OF READING ACTIVITIES IN A COMMUNITY

Throughout this textbook, we have been making the assumption that reading is an important activity in the daily lives of many adults. In this section, we look more closely at the kinds of reading adults actually do, as shown in recent research. The purpose of providing this information is to make you more

first key concept. Workplace uses of literacy are much different from typical school reading activities. It may be valuable, then, for teachers to have children participate in some classroom activities similar in certain respects to those of the workplace.

In the second key concept, we look at recreational reading. We see that many adults engage in leisure time reading and look at children's patterns of recreational reading. Means the teacher can use to foster recreational reading are discussed, for books, newspapers, and magazines.

The third key concept has to do with using two types of resources, the library and children in other classes, to help children learn to read. In this section, we offer teachers suggestions which carry the developmental reading program beyond the walls of the single classroom, by involving others in the school.

In the fourth key concept, we discuss how teachers can promote children's reading development by making connections between the home and school. The importance of enlisting family support for reading is discussed. We describe different means of communicating with parents about the classroom reading program and their child's reading progress. Finally, we describe ways of enlisting the help of parents to foster students' recreational reading. The key concepts in this final chapter are:

Key Concept #1: Given what is known about the nature of reading in the workplace, teachers should involve students in a wide variety of reading activities requiring problem-solving with different kinds of materials.

Key Concept #2: Teachers should know how to encourage recreational reading, so students will choose to read independently for their own enjoyment and information.

Key Concept #3: Teachers should know how to encourage students' reading development in school by making use of resources such as the library and students in other classes.

Key Concept #4: Teachers should foster students' reading ability and interest by strengthening connections between reading at home and at school.

EXERCISE

In this exercise you will be comparing your own patterns of reading with those of two other people.

(1) Divide a blank sheet of paper into three columns, with headings as indicated below.

Time   Types of Material   Setting

(2) In the column labeled *Time*, record the times of the day in half-hour segments, beginning with the time you awaken on a typical weekday, to the nearest hour or half hour (e.g., 7:00 a.m., 7:30 a.m.). End with the last half hour before you go to sleep.

(3) For each of these half-hour segments, list in the second column the types of material you would normally read on a weekday. Use the following categories of material only: (1) newspapers, (2) books, (3) magazines (including comic books), and (4) brief documents. The category of brief documents includes labels, billboards, invoices, maps, forms, and similar items.

(4) Under setting, use the following categories to indicate where you did the reading: home, school, workplace, or other (while outdoors, for example, or in a store).

(5) Consider your list. In how many half-hour time slots did your reading occur? What types of materials do you seem to spend the most time reading? In what setting is most of your reading done?

(6) Try to gather this same type of information on two other individuals, one an adult (preferably, one who is not a full-time student) and one an elementary school student. Prepare a form for each individual, as you did for yourself, and ask them to give you the information for each time segment, considering the kinds of reading they would do on a typical weekday.

(7) What similarities and differences do you observe between yourself and the other adult, in terms of time segments when reading occurred, types of materials read, and setting for reading? What similarities and differences do you find between the results for the adults and those for the child?

From this exercise you should have gained some sense of the differences which exist between children's reading patterns and those of adults. Possibly, you also discovered something about the reading patterns shown by different groups of adults. Keep these results in mind as you read of the findings of large-scale studies of the reading patterns of adults and children, and think of the factors which might explain the results you obtained.

aware of how your students may eventually be using literacy, and of how the classroom reading program may be designed to prepare students for these uses.

Guthrie and Seifert (1983) conducted an extensive study of reading activity in a community. People in this community had somewhat more education than the average but were similar in occupational characteristics to people in the United States as a whole. Reading was defined as "gaining meaning from written messages," and adult wage earners were asked how much reading they did each month, while at home and at work, whether dealing with newspapers, books, magazines, or brief documents. Wage earners in this community were found to spend a considerable amount of time reading; an average of 157 minutes (between two and three hours) per day.

What kinds of reading material occupied these adults during the several hours they spent reading each day? Guthrie and Seifert discovered that adults most often dealt with brief documents. That is, they spent an average of 37 minutes reading such materials as newsletters, business correspondence, billboards, and directions. Guthrie and Seifert speculated that the use of literacy to read brief documents is important in urban settings where adults must deal with large organizations, such as businesses and government agencies.

The second most commonly read content was news and business, which was dealt with for an average of 17.8 minutes per day. According to Guthrie and Seifert, using literacy in this way points to a widespread interest in accomplishing economic, domestic, and personal goals. Fiction (including literature, short stories, and humor found in books, magazines, and newspapers) was read for 7.4 minutes per day. When reading this type of content, adults seem to be using literacy primarily for an aesthetic function, enjoying the experience of reading as an end in itself. Finally, adults in this study read material with a sports and recreation content for 4.1 minutes per day. In short, adults read a range of different materials, for a variety of purposes, spending much more time with some types of materials than with others.

Reference materials (such as manuals, directories, and newspaper classified ads) were read for an average of 11.3 minutes per day. Guthrie and Seifert saw this kind of reading as serving a utilitarian function, aiding adults in government and economic matters. Adults spent a similar amount of time, 17 minutes per day, reading about social issues, including topics such as health, psychology, and education. This kind of reading suggests that many people may want to increase their knowledge in areas such as the physical, medical, and social sciences.

Guthrie and Seifert also discovered that reading activities differed among occupational groups. For example, professionals and managers read about 224 minutes per day and spent more time than other workers' reading brief documents and news and business content. They seemed highly oriented to institutions and politics. Another group, workers in unskilled occupations, read about 60 minutes per day, largely brief documents and reference materials. This suggests literacy being used for utilitarian benefits, as well as to support an orientation toward institutions. Guthrie and Seifert emphasize:

The popular image that unskilled workers are nonreaders or are limited to the reading required by employment applications is contradicted by these findings. News and business, social issues, fiction, and sports were also read in moderation. In other words, political awareness, social development, aesthetic experience, and amusement were among the functions of reading in this group as well as others. (pp. 507–508)

There is an important practical implication growing from this study, which has given us a picture of how adults in a community use literacy. We see that people in different occupations will need or want to use literacy in different ways, and perhaps for somewhat different purposes. Teachers should be aware of the kinds of occupations and life-styles that their students have an interest in pursuing, and of the expectations for literacy that are likely to come from the home and community. But, while having this awareness, teachers will want to prepare students to use literacy for a wide variety of purposes, to make it possible for students to pursue a variety of life options.

KEY CONCEPT 1

Given what is known about the nature of reading in the workplace, teachers should involve students in a wide variety of reading activities requiring problem-solving with different kinds of materials.

LITERACY IN THE WORKPLACE

Recent analyses of the job market in the United States suggest that employment opportunities are to be found largely in occupations requiring rather high levels of skill in reading and writing. Few occupations at present require little or no use of literacy, and these are quickly disappearing (Mikulecky, 1984).

If literacy is so important in the workplace, we need to know more about the kinds of reading skills workers actually use on the job. To find out, Diehl and Mikulecky (1980) studied people in 100 occupations, ranging from stonecutter to vice president of a large corporation. They looked at the reading tasks people faced, the different kinds of reading material encountered and the strategies used to complete tasks.

Diehl and Mikulecky's first major finding was that reading at work is an almost universal activity. Almost 99 percent of the people studied reported reading at work every day, for an average of almost two hours. These results suggest that, on most days, workers probably spend more time reading job-related materials than any other kind. Furthermore, reading seemed to be an important aspect of all kinds of jobs, blue-collar as well as white-collar. In general, workers seemed to think that reading helped them complete tasks more easily and efficiently.

What kinds of reading tasks did workers do? Tasks were placed in one of four categories (based on earlier work by Sticht, 1977):

"Reading-to-learn" in which the subject reads with the intention of remembering text information and applies some learning strategy to do so;

"Reading-to-do with no learning" in which the subject uses the material primarily as an aid to do something else (e.g., fix a machine) and later reports not remembering the information; these materials thus serve as "external memories" (Sticht, 1977);

In workplace settings, such as this construction site, the need for literacy is almost universal. Notice the signs in the background, as well as the plans these men are referring to.

"Reading-to-do with incidental learning" in which the subject uses the material primarily as an aid to do something else, but in the process learns (remembers) the information;

"Reading-to-assess" in which the subject quickly reads or skims material to determine its usefulness for some later task or for some other person; the material is then filed or passed on. (Diehl & Mikulecky, 1980, p. 222–223)

Diehl and Mikulecky found that only 11 percent of the tasks involved reading-to-learn, 40 percent involved reading-to-do with no learning, 23 percent involved reading-to-do with incidental learning, and 26 percent involved reading-to-do tasks (63 percent of the time, when the categories of reading-to-do with no learning and reading-to-do with incidental learning are combined). This indicates that workers generally use reading material as a form of external memory, applying the information immediately and directly to complete the task. Workers did not usually learn the information and expected to refer to the same material when they faced the task again the next day.

How does reading at school match with this picture of reading in the workplace? There seem to be wide differences between the kinds of reading done by students and workers, as shown in a study by Mikulecky (1982). Students apparently spend much less time reading than workers. Also, students generally read textbooks, while workers deal with manuals, product directions, labels, computer printouts, and many other materials, often moving among formats. High school students reported reading-to-learn (66%) as the purpose of most of their tasks, with few tasks involving reading-to-do with no learning (2%) or reading-to-do with incidental learning (13%), and no tasks involving reading-to-assess (0%). The remaining 11 percent of the tasks fell into other categories, not discussed in Mikulecky's report.

Still another difference between reading at school versus on the job is in the degree to which the environment provides cues about how text information is to be applied. Many more of these cues are generally available in the workplace than at school. As Diehl and Mikulecky (1980) point out, much of the reading-to-do by workers is highly specific to a particular task and setting. For example, workers may be following a set of directions and diagrams to assemble a lathe, with its parts sitting right in front of them. Being able to refer to these physical objects helps the workers to read much more efficiently. Their task has become that of finding the match between the objects and their representation in the text.

On the other hand, students in school, who are often engaged in reading-to-learn tasks, usually do not have these physical cues in the environment. Thus, students must rely more on the text and on their own background knowledge. It seems, then, that school reading-to-learn tasks may require different kinds of problem-solving strategies from workplace reading-to-do tasks.

What are the practical implications of these analyses of the disparity between school and workplace literacy? The answer to this question is not a simple one. School should not be seen merely as a place to prepare students for the world of work, so the findings above should *not* be interpreted to mean that teachers should try to make school literacy activities identical to those of the workplace. Yet we wish students to have knowledge of the many different functions of literacy, including the functions of literacy in the workplace. Thus, we recommend that teachers at least introduce students to these functions.

INSTRUCTIONAL GUIDELINES

The two kinds of reading tasks often faced by workers, but rarely by students, appear to be reading-to-do and reading-to-assess. Now that you are aware of this gap, you should look for opportunities to highlight these tasks, particularly when teaching content area lessons. For example, here are two situations in which reading-to-do can be highlighted. During a science lesson students might be asked to carry out an experiment following written directions. Such directions are often found in science kits or textbooks, or the teacher may write them out on task cards. For example, primary grade students may carry out experiments to see which objects sink or float in a pan of water, while upper grade students may work with batteries and wires to create electrical circuits. Children can work either individually or in small groups, while the teacher circulates around the room to provide assistance.

Children could also be given written directions for a craft or cooking project. For example, written directions for making a mask out of a large paper sack and construction paper might be given to primary grade children. To make the task somewhat easier for younger children, drawings might be used to illustrate some of the steps. For cooking projects, recipes can be written on task cards for the children. Some foods can be prepared which do not require baking or frying, for example, snacks such as trail mix, sandwiches, jello, and lemonade. Cooking projects often go more smoothly if parents come to the classroom to help. Later, children can take copies of the recipes home.

Reading-to-assess might be highlighted when the children are doing research for reports in one of the content areas. For example, suppose that the children in a group are looking for information on different kinds of insects (i.e., one child is writing a report on ants, another on bees, another on grasshoppers, and so on). The children could be made aware of one another's topics and asked to pass along information about books or magazine articles other students might find useful. Or the teacher can lead the children in a discussion comparing the merits of various sources when one is seeking answers to particular questions (e.g., which provide detailed information, which are more general).

The teacher may also wish to be sure that students are acquainted with certain practical uses of literacy that may be related to finding and keeping a job. These include being able to read the newspaper and notices, filling out application forms, using the telephone directory, using a building directory to locate a particular store or office, and reading a bus schedule. By the time they are in the upper elementary grades, some students may already have these skills. Others, however, may be able to benefit from instruction in these areas. For example, the building directory could be pointed out, and information from it used when the children are visiting an office building.

INSTRUCTIONAL ACTIVITIES

Mikulecky (1984) suggests that classroom teachers can best prepare students to meet workplace demands for literacy by increasing the amount of reading and writing students do and involving them in activities which include real-world materials and problem-solving strategies similar to those workers use. Real-world materials include newspapers, advertisements, correspondence, and instruction manuals. The problem-solving strategies should center on the completion of a specific task in which reading and writing are absolutely necessary. Most activities should require students to work with others, since workplace literacy often involves the exchange of information and pooling of ideas among workers.

Realistic literacy experiences

To give elementary students realistic literacy experiences, Mikulecky (1984) recommends the following activities, which appear suitable for use with fourth through sixth graders:

1. The teacher makes the following suggestions: (a) Pretend you have just won a puppy in a raffle. How are you going to take care of your new pet? Find information by calling the veterinarian, reading pamphlets, finding library books. Make a schedule, based on your readings, to show what kinds of vaccinations your pet will need. Make a feeding timetable. What types and how much exercise will the dog need? How big will it get and what size house will it need? (b) Plan to build a dog house. What materials would you use? Make a sketch or blueprint of the house you propose.

2. The children are to decide on a class mascot to be built life-size out of papier-maché. After choosing a character, the children research how to design and build the structures and how to make papier-maché. When enough information is gathered and plans written down, the children do the project.

3. Sooner or later most elementary schools have playground problems. Children can help solve them by gathering information, and considering alternative solutions. Groups of children can write, in their own words, what they see as major problems. Other groups can interview and write up opinions of teachers on playground duty. Still other students can read copies of school rules or books and pamphlets on playground and park safety. From this information, a selected group of students can compile a list of possible solutions and how each could be employed. This list can serve as a basis for school discussion and decision making.

4. The teacher arranges for students to have pen pals from different countries. Over the school year, students can plan all the details of a trip to visit pen pals. This would include using an atlas, maps, travel schedules, and estimating accommodation and travel costs. Follow-up activities could include developing ways to fund such trips.

5. Students collect local restaurant menus and advertisements for restaurant discounts. Then they draw envelopes with differing amounts of pretend money. Each student must now decide what to order with the allotted money at each of five restaurants. (pp. 256–257)

Group tasks

Mikulecky also recommends having students work together on assignments, as workers often do on the job. Here are activities for upper grade students, which might be adapted for second and third graders:

Have students use telephone directories to find business addresses.

Appoint students to write and post instructions to absent students on how to do class assignments (the teacher can check these for accuracy).

Involve students in some classroom record-keeping and form-filling.

Have students skim current periodicals for articles on specific topics. (pp. 255–256)

Problem-solving activities using several types of materials

In the following activities, students are required to read and write and collect information from more than one printed source. They also become involved in setting their own goals and in addressing an audience other than the teacher. With guidance from the teacher, many fifth and sixth graders, and perhaps some fourth graders, will be able to carry out these activities.

Students write a letter requesting information on a product.

Students choose a place they wish to visit. They gather information on costs of travel, lodging, food, etc. for the trip. (Automobile association maps and booklets are particularly helpful.)

Students interview three adults about the sorts of reading and writing they must do on their jobs. They write a letter to the principal, superintendent, or counselor explaining what one must learn to perform these jobs, or write a story for the class newspaper or magazine.

Students summarize the main idea from several different materials they have read on a topic of their choice. They make the summary into a booklet or article a younger reader could understand.

The teacher delegates authority. Students who have done well in class are allowed to determine what is needed to set up a terrarium, get a speaker to come to class and explain microcomputers, or whatever else is needed.

Students plan to accomplish a goal or personal dream. This may involve writing letters and using catalogs, maps, advertising, price lists, and reference books. A final businesslike report can outline the resources needed and the steps required to make the dream come true. (Mikulecky, 1984, p. 256)

KEY CONCEPT 2

Teachers should know how to encourage recreational reading, so students will choose to read independently for their own enjoyment and information.

ENCOURAGING RECREATIONAL READING

With this key concept, we turn our attention away from the kinds of reading which may have relevance in the workplace to the kinds of reading people do in their leisure time, or *recreational reading*. Recreational reading may be defined as "voluntary reading of self-selected materials, either for information or for pleasure" (Spiegel, 1981, p. 3).

Some children and adults may spend several hours of leisure time a day reading, while others spend only a few minutes or no time at all (e.g., Greaney, 1980). Obviously, this is because reading is only one of many recreational activities available to people away from the workplace or the school. Competing activities include watching television, listening to music, participating in sports, attending religious activities, and socializing with friends. Yet both children and adults often choose to read, and older, literate adults indicate that reading is an activity to be valued across an entire lifetime (Ribovich & Erickson, 1980).

The goal of a teacher-initiated recreational reading program is to bring students to enjoy reading and practice it as a leisure-time activity. A recreational reading program can be justified on the grounds that reading for one's own information and pleasure has value in and of itself. For the developing elementary school reader, recreational reading has many other important benefits. For example, Spiegel (1981) suggests that recreational reading helps students develop positive attitudes toward reading, expand their base of knowledge, develop automaticity in the use of word identification strategies, learn to use context cues, and increase their vocabulary.

Teachers who wish to encourage children's recreational reading will find it useful to know something about what motivates adults and children to read during their leisure time. They will also want to be aware of factors affecting people's reading of the different major print media. The adults surveyed by Guthrie and Seifert (1983) spent the most time reading newspapers, followed by books, and then magazines. Children appear to spend more time reading books and magazines and less time reading the newspaper (Guthrie, 1981). Thus, the sections below include instructional guidelines and activities for encouraging children's recreational reading of newspapers and magazines, as well as of books.

Checklist to assess attitudes toward reading

Children who develop a positive attitude toward reading are more likely to acquire a lifelong reading habit. For this reason, teachers want to be able to identify children who seem to dislike reading and need extra teacher attention to become involved in recreational reading.

Heathington and Alexander (1978) present a simple checklist teachers can use to assess children's attitudes toward reading, as shown in Figure 13.1.

FIGURE 13.1   Observation Checklist to Assess Reading Attitudes

In the two-week period has the child:

		yes	no
1.	Seemed happy when engaged in reading activities?	___	___
2.	Volunteered to read aloud in class?	___	___
3.	Read a book during free time?	___	___
4.	Mentioned reading a book at home?	___	___
5.	Chosen reading over other activities (playing games, coloring, talking, etc.)?	___	___
6.	Made requests to go to the library?	___	___
7.	Checked out books at the library?	___	___
8.	Talked about books he/she has read?	___	___
9.	Finished most of the books she/he has started?	___	___
10.	Mentioned books she/he has at home?	___	___

From "A Child-Based Observation Checklist to Assess Attitudes Toward Reading" by B. Heathington and J. E. Alexander, April 1978 in *The Reading Teacher*. Reprinted with the permission of the authors and the International Reading Association.

They developed the checklist by interviewing sixty children in grades one through six. The children were asked about the behaviors of children who liked reading, as well as those of children who disliked it. The ten checklist items stemmed from their responses.

By using this checklist, teachers can identify children who appear to have negative attitudes toward particular types of reading activities, especially in the area of recreational reading. Steps can then be taken to improve attitudes in problem areas. A two week period of observation should be sufficient, according to Heathington and Alexander. During this time, the teacher will usually have the opportunity to observe the child in both structured and free reading situations and at the library. In addition, the teacher will probably have spoken to the child about his or her recreational reading and been able to note whether the child has finished reading any books.

INSTRUCTIONAL ACTIVITIES

RECREATIONAL READING

Reading for Pleasure: Guidelines, a booklet written by Spiegel (1981), provides many practical suggestions teachers can use to promote recreational reading. Most of the ideas below are discussed in more detail in this booklet.

Helping students set goals for recreational reading

Spiegel recommends that teachers who wish to give a special emphasis to recreational reading discuss with their classes the purposes for having a recreational reading program. Teachers may establish goals for the class as a whole and have students react to these goals. Within this general framework, the students could also be asked to set their own personal goals. Figure 13.2

shows an example of some class and personal goals. In later group discussions, the teacher and children can assess how well the recreational reading program is working, and the teacher can help the children arrive at new class and personal goals.

A slightly different approach is recommended by Indrisano (1978, cited in Spiegel, 1981). Each month, the teacher asks the students to list one goal they would like to meet through reading. These goals can be as varied as the students' own interests and reading proficiency. For example, a primary grade child may set the goal of reading another book by Dr. Seuss, while an upper grade student may choose to read several magazine articles about computers. Once goals are set, the teacher aids the students in achieving their goals. The teacher may wish to encourage students to set different types of goals from one month to the next, so that they will develop a range of interests.

Initiating recreational reading

Spiegel suggests that the teacher start recreational reading by reading aloud to the class for a short period of time, perhaps ten minutes. Following this time, the children read on their own for a brief period (this time may be structured as sustained silent reading, as discussed in Chapter 6). Gradually, the period for the teacher's reading aloud may be shortened, while that for the students' silent reading is lengthened. It is recommended, however, that teachers always do some reading aloud to their classes.

Forming groups to encourage recreational reading

In *jigsaw grouping* (Aronson, Blaney, Sikes, Stephan, & Snapp, 1975, cited in Spiegel, 1981) each student belongs to two different groups. The first group is based on interest. For example, a student might be interested in sports and so

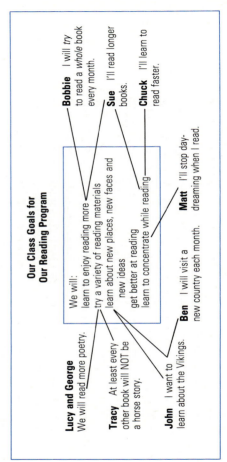

FIGURE 13.2   Class Goals Chart

joins a group reading about the history of the Olympic games. Another student interested in popular music might join a group reading about recording stars. There might be four or five such groups in a classroom. The members of each interest group read independently to collect information on their topic. They then meet to discuss what they have learned and to generate a group outline organizing major pieces of information.

After the outlines have been produced, new groups are formed. These consist of one member of each of the original interest groups (i.e., if there were four interest groups, each new group has four members). Children in the group share information following their interest group outline. This arrangement gives all children the opportunity to discuss their reading, as well as to learn information about another topic.

Interest groups might also be formed on an ad hoc basis, as two or more children seem to be interested in exploring the same topic. The volunteers meet in the group only as long as they want to, and the group can be dissolved at any time. At any given time, just one or two of these groups might be in existence in a classroom.

Another approach is to assign students to a "reading buddy" (Roeder & Lee, 1973; cited in Spiegel, 1981). The partners may read aloud to one another, present a book report prepared together, or help one another choose books for independent reading.

According to Spiegel, mixing children in different groups for the purposes of talking about their independent reading can also be a boon in classrooms with sustained silent reading. Having children meet and interact keeps interest high. Children can get ideas of what to read by talking to other children and be recognized for the reading they themselves are doing.

Voluntary sharing

Spiegel argues convincingly that students *not* be required to share the reading they have done through book reports or other means. She believes the motivation for recreational reading should be the students' own interest in reading, rather than external forces, such as teachers' requirements. On the other hand, she strongly recommends voluntary sharing, because many students enjoy sharing their reading experiences with other children and with adults. Encouraging voluntary sharing contributes to the development of a community of readers in the classroom.

Spiegel offers two sensible guidelines for voluntary sharing. According to the first guideline, teachers should be sure that the amount of time the student spends on a sharing project is much less than that spent on the original reading of the material. For example, if a child took about an hour to read a storybook, the sharing project should take up much less than an hour. Art projects such as murals or models frequently take up a great deal of time. Even though students often enjoy these projects, Spiegel points out that the projects may have more to do with artistic expression than with developing the habit of recreational reading.

The second guideline is that teachers have children use techniques for

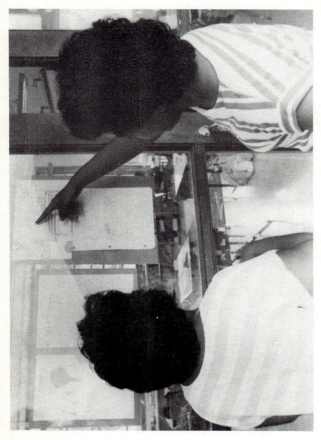

These girls get ideas for future reading from classmates' book reports, posted on the sliding glass doors.

sharing that promote the recreational reading of other students. One way to do this is to have the children add pages to a catalogue of recommended books (Criscuolo, 1977, cited in Spiegel). When children have read a book they think will be interesting to their classmates, they write a synopsis or advertisement for it on a piece of 8″ × 10″ tagboard, perhaps including an illustration. The teacher makes sure the children include information such as the title, author, and where the book may be found (e.g., school or classroom library).

Another method of sharing, which may boost the confidence and interest of a poor reader, is to have the student read aloud to younger children from a favorite book he or she has just finished. This method allows the student to read from an "easy" book that few classmates are likely to find appealing, while at the same time encouraging the reading interests of the younger children.

INSTRUCTIONAL ACTIVITIES

BOOK READING

On the average, American adults may spend only five minutes per day reading books (Guthrie, 1982). Older adults, however, appear to spend more time and read an average of almost a book a month (Ribovich & Erickson, 1980). Factors affecting the amount of book reading by adults include occupation, level of education, and leisure time available, as well as the individual's tastes and interests.

Encouraging book reading

In reviewing studies of the extent of children's book reading, Greaney (1980) reports that children appear to do the greatest amount of reading near the end of elementary school. After this they seem to do less and less leisure reading, especially of books. Children from more privileged backgrounds, with better educated parents, seem to read books more than those from working class backgrounds. Children's level of reading proficiency also appears to affect how much they read books, with poor readers doing much less than good readers.

Children seem to spend surprisingly little time reading books in comparison to time spent on other leisure time activities. Fifty percent of the fifth graders studied by Fielding, Wilson, and Anderson (in press) read books for less than four minutes a day, while 30 percent read only two minutes a day or less and 10 percent never reported reading a book at all. A majority of the children spent 1 percent or less of their free time reading books.

The children were perfectly capable of reading books, for example, spending two hours or more reading when they had to prepare a book report. But on the average, children read books on only one day in five. "The problem," according to Fielding et al., "is not that students can't read, but that on most days they don't."

Fielding et al. suggest that substantial increases in reading achievement might be seen if children could be encouraged to read books for even ten minutes per day. Of all the children's leisure-time activities, book reading was found to be the single best predictor of reading achievement as measured by standardized tests, of size of vocabulary, and of gains in reading achievement from the second to fifth grade.

Why should book reading, in particular, be so strongly related to overall reading proficiency? First, according to Fielding et al, book reading can build background knowledge of many different topics. Second, it can acquaint children with the various structures of narrative and expository text. When reading tradebooks, children can gain experience with well-organized, well-written text, rich in information. This experience is not necessarily gained in work with basal readers and content area textbooks. Third, vocabulary growth is promoted in the manner discussed in Chapter 4. Finally, book reading serves as self-initiated practice, an opportunity for children to orchestrate all of the reading skills they have been taught, so that use of these skills becomes automatic.

Fielding et al. looked at the question of why some children become avid readers. They discovered that parents of avid readers created environments where reading would seem attractive to their children, but otherwise did not worry too much about it. For example, the parents made sure there were many books in the home and acted as models because they themselves enjoyed reading, but they did not have scheduled times for the children to read.

Interviews with the young avid readers themselves revealed other factors contributing to their interest in reading books.

Most interesting was that avid readers seemed to belong to *communities of readers.* They reported talking to peers, siblings, parents, or teachers about books they had read and getting recommendations for future reading from these same people. The avid readers never seemed to be at a loss for something to read. Though only a few of them read more than one book at a time, they all had plans for what they would read next.

The avid readers were more aware than their parents of past or present teachers' influence on their reading habits. They mentioned teachers having books available in the classroom, reading out loud to the class, recommending books to them, talking to them about books they had read, requiring them to read a certain number of books in a grading period, or just being such good teachers that children came to love reading by being in their classes. According to the children themselves, teachers can have a significant influence on the development of avid reading.

A noteworthy observation from the children's interviews is their admission that, except for one or two of them, reading is not always their number-one favorite way to spend free time. Watching television, playing video or computer games, and participating in sports were often favored over reading. But for these children, reading remained a frequent activity, perhaps because it is something they can do at any time, without involving anyone else. As one child put it, "It's always been there, and it always will be."

Making books accessible

In promoting children's independent reading of books, Fielding et al. suggest that the first step is to increase the children's access to books. Setting up a classroom library, as described in Chapter 12, can be a big help, particularly if

To give children extra time to find books they will enjoy reading, this girl's teacher takes a small group to the library every day at recess.

the teacher gives brief talks to "sell" children on the books being placed there. "Flooding" classrooms with books is also a powerful technique (for more information about book floods, see Chapter 9).

Children may also gain access to books during visits to school or community libraries, but these do not offer the convenience of a classroom library. For example, as Fielding et al. point out, children may be absent on the day the class visits the library, or find that they are not really enjoying the books borrowed. With a classroom library, these problems do not arise because books can be borrowed or exchanged at any time.

If the school or community library is the primary source of books, special steps may have to be taken to be sure that less avid readers have suitable books. Spiegel (1981) points out that some children may benefit from extra time to browse among books in the school library. For these children, a brief, once-a-week class visit may not allow enough time for appropriate books to be located.

Helping children to build up a small home library may also increase book reading. Spiegel suggests that teachers look into ways that children can obtain books at little or no cost. The federally funded Reading is Fundamental (RIF) program, which has the goal of distributing free books to children, operates in many communities. Also, children may order books inexpensively through book clubs. Some textbooks being discarded by the school may provide children with books for their home libraries. Teachers may organize sessions when the children may swap books with one another. Lowe (1977, cited in Spiegel) describes one method for conducting a book swap. The swapping is done in a single large room. The number of books each child brings to the room is recorded. He or she is then allowed to take that same number of books from the room.

Summer loss of reading proficiency is sometimes of concern to teachers, particularly those who work with children from low-income families. Crowell and Klein (1981) suggest that giving these children access to books over the summer vacation is one way to prevent a decline in reading proficiency. They designed a program which involved mailing paperback books to children who had just completed the first and second grades. Children received books at their own reading levels, which ranged from readiness to the third grade. One book was mailed each week for ten weeks during the summer vacation, and the children were allowed to keep the books. All of the children appeared to benefit from the program, but positive effects were greater for the first graders.

A procedure like the one used by Crowell and Klein is a good way to ensure that children have reading material over the summer, a natural extension to a recreational reading program carried out during the school year. Parents who ask what they can do to help their children over the summer could be told to take the children on regular visits to the library, help them select and purchase a number of paperback books, and otherwise make sure they have plenty of high-interest reading material.

Helping children find interesting books

Some children may be doing little book reading because they are having trouble finding books they like. In this case, mechanisms should be used which allow the teacher and classmates to assist them in finding books they will enjoy. Spiegel suggests that teachers keep a folder where students can record the kind of reading material they would like to find. Periodically, the teacher can give the child help in locating these materials or ask the librarian to do so.

The teacher could also have the children complete brief forms describing their reading interests, as recommended by Criscuolo (1977, cited in Spiegel) and shown in Figure 13.3. The forms can be posted so that the children will be aware of one another's interests and can let classmates know of relevant books. This method engages students in the task of "reading-to-assess" since they are deciding whether particular books match a classmate's interests. Children also become naturally involved in supporting one another's recreational reading.

Teachers should also be aware of books which can turn reluctant readers into avid readers. Being able to make suitable recommendations may be especially important for teachers working with upper elementary students who have had difficulty learning to read. Bennett and Bennett (1982) provide a bibliography of humorous children's books found to be favored by fourth, fifth and sixth graders. Other high-interest books are recommended by Cunningham (1983a, 1983b). In the first article she discusses books where children can choose their own adventures, while in the second she identifies books children can read for information, for carrying out projects, or for entertainment and escape.

Teachers are sometimes interested in expanding children's reading interests and leading them to read more challenging books. Spiegel (1981) takes the position that teachers' first priority should be to make sure that children *will* read. In her view, improving the quality of children's book reading is of less importance, in part because most children prefer choosing books for themselves and may become less motivated to read if teachers seem to be forcing specific books on them. To get around this problem, Spiegel recommends that the teacher use a group rather than individual approach. For example, the

<u>**FIGURE 13.3**</u>   *Reading Interest Form*

Name _____

Hobbies _____

Favorite TV Program _____

Last Book I Read _____

Types of Books I Like _____

Age _____

INSTRUCTIONAL ACTIVITIES

NEWSPAPER READING

teacher can introduce the whole class to a variety of challenging books, differing in genre and topic from those most children are choosing to read. The teacher may give brief book talks or read short sections of the new books out loud. By using procedures such as this one, the teacher can get around the problem of appearing to prescribe a certain book for a certain child.

It is likely that almost all American adults read the newspaper, and according to Guthrie (1981), 60 to 70 percent of adults in the United States say they read the newspaper daily. By comparison, few children appear to read the newspaper every day: 5 percent of 6-year-olds, 10 percent of 9-year-olds, and 40 percent of 12-year-olds. The newspaper content children choose to read changes as they grow older. Boys start by reading the comics, then add sports, and then the news. Girls begin with the comics, then add information relevant to personal and social development and the news.

According to Guthrie, teachers can increase children's newspaper reading by using the newspaper in classroom activities. Presumably, homework assignments which required use of the newspaper would have similar effects. Both school and home newspaper activities could be designed to promote children's interest in contents, such as national and local news, which they generally would not read on their own.

Stimulating interest in current events

Frequently, teachers are able to generate a great deal of interest in current events in classes from the third grade on up. An effective technique is to hold class discussions based on information in the newspaper and to allow children to share and post news articles. In almost every community, children's interest in local news can be stimulated by having them begin by reading about issues of concern to their families and neighbors. For example, a farming community may be experiencing a shortage of water, or a suburban community may be concerned about the lack of ambulance service to the nearest city hospital. At other times, the children's interest may be captured by the national news, for example, in the year of a presidential election. Older children may become involved in clipping newspaper articles on international news, perhaps for a particular country being covered in a social studies unit.

Children who do not have access to a newspaper at home may be encouraged to read the newspaper if one is delivered to the classroom. At the end of the school day, these children might be allowed to take sections home to read.

Homework assignments

Criscuolo (1981) suggests a number of homework assignments which encourage children to read the newspaper. He recommends giving a newspaper assignment perhaps once a week, with about ten minutes of work for primary grade students and twenty minutes for sixth graders. Here are three ideas:

Sale items. Ask children to select one of their possessions they would like to sell. As a homework assignment, have them read some classified ads under Merchandise for Sale to see what kind of information is given. Have them count the words in a four-line ad and write a four-line ad that will help sell their items. When the children turn in their ads, let them share them with each other.

Check the reviews. Reviews of current books and movies are printed in the newspaper. Ask the children to write a review of a recently published book they've read or a newly released movie they've seen. As a homework assignment, have them cut out the reviews published in their newspapers and compare them to their own written reviews.

Celebrities. Ask children to select someone who is frequently in the news, e.g., an entertainer or a national figure. Ask them to keep a scrapbook of clippings on the exploits or experiences of the famous personality they select. As a follow-up activity, children can go to the library and write a biographical sketch of this famous person using a variety of reference aids. (pp. 921–922)

INSTRUCTIONAL ACTIVITIES

MAGAZINE READING

Probably over 90 percent of American adults read magazines (e.g., Monteith, 1981; Ribovich & Erickson, 1980). In reviewing evidence of children's interests in magazines, Monteith (1981) reports that quite a number of magazines for young people are currently being published, and several are among the top 100 in the country in terms of subscriptions and newsstand sales. These include *Mad Magazine, Boy's Life, Seventeen Magazine,* and *Highlights for Children.* Children seem to be interested primarily in magazines containing either nonfiction or humor. Even poor readers appear to be motivated to read magazines, including those such as *Sports Illustrated* or *People* which consist of text they are likely to find quite difficult. Monteith suggests that teachers should capitalize on children's interests in magazines as a natural way of developing motivation and encouraging the habit of recreational reading. Interests developed in reading magazine articles may also lead children to read books on the same topics.

Classroom use of magazines

Occasionally, the teacher may conduct either large or small group reading lessons based on high-interest magazine articles instead of basal reader selections or other texts. For example, articles from the *Weekly Reader* may be read and discussed by the whole class. With a small group of proficient readers, even articles from magazines for adults, such as *Reader's Digest*, may be used. Often, magazine articles are suitable for content area reading lessons. For example, an article from *Ranger Rick* may fit well in a science unit.

Some children may not have access to magazines at home. If the teacher has subscriptions to children's magazines, copies of past issues could be sent home with these children.

Homework assignments

Unlike most newspapers, many magazines are designed to appeal to readers with certain special interests. Thus, homework assignments involving magazines might serve the purpose of giving children time to become familiar with magazines they might enjoy reading. The teacher could introduce the home-work assignment by having the children discuss interests, such as jokes, wild animals, fashion, or sports, which might be covered in magazine articles. Children can suggest magazines they already know of which contain such articles, and other magazines might be sought at the library. The children could then read one or two articles for homework and share the information learned with the class.

ENCOURAGING LITERACY BY USING OTHER RESOURCES IN THE SCHOOL

In this section we discuss two means the teacher can use to strengthen the classroom reading program. The first involves using the library, and the second, sharing reading and writing experiences with students in other classes. These are both ways of encouraging literacy within school settings, but by making use of resources beyond the walls of a single classroom.

Making use of the school or community library

Class visits to the school or community library are regularly scheduled events in many schools. These visits provide children with the opportunity to learn about the wide range of books and other reading materials available to them. Keep in mind that visits to the library can serve two broad goals of the classroom reading program. They can be a way of furthering children's appreciation of literature and enjoyment of books. They can also be a way of strengthening study skills and the ability to work with expository text.

The teacher should try to work together with the librarian to develop plans for familiarizing students with the library so that these goals can be achieved. In the case of recreational reading, the teacher could ask the librarian for suggestions about books and authors the children might find especially interesting. In the classroom, the teacher could then read several of these books, or parts of them, to the children, before their next visit to the library. If they are interested in them, the children could then be reminded to look for these books while they are at the library. Some librarians carry out programs like this, reading aloud or giving book talks in the library itself.

The teacher and librarian can also work together to help the children learn basic library skills, such as how to use the card catalogue or the *Reader's Guide to Periodical Literature* to locate materials of interest, and where in the library those materials are located. In some libraries information is stored on microfiche or computers, and children may also be taught to look up information by using these media. The children will need to learn how to check out and return materials to the library, and they should also be made aware that the librarian is available to answer their questions.

Once the children have these basic library skills, the teacher and librarian can also carry out a coordinated program of helping the children develop library research skills. For example, suppose that the class is working on a unit about the different states in the union, and that each child in the class is going to prepare a report on a different state. The teacher might arrange with the librarian to have small groups of children visit the library and work independently, locating sources of information and taking notes for their reports. A librarian who knows in advance the content the children are studying and the research skills they will be required to use can be a valuable resource to the children.

In other cases, the teacher may not be able to send the children to the library but will want them to work with materials in the classroom. The librarian might be able to help the teacher with information about materials suitable for this purpose.

Sharing with students in other classes

In Chapters 6 and 8 we mentioned how children in the classroom might form a *community of readers*, exchanging information about books they each enjoyed reading. This community can be extended beyond a single class, if the children share the joys of reading with students in other classes.

Sharing a language experience library. This activity, developed by Powers (1981), allows children to share books with other classes and, at the same time, to develop library skills. A language experience library consists of books (stories put into booklets) the children have written themselves, following the language experience approach, as discussed in Chapters 2 and 11. Powers worked with a class of first graders, but the activity can be adapted for use with older children, as well.

From start to finish, the process of writing the books and of learning about the library takes about six weeks. Two different sets of goals are pursued with the children. The first set involves acquainting the children with different genres of literature, such as folktales, fairy tales, and poetry. The second involves teaching the children about how libraries work.

Starting off. For the first set of goals, begin by reading books of different genres aloud and discussing them with the children. Then have the children start writing their own stories. Powers had the children begin with group language experience stories, patterned after folktales, before having them write stories individually.

For the second set of goals, prepare the children to visit the library. Before going there, have the children generate a list of questions. For example, Powers' students wanted to know if the library had books about such topics as monsters and baseball; where the books of folktales were located; how they could take books out of the library; and what kind of system was used for organizing the books. Begin with a visit to the school library. Follow up, if possible, with a visit to the public library. With the help of librarians, introduce the children to the card catalog and the concept of alphabetical order, and the terms fiction and nonfiction. Be sure to discuss the information learned with the children when you are back in the classroom.

Putting the library together. At this point, the two sets of goals start to converge. The class is now ready to begin putting together its own library. Discuss with the children what will be needed for a classroom library, beginning with the space for keeping the books and how it should be arranged.

Then have the children begin writing the stories and making the books for the library. Powers had her students dictate stories, but the children could, of course, write the stories themselves, if they are able to. Try to have each child contribute at least one story, and be sure to accept all of their work. Have the children make books from their stories, for example, by stitching the pages between cardboard covers. To prepare the books, Powers worked with her class about one to two hours a day for a period of three weeks. Her 23 first graders wrote 35 books.

Show the children how to paste pockets in the completed books and make a card for each one. Develop some kind of card catalog system. For example, Powers' students used the initial of the author's last name in cataloging fiction books and a Dewey Decimal number assigned by the school librarian for nonfiction books.

Running the library. Discuss with the children the different kinds of jobs they will need to do to run the library. Encourage them to think the issues through on their own. The children in Powers' class worked out the following jobs:

(1) The *bringers* went to the visiting class and brought the students to the [class-room] library. Class visits were prearranged. (2) The *reference librarians* showed the children the books and answered questions about the kinds of books available in our library. (3) The *check out librarians* showed the children how to sign out the books. They stamped the due date on the card and in the book and then filed the cards alphabetically in the card box. (4) *Readers* were assigned to read to the kindergarten children, but all children were called upon at times to read their own books to older children. (5) *Check in librarians* took the returned books from the book box and put the cards back in the books. (6) *Returners* put the books back on the shelf and did other necessary straightening.   (Powers, 1981, p. 894)

Keep the library open for about a week. Powers and her students opened their library for six days, 45 minutes in the morning and 45 minutes in the afternoon. Be sure to allow time for the children to share their experiences with the class. Such topics as how to deal with older and younger children may require considerable discussion. If possible, schedule a visit by a class of younger children first, so that your students will develop some confidence. Have visits by classes of older students occur after this. Older students may also wish to read stories of their own to your class. Invite the principal, school librarian, resource room teachers, and other adults to visit the class library, too.

After the children have had the opportunity to work at a number of different jobs in the library, help the children close the library and allow them to take their own books home. As a follow-up activity, if the children are interested, have them write about working in the library and what they learned.

Other ways of sharing books with other classes. Children may also be interested in giving *book talks*. During a book talk, a student tells about a book he or she especially enjoyed reading, with the aim of encouraging other students to read the book, too. A book talk might include reading a short portion of the book aloud. Begin by setting aside a time each week when your students can give book talks to their classmates. After they become familiar with this routine, arrange for them to give their book talks to another class.

Children can share the books they have written and published with students in other classes. For example, fourth and fifth graders might be allowed to read their own published books aloud to a class of first graders. After reading, they can receive comments and answer questions from the younger children. Experiences such as these help children to feel pride in their literary accomplishments. There can be benefits, too, for the younger children, who may be motivated to do more reading and writing of their own.

As described in Chapter 6, children can serve as tutors to younger chil-dren, by reading published books or their own writing aloud. The older children can also encourage the younger ones to read aloud and to write. Refer to Nevi (1983) for a discussion of how cross-age tutoring can be beneficial to the tutor.

KEY CONCEPT 4

Teachers should foster students' reading ability and interest by strengthening connections between reading at home and at school.

ENCOURAGING LITERACY BY MAKING CONNECTIONS TO THE HOME

As Taylor's (1983) work shows, the home provides many children with the foundation for becoming literate. Teachers should be aware of ways in which children's learning to read in school may interact with literacy experiences already available in the home. As pointed out in Chapter 1, it is important for the school to broaden children's literacy experiences and not to narrow them. For this reason, teachers should be sensitive to the fact that communication needs to flow in both directions. That is, information about children's school progress in learning to read needs to be sent to parents, but parents should also be encouraged to communicate with teachers about their knowledge of their children's progress. For example, children sometimes enter school already knowing how to read a number of storybooks. Asking parents for information like this may enable teachers to plan more challenging activities for certain children.

In general, the teacher should be sensitive to children's family circumstances and look for signs that parents are interested in encouraging their children's reading at home. Suggestions made in response to a parent's request are quite likely to be followed. On the other hand, in some instances parents may be put off by uninvited suggestions which they see as conflicting with family routines or values.

In some cases, too, the teacher may find that it is another family member, perhaps a grandparent or an older sister or brother, rather than a parent, who is willing and able to support the child's recreational reading. Sometimes it is a neighbor, or the parent of another child in the class, who can be enlisted to take a child to the library. In some cases, however, the teacher should be aware that a high degree of home support for reading is not readily available to particular children. An extra dose of teacher attention may be the key to encouraging the recreational reading of these children.

Discussed below are two major means that teachers can use to strengthen the connections between the home and school for the purpose of improving children's opportunities for learning to read. These have to do with communicating with parents and enlisting parents' help in encouraging children's recreational reading by reading aloud to them, taking them to the library on a regular basis, and being involved in classroom activities. Many of the same ideas are easily adapted to situations where the teacher is trying to work with a family member other than the child's parents.

Communicating with parents about children's learning to read

Written communication. Schools generally rely on report cards as the chief means of communicating with parents about children's progress in learning to read, as well as in other academic and social areas. Because report cards are usually sent home only about four times a year, they generally can provide only a very broad overview of children's accomplishments. Thus, the teacher will probably wish to supplement report cards with other written reports to parents.

One option is *progress letters*, in which the teacher can describe in more detail the kinds of stories or expository selections the child is able to comprehend, some of the areas in which new vocabulary has been learned, and the kinds of books the child seems interested in reading on his or her own. Brief notes may be sent home with certain children on days when they have accomplished something special (for example, read their first published book to the class).

The teacher might also wish to send a letter home describing the goals of the classroom reading program and the types of activities planned for the children. Or the children themselves may write letters to their parents, describing their reading and writing activities and perhaps stapling to the letter a sample of work recently completed. Refer to Vukelich (1984) for further discussion of these and other ways of communicating with parents in writing.

Conferences, open houses, and classroom visits.   While the work schedule of many parents makes it difficult for them to serve as classroom volunteers, they often are able to attend conferences and open houses. In many schools, parent conferences are scheduled at two times during the year (practical guidelines for scheduling and planning parent conferences are given by Granowsky, Rose, & Barton, 1983). On these occasions parents usually meet with the teacher to discuss their child's progress. The child's progress in learning to read, of course, should be an important part of this discussion. The teacher should be sure to give parents the chance to raise questions (for a listing of frequently asked questions and ideas for sensible responses, see Koppman, 1983).

Showing parents samples of the selections the child is reading and of the child's writing often gives them a better idea of how the child is progressing. Parents may be able to appreciate the progress a child has made if they are shown materials the child was working with earlier in the year, and then have the opportunity to contrast them with materials the child is presently using. The teacher should encourage parents to appreciate their children as individuals, with unique abilities and interests in reading and writing, and discourage what may be inappropriate comparisons with other children.

Open houses can serve as an occasion for the teacher to explain the classroom reading program to the parents as a group. The teacher may wish to display the children's reading materials, basal readers as well as content area textbooks and tradebooks, and have samples of the children's writing in folders for their parents to peruse.

Some schools hold "back to school" sessions when parents come to school and participate with their children in typical school activities. Or parents can be invited to visit the classroom during the school day to observe reading and writing activities. The teacher, principal, or reading specialist should try to be available to meet with the parents as the visit is being concluded, to answer any questions.

Conferences, open houses, and other visits by parents may provide the teacher with opportunities to offer suggestions about ways that reading and writing can be encouraged at home. Figure 13.4 shows the suggestions most frequently made, according to Vukelich (1984).

Parental concerns

Homework. Many parents want even their primary grade children to be given homework assignments and are happy to help with homework. Teachers should be certain to design homework to support the major goals of the classroom reading program, not to serve as busywork, and to help parents understand the reasons for giving certain kinds of homework assignments rather than others.

Homework will generally prove most valuable if it encourages children to use reading and writing in real-world ways. For example, independent reading of a book chosen by the child is a good substitute for paper-and-pencil activities. As mentioned earlier, another sound homework activity is to have the child read the newspaper for particular kinds of information. Corresponding with a pen pal is another example of a type of homework that teaches

---

FIGURE 13.4   *Suggestions Most Frequently Made for Parent Reading Involvement*

Activity or behavior	Number of times suggested, out of 24
Read to your child	22
Be a good literate model	14
Provide books, magazines, etc. for the child to read	13
Build a reading atmosphere at home (place, time, library area)	11
Talk and listen to your child	7
Exemplify a positive attitude toward reading, including praising your child for reading	7
Provide experiences for children that are reading related, e.g., library trips, or that can be used to stimulate interest in reading	7
Read environmental signs; capture reading opportunities in the environment	5
Provide contact with paper and pencils	4
Be aware of your child's interests	4
Point out similarity and differences in objects in the environment	4

Figure from "Parents' Role in the Reading Process" by Carol Vukelich, February 1984 in *The Reading Teacher*. Reprinted with permission of Carol Vukelich and the International Reading Association.

children about an important use of literacy. Parents could also help children write letters to relatives and friends. Still another possibility is to have children write in journals (refer to Chapter 8).

Television viewing. Teachers may wish to alert concerned parents to the possibly negative effects of a great amount of television viewing on children's reading achievement. In a metaanalysis of 23 studies, Williams, Haertel, Haertel, and Walberg (1982) found a small but consistently negative relationship between hours of television viewing and school achievement. There seems to be no problem at all if children watch television for up to ten hours per week. However, watching television for longer amounts of time is related to lower levels of school achievement, especially for girls and for children of higher ability.

In general, the time children spend watching television is far greater than that spent reading books. The children studied by Fielding, Wilson, and Anderson (in press), for example, spent an average of two hours a day watching television, compared to only four minutes reading books.

Of course, the amount of time children spend watching television may reflect other home values and does not necessarily indicate a negative view toward reading and books. While teachers should handle the issue carefully, they might wish to encourage parents to monitor the amount of time their children spend watching television, to be sure that there is adequate time for recreational reading and homework. Telfer and Kann (1984) suggest that it may also be important for teachers and parents to be concerned about the amount of time students spend listening to the radio, records, and tapes.

Literate home environment. The worries that some parents have about supporting their children's learning to read at home may be reduced if teachers help them understand that one of the best things they can do is simply continue modeling for their children the many uses of literacy in the home. Parents who read the newspaper, make shopping lists, write letters, or talk about favorite books are creating a literate home environment. In this perfectly natural way, they are giving their children the opportunity to see how valuable reading and writing can be in everyday life.

Involving parents in a recreational reading program

Introducing the program. Spiegel (1981) reminds us that parents may need to be convinced of the value of a recreational reading program. She warns that teachers may need to clarify for some parents the fact that recreational reading is not a frill but a key component in a complete developmental reading program. To gain the support of parents, teachers may wish to send out a series of short newsletters explaining the reasons for having a recreational reading program and how it will work. Spiegel offers the following suggestions:

Newsletter 1. Explanation of what a recreational reading program is and how it will work in your class. Schedule of what information will be contained in subsequent newsletters.

Newsletter 2 (two days later). Rationale for having a recreational reading program, with emphasis on how it fits into the basic curriculum. Short statement of support from your principal and reading teacher.

Newsletter 3 (two days later). List of suggestions of ways parents can help support the program through their efforts at home.

Newsletter 4 (two days later). List of ways parents can volunteer their time in the classroom to support this program.   (p. 58)

The recreational reading program could also be discussed at an open house and during parent conferences. As Spiegel points out, asking parents to support recreational reading gives them a positive, pleasant, and low-pressure way of helping their children at home.

Parents' reading aloud to children.   Judging from teachers' reports, having parents read aloud to their children, or listen to their children read, is probably the most common method of parent involvement (Epstein & Becker, 1982). For the purposes of promoting recreational reading, this practice has much to recommend it. Many parents are reading aloud to their young children already, and others find that they can easily fit it into the family's routine. However, parents may differ in the way that they handle the reading aloud of storybooks. For example, research by Heath (1982) suggests that some parents may attempt to relate story ideas to the children's own experiences, while others do not. Heath also found that some parents expect their children to be able to answer questions about the story, while others do not. Findings such as these suggest that parents' reading aloud of storybooks may have a number of different effects on their children's learning to read (Teale, 1981).

Perhaps the best approach the teacher can take is to offer parents suggestions about books their children might especially enjoy hearing. This would seem preferable to recommending specific procedures that parents should follow in reading stories to their children, or a particular schedule or amount of reading to be done. As mentioned in Chapter 11, a good place to gather ideas is from the lists of Children's Choices published in *The Reading Teacher*.

Making use of the library.   Another step teachers can take is to encourage parents to take their children to the library. Specifically, teachers may be able to collect applications for library cards, provide parents with information on the location and hours of public libraries, and pass on announcements of special events (such as story hours). Teachers may also give parents ideas about books their children would enjoy borrowing. For example, parents of reluctant readers might appreciate knowing about books their children have enjoyed, so they can help them find other books by the same authors.

Asking children to involve their parents. The teacher may also encourage children to involve their parents if it seems appropriate to do so. For example, when the children have borrowed books from the library, the teacher may ask them to see if their parents would be interested in hearing them read aloud. Or the child might be asked to read to a younger sibling for a few minutes. Older children might be asked to see if their parents would be interested in discussing a library book with them.

Using parents' help in the classroom. Some easy ways to involve parents who volunteer to help in the classroom are the following: Parents may be asked to read aloud to the whole class or to small groups of children, or to listen to children read aloud from favorite books. Or parents may wish to begin simply by serving as a second adult model (in addition to the teacher) during sustained silent reading. Later, they may be willing to give book talks. Parents are often willing to accompany the class on visits to the public library, and then to help the children select and sign out books.

Some parents would like to assist in the classroom but are unable to do so because of work or family responsibilities. These parents, however, may be able to help collect materials for the classroom library. Among contributions many teachers welcome are children's books, old sets of encyclopedias, and magazines such as *National Geographic.*

SUMMARY

Studies of reading in the community show us that most adults do more reading in the workplace than anywhere else. In the first key concept we discussed this fact further. We also looked at the instructional implications growing from it, which is that teachers will probably want to give students reading experiences that in some way parallel those of the workplace, for example, tasks which require reading-to-do and reading-to-assess. Reading activities involving students in sharing ideas and in working with several types of material, also common features of reading in the workplace, were described as well.

The value of promoting the habit of recreational reading was discussed under the second key concept. We described adult and child patterns in the leisure reading of books, newspapers, and magazines, along with instructional activities designed to encourage children's recreational reading. These ranged from working with students to set goals for recreational reading, to making books accessible to children, to involving students in encouraging the recreational reading of their peers.

In the third key concept we looked at ideas for building library activities into the classroom reading program. These included using the school library's help and having children run their own library within the classroom. We also discussed the sharing of books with children in other classes as a means of extending the community of readers beyond a single classroom.

The topic of the fourth key concept was fostering reading by strengthening connections between the home and school. We discussed the importance of communicating with parents about the classroom reading program and their child's progress in learning to read. We then provided suggestions parents might be willing to follow to boost a student's reading development and interest in reading. Particular attention was given to methods of involving parents in promoting children's recreational reading.

BIBLIOGRAPHY

REFERENCES

Aronson, E., Blaney, N., Sikes, J., Stephan, C., & Snapp, M. (1975). The jigsaw route to learning and liking. *Psychology Today, 8*, 43–50. [cited in Spiegel, 1981]

Bennett, J. E., & Bennett, P. (1982) What's so funny? Action research and bibliography of humorous children's books—1975-1980. *Reading Teacher, 35*, 924-927.

Criscuolo, N. P. (1977). Book reports: Twelve creative alternatives. *Reading Teacher, 30* (8), 893-895.

Criscuolo, N. P. (1981). Creative homework with the newspaper. *Reading Teacher, 34* (8), 921-922.

Crowell, D. C., & Klein, T. W. (1981). Preventing summer loss of reading skills among primary children. *Reading Teacher, 34* (5), 561-564.

Cunningham, P. (1983a). The clip sheet: Adventures in reading and writing. *Reading Teacher, 36* (6), 578-581.

Cunningham, P. (1983b). The clip sheet: Why should I read? *Reading Teacher, 36* (7), 698-700.

Diehl, W. A., & Mikulecky, L. (1980). The nature of reading at work. *Journal of Reading, 24,* 221-227.

Epstein, J. L., & Becker, H. J. (1982). Teachers' reported practices of parent involvement: Problems and possibilities. *Elementary School Journal, 83* (2), 103-113.

Fielding, L. G., Wilson, P. T., & Anderson, R. C. (in press). A new focus on free reading: The role of trade books in reading instruction. In T. E. Raphael (Ed.), *Contexts of school-based literacy.* New York: Random House.

Granowsky, A., Rose, A., & Barton, N. (1983). Parents as partners in education. Ginn Occasional Papers, Writings in reading and language arts, No. 2. Columbus, OH: Ginn.

Greaney, V. (1980). Factors related to amount and type of leisure time reading. *Reading Research Quarterly, 15* (3), 337-357.

Guthrie, J. T. (1981). Acquisition of newspaper readership. *Reading Teacher, 34,* 616-618.

Guthrie, J. T. (1982). Corporate education for the electronic culture. *Journal of Reading, 25,* 492-495.

Guthrie, J. T., & Seifert, M. (1983). Profiles of reading activity in a community, *Journal of Reading, 26* (6), 498-508.

Heath, S. B. (1982). What no bedtime story means: Narrative skills at home and school. *Language in Society, 11* (2), 49-76.

Heathington, B. S., and Alexander, J. E. (1978). A child-based observation checklist to assess attitudes toward reading. *Reading Teacher, 31* (7), 769-771.

Indrisano, R. (1978). Reading: What about those who can read but don't? *Instructor, 87,* 94-98. [cited in Spiegel, 1981]

Koppman, P. S. (1983). Questions parents ask—Answers teachers give. Ginn Occasional Papers, Writings in reading and language arts, No.16. Columbus, OH: Ginn.

Lowe, B. R. (1977). Book swap shop. *Instructor, 87,* 47. [cited in Spiegel, 1981]

Mikulecky, L. (1982). Job literacy: The relationship between school preparation and workplace actuality. *Reading Research Quarterly, 17,* 400-417.

Mikulecky, L. (1984). Preparing students for workplace literacy demands. *Journal of Reading, 28* (3), 253-257.

Monteith, M. K. (1981). The magazine habit. *Language Arts, 58,* 965-969.

Nevi, C.N. (1983). Cross-age tutoring: Why does it help the tutors? *Reading Teacher, 36* (9), 892-898.

Powers, A. (1981). Sharing a language experience library with the whole school. *Reading Teacher, 34* (8), 892-895.

Ribovich, J. K., & Erickson, L. (1980). A study of lifelong reading with implications for instructional programs. *Journal of Reading, 24,* 20-26.

Roeder, H. H., & Lee, N. (1973). Twenty-five teacher-tested ways to encourage voluntary reading. *Reading Teacher, 27,* (1), 48-50.

Spiegel, D. L. (1981). *Reading for pleasure: Guidelines.* Newark, DE: International Reading Association.

Sticht, T. G. (1977). Comprehending reading at work. In M. A. Just & P. A. Carpenter (Eds.), *Cognitive processes in comprehension.* Hillsdale, NJ: Erlbaum.

Taylor, D. (1983). *Family literacy: Young children learning to read and write.* Exeter, NH: Heinemann.

Teale, W. H. (1981). Parents reading to their children: What we know and need to know. *Language Arts, 58* (8), 902-912.

Telfer, R. J., & Kann, R. S. (1984). Reading achievement, free reading, watching TV, and listening to music. *Journal of Reading, 27* (6), 536-539.

Vukelich, C. (1984). Parents' role in the reading process: A review of practical suggestions and ways to communicate with parents. *Reading Teacher, 37* (6), 472-477.

Williams, P. A., Haertel, E. H., Haertel, G. D., & Walberg, H. J. (1982). The impact of leisure-time television on school learning: A research synthesis. *American Educational Research Journal, 19,* 19-50.

FURTHER READINGS

Heath, S. B. (1980). The functions and uses of literacy. *Journal of Communication, 30* (1), 123-35.

Ingham, J. (1981). *Books and reading development.* London: Heinemann.

Lapp, D., & Flood, J. (1983). Developing students' interest in reading. Chapter 11 in *Teaching reading to every child.* New York: Macmillan.

Larrick, N. (1980). *A parents' guide to children's reading.* Garden City, NY: Doubleday.

Lehr, F. (1982). Identifying and assessing reading attitudes. *Journal of Reading, 26* (1), 80-83.

Suhor, C. (1984). The role of print as a medium in our society. In A. C. Purves & O. Niles (Eds.), *Becoming readers in a complex society.* 83rd yearbook of the National Society for the Study of Education. Chicago: University of Chicago Press.

Acknowledgments

This is an extension of the copyright page.

From *The Little Park* by Dale Fife. Reprinted by permission of Curtis Brown Ltd. © 1973 by Dale Fife.

From "Vocabulary Language and Prediction" by Karen D. Wood and Nora Robinson, January 1983, *The Reading Teacher*. Reprinted by permission of the authors and the International Reading Association.

From "Oral Reading for Meaning" by Barbara Taylor and Linda Nosbush, December 1983, *The Reading Teacher*. Reprinted by permission of the authors and the International Reading Association.

From "Preparing Students for Workplace Literacy Demands" by Larry Mikulecky, December 1984, *Journal of Reading*. Reprinted by permission of the author and the International Reading Association.

From "Sharing a Language Experience Library with the Whole School" by Anne Powers, May 1984, *The Reading Teacher*. Reprinted by permission of the author and the International Reading Association.

From "Concept Definition: A Key to Improving Students' Vocabulary" by Robert M. Schwartz and Taffy E. Raphael, *The Reading Teacher*, November 1985. Reprinted with permission of the authors and the International Reading Association.

Photo Credits

Elizabeth Crews: pages 38, 91, 171

Elizabeth Crews/Stock Boston: page 375

Robert G. Gaylord: page 424

IBM Corporation: page 375

Eugene Kam: pages 115, 148, 173, 185, 202, 204, 249, 251, 266, 281, 303, 327, 341, 370, 399, 414, 433, 435

Jean-Claude Lejeune: page 17

Howard Simmons: page 151

Scott, Foresman: pages 11, 33, 77, 100, 167

Index

Also Available from
Scott, Foresman and Company
Good Year Books

Good Year Books are reproducible resource and activity books for teachers and parents of students in preschool through grade 12. Written by experienced educators, Good Year Books are filled with class-tested ideas, teaching strategies and methods, and fun-to-do activities for every basic curriculum area. They also contain enrichment materials and activities that help extend a child's learning experiences beyond the classroom.

Good Year Books address many educational needs in both formal and informal settings. They have been used widely in preservice teacher training courses, as a resource for practicing teachers to enhance their own professional growth, and by interested adults as a source of sound, valuable activities for home, summer camp, Scout meetings, and the like.

Good Year Books are available through your local college or university bookstore, independent or chain booksellers, and school supply and educational dealers. For a complete catalog of Good Year Books, write:

Good Year Books
Department PPG-T
1900 East Lake Avenue
Glenview, Illinois 60025